Looking Back and Living Forward

TRANSGRESSIONS: CULTURAL STUDIES AND EDUCATION

VOLUME 125

Series Editor

Shirley R. Steinberg, *Werklund School of Education, University of Calgary, Canada*

Founding Editor

Joe L. Kincheloe (1950–2008), The Paulo and Nita Freire International Project for Critical Pedagogy

Editorial Board

Rochelle Brock, *University of North Carolina, Greensboro, USA*
Annette Coburn, *University of the West of Scotland, UK*
Kenneth Fasching-Varner, *Louisiana State University, USA*
Luis Huerta-Charles, *New Mexico State University, USA*
Christine Quail, *McMaster University, Canada*
Jackie Seidel, *University of Calgary, Canada*
Cathryn Teasley, *University of A Coruña, Spain*
Sandra Vega, *IPEC Instituto de Pedagogía Crítica, Mexico*
Mark Vicars, *Victoria University, Queensland, Australia*

This book series is dedicated to the radical love and actions of Paulo Freire, Jesus "Pato" Gomez, and Joe L. Kincheloe.

The titles published in this series are listed at *brill.com/tcse*

Scope of Series

Cultural studies provides an analytical toolbox for both making sense of educational practice and extending the insights of educational professionals into their labors. In this context *Transgressions: Cultural Studies and Education* provides a collection of books in the domain that specify this assertion. Crafted for an audience of teachers, teacher educators, scholars and students of cultural studies and others interested in cultural studies and pedagogy, the series documents both the possibilities of and the controversies surrounding the intersection of cultural studies and education. The editors and the authors of this series do not assume that the interaction of cultural studies and education devalues other types of knowledge and analytical forms. Rather the intersection of these knowledge disciplines offers a rejuvenating, optimistic, and positive perspective on education and educational institutions. Some might describe its contribution as democratic, emancipatory, and transformative. The editors and authors maintain that cultural studies helps free educators from sterile, monolithic analyses that have for too long undermined efforts to think of educational practices by providing other words, new languages, and fresh metaphors. Operating in an interdisciplinary cosmos, *Transgressions: Cultural Studies and Education* is dedicated to exploring the ways cultural studies enhances the study and practice of education. With this in mind the series focuses in a non-exclusive way on popular culture as well as other dimensions of cultural studies including social theory, social justice and positionality, cultural dimensions of technological innovation, new media and media literacy, new forms of oppression emerging in an electronic hyperreality, and postcolonial global concerns. With these concerns in mind cultural studies scholars often argue that the realm of popular culture is the most powerful educational force in contemporary culture. Indeed, in the twenty-first century this pedagogical dynamic is sweeping through the entire world. Educators, they believe, must understand these emerging realities in order to gain an important voice in the pedagogical conversation.

Without an understanding of cultural pedagogy's (education that takes place outside of formal schooling) role in the shaping of individual identity – youth identity in particular – the role educators play in the lives of their students will continue to fade. Why do so many of our students feel that life is incomprehensible and devoid of meaning? What does it mean, teachers wonder, when young people are unable to describe their moods, their affective affiliation to the society around them. Meanings provided young people by mainstream institutions often do little to help them deal with their affective complexity, their difficulty negotiating the rift between meaning and affect. School knowledge and educational expectations seem as anachronistic as a ditto machine, not that learning ways of rational thought and making sense of the world are unimportant.

But school knowledge and educational expectations often have little to offer students about making sense of the way they feel, the way their affective lives are shaped. In no way do we argue that analysis of the production of youth in an electronic mediated world demands some "touchy-feely" educational superficiality. What is needed in this context is a rigorous analysis of the interrelationship between pedagogy, popular culture, meaning making, and youth subjectivity. In an era marked by youth depression, violence, and suicide such insights become extremely important, even life saving. Pessimism about the future is the common sense of many contemporary youth with its concomitant feeling that no one can make a difference.

If affective production can be shaped to reflect these perspectives, then it can be reshaped to lay the groundwork for optimism, passionate commitment, and transformative educational and political activity. In these ways cultural studies adds a dimension to the work of education unfilled by any other sub-discipline. This is what *Transgressions: Cultural Studies and Education* seeks to produce – literature on these issues that makes a difference. It seeks to publish studies that help those who work with young people, those individuals involved in the disciplines that study children and youth, and young people themselves improve their lives in these bizarre times.

Looking Back and Living Forward

Indigenous Research Rising Up

Edited by

Jennifer Markides and Laura Forsythe

BRILL
SENSE

LEIDEN | BOSTON

Cover illustration: Christi Belcourt and Isaac Murdoch in collaboration with the students of St. Thomas Aquinas Secondary School in Brampton, Ontario.

All chapters in this book have undergone peer review.

The Library of Congress Cataloging-in-Publication Data is available online at http://catalog.loc.gov

ISBN: 978-90-04-36739-5 (paperback)
ISBN: 978-90-04-36740-1 (hardback)
ISBN: 978-90-04-36741-8 (e-book)

Copyright 2018 by Koninklijke Brill NV, Leiden, The Netherlands.
Koninklijke Brill NV incorporates the imprints Brill, Brill Hes & De Graaf,
Brill Nijhoff, Brill Rodopi, Brill Sense and Hotei Publishing.
All rights reserved. No part of this publication may be reproduced, translated,
stored in a retrieval system, or transmitted in any form or by any means, electronic,
mechanical, photocopying, recording or otherwise, without prior written
permission from the publisher.
Authorization to photocopy items for internal or personal use is granted by
Koninklijke Brill NV provided that the appropriate fees are paid directly to The
Copyright Clearance Center, 222 Rosewood Drive, Suite 910, Danvers, MA 01923,
USA. Fees are subject to change.

This book is printed on acid-free paper and produced in a sustainable manner.

To our brothers,
Will Foster and Mark MacDermott,
gone too soon from this world.
You are sadly missed.

Love, your sisters,
Laura Forsythe (nee Foster) and
Jennifer Markides (nee MacDermott)

CONTENTS

Foreword   xiii
Dwayne Donald

Acknowledgements   xv

Introduction   xvii
Jennifer Markides

Part 1: Defending the Sacred: Land and Relationships

1. The Cold War, the Nuclear Arctic, and Inuit Resistance   3
   Warren Bernauer

2. Working Together: Recommendations for Indigenous and Archaeological
   Custodianship of Past in Canada   13
   April Chabot

3. Indigenous Knowledge on Nguni Cattle Uses: Breed of the Past for the
   Future   25
   Saymore Petros Ndou and Michael Chimonyo

4. Early Indigenous North American Cartography as Performance Texts   35
   Waylon Lenk

5. The Gradual Rise of Manitoba's Northern Hydro-Electrical Generation
   Project   45
   Victoria Grima

6. First Nations, Municipalities, and Urban Reserves: Shifting
   Intergovernmental Power Balance in Urban Settings?   55
   Charlotte Bezamat-Mantes

7. Indigenous Food Sovereignty Is a Public Health Priority   63
   Carly Welham

Part 2: Sharing Intergenerational Teachings: Language and Stories

8. Using Language Nests to Promote the Intergenerational Transmission
   of Tāłtān   73
   Kāshā Julie A. Morris (Tahltan Nation)

CONTENTS

9. Bibooniiwininii: Miigaazoo-Dibaajimowin – Winter Spirit: Fight Story 81
   Isaac Murdoch (Narrator) and Jason Bone (Editor)

10. In Defense of the Oral Tradition: The Embodiment of Indigenous
    Literature and the Storytelling Styles of Dovie Thomason and Louis Bird 91
    Michelle Lietz

11. An Elaborate Educational Endeavour: The Writing of Basil H. Johnston 97
    Paul M. R. Murphy

12. Korean Indigenous Epistemologies with Notes on the Corresponding
    Epistemologies of Indigenous Scholarship 105
    Jusung Kim

13. Channelling Indigenous Knowledge through Digital Transmission:
    The Opportunities and Limitations of Indigenous Computer Games 115
    Melanie Belmore and Melanie Braith

14. Knowledge and Practices in Conflict: Indigenous Voice and Oral
    Traditions in the Legal System 123
    Monica Morales-Good

Part 3: Re-Dressing Colonial Legacies: Counter-Narratives of Resistance

15. Self-Determination Undermined: Education and Self-government 135
    Laura Forsythe

16. Daniels v. Canada: The Supreme Court's Racialized Understanding
    of the Métis and Section 91(24) 145
    Karine Martel

17. Canadian Cyber Stories on Indigenous Topics and White Fragility: Why
    is the Online Comment Section So Volatile and Divisive? 155
    Belinda Nicholson

18. How Imperial Images Demonize Indigenous Spiritualities 163
    Timothy Maton

19. An 'Indian' Industry: Tourism and the Exploitation of Indigenous
    Cultures in the Canadian West 177
    Miriam Martens

20. Celebrating Canada 150 by Exploiting Coast Salish Culture 187
    Irwin Oostindie

21. Reclaiming Indigenous Schooling Process against Colonization   197
Eduardo Vergolino

22. Surveying Undergraduate Students' Perceptions on the Indigenous
Course Requirement   205
Amanda Appasamy, Cassandra Szabo, and Jordan Tabobondung

Part 4: Communities of Healing and Strength: Redirection to Resurgence

23. Moccasin Making for Community Development: In York Factory
First Nation   219
Charlene Moore

24. Elders and Indigenous Healing in the Correctional Service of Canada:
A Story of Relational Dissonance, Sacred Doughnuts, and Drive-Thru
Expectations   231
Robin Quantick

25. Indigenous Voices for Well-Being in Northern Manitoba: An Exploratory
Study   245
Miriam Perry

26. Scaling Deep: Arts Based Research Practices   255
Kara Passey

27. Drawing Back the Curtain: Community Engagement Prior to Basic
Science Research Improves Research Questions and Assists in Framing
Study Outcomes   263
*Monika M. Kowatsch, Courtney Bell, Margaret Ormond, and
Keith R. Fowke*

28. Research Ethics Review, Research Participants, and the Researcher
in-between: When REB Directives Clash with Participant Socio-Relational
Cosmologies   273
Marion J. Kiprop

29. An Act of Anishinaabe Resistance   283
Patricia Siniikwe Pajunen

30. Reconciling an Ethical Framework for Living Well in the World of
Research   291
Jennifer Markides

DWAYNE DONALD

FOREWORD

In June 2013, I attended the *Canada-Mexico Round Table on Aboriginal Higher Education* hosted by the University of Lethbridge. This *Roundtable* brought together an interesting assemblage of program leaders and instructors from ten Indigenous universities in Mexico and fifteen primarily undergraduate universities in Canada. For me, the most intriguing attendee was a Mayan woman Elder from southern Mexico who was invited to the podium to address the delegates. With the help of a translator, the Elder provided us with a beautiful message of love and perseverance. She spoke specifically on the misinterpretations of the Mayan calendar and the spreading of the popular culture myth that ancient Mayan visionaries had predicted that the world would end in 2012. With a smile, the Elder confirmed for us that they did not expect an apocalyptic ending; rather, for them the year 2012 marks the time when a new era would begin. She finished her address by telling us that the Mayan people have resisted over 500 years of Spanish domination of their lands and lives by secretly teaching their children traditional ancestral knowledge in hidden caves. She explained that for Mayans, this new era means that it is now time for them to emerge from their secret caves and begin sharing the wisdom teachings that they have so lovingly cherished and sustained all these years.

This memory instantly came to my mind when I first read the title for this exciting book. This title captures beautifully the spirit and intent of the message that the Elder shared on that day. If the Mayans, and other Indigenous peoples around the world who held similar visions, were indeed tapping into a mysterious wisdom understanding of an important shift in the energy circulating in the world, then we would be wise to carefully attend to the lessons on life and living being passed on to us. For me, the key insight that flows from this vision is that a new era has begun during which Indigenous peoples around the world must emerge from own 'caves' and begin sharing their ancestral wisdom teachings that have survived the many years of colonial oppression. We must begin to interrogate the ways and means by which we have been carefully trained to disregard wisdom teachings and insights from earlier eras and accept without question the assertion that human beings really only began to live good lives in the past few centuries. It is this faith in the cultural mythology of a techno-scientific version of Progress that blinds us to the truth that we are enmeshed in a whole series of relationships – human and more-than-human – that we are fully dependent upon for our survival. The most urgent challenge facing human beings today is to remember sacred ecological wisdom teachings regarding

xiii

DWAYNE DONALD

how to live in ways that honour those relationships and sustain them so that our extended more-than-human relations can also continue to live.

So, for me, *Looking Back and Living Forward: Indigenous Research Rising Up* is a beautiful compilation of chapters that address these challenges in unique and inspiring ways. As the many contributing authors exemplify through their textual offerings, the possibility of a *Rising Up* arises from a (re)newed commitment to an ethic of wisdom relationality. It is this form of ethical relationality that will help heal us from the violent divisiveness of colonial logics and inspire us to (re)imagine ourselves as human beings. As such, this book is healing medicine.

Dwayne Donald
Faculty of Education
University of Alberta
Edmonton, Alberta

ACKNOWLEDGEMENTS

We are grateful for the privilege to first come together with this collection of work on the original lands of Anishinaabeg, Cree, Oji-Cree, Dakota, and Dene peoples, and on the homeland of the Métis Nation. Much of the editing for the book took place on this territory and the original lands of Siksika, Piikuni, Kainai, Tsuut'ina, Nakoda and the Métis.

Looking Back and Living Forward: Indigenous Research Rising Up is inspired by the strong scholarship shared by presenters and speakers at Rising Up: A Graduate Research Conference on Indigenous Knowledge and Research in Indigenous Studies 2017. The second annual international conference hosted by the University of Manitoba Native Studies Graduate Students Association (NSGSA), graduate students from within the Department of Native Studies at the University of Manitoba who culturally, personally and academically support students pursuing Indigenous studies across the University as well as throughout Turtle Island.

We are thankful to the conference committee for their continued perseverance and tenacity to organize an enterprise of this magnitude alongside their studies. Special thanks go to the following committee members: Belinda Nicholson, Naithan Lagace, Laura Forsythe, Charlotte Bezamat-Mantes, Richard Stecenko, Leo Baskatawang, Karine Martel, and Sharon Dainard. Their commitment to providing a space to bring both the grassroots community and graduate students to all to share knowledge, present research, network, and acquire critical feedback is inspiring.

We would like to express gratitude to Brill | Sense for believing that the work of graduate students has a place on the global stage by providing the publishing opportunity in the series Transgressions: Cultural Studies and Education, and making *Looking Back and Living Forward: Indigenous Research Rising Up* available to a wide audience of scholars, teachers, teacher educators, and students seeking works in Indigenous research. Under the guidance of Shirley R. Steinberg we have been able to actualize the dream of creating this book, we are truly thankful for all that has been imparted with us.

Our deepest thanks to those who labour diligently to preserve histories and arts, who have accommodated our requests to share their images: The William Ready Division of Archives and Research Collections, McMaster University Library, and the Glenbow Archives, Calgary, Alberta.

Thank you to all the contributors for sharing their distinct voices from across disciplines in a comprehensive range of topics and approaches that serve to further Indigenous research. We offer our profound appreciation for trusting us with their work and for their confidence in us as editors to bring their work to the world.

JENNIFER MARKIDES

INTRODUCTION

Since the Truth and Reconciliation Commission (TRC) released its 94 "Calls to Action" in June 2015, organizations – including the government, universities, private businesses, and public sector employers – across Canada have been consciously making efforts to indigenize their practices. We can see this in media statements, Indigenous consultation committees, acknowledgements of the land, educational initiatives, and increased hiring of Indigenous peoples, to name a few. There is a growing need for Indigenous voices and Indigenous scholarship to inform new and renewed practices in all areas of our society. Correspondingly, research involving Indigenous studies and Indigenous Knowledges (IK) is thriving. The scholarship around Indigenous ways of knowing and being spans all disciplines and informs broad audiences.

The *Rising Up* conference, hosted by the University of Manitoba in March of 2017, showcased the work of Indigenous and non-Indigenous scholars from around the world. Presenters shared their research and explorations of Indigenous philosophies, methodologies, histories, resurgences, theories, and practices. While the conference was small and intimate, it seemed imperative that the scholarship shared should reach a broader audience. The publication of these works provides a unique and timely collection of knowledge, stories, and ideas – teachings and learnings – with Indigenous foci.

Looking Back and Living Forward: Indigenous Research Rising Up is an interdisciplinary and collaborative project. The contributors were encouraged to stay true the writing style and formatting that is germane to their field. This means that the citations and referencing may vary from chapter to chapter. The decision to do so was made consciously. We hope that anyone can pick up this book, regardless of discipline, and find some offerings that align with their interests and discover other readings that they might not have otherwise come across.

The book is organized into four overlapping and interrelated parts: Defending the Sacred – Land and Relationships; Sharing Intergenerational Teachings – Land and Stories; Re-Dressing Colonial Legacies – Counter-Narratives of Resistance; and Communities of Healing and Strength – Redirection to Resurgence. The chapters include topics such as: archaeological custodianship; arts-based research; cartography; cattle systems and traditions; community health sciences; cultural exploitation; economic development; education; education as continued oppression; Elders healing in federal prisons; ethical considerations in research relationships;

xvii

JENNIFER MARKIDES

food sovereignty; healing and well-being; health; history and colonization; hydro-electric power generations; identity; inclusive and transparent research practices; Indigenous epistemologies; Indigenous knowledge; Indigenous literature; Inuit resistance; land use; language revitalization; oral traditions in the legal system; racialization of legal precedents/cases; racism in cyber spaces; reconciliation; resistance and oppression; responses to Indigenous course requirements; self-determination; tourism; spirituality; storytelling; urban treaty territories; and video-games for cultural learning.

Readers are encouraged to follow their own path through the book. The layout is not intended to be prescriptive, but open. The collection aspires to move Indigenous research and conversations forward, while honouring and learning from those who came before us. Indigenous research is not a shadow of the past; it illuminates the future – *rising up*.

PART 1

DEFENDING THE SACRED: LAND AND RELATIONSHIPS

WARREN BERNAUER

1. THE COLD WAR, THE NUCLEAR ARCTIC, AND INUIT RESISTANCE

The history of the cold war in the North American Arctic has remained a popular topic in academia, with books and journal articles on the topic published regularly. These studies range from discourse analyses of the 'imaginative geography' of the cold war Arctic (Farish, 2010), to examinations of the relationship between cold war militarization and the Canadian state's territorial claims (Coates et al., 2008). Other contributions have discussed the role of technical discourses in Arctic militarization (Farish & Lackenbauer, 2017), and the role of indigenous peoples in asserting Canadian sovereignty during the cold war (Lackenbauer, 2007a, 2007b, 2009).

From the perspective of indigenous studies, much of this work is useful – it has brought to light important aspects of Arctic history, and therefore provides important context for Arctic indigenous histories. However, by and large, recent writing on the cold war in the Arctic has generally ignored, or paid insufficient attention to, Inuit resistance. Some studies of debates over weapons testing in the Canadian Arctic have ignored the role of Inuit entirely (Clearwater, 2006). Other cold war histories depict Inuit as loyal subjects of empire, helping to assert Canadian sovereignty (Lackenbauer, 2007a, 2007b, 2009). While some contributions discuss calls by Dene and Inuit leaders to demilitarize the Arctic, they do not capture the extent of Inuit resistance to militarization (Lackenbauer & Farish, 2007; Coates et al., 2008).

This chapter contributes to the academic study of the cold war Arctic by centering Inuit resistance to the militarization and of the Arctic. To properly understand the extent of Inuit resistance to cold war militarization, I argue, we must consider the close relationship between the nuclear industry and cold war militarization. Indeed, for many Inuit politicians, these two issues were inseparable. My focus is on discursive resistance – what Inuit call *Kiumajut* ('talking back'), and what western activists sometimes call 'speaking truth to power' (Kulchyski & Tester, 2007). I examine statements made by Inuit politicians which criticized the way the cold war manifested in Inuit Nunangat (the Inuit homeland).

I begin with an overview of the militarization of Inuit Nunangat, with a focus on nuclear weapons and nuclear military technology. Next, I document several examples of Inuit resistance to militarization, including through the Inuit Circumpolar Conference, the Government of the Northwest Territories Legislative Assembly, the Canadian House of Commons, and opposition to uranium mining. I end with some brief conclusions regarding the relevance of these events to cold war history.

© KONINKLIJKE BRILL NV, LEIDEN, 2018 | DOI 9789004367418_001

WARREN BERNAUER

THE COLD WAR AND THE NUCLEAR ARCTIC

The cold war nuclear arms race began in 1949, when the USA and USSR began to compete in the development of larger nuclear explosives, as well as delivery, and defense systems (Heller, 2006; Farish, 2010). It quickly spilled into Inuit Nunangat, as the Inuit homelands assumed a new strategic significance. The shortest air route between the continental USA and the USSR crossed Greenland and the Canadian Arctic, which led to anxieties that either the USSR or USA would launch a nuclear strike across that airspace (Coates et al., 2008; Eyre, 1989).

The strategic significance of the Inuit homeland led to the rapid militarization of the region. A line of military radar bases was constructed across the North American Arctic. Stretching from Alaska to Greenland, the Distant Early Warning Line (DEW Line) was a collaboration between the Canadian and American militaries, designed to give the United States advanced warning of a Soviet nuclear attack (Coates et al., 2008).

Both major powers deployed nuclear weapons in the Arctic. The United States' military began deploying nuclear weapons to bases in the Arctic in the 1950s, including in bases in/near Inuit territory in Alaska, Canada, and Greenland (Clearwater, 1999; Dragsdahl, 2001). During the cold war, American, British, French and Soviet nuclear submarines, often armed with nuclear missiles and torpedoes, regularly patrolled the Arctic ocean (Eyre, 1989). Throughout the 1960s, the American military *constantly* flew long-range bombers, armed with nuclear weapons, over Greenland, Alaska and Arctic Canada. The purpose of this program was to ensure that the American military had the means to inflict a swift nuclear attack against the Soviet Union, by ensuring that bombers were perpetually flying within range of Moscow (Petersen, 2011). In 1968, an American bomber carrying four nuclear weapons crashed on the sea ice between Greenland and Baffin Island. While a cleanup effort recovered substantial radioactive material, there is speculation that the second stage of one warhead remains at the bottom of Baffin Bay (Petersen, 2011; Dragsdahl, 2001).

Both the United States and the Soviet Union conducted nuclear weapons testing in the Arctic, at the Amitchka and Novaya Zemlya sites respectively (Gizewski, 1993; Khalturin et al., 2005). Both sites lay outside of Inuit territory, and detonations of nuclear explosives have never been carried out in Inuit Nunangat. Two proposals for the testing of nuclear explosives in Inuit Nunangat were developed, but ultimately abandoned. Britain considered, but later abandoned, plans to test its first nuclear weapons near Churchill Manitoba (Clearwater & O'Brien, 2003). The United States developed a rather peculiar proposal to use nuclear weapons for civil engineering purposes in Alaska. In 1962, it was forced to abandon plans to excavate a harbour with nuclear explosions, due to opposition from Alaskan Inuit and scientists (O'Neil, 1994).

While nuclear weapons were not detonated on Inuit lands, the region still encountered the atmospheric fall-out from nuclear weapons testing. Atmospheric detonations carried out across the globe dispersed a significant amount of radioactive fallout into the atmosphere, some of which settled on Inuit territory. This fallout resulted in the contamination of the Inuit food supply in the 1960s. Due to a very efficient uptake pathway, radioactive cesium, which landed on lichen, was rapidly transferred to caribou. As a result, Inuit caribou hunters received significant doses of radiation in the 1950s and 1960s (AMAP, 2004).

Arctic military activities during the 1950s and 1960s were mostly carried out in secret, and it was not until much later that many of these events became public knowledge. Further, they largely took place before Nunavut Inuit had become organized into formal political institutions. As such, there is little record of resistance by Inuit to the militarization of the Arctic in this era, with the exceptions of Alaskan Inuit resistance to Project Chariot and Greenlandic outrage over the nuclear bomber which crashed off its coast. However, it clearly influenced the Inuit perception of the military and nuclear industry in later decades, and numerous Inuit have since made retroactive critiques. For example, Greenlandic politician Aqquluk Lynge wrote,

> The nightmare of the Cold War had a most powerful effect on us. We were whisked into the rivalry of the two great superpowers…Suddenly, we found our settlements and hunting grounds invaded and airfields established, not to mention the test detonations of atomic weapons which polluted the air we breathe. Toxic chemicals were on our land, from one DEW line base to the other, from Alaska to the Greenland ice cap. (Lynge, 1992; see also: Simon, 1989, 1992)

The nuclear arms race deescalated in the early 1970s, a decade which saw some relative *dente* between Washington and Moscow, and the negotiation of treaties to scale-back the nuclear buildup of the 1960s. By the 1970s, the United States had removed its nuclear weapons from Greenland and the Canadian North, and ceased its constant bomber flights over Arctic airspace.

However, Inuit encounters with military nuclear technology continued. In 1978, the Soviet COSMOS 954 nuclear-powered surveillance satellite crashed into the Canadian Arctic, near the Inuit community of Baker Lake, dispersing radioactive material across the tundra (Aftergood, 1986). There was serious concern among Inuit in Baker Lake that the crash had resulted in the radioactive contamination of caribou (ITC, 1978). A cleanup operation, undertaken jointly by the Canadian Department of National Defense and Atomic Energy Control Board retrieved significant amounts of debris, although most of the satellite and its fuel were ultimately unaccounted for (Gummer et al., 1980).

Beginning during the Carter presidency, and accelerating greatly during Reagan administration, the "thawing" of relations between the United States and Soviet Union was reversed, and the cold war again intensified. Reagan explicitly rejected the goal of disarmament, and began to escalate the nuclear arms race (Heller, 2006, pp. 250–265). New cruise and ballistic missiles were developed to bypass Soviet defenses and deliver nuclear payloads to Moscow.

WARREN BERNAUER

The USA planned to station new MX ballistic missiles in Inupiat homeland in Alaska, and expanded its Thule air force base in Greenland. In Arctic and subarctic Canada, it began testing its new cruise missiles in 1984. The tests became a focal point of activism for the anti-war movement, and a wave of protests spread throughout Canada (Clearwater, 2006, pp. 50–54).

INUIT CIRCUMPOLAR CONFERENCE CALLS FOR DEMILITARIZATION AND A NUCLEAR-FREE ZONE

The Inuit Circumpolar Conference (ICC), later renamed the Inuit Circumpolar Council, was created in 1977. With membership in Siberia, Alaska, Canada, and Greenland, the ICC provides a forum through which Inuit can develop unified positions on international issues (Lynge, 1993; Simon, 1996). In its formative years, the ICC adopted policies opposing militarization and the use of nuclear technology in the Arctic.

At its first meeting a resolution was passed calling for a ban on all military activity in the Inuit homeland. It declared,

...the Arctic shall be used for peaceful and environmentally safe purposes only, and that there should be prohibited any measure of a military nature such as the establishment of military bases and fortifications, the carrying out of military manoeuvres, and the testing of any type of weapon. (ITC, 1977, p. 35)

At its 1983 general meeting, the ICC passed a resolution calling for the Arctic to be declared a "nuclear-free zone". The resolution reiterated ICC's opposition to Arctic militarization, and resolved:

1. that the arctic and subarctic be used for purposes that are peaceful and environmentally safe;
2. that there shall be no nuclear testing or nuclear devices in the arctic;
3. that there should be no nuclear dump sites in the arctic and subarctic;
4. that exploration and exploitation of uranium, thorium, lithium, or other materials related to the nuclear industry in our homeland be prohibited (ITC, 1984, p. 4).

The ICC consistently called for the demilitarization of the Arctic and nuclear disarmament through the 1980s. General assemblies reaffirmed this position, and ICC's political leaders – including Hans Pavia-Rosing, Aqqaluk Lynge, and Mary Simon – made public statements protesting militarization and the nuclear arms race (*Arctic Policy Review*, 1983, 1985; Simon, 1989, 1992; Lynge, 1993).

GOVERNMENT OF THE NORTHWEST TERRITORIES DEBATES NUCLEAR ISSUES

The Government of the Northwest Territories (GNWT) is the 'public' representative body that governed Inuit territory in the Central and Eastern Arctic until the new

Nunavut Territory was created in 1999. The NWT Council originally consisted entirely of members appointed by the Prime Minister of Canada. However, it began a transition into an elected body in the 1950s. Inuit politicians have served in the NWT council (later renamed the Legislative Assembly of the NWT) since 1966 when Simionie Michael was elected (Dickerson, 1991). Through the 1980s, military and nuclear issues were debated in the Legislative Assembly of the GNWT. Inuit Members of the Legislative Assembly (MLAs), and non-Inuit MLAs representing Inuit-majority ridings, played important roles in these debates.

In 1986, following the Chernobyl nuclear disaster, MLA Tom Gargan, tabled a motion entitled "Declaration of a Nuclear Free Zone" in the GNWT legislative assembly. The motion was seconded by Joe Arlooktoo, an Inuk representing the riding of South Baffin. Its preamble cited anti-nuclear and anti-nuclear weapons stances adopted by the Inuit Circumpolar Conference and other northern indigenous organizations. It called for the legislative assembly to "declare the Northwest Territories, land, coastal waters, and airspace a nuclear weapons free zone." It further declared its opposition to the "exploration and exploitation of other materials related to the nuclear weapons industry" as well as to "the testing and/or establishment of nuclear weapons, nuclear weapons related technology, and nuclear waste dump sites" in the Northwest Territories. Arguing in support of the motion, Gargan and Arlooktoo cited the Chernobyl disaster, the rising global anti-nuclear movement, cruise missile testing in the Mackenzie Valley, and the possibility of basing nuclear weapons in the High Arctic. They also referred to numerous Inuit and Dene communities in the Northwest Territories that had declared themselves nuclear-free zones.

During debate, the motion was amended several times by the assembly. Responding to pressure from the mining industry, some members claimed the motion's opposition to the extraction of materials related to nuclear weapons was too broadly cast. As a result, an amendment was tabled, to remove the sections of the motion that referred to the extraction of materials used in nuclear weapons. Dennis Patterson, a non-Inuit member for the Inuit-majority riding of Frobisher Bay, responded to the amendment, declaring that he was "opposed to the exploration and mining of uranium in the Northwest Territories." In defense of his position, Patterson cited the use of uranium in nuclear weapons, telling the assembly "the truth is, that Canadian uranium goes into nuclear weapons." The amendment removing references to uranium mining was passed by the assembly, as was a second amendment retitling the resolution to "Declaration of a Nuclear *Weapons* Free Zone." The motion ultimately passed with fifteen in favour, no opposed, and one abstention.

CANADIAN PARLIAMENT DEBATES CRUISE MISSILE TESTING

Prior to the 1950s, Inuit were legally barred from participating in federal elections. While this legislation was revoked in 1950, the design of federal electoral ridings prevented Inuit from substantially influencing election outcomes. As a result, it was not until the electoral riding of Nunatsiaq was created in 1979, that Peter Ittinuar was elected as the first Inuk Member of Parliament (Dickerson, 1991).

When Liberal Prime Minister Pierre Trudeau first agreed to allow cruise missile testing in the early 1980s, members of the New Democratic Party introduced a private members bill to reverse the government's decision. Peter Ittinuar was one of several liberal MPs who broke party ranks by abstaining from voting on the legislation. However, despite this silent protest, the bill was defeated, and tests continued through the 1980s despite the clear opposition of northerners (Clearwater, 2006).

After coming to power in 1993, Jean Chretien's Liberal government agreed to allow tests to continue, despite significant opposition to the tests within the Liberal Party. However, Chretien allowed the issue to be openly debated in the House of Commons, and many party members spoke out against cruise missile testing (Clearwater, 2006).

Jack Anawak – the Inuk MP for Nunatsiaq and Liberal Party member – gave a passionate speech against continued testing. Anawak referenced clear and repeated statements of opposition to cruise missile testing by the GNWT, as well as Inuit and Dene organizations. He claimed that northerners were "shocked" by the government's renewal of testing agreements, which he called a "total disregard for their concerns." He went on to proclaim that northerners are "peaceful people" who "do not feel comfortable with [their] land being used as testing grounds for weapons of war." Anawak concluded his speech with a call for action: "Let us take a bold step, let us cancel the cruise missile testing" (Canada, 1994, pp. 437–439).

One further test of the cruise missile in the Northwest territories took place later that year. Afterwards, an upwell of opposition within Liberal Party ranks began to exert further pressure to cancel agreement. Before this came to a head, the USA unilaterally ended the testing program in 1994 (Clearwater, 2006).

BAKER LAKE INUIT RESIST URANIUM MINING

Inuit also resisted cold war militarization through debates about uranium mining in the Arctic, especially the Inuit response to the proposed Kiggavik uranium mine. Canadian Inuit first confronted the uranium industry in the early 1970s, when a uranium exploration rush descended on the Kivalliq region of the Northwest Territories. Throughout that decade, Inuit community of Baker Lake repeatedly (and ultimately unsuccessfully) attempted to halt uranium exploration near their community, with letters, petitions, and litigation. Their primary grievance with exploration was the impact it was having on the community's caribou hunt (Bernauer, 2015). In the late 1970s, Labrador Inuit were likewise led into a political confrontation when a uranium mine was proposed near the community of Makkovik. Concerns with disturbance to wildlife and radioactive contamination spurred the Labrador Inuit Association and Inuit Tapirisat of Canada to (successfully) oppose the proposal (Proctor, 2015). By the late 1980s, Urangesellschaft, a West German mining firm, had delineated an economically viable uranium deposit west of Baker Lake. In 1988, Urangesellschaft submitted a proposal for the "Kiggavik" uranium mine to federal regulators. The Kiggavik proposal was met with firm opposition from Inuit political organizations and the Inuit of Baker Lake. However, unlike previous confrontations with the industry in the 1970s and early 1980s, a substantial factor in Inuit opposition to Kiggavik was related to the use of uranium in nuclear weapons.

The Kiggavik proposal was met with firm opposition. Baker Lake residents formed the Baker Lake Concerned Citizens Committee to organize local opposition to the proposal. Several Inuit organizations and regional boards came together to form a coalition opposing the proposed mine – the 'Northern Anti-Uranium Coalition' (NAUC). The coalition participated as an intervenor in the review of the Kiggavik proposal, and helped coordinate a broader public campaign against the proposal. NAUC held public events in Rankin Inlet and Baker Lake, featuring presentations from prominent spokespeople in the anti-nuclear movement. NAUC produced plain-language information sheets – about uranium mining, the nuclear industry, and the health risks of radiation – and distributed them in Kivalliq communities. A common theme in many of NAUC's submissions and presentations concerned the connection between nuclear weapons and uranium mining (Harding, 2007; McPherson, 2003).

While the Inuit political organizations were quick to choose a side on the Kiggavik question, GNWT government leader Dennis Patterson claimed to be "neutral" on the question of the Kiggavik mine, and repeatedly insisted that the future of the proposal should be decided through a technical environmental review. In March 1990 Peter Irniq, MLA for Rankin Inlet, introduced a motion in the GNWT legislative assembly opposing the Kiggavik mine. The motion included an extensive preamble, citing opposition to the proposed mine in the form of petitions Notably, the resolution directly connected the question of uranium mining to moral and political concerns with nuclear weapons.

> ...economic development which makes a contribution to the production of nuclear weapons and also generates dangerous waste which threatens the health of people and wildlife for thousands of years CANNOT be considered a form of sustainable development which is acceptable to Inuit and Dene values. (GNWT, 1990)

Irniq's motion was never acted upon, as government ministers referred it to committee for discussion (ensuring it could not be voted on for months) (*Nunatsiaq News*, 1990). However, the proponent soon shelved the Kiggavik proposal in the face of scathing criticisms of its environmental assessment, poor markets for uranium, and clear and coordinated local resistance. Notably, in a public plebiscite in Baker Lake, over 90% of participating residents voted 'no' to the proposed mine (McPherson, 2003).

WARREN BERNAUER

CONCLUSION

Inuit resistance to cold war militarization is more extensive than is generally acknowledged in recent academic analyses. One reason for this oversight seems to be a failure to understand that, for many Inuit, the nuclear industry was inseparable from the cold war nuclear arms race and the militarization of the Arctic. As such, much of the Inuit opposition to uranium mining should be understood (in part) as resistance to militarization and the cold war.

It is important that Inuit resistance be given proper attention in cold war histories. The depiction of Inuit as loyal subjects working to promote and enforce Canadian sovereignty in the Arctic are important. These depictions are in line with how many Inuit political leaders have understood the relationship between Inuit and Canadian identities, summarized in Jose Kusugak's famous slogan, "first Canadians, but Canadians first". However, portrayals of Inuit as loyal Canadians often obscures the critical dimensions of Inuit political consciousness. More attention to Inuit resistance to the cold war can help bring this critical consciousness to light.

REFERENCES

Arctic Policy Review. (1983). ICC protest against US military buildup. *Arctic Policy Review.*
Arctic Policy Review. (1985, January). Three cruise tests scheduled, ICC opposed. *Arctic Policy Review.*
Aftergood. (1986, October). Nuclear space mishaps and starwars. *The Bulletin of the Atomic Scientists, 42*(8), 40–43.
Arctic Monitoring and Assessment Program (AMAP). (2004). *AMAP assessment 2002: Radioactivity in the arctic.* Oslo: Arctic Monitoring and Assessment Program.
Canada. (1994, January 28). *House of commons. Debates, 35th parliament, 1st session, 1994–1996.* Ottawa: Canadian Government Publishing.
Clearwater. (1999). *US nuclear weapons in Canada.* Toronto: Dundurn Press.
Clearwater. (2006). *Just dummies: Cruise missile testing in Canada.* Calgary: University of Calgary Press.
Clearwater, & O'Brien. (2003). O lucky Canada. *Bulletin of the Atomic Scientists, 59*(4), 60–65.
Coates, Lackenbaur, Morrison, & Poelzer. (2008). *Arctic front: Defending Canada in the far north.* Toronto: Thomas Allen.
Dickerson, M. (1992). *Whose north?* Vancouver: UBC Press.
Dragsdahl. (2001). The Danish Dilemma. *Bulletin of the Atomic Scientists, 57*(5), 45–50.
Farish, & Lackenbaur. (2017). Western electric turns north: Technicians and the transformation of the cold war arctic. In Bocking & Martin (Eds.), *Ice blink: Northern environmental history.* Calgary: University of Calgary Press.
Gizewski, P. (1993). Military activity and environmental security: The case of radioactivity in the arctic. *Canadian Arctic Resources Committee, 21*(4), 16–21.
Government of the Northwest Territories. (1986, June 19). *Hansard of the 10th assembly, 7th session of the legislative assembly of the northwest territories.* Ottawa: Government of the Northwest Territories.
Government of the Northwest Territories. (1990). *Opposition to exploration and mining of uranium in the N.W.T. Motion.* Retrieved from https://makitanunavut.files.wordpress.com/2012/04/13.pdf
Gummer, Campbell, Knight, & Ricard. (1980). *COSMOS 954: The occurrence and nature of recovered debris.* Ottawa: Atomic Energy Control Board.
Harding. (2007). *Canada's deadly secret: Saskatchewan uranium and the global nuclear system.* Halifax: Fernwood Publishers.
Heller, H. (2006). *The cold war and the new imperialism: A global history, 1945–2005.* New York, NY: Monthly Review Press.

THE COLD WAR, THE NUCLEAR ARCTIC, AND INUIT RESISTANCE

ITC. (1977, September). The Inuit circumpolar conference. *Inuit Today, 6*(7).

ITC. (1984, September). Inuit protest war's madness. *Inuit Today, 12*(3).

Khalturin, Rautian, Richard, & Leith. (2005). A review of nuclear testing by the Soviet Union at Novaya Zemlya. *Science and Global Security, 13*(1–2), 1–42.

Kulchyski, & Tester. (2007). *Kiumajut/talking back.* Vancouver: UBC Press.

Lackenbauer, P. W. (2007a). Canada's northern defenders: Aboriginal peoples in he Canadian rangers. In Lackenbauer & Mantle (Eds.), *Aboriginal peoples and the Canadian military: Historical perspectives.* Kingston: Canadian Defense Academy Press.

Lackenbauer, P. W. (2007b). Teaching Canada's indigenous sovereignty soldiers...and vice versa. In Lackenbauer, Sheffield, & Mantle (Eds.), *Aboriginal peoples and military participation.* Kingston: Canadian Defense Academy Press.

Lackenbauer, P. W. (2009). The Canadian rangers: Sovereignty, security, and stewardship rom the inside out. In R. Heubert (Ed.), *Thawing ice – cold war: Canada's security, sovereignty, and environmental concerns in the arctic.* Winnipeg: Centre for Defense and Security Studies.

Lackenbaur, P. W., & Farish, M. (2007, October). The cold war on Canadian soil: Militarizing a northern environment. Environmental History, 12(4), 920–950.

Lynge, A. (1993). *Inuit: The story of the Inuit circumpolar conference.* Nuuk: Atuakkiorfik.

McPherson. (2003). *New owners in their own lands: Minerals and Inuit land claims.* Calgary: University of Calgary Press.

Nunatsiaq News. (1990, March 9). Motion opposing Kiggavik stalled by legislative assembly.

O'Neil. (1994). *The firecracker boys: H-bombs, Inupiat Eskimos, and the roots of the environmental movement.* New York, NY: St. Martin's Press.

Petersen. (2011). SAC at Thule – Greenland in the US polar strategy. *Journal of Cold War Studies, 13*(2), 90–105.

Proctor, A. (2015). Uranium, Inuit rights, and emergent neoliberalism in Labrador: 1956–2012. In Keeling & Sandlos (Eds.), *Mining and communities in Northern Canada: History, politics, memory.* Calgary: University of Calgary Press.

Simon, M. (1989). Security, peace, and the natives peoples of the arctic. In T. Berger, A. Rodionov, & D. Roche (Eds.), *The arctic: Choices for peace and security.* Vancouver: Gordon Soules.

Simon. (1992). Militarization and the aboriginal peoples. In Griffiths (Ed.), *Arctic alternatives: Civility or militarism in the circumpolar north.* Toronto: Dundurn.

Simon. (1996). *Inuit.* Peterborough: Cider Press.

Warren Bernauer
Department of Geography
York University
Toronto, Ontario

APRIL CHABOT

2. WORKING TOGETHER

Recommendations for Indigenous and Archaeological Custodianship of Past in Canada

> Both Colonialism and culture contact are suited to anthropological and archaeological analyses…a key aspect of colonialism is material, as objects themselves are part of power and status differentials.
>
> (Paterson, 2009, p. 245)

In Canada, an archaeological investigation is guided by policy and legislation that governs practices (in the private as well as the public sphere) known as cultural resource management (CRM). Most archaeological work is conducted by archaeologists working for (CRM) firms in the private sector. Private CRM companies liaise with clients who are often private land developers, as well as Indigenous groups or the government sector. Archaeology is both a creative and destructive process. There is only one chance to do an excavation properly. Once the fieldwork is complete, an archaeological record is created to be shared by all. However, in the process of obtaining the data that constitutes this archaeological record, the site as it once was is destroyed forever.

Before an archaeologist enters the field, there is much planning and preparation involved. Background research of an area must be done, as well as a myriad of other project management tasks completed. Professional standards and guidelines along with policy and legislation dictate what is or is not allowed to happen during an archaeological investigation or excavation and specific requirements are laid out for all personnel working on the site. Permits are received based upon often stringent criteria, which vary, by province and territory within Canada. Every step taken in the field is negotiated in meetings throughout the process. Fieldwork ultimately represents only a fraction of the duties that archaeologists perform on any given project. In this study, groups involved in the various stages of land development and archaeological inquiry shall be referred to as "stakeholders" due to their vested interests in the outcome of a project.

This chapter argues for the need to move past the current bare minimum requirement of engagement with Indigenous communities currently in place within Canada, toward being reflexively and truly inclusive at each step throughout the process. It is a disservice to everyone involved in the archaeological process to

© KONINKLIJKE BRILL NV, LEIDEN, 2018 | DOI 9789004367418_002

simply pay lip service to the notion of engagement and inclusivity while practices remain unchanged.

Recovery of Canadian Indigenous cultural heritage is situated within a context of colonialism insofar that it cannot be separated from the struggle of indigenous populations to obtain control and exercise influence over their cultural heritage. In order to appreciate the position of both archaeologists and Indigenous people working together toward a truly postcolonial period, it is necessary to recognize the legacy of colonialism that continues to impact both policy and practice. Atalay (1996, p. 282) outlines how a colonial past continues to inform the present reality faced by Indigenous people in stating:

> The colonial past is not distinct from today's realities and practices, as the precedents that were set continue to define structures for heritage management practices and have powerful continuing implications for Indigenous peoples in North America and elsewhere precisely because they disrupted the self-determination and sovereignty of Indigenous populations with respect to their abilities to govern and practice their own traditional forms of cultural resource management.

To indicate the continued influence and impacts of colonialism in contemporary Canadian society, I introduce the term "Colonial Present" to the chapter. It is imperative that Indigenous interests as primary stakeholders in any archaeological investigation are included in any future considerations of government policy and legislation at all levels. Equally imperative is that Indigenous voices and principles are given *equal weight* in the process of developing heritage policy and legislation going forward.

Canada lacks cohesive federal policy and legislation regarding Indigenous cultural heritage material. Thus, policy initiatives and resulting legislation have been left to the individual provinces and territories. Consequently, Watkins (2003, p. 277) quoting Syms, emphasizes that "...there is no leverage to hold the province accountable for bilaterally funded projects, no precedents for the provincial politicians to become used to funding large scale mitigations projects and no heritage legislation for federal lands, including reserves". This point is exemplified by the archaeological case study under examination: the excavation and construction of the Canadian Human Rights Museum (CMHR) at the Forks site in Winnipeg.

The CMHR was chosen for the case study because the location was initially owned by the province and changed hands midway through the archaeological investigations to become Federal land. This sale was necessary for the museum is designated as a "National" museum; the first one outside of the Nation's capital, and as such, must reside on federal lands. The fact that the CMHR was subject to both provincial and federal jurisdictions while archaeological investigations were taking place positions it as the ideal case study to examine the impact of provincial and currently non-existent federal policy and legislation.

Significantly, this research took place within Manitoba where many consider little cultural heritage regulation to be in effect and where awareness of Indigenous worldviews are not necessarily taken into account, particularly in northern regions. Where there are competing or conflicting interests between Indigenous groups and other stakeholders, resolutions are yet to be found. The development of a best practices model that is broadly applicable to Canada provides a way forward with new solutions.

The call for Canadian federal level heritage policy and legislation has stagnated for well over two decades. Previous attempts to address this serious issue have failed, no doubt in part due to a lack of knowledge or agreement about the best way to proceed. Many scholars and CRM specialists have noted the lack of federal policy regarding these interests and issues as a detriment to Canadian archaeological standards (Bell, 1992; Ferris, 2003; Watkins, 2003). This lack of federal policy is simply not acceptable in a country rich with history, traditional knowledge, and Indigenous cultural heritage material. A comprehensive best practices model seeks to correct this problem, heal the current paralysis, and provide the mechanism to move forward with the creation of federal policy and legislation that protects Canada's precious cultural heritage material.

In order to reflect the richness of cultural diversity in Canada, our policies and legislation, particularly those that aim to protect cultural heritage material, must move beyond colonial influence into a future that includes the multiple worldviews informing the core of Canadian experience.

Manitoba has a long and rich history of archaeological exploration and investigation that predates the incorporation of the province into Canada. Manitoba began archaeological explorations as early as 1859, taking off after 1879 with the help of government sponsorship and the aid of the Historical and Scientific society (Dyck, 2009, p. 1). By contrast, it is thought that the rest of the prairie provinces did not start explorations until the late 1930s (Dyck, 2009, p. 1). With the passing of the 1867 British North America Act in London, most of its eastern colonies were consolidated into a single federation that became the Dominion of Canada (Dyck, 2009, p. 11). In the 1860s a small village of settlers had been established next to Fort Garry. By 1866, that village became Winnipeg (Dyck, 2009, p. 11).

Waves of settlers in the 1870s brought growth, resulting in two significant events (Dyck, 2009, p. 11). First, the Geological Survey of Canada (GSC) was created in 1877; charged with the assignment to begin "a full and scientific study of the natural history of the country, including aboriginal history" (Dyck, 2009, p. 12). Second, the Historical and Scientific Society Manitoba (HSSM) was established on January 23, 1879, in the courthouse of Winnipeg. This represented the first "public enterprise...operating under a provincially incorporated and funded body" (Dyck, 2009, p. 17). Dr. Robert Bell was the first visiting scientist, a geologist with GSC, to join the HSSM in 1879. He later supervised archaeological excavations of a mound in St. Andrews on the west bank of the Red River (Dyck, 2009, p. 12). Bell's team included traditional knowledge in their undertaking by learning about the mound legends from local "elderly Native women" from nearby communities (Dyck, 2009, p. 13). Dr. Bell's efforts are most likely the earliest incorporation of traditional knowledge within archaeological fieldwork in Manitoba.

However, there are parallels between Manitoba and the other prairie provinces, such as the period of sporadic archaeological work and private collecting that characterized interest in the last half of the 19th and early 20th century (Dyck, 2009, p. 2). The post-World War II era brought change when the HSSM "employed Chris Vickers as a part-time archaeologist in the late 1940s and early 1950s" which added "considerable new information and systemization of archaeology" to the province (Dyck, 2009, p. 2). Vickers became the first full-time professional archaeologist in Manitoba. This also brought about the hiring of J. William Oakes by the University of Manitoba in 1962 (Dyck, 2009, p. 2).

The period of 1960–1975 was a "Boom" period in Canadian archaeology (http://www.thecanadianencyclopedia.ca/en/article/archaeology/#h3_jump_2, accessed February 5, 2017). The trends at the time were aimed toward the expansion of museum programs and increased funding for archaeological research (http://www.thecanadianencyclopedia.ca/en/article/archaeology/#h3_jump_2, accessed February 5, 2017). Jobs in the field of archaeology were plentiful coinciding with an increased interest in conservation issues at the federal level (http://www.thecanadianencyclopedia.ca/en/article/archaeology/#h3_jump_2, accessed February 5, 2017). The Canada Council began supporting archaeological endeavours in 1961, "followed by the National Research Council (briefly) and the Social Sciences and Humanities Research Council of Canada" (http://www.thecanadianencyclopedia.ca/en/article/archaeology/#h3_jump_2, accessed February 5, 2017). Due to this robust boom period in archaeology, professional archaeologists across Canada "came together to form the nationwide Canadian Archaeological Association (CAA) in 1968, which continues to be a vital organization allowing the sharing of archaeological research among peers (http://www.thecanadianencyclopedia.ca/en/article/archaeology/#h3_jump_2, accessed February 5, 2017).

1971 marked a "substantial increase in its operating budget to launch a country-wide archaeological salvage program", and the "Federal Archaeology Department was renamed the Archaeological Survey of Canada" (http://www.thecanadianencyclopedia.ca/en/article/archaeology/#h3_jump_2, accessed February 5, 2017). Out of the increased budgets for archaeological salvage programs and greater interest in conservation, grew the field of "salvage archaeology," or cultural resource management (CRM). Other outgrowths of this boom were industry-driven changes such as better quality dating techniques for artifacts and the sheer quantity of research produced. For example, the James Bay Project in Québec, the Nipawin Reservoir Heritage Study in Saskatchewan, the Site C Dam Project on the Peace River, BC, and the Northern Oil and Gas Action Plan in the Mackenzie Delta (http://www.thecanadianencyclopedia.ca/en/article/archaeology/#h3_jump_2, accessed February 5, 2017).

The 1980s saw less funding for academic projects but still provided funding for CRM projects (http://www.thecanadianencyclopedia.ca/en/article/archaeology/#h3_jump_2, accessed February 5, 2017). The trend now moved toward "increasing public awareness and appreciation of our nation's cultural heritage" (http://www.thecanadianencyclopedia.ca/en/article/archaeology/#h3_jump_2, accessed February 5, 2017). Since the 1990s, declining government support and funding has led to stringent funding cuts resulting in fewer professional positions within offices such as Parks Canada as well as fewer grants for student researchers.

Watkins (2000, p. 156) presents the outcome of the Canadian Archaeological Association's Committee on Archaeology and Aboriginal Heritage in 1992, which examined the "relationships between professional archaeologists and aboriginal people." The committee produced a mandate that included the following three points:

1. To develop, through extensive consultation with the aboriginal and archaeological communities, a draft statement of principles for ethical archaeological practice and minimum standards for intercommunity communication.
2. To examine policies and concepts to assist all levels of government (including aboriginal governments) to realize consensual management of aboriginal heritage features.
3. To encourage direct involvement of aboriginal people, through active recruitment programs, in professional archaeology.

The best practices model presented here builds on the first two recommendations while the third recommendation is addressed within my original thesis.

Archaeological work is split between fieldwork carried out by academics and students who are funded through their universities or other grant sources on the one hand, and private cultural resource management companies (CRM) on the other. Within the corporate nature of CRM, reporting findings to local communities or presenting findings at professional conferences is rare; viewed as a luxury not available to many companies as they must move on to their next client once their project is complete. Summary reports of archaeological findings are submitted to the client and local heritage branch. Although such reports are usually publicly available on the website of the local heritage branch, there is often little awareness of them among the general public. Most CRM companies do send archaeological material for curation and storage to the local museum or university, which allows students and researchers access to the collections.

In Manitoba, archaeologists working in the private or public sector must apply for a permit from the Historic Resources Branch (HRB) to begin work. There are four stages of archaeological investigation in Manitoba, each requiring a different permit. Stage One is a Heritage Resource Impact Assessment (HRIA), Stages Two and Three are increasing levels of testing of a defined area, and Stage Four is the full mitigation or excavation, of a site.

The archaeological site now sitting under the Canadian Museum for Human Rights (CMHR) is designated by the Provincial Borden number DiLg-33. The

APRIL CHABOT

site is located in an area with several other archaeologically rich sites collectively known as The Forks National Historic Sites (NHSC). The Forks has been a meeting place for Indigenous groups and later European settlers for the past 6000 years (www.theforks.com, accessed February 1, 2017).

Site DiLg-33 represents one of the largest and most significant archaeological excavations undertaken in the province of Manitoba to date. Constructing the Canadian Museum for Human Rights on this site has been socially and politically contentious from the start; not only because of its culturally significant location, but also due to concerns raised by archaeologists, academics and the public as to the fate of the recovered artifacts and the measures taken to protect the cultural heritage not yet recovered. Many regard the construction of the museum on such culturally rich and significant ground to be culturally insensitive to Indigenous people, for whom the landscape of their ancestors has been forever altered. Again.

The Canadian Museum for Human Rights could be the ideal platform to address the human rights abuses that have plagued and continue to plague, Indigenous people in Canada. It is impossible to showcase the advancement of human rights without serious discussions about the violations of those rights that have necessitated change and enlightenment. It is unclear at the time of writing whether the Canadian Museum for Human Rights is up to the task.

Archaeological investigations that took place at the CMHR site in 2008–2009 revealed 379,941 artifacts, as well as a perfectly preserved 800-year-old human footprint (Kroker, 2010, p. 118). Despite rumour of human burials, none were found at the site.

According to Parks Canada, the law provides that "protected archaeological resources include *all evidence of human occupation that comes out of the ground (or underwater)*" except Nova Scotia (Parks Canada http://www.pc.gc.ca/docs/r/pfa-fap/ap-an.aspx, accessed July 11, 2014). Since the protection of "property" comes under provincial jurisdiction according to the Constitution in Canada, provincial and territorial governments have each enacted specific legislation to protect archaeological material (Parks Canada http://www.pc.gc.ca/docs/r/pfa-fap/ap-an.aspx, accessed July 11, 2014). Parks Canada notes that every jurisdiction has in place a "single workable scenario" for the management of cultural materials or liaison among authorities and although they "all follow the same basic pattern", it is generally not outlined in written form (Parks Canada http://www.pc.gc.ca/docs/r/pfa-fap/ap-an.aspx, accessed July 1, 2016). The vague and informal nature of this commitment is likely the basis for the wide variation in the management of cultural heritage materials seen across Canada's provinces and territories.

There are two federal statutes under which archaeological concerns are addressed in Canada. These are the Canadian Environmental Assessment Act (CEA) and the Cultural Property Export and Import Act, which serve as an umbrella for concerns including environmental, marine and import/export among others. Under the CEA, the terms "archaeological" and "cultural heritage" appear only twice and no section exists which deals with archaeological artifacts or cultural heritage material specifically. In Manitoba, a Stage One environmental assessment is required before progressing to more aggressive testing or excavation. As an environmental assessment, this step falls under the purview of the CEA legislation.

The Cultural Property Export and Import Act is designed to protect against the removal of cultural heritage artifacts from the country without appropriate permits. Perpetrators may be subject to further penalties under UNESCO sanctions (Cultural Property Export and Import Act: 12). Neither piece of legislation deals with the protection of, for example, cultural landscapes, sacred land or human remains. The term "archaeology" appears only once under the Cultural Property Export and Import Act in the context mentioned above.

As early as 1950, the need for Canadian federal heritage legislation was recognized and tasked to the Massey Commission. The resulting report stated, "if the government took charge and provided adequate funding and a comprehensive policy, the "precarious state" of Canadian culture as indicated in its findings would change for the better" (Klimko, 1998, p. 205). These findings were not followed up until 40 years later when in 1990 a renewed attempt at Canadian federal heritage legislation was drafted and very nearly came into being. The proposed legislation, known as the "Proposed Act respecting the protection of the archaeological heritage of Canada" (Minister of Communications, 1990), was the outcome of concerns raised by the archaeological and heritage communities.

Seidemann (2003, p. 575) quotes Neal Ferris to suggest the underlying reasons for the absence of federal law in Canada which:

[I]n part due to jurisdiction issues (provinces like states, are responsible for heritage off federal lands)...partly due to the lack of willingness [of the federal government] to grapple with such a complex issue, and partly due to major research institutions...being proactive and developing their own repatriation policies in [t]he absence of legislation...Part of this void in legislation is also filled by ethical mandates of national professional organizations such as the Canadian Archaeological Association and the Canadian Museums Association.

Any federal legislation must resolve the issue of locality, wherein federal jurisdiction accommodates specific provincial or territorial issues. Many types of cultural remains may be held to be as sacred and/or as valuable as human remains within an Indigenous culture in Canada and these should receive no less protection. The Cultural material should enrich broader living descendant communities, providing links between culture and identities of the past and cultural identities of the present. Recognition of these identities is crucial not only to the material record but to local communities. As Ross (2010, p. 124) has stated,

It is only by having Aboriginal people and heritage professionals working together to challenge out-dated legislation acknowledged and acted upon by bureaucracies, that Aboriginal voice can, once again, be heard.

Without meaningful changes to policy and legislation at the federal and/or provincial level, the inclusion of Indigenous communities and values remains only theoretical in Canada.

An overarching theme taken from interviews with participants of the Indigenous group is that respect for their cultural heritage material is key. Many expressed concerns and deep anxiety at the thought that artifacts in general and from the site of the CMHR in particular (especially sacred objects such as those with ceremonial significance), would not be treated with the traditional respect accorded to them or ever seen again by their communities. The fear was that these materials would be left to gather dust in the basement of a museum or government building. To my knowledge, these fears have become reality; the artifacts have been left in less than ideal conditions in the basement of a government building. The participants I spoke to were happy to share their cultural heritage with any group as long as the proper protocols demonstrating sensitivity and respect for their communities and the objects were genuinely followed. Their requests do not seem too much to ask.

This group unanimously supported the location of the site of the CMHR as the continuation of a meeting place from ancient to modern times. One of the wishes expressed was for The Forks location to represent Indigenous cultures as it expands, recognizing the importance of the land to people long ago as well as today.

The concept of "ownership" of cultural heritage was another theme touched upon in the interviews with this group of participants. Ownership is a distinctly capitalistic aspect of colonialism. In contrast, it was pointed out to me that Indigenous people regard the land and anything on or in it as under their guardianship, rather than "owned" by them. The land and its resources are for everyone, to be shared by all. In order to regain guardianship of their cultural heritage, Indigenous people must face a system that is based on different notions of possession and sovereignty, vestiges of the colonial mindset, placing them at a serious disadvantage.

The notion of Indigenous ownership of cultural heritage material, engagement and control in Canada is non-existent since all cultural heritage material is automatically considered to be vested in the Crown. Bell (1992, p. 502) argues that "Recent trends in Canadian aboriginal rights law appear to support the expansion of aboriginal rights to include collective or communal ownership of moveable cultural property." All of the Indigenous people interviewed described their inclusion at all in the development process of the CMHR in particular and development in general as appearing to be an "afterthought" by development, or a way to "cover themselves" that appeared to be little more than simple tokenism. After an initial blessing ceremony of the CMHR excavation, Indigenous people were not further engaged as development proceeded, nor were they informed of any of the outcomes of the excavation process by the museum or its representatives.

One proposed solution is that the concept of custodianship rather than ownership be used in reference to cultural heritage material providing a symbolic acknowledgment that Indigenous cultural heritage is under the guardianship of Indigenous communities and on loan from them to local museums, universities, etc. This proposed solution alleviates the stress of not being in physical possession of cultural heritage materials, and that alone would be a significant step to building trust between Indigenous communities and other stakeholders. As a symbolic gesture it is incredibly important because it shifts the focus away from the notion of "ownership," which becomes bogged down in legality, instead focusing on cooperative relationships built on mutual interests, trust, and respect. All groups interviewed demonstrated considerable interest in moving away from the concept of ownership applied to cultural heritage materials. Instead, custodianship and respect through proper conservation were emphasized by all as key when dealing with current issues in cultural heritage management.

The notion of "ownership" of cultural heritage in the legal sense has created adversarial legal and political relationships between competing interests that have characterized disputes over cultural heritage material. By moving away from a concept of "ownership," these adversarial relationships are no longer necessary. When stakeholders work together to protect and conserve cultural heritage material as set out in formal policy and legislation, their actions work as the much-needed form of checks and balances to counteract the main issue: a lack of political will.

Another proposed solution is the adoption of OCAP principles (Ownership, Control, Access, and Possession) for archaeological research (OCAP, 2017). OCAP principles seem uniquely amenable to the idea of replacing ownership with custodianship while maintaining the intent of research protocols. Although originally developed by Indigenous researchers studying health in northern communities, its principles are currently applied by other disciplines researching within Indigenous communities. In fact, the voluntary adoption of these principles is now standard practice for any research conducted by Indigenous researchers and cultural anthropologists working in northern communities. Many chiefs already insist that this model is used whenever research is conducted in their communities. For these reasons and due to the suitability of OCAP principles to archaeological research within Canada, this represents an ideal starting point to address new policy and legislation initiatives for cultural heritage research and management. As a best practices model, it presents an opportunity for archaeologists and government representatives to collaborate with Indigenous researchers and communities to create a set of meaningful and inclusive research protocols:

The First Nations Principles of OCAP™ (ownership, control, access, and possession) mean that First Nations control data collection processes in their communities. The right of First Nations communities to own, control, access, and possess information about their peoples is fundamentally tied to

APRIL CHABOT

self-determination and to the preservation and development of their culture. OCAP™ allows a community to make decisions regarding why, how and by whom information is collected, used or shared. (http://www.rhs-ers.ca/node/2, accessed September 16, 2013)

Instead of ownership vested in the Crown, future policy and legislation development or amendment at all levels will fully and automatically recognize that cultural heritage material is under guardianship of Indigenous communities who allow researchers, government or private museums to take responsibility (act as custodian) for the conservation and protection of these cultural materials when local communities do not have the capacity to do so themselves. For more information regarding the four components of the OCAP principles, see http://fnigc.ca/ocap.

Regarding archaeological research, adoption and amendment of the OCAP principles would thus reflect new collaborative relationships between the stakeholder groups based on mutual respect and accountability.

A global crisis of destruction of cultural heritage sites exists due to rapid development, outpacing the ability of available archaeologists as well as existing protective measures to contend with it (Allen, 2010, p. 162). Unfortunately, it is still not even recognized as a crisis in Canada. As a result, legislation and protective measures have not entered into the discussion for over two decades.

The ideas and best practices model presented here have been available in various forms for many decades and are intended as a starting point for future consideration when designing new policy or legislation. A cohesive statement of best practices aims to ensure imperviousness (to whatever degree possible) to a lack of political will, exempting it from the passing whims of whichever federal or provincial political party happens to be in power. In total, eight recommendations for best practices are included here, in point form:

- Establishment of federal heritage policy and legislation flexible enough to work with existing provincial and territorial policy and legislation
- Establishment of Archaeology as a Profession with professional standards and guidelines encoded within heritage policy and legislation (i.e. must meet professional and educational requirements to obtain permits)
- Seven Teachings provides basis for interactions or engagement between archaeologists or government representatives and Indigenous communities
- OCAP Principles shall be adopted and practiced whenever archaeological research is conducted anywhere in Canada
- Establishment of position for Indigenous Elder chosen by their community to represent City/Province (as applicable) to work with provincial or territorial Heritage Branch, ensuring compliance with OCAP Principles
- Establishment of a database accessible to the public that tracks archaeological data as well as traditional knowledge by province/territory
- Permit Compliance: Specific standards of engagement with Indigenous communities set out in permit requirements

- Reporting: Permit requirement to document oral traditions of area in formal report along with archaeological data/findings

Federal legislation and policy guidelines must be drafted to reflect these elements and to provide coverage of gaps in cultural heritage regulation, which currently exist, such as in airports and some waterways. Thus, federal legislation is necessary in order to adequately conserve and protect cultural heritage materials, wherever they are recovered.

The fact that Canada has no federal legislation in place to protect its rich heritage resources is nothing short of a global embarrassment. Could it be (the reason that there have been no further attempts at federal legislation for heritage) that our proud nation is bending under the shame of both our colonial past and the enduring colonial present?

Moving forward requires a look back while charting a new path into unknown territory and rebuilding relationships. Legal definitions and Indigenous sovereign rights must be fully established and codified. Indigenous people have been fighting since day one to establish their human rights in a now hostile land that once provided both home and livelihood long before settler colonialists set up house. Moving forward requires recognition of this complex and horrific past, which defies the carefully moulded national identity of Canada as a multi-cultural success on the global stage. I leave these results for future researchers with a quote from the final chapter of my thesis to emphasize that we cannot afford to leave anyone behind on the path we must take forward: This strange road we find ourselves on can only be traveled together (Sleepy Hollow TV series, 2013).

REFERENCES

Allen, H. (2010). The crisis in 21st century archaeological heritage management. In C. Phillips & H. Allen (Eds.), *Bridging the divide indigenous communities and archaeology into the 21st century.* Walnut Creek, CA: Leftcoast Press, Inc.

Atalay, S. (1996). Indigenous archaeology as decolonizing practice. *American Indian Quarterly, 30*(3–4), 280–310.

Bell, C. (1992). Aboriginal claims to cultural property in Canada: A comparative legal analysis of the repatriation debate. *American Indian Law Review, 17*(2), 457–521.

Dyck, I. (2009). Canadian prairies archaeology, 1857–1886: Exploration and self development. *Canadian Journal of Archaeology, 33*, 1–40.

Ferris, N. (2003). Between colonial and indigenous archaeologies: Legal and extra-legal ownership of the archaeological past in North America. *Canadian Journal of Archaeology, 27*, 154–190.

Klimko, O. (1998). Nationalism and the growth of fur trade archaeology in Western Canada. In P. Smith & D. Mitchell (Eds.), *Bringing back the past historical perspectives on Canadian archaeology.* Gatineau: Canadian Museum of Civilization.

Kroker, S. (2010). *Archaeological mitigation for the Canadian museum for human rights at the Forks, Winnipeg, Manitoba.* Winnipeg: Quaternary Consultants Ltd.

OCAP™. (2014, May). *The path to first nations information governance.* Ottawa: The First Nations Information Governance Centre.

Parks Canada. (2016). *Law and terminology in archaeological resource management.* Retrieved June 29, 2016, from http://www.pc.gc.ca/docs/r/pfa-fap/ap-an.aspx

APRIL CHABOT

Ross, A. (2010). Defining cultural heritage at Gummingurru, Queensland, Australia. In C. Phillips & H. Allen (Eds.), *Bridging the divide indigenous communities and archaeology into the 21st century.* Walnut Creek, CA: Leftcoast Press, Inc.

Seidemann, R. M. (2003/2004). Bones of contention: A comparative examination of law governing human remains from archaeological contexts in formerly colonial countries. *Louisiana Law Review, 64*, 545–588.

Sleepy Hollow [Television series]. (2013, September 16). Hollywood, CA: Fox.

Watkins, J. E. (2000). Repatriation in a global perspective. In *Indigenous archaeology American Indian values and scientific practice.* Walnut Creek, CA: Alta Mira Press.

Watkins, J. E. (2003). Beyond the margin: American Indians, first nations and archaeology in North America. *American Antiquity, 68*(2), 273–285.

Website. Retrieved February 5, 2017, from thecanadianencyclopedia.ca

Website. Retrieved February 1, 2017, from www.theforks.com

April Chabot
Department of Anthropology
University of Manitoba
Winnipeg, Manitoba

SAYMORE PETROS NDOU AND MICHAEL CHIMONYO

3. INDIGENOUS KNOWLEDGE ON NGUNI CATTLE USES

Breed of the Past for the Future

INTRODUCTION

Resource-poor farmers possess undocumented Indigenous knowledge (IK) on use of Nguni cattle and their by-products that can be used in the future. Indigenous knowledge systems (IKS) are bodies of undocumented skills, experiences, ideas, information and insights about survival and livelihood developed naturally over generations by local people within their community (Kaya & Masoga, 2005). Indigenous knowledge is dynamic, relies on memory and is transmitted systematically and orally from generation to generation. Approximately 70% of the communal households in southern Africa depend on low-input livestock production. Livestock production including rearing cattle for multipurpose is an important component of their livelihood because their land is marginal and not quite suitable for cropping (Ndou et al., 2011). Of these, between 35 and 75% are food-insecure. However, as a low-input coping strategy, resource-poor farmers have developed IK to manage livestock and handle livestock products with efforts to address socio-economic challenges, improve their livelihood and celebrate life. Use of IK to address food insecurity among poverty-stricken communal farmers is under-exploited and scantily documented. Sustainability of IKS is, therefore, at stake, unless concerted efforts are made to preserve it.

Among other livestock species, cattle are the most valued across the southern Africa region. One of the dominant indigenous cattle breeds in Southern Africa is the Nguni breed, which has been skillfully bred and subjected to natural selection to meet a plethora of socio-economic and cultural needs of the poor. Uses of Nguni cattle include the provision of animal traction, and playing key roles in socio-cultural ceremonies. Nguni cattle products and terms had been transformed into a rich art of unexpected beauty, and now form part of the stock of IK. This is the cultural heritage of the Zulu people (Poland, 2003). Therefore, it is crucial to document the IK of Zulu people on cattle production and actively engage them in livelihood development programs. The article emphasizes that the transfer of IK on cattle production will ensure that the utilization of cattle products will be maintained as a source of food or healing for resource-poor rural farmers. Moreover, the transfer of the IK associated with cattle production to the younger generation opens the way to the potential future

© KONINKLIJKE BRILL NV, LEIDEN, 2018 | DOI 9789004367418_003

use of traditional cattle products. Therefore, the objective of this study is to give an overview of Zulu resource-limited farmers' IK on the socio-economic importance and cultural significance of indigenous Nguni cattle products in rural households.

MATERIALS AND METHODS

The experimental procedures were performed in accordance with the ethical standard guidelines approved by the University of KwaZulu-Natal's Research Ethics Committee (Clearance certificate: HSS/0164/013D).

Description of Study Sites

The study was conducted in five villages in the Jozini local municipality in UMkhanyakude district situated in the extreme north-eastern part of the KwaZulu-Natal Province, South Africa. The villages are Biva, Gedleza, Mkhayane, Mamfene, and Nyawushane. The villages are located on flatlands at an altitude of 77 m above sea level. The mean annual rainfall is 600 mm. The rainfall patterns around the district are unreliable with peaks occurring during the hot wet season. Temperature ranges from a minimum of 11°C to a maximum of 30°C. The vegetation around the district is typical coastal sand veld, bushveld and foothill wooded grasslands. Due to the diversity of its vegetation, the district favored a broad range of socio-cultural conditions of the Zulu ethnic groups who occupied these areas for more than 100 years ago.

The villages were selected to represent the diversity in natural conditions around the district. Therefore, in some parts of the district mixed (crop and livestock) farming is practiced whilst natural conditions in other parts of the district entirely favor livestock production. The study area was selected because it is fairly isolated, remote and is still governed by traditional leaders and royal families of the pre-colonial era. Therefore, villagers from UMkhanyakude district represent the Zulu people who are a distinct social group with unique IK of rearing cattle and methods of processing or handling livestock products. The villagers are linked with the urban center through gravel roads with no bridges, and households are not electrified. The remoteness of the villages boosts the use of IK in addressing household challenges by making it difficult to have a constant supply or processing of commercialized cattle products through modern technology, especially during the rainy season. Other communal farmers within UMkhanyakude district occupied these villages as a result of the post-colonial evacuations from other districts within the KwaZulu-Natal Province and were also engaged in local livelihood strategies.

Experimental Design and Data Collection

The study adopted the structural functionalism theory, which points out that a sustainable system is composed of interrelated components which work hand in hand in achieving a primary goal (Babbie, 2008; Dweba & Mearns, 2011). Data were collected through face-to-face interviews and focus group discussions conducted by trained interviewers using a tape recorder. Interviews were conducted in their local Zulu language and at their homesteads. Selection of respondents for both face-to-face interviews and focus groups discussions were based on snowball sampling technique and a willingness by interviewees to participate in the research. The respondents included 72 (Age ≥ 60) male and married, 36 (Age ≥ 55) female and married, 50 (Age 18–35) youths and 18 traditional healers (Age ≥ 57) and 15 (Age ≥ 65) traditional leaders. Twelve focus discussion groups, which were made up of elderly females, elderly males and youths, that is, four focus groups per social group were conducted. Each focus discussion group would comprise of at least four members. The principle of adaptive collaborative investigations/questioning was adopted to guide interviewees and ensure that differences between IK, TK, and CK are taken care of.

In the current study, persons with more than 65 years of age were selected because they are regarded as sole proprietors, repositories and reliable fundamental sources of IK. Apart from being sole proprietors of the knowledge of the past, the elderly, especially traditional leaders and healers, were also selected because they play a central role in addressing household socio-economic and cultural needs, illiteracy and that they have remained localized within that habitat. The youth were also selected, and their perceptions were considered to be major determinants of the potential use of IK of the past, in the future. Thus, the constituents within the district possess a unique Indigenous knowledge about the socio-cultural significance, economic importance and management practices of local cattle breeds in relation to household food security.

Although most of the respondents were interviewed individually, however, for very old informants, video recordings were adopted and other household members were allowed during the interview only to supplement with information. Video recording covered interview sessions for 12 male and 9 female respondents. The youths were also interviewed to determine the potential future use of IK in cattle production and processing of cattle products. Information obtained from the youths was also used to assess the extent to which the IK is passed through generations. Data obtained through video recording, audio-scoping, and photography was subjected to qualitative analysis.

RESULTS AND DISCUSSION

Indigenous Knowledge about Ownership Patterns of Cattle

There was substantial concordance among farmers in that, regardless of the source, all cattle within a kraal belonged to the head of household – *uBaba* (the father). After the death of the household head, the eldest son formally inherits and becomes in charge of all cattle (Andrew, 2003; Mapiye, 2009). In a polygamous household, however, other farmers mentioned that cattle that came directly from the bride's family would be inherited by the youngest son of the bride. Cattle that were linked to social beliefs or ancestral rituals such as *inkomo eyamadlozi* (cow used to worship ancestors) were respected, and even though the household head owns them, he would use them, if and only, after performing rituals to ask permission from the ancestors. The observations support the common phenomenon that unlike other Southern Bantu language-speaking peoples, the Zulu people attach their traditional values and lifestyles to their cattle (Poland et al., 2003).

Some farmers pointed out that cattle were shared amongst household members following the death of the household head, but the chief-heir would be the eldest son. Farmers mentioned that for a herd to meet the socio-economic and cultural needs of the household, it should have all classes of cattle namely cows, heifers, bulls, oxen, and calves. The classifications were based on farmers' knowledge on the cattle's parentage history (incidences associated with days of calving), physiological status (parity and gestation) and the phenotypic traits (sexual organs and horns). While heifers were mainly used as replacements to substitute old cows that are used for breeding purposes, other classes of cattle were reared to meet several of household needs.

Indigenous Knowledge of Roles of Cattle Classes

Farmers possessed knowledge about diversified roles played by classes of Nguni cattle to meet various socio-economic and cultural needs of rural communities. Cattle played significant roles during social gatherings and traditional ceremonies (collectively identified as *imisebenzi*), such as wedding ceremonies (*umshado*), dowry (*lobola*), funerals (*isifo*), *ukweshwama*, *ukuqolisa*, memorial service (*umbuyiso*) and in settling disputes either as live animals or using products such as meat and skins. Animal welfare concerns had been raised during some of these ceremonies, as the animal is subjected to inhumane handling, as viewed by the international community (Ndou et al., 2011). All cattle classes were used in social gatherings and dowry. Dowry settlements were considered a token of appreciation and a way of strengthening relations between in-laws. There was a mutual agreement among farmers that the process of marriage was cherished and supported by exchange of precious gift while a divorce is now acceptable, the Zulu culture shuns divorce. Each household had draught cattle in the form of oxen or dry cows to assist is doing heavy work such as hauling farm produce, stones, cuts, timber and firewood.

Indigenous Knowledge of Cattle Uses and Products

Milk.   The respondents revealed that milk plays an important role as a cheap, readily accessible, and alternative source of protein in rural communities. Indigenous cattle are reared by communal farmers under less benign conditions to meet multiple objectives including a provision of quality milk that is essential for human health

(Mapekula et al., 2011). Most of the participants mentioned that indigenous cows, such as the Nguni breed reproduce remarkably, each cow produces a calf every year. In this respect, cattle have an enormous potential to provide milk throughout the year, thereby contributing towards food security. As a low-input coping strategy, resource-poor farmers in KwaZulu-Natal are custodians of IK for managing milking herds, processing and use practices of milk to celebrate life. Farmers claimed that milk could be consumed raw (*ubisi oluhlaza*) or can be processed using different methods to produce indigenous products, namely *isthubi, amasi, umlaza* and *ihongo*. Indigenous knowledge on milk production within the poverty-stricken communities occupied by the Zulu people is under-exploited and ignored in research.

Slaughtering for meat, leather and ritual purposes. Cattle were slaughtered for various reasons, including meat production, leather production, culling purpose and traditional gatherings (settling disputes, thanking ancestors for the change of seasons especially in winter, wedding ceremonies, ummbuyiso (memorial services) and comforting widows or widower. Farmers mentioned that different slaughtering techniques were adopted depending on the reasons for slaughter. For instance, under normal circumstances, a spear is used to put down the beast by stabbing straight into the heart (located just behind the right foreleg) in the kraal. Another way was through bare hands by warriors using bare hands during the inauguration ceremony of the Chief or King, a social gathering known as *ukweshwama* out of the kraal. The third slaughtering method was for *inkomo yokuqolisa* which required the animal to die in pain by first tearing its tail. During this slaughtering method people would bet for the animal to die quickly while others would want it to die slowly, and rewards were provided for that.

In the first method, the spear is immediately inserted and removed to let blood out. Slaughtering was done by experienced slaughter-man specialist following consultation with ancestors. Farmers emphasized that a specialist was chosen within a community for the belief that meat eating quality (flavor) would be improved, however, 'the stabber' was required to render the animal dead within the shortest possible time. Just before stabbing, slaughter-men were encouraged to eat salt because farmer believed that it cleans the slaughter-man in eliminating aberrant beef quality traits. Although slaughtering was done anytime depending on the need except at night, it was solely directed by the household head or village elders, following a traditional saying to ask for permission from ancestors. Cattle were slaughtered inside the kraal in the presence of the whole herd. Henceforth, this further augmented the need for stabbing to be quick and peaceful so that they do not frighten other cattle within the herd. Cattle that were associated with evil spirits were slaughtered outside the kraal, and the meat will be cooked closer to the kraal and consumed there, any member of the community is welcome to enjoy the meat. During slaughter, cattle were not supposed to be restrained. Therefore, behavioral responses such as urinating and relaxation were used as indicators that the animal is ready for slaughter.

It was of paramount importance that slaughter and skinning procedures should minimize damage to the skin or living some muscle or meat attached to the skin. There was a general concordance by farmers that proper slaughtering and skinning techniques prevent losses of meat. At the same time, a hide will be used effectively when it is not damaged.

After the slaughtering process, bile (*inyongo*) will be spilled on the blood spilled on the ground for the belief that it would cool down ancestors and prevent remaining herd from fleeing the habitat. After slaughter, just like milk, respondents pinpointed that it was a taboo to consume meat anywhere else except within the household. The carcass was distributed according to gender and age, but different body parts were cooked by man at the same time without cutting the meat into small pieces. While cooking meat during social meetings was performed by a man, the women would partake in beer making. Slaughtering was the most interesting scenario for herd boys because it gives an opportunity for herd boys to elect new leaders. In this way, some cattle organs such as heart, lungs, and ears were used by herders as prizes for their fighting games. These organs were given to the household leader (*inqgwele*) of the herd boys to take to the grazing fields to defend his household by fighting for it. Boys would cut the heart into small pieces and insert it into the bronchi and grill. The grilled meat product will be used as a prize for the herd boys who win during fighting games.

Skin. It is given first preference to milk in case a calf is born with beautiful or uniquely coat characteristics. The Nguni skin was also used to make (*ibhetshu*). Therefore, when a nice calf is born, regardless of the goodness of other traits from its parents, the calf will be slaughtered for the provision of the skin. Apart from clothes, the skin was also used to make mats, ropes, clothes, blankets, drums, shields and for performing a ritual or traditional procedures. The coat characteristic will be used as a way to identify the use of the skin. Some people would exchange a matured animal for beautiful skin. Traditional healers use the tail end.

Reasons for Losses in Indigenous Knowledge

A plethora of respondents indicated that IK of use of cattle and their products is diminishing in rural communities. The findings agree with previous reports that IK on agriculture is at risk of getting extinct (Dweba & Mearns, 2011). Furthermore, these losses have inevitably contributed to the reduction in the use of cattle in social gatherings and consumption of traditionally processed cattle products, and consequently leading to lack of diet diversity. Eventually, food security and availability of traditional cattle products is ultimately compromised, especially among resource-poor farmers in rural communities. The respondents repeatedly mentioned the reasons for losses in IK are linked more with modern civilization and the migration of people from one community to the other. These include the lack of proper documentation, globalization and modern lifestyle, habitat loss, climatic change and deforestation, migration to urban areas, govern policies and post-colonial effects, prejudice, and stigma attached to use of IK by the youths.

Lack of Proper Documentation and Standardisation

Respondents pinpointed that the knowledge of the past on cattle products is possessed by the elderly age. Of these, a few are able to read and write. The application of IK relies on memory, and the households do not record any information. Due to a reduction in the life expectancy, the elderly population is decreasing; this further puts pressure on the sustainability or future existence of IK to address challenges faced by communal cattle farmers. Apart from this, the IK is often sidelined in scientific research programs. The 'science' behind resource-poor farmers' knowledge can be validated and standardized for future use. The lack of standardized products of the past has led to lack of the interest in the use of IK-based products and sometimes inefficiencies of such products or IK-orientated ideas.

Globalisation and Modern Lifestyle

In this era of globalization, the rural communities are the most susceptible parts of the world that are prone to losses of some individual cultural identities. Eventually, the worldwide integration and developments have also introduced other substitute forms of knowledge and products that lead to shunning of the local ways of meeting socio-economic and cultural needs. For example, long ago milk was handled by use of plant-derived material, but nowadays, plastic containers are being introduced. With this new phase of globalization looming, the introduction of television and other forms of entertainment from the west has led to that people to rebuke their traditional social gatherings that were crucial to allow sharing of IK among community members. Cattle farmers have developed negative attitudes and stigma against the use of IK in fear of being labelled as old-fashioned and backward. Considering that youth do not attend traditional gatherings and they attend modern education institute that follow curriculums that are not culture-fit, they do not contribute much to the preservation of IK. Before young boys and girls, would be allowed to first attend home chores before attending schools but nowadays things have changed. People have lost trust on things that are said and not taught at school. The introduction of foreign or scientifically proven interventions has also contributed to the loss in the knowledge of the past.

Pre-Colonial and Government Policies

Owing to the occupation of land by the colonial settlers, climatic change and deforestation, natural ecosystems that were previously managed by local sustained the exhibition of knowledge of the past in cattle production, is rapidly disappearing. Cattle farmers were forcibly moved by colonial settlers to new habitats eventually, their livelihood strategies changed leading to alterations of natural ecosystems.

Within new habitats, cattle herd sizes were reduced and demarcation fences were introduced which further restricted the ancestral occupants their freedom to apply IK. The IK about management of cattle could have thrived into new habitats, but more specialized organisms or plant species may not be able to adjust to the new interventions when occupants are changed or disappear as a result of land development. On the other hand, the current post-colonial government policies in the judiciary, education systems, and natural resources management do not go hand in hand with the old ways of implementing instructions or management of natural resources. For instance, the current education and the judiciary systems, which protect have been identified to be not 'culture fit'. These situations have negative impact on the sustainability of biodiversity, which supports cattle production and has caused the deterioration of the associated Indigenous knowledge.

Climatic Change and Deforestation

In its most general sense, any forms of human-nature interactions alter the natural ecosystems. Many farmers have identified deforestation and climatic change as two factors that have contributed to losses in IK in cattle in two ways. Firstly, there are direct effects on habitat losses for both cattle and farmers, for example, loss of vegetation that is used for feeding animals, building kraals, design handling facilities and provision of ethno-veterinary medicines. Secondly, changes in cattle management practices in response to hazards that stem from climatic change and deforestation indirectly fail the IK to adapt to new living conditions. For example, respondents pointed out that nowadays the use of purchased supplementary feeds and modern veterinary medicines which are not within the framework of their cultures has extremely led to IK being side-lined, consequently exacerbating its loss.

Migration to Urban Areas

The movement of people to urban areas in search of jobs have also been cited as one of the main reasons that contributed to the loss of knowledge of the past about rearing cattle. Previously, the youths would migrate to urban areas and work in order save money so that he can build a herd and come back and was encouraged not to inherit foreign ideologies for fear of being punished by ancestors. Nowadays, the youths stay for long period of time in fear of losing jobs thereby changing lifestyle and ignoring IK. The household head trains the eldest son with the hope that he will succeed him, but nowadays the heir migrates to urban areas and may not share the knowledge with their youngsters.

SUMMARY AND CONCLUDING REMARKS

The discussion above has demonstrated the importance of IK in cattle production. Given the responses of most of the farmers, implementation of IK could play a major role in achieving food security, alleviating poverty, and facilitates efficient use of natural resources. The IK of Zulu cattle farmers contribute to herd dynamics, subsequently influencing ways in which cattle products contribute to food security and poverty alleviation. Characterization, integration of local knowledge with modern technology and education of resource-limited farmers through veterinary and agricultural extension would ultimately result in improved animal husbandry techniques. Application of IK in utilization of cattle will also open an opportunity to increase production of cattle products and celebration of life by rural communities. Furthermore, evidence exists that IK on cattle products is gradually getting extinct. Although the knowledge is at risk of getting diminished, if documented and implemented, it could be a culmination of rural people's varied interests in addressing livelihood challenges, healing and celebrating life through livestock production. Therefore, the needs for awareness programs to capture, preserve, transfer and use easily accessible, cheap and locally available knowledge for cattle production to develop rural communities, and alleviate poverty and food insecurity cannot be undermined.

ACKNOWLEDGEMENTS

We are grateful to University of KwaZulu-Natal Competitive grant for supporting this research and UMkhanyakude district farmers for their invaluable information. Many thanks also go to Mr. Nkosi of the Jozini Livestock Association, Department of Agriculture for assisting the authors during data collection and language translation.

REFERENCES

Andrew, M., Ainslie, A., & Shackleton, C. (2003). *Evaluating land and agrarian reform in South Africa* (Occasional paper series No. 8). Cape Town: Programme for Land and Agrarian Studies, School of Government, and University of the Western Cape.

Babbie, E. (2008). *The basis of social research* (4th ed.). Belmont, CA: Thomson Wadsworth.

Dweba, T. P., & Mearns, M. A. (2011). Conserving indigenous knowledge as the key to the current and future use of traditional vegetables. *International Journal of Information Management, 31*(6), 564–571.

Kaya, H. O., & Masoga, M. (2005). *Balanced literacy: Enhancing the school curriculum through African indigenous knowledge system.* Potchefstroom: North West University.

Mapekula, M., Chimonyo, M., Mapiye, C., & Dzama, K. (2011). Fatty acid, amino acid and mineral composition of milk from Nguni and local crossbred cows in South Africa. *Journal of Food Composition and Analysis, 24*, 529–536.

Mapiye, C., Chimonyo, M., Dzama, K., Raats, J. G., & Mapekula, M. (2009). Opportunities for improving Nguni cattle production in the smallholder farming systems of South Africa. *Livestock Science, 124*, 196–204.

Ndou, S. P., Muchenje, V., & Chimonyo, M. (2011). Animal welfare in multipurpose cattle production systems and its implications on beef quality. *African Journal of Biotechnology, 10*(7), 1049–1064.

Poland, M., Hammond-Tooke, D., & Voigt, L. (2003). *The abundant herds: A celebration of the Nguni cattle of the Zulu people.* Vlaeberg: Fernwood Press.

SAYMORE PETROS NDOU AND MICHAEL CHIMONYO

Saymore Petros Ndou
Department of Animal Sciences
University of Manitoba
Winnipeg, Canada

Michael Chimonyo
Discipline of Poultry and Animal Sciences
University of KwaZulu-Natal
Durban, South Africa

WAYLON LENK

4. EARLY INDIGENOUS NORTH AMERICAN CARTOGRAPHY AS PERFORMANCE TEXTS

INTRODUCTION

What's a map? If the International Cartographic Association (ICA) has anything to say about it, it's "a symbolized representation of *geographic reality...*" ("International Cartographic Association Mission") Emphasis is mine, because, if indeed maps depict geographic reality, then La Vérendrye's 1728, 1729 or 1730 map compositing information from Indian informants – Ochagach, Tacchigis, Le Marteblanche, Pako, an unnamed slave of the Cree, and an unnamed Monsoni chief – is as much a map as Tolkien's illustrations of Middle Earth. La Vérendrye's composite is the point of entry for the English language historiography of North American Indian maps prior to 1800, starting with Lawrence J. Burpee in 1935. That historiography is loaded with Eurocentric notions of reality and how space works that need to be unpacked if we're to talk intelligently and rigorously about the cartography under consideration. The key in the historiography is about whom is the story told? Is it about European expansionists with Indian cartographers relegated to roles as deuteragonists, or is it about Indian cartography in which Indians and Europeans sometimes collaborate on mapping the continent?

(A note on terminology: I use "Indian" through this chapter for two reasons. The first is that that is how indigenous peoples of the Americas are generally referred to in the historiography that forms the backbone of this chapter. The second is that I am Karuk, one of the tribes of the Klamath River in northwest California. In addition to family, village and tribe, my elders use "Indian" or "Injun" to refer to ourselves. I grew up around skepticism towards "Native" or "Native American" – the reason for which is that white people can't just make us change how we refer to ourselves to make themselves feel better about genocide. While I acknowledge that others may hear it as a pejorative, as I live with it, "Indian" is an act of sovereignty.)

HISTORIOGRAPHY

Prior to the 1980s, the scholarly conversation on the La Vérendrye map – one of the most studied of all Indian maps – landed squarely on the initial answer: the story of Indian cartography is a subplot in the tale of Aryan exceptionalism. Lawrence J. Burpee began the conversation in 1935:

© KONINKLIJKE BRILL NV, LEIDEN, 2018 | DOI 9789004367418_004

> A thousand years ago the Northmen, responding to that mysterious attraction which has exercised such a compelling power over men of Aryan blood, pushed their way across the Atlantic to Iceland, from Iceland to Greenland, and from Greenland to America, where they stood first of white men on the shores of a new world. That they were quite unconscious of the magnitude of their discovery does not detract from its interest. The world's greatest discoveries have generally been made unwittingly. (Burpee, 1935)

The import of his use of "Aryan" in 1935 shouldn't be overlooked: by using a shared vocabulary, Burpee's story about Canadian history exists in conversation with Goebbels' story about German identity in a way that analogizes the two. Burpee casts Ochagach, one of La Vérendrye's Indian cartographers, as a Tonto-esque sidekick to the commandant of the Nipigon trading post. As Burpee puts it, "Ochagach's visit had put the torch to La Vérendrye's enthusiasm, and he was now determined at all costs to follow the search which he had so much at heart." Burpee's Ochagach's function is to inspire the Aryan hero to pursue his destiny west.

A shift occurs in the 1980s. In his "Indicators of Unacknowledged Assimilations from Amerindian 'Maps' on Euro-American Maps of North America," George Malcolm Lewis attempts a sort of cartographical archaeology to resurrect the lost maps drawn by Ochagach and others for La Vérendrye (Lewis, 1986). Lewis posits an appealing five-part process for the creation of the La Vérendrye map by juxtaposing archived accounts of the cartography with the map itself:

- "interpreting information received from Indians,"
- "mosaicking information received from several sources,"
- "transforming the mosaic according to some concept of scale,"
- "incorporating the transformation into an existing map of a wider area derived from a different source," and
- "accommodating the original incorporation on other maps."

Lewis' contribution remains untested on other maps drawn by Europeans based on Indian information. As such, it's not clear whether or not it can add Indian material to the archive. His use of quotations in his title echoes De Vorsey's apprehension of indigenous reliability calls his good faith into question. However, his subsequent article suggests that the indigenous maps had much more in common with "geographic reality" than La Vérendrye's composite and the later European "maps" derived from it (Lewis, 1987).

In that subsequent article, Lewis traces the surging French desire for a water route from the Atlantic to the Pacific through North America, and how they then mapped one based on Indian sources who were describing something else. He introduces the metaphor of a mirage. Like when we're driving down the road on a sunny day and vaguely see something in the distance that, upon closer proximity is found to not exist, the Frenchmen mapping a river to the Pacific saw water where there was none. Lewis describes their mirage "incorporating a red river, a mountain of bright stones,

EARLY INDIGENOUS NORTH AMERICAN CARTOGRAPHY AS PERFORMANCE TEXTS

and a river of the west that flowed to a place where its water began to ebb and flow," recalling my comparison to Tolkien above. Just like Tolkien's maps take things that exist in the real world and then jumble them up into something that's never existed anywhere, so La Vérendrye and his successors took aspects of the real world as described by their Indian informants and mapped a fantasy.

Four years later, Lewis places blame for the Frenchmen's creative cartography squarely at the feet of Ochagach and the others (Lewis, 1991). He cites John Long's observation that, based on Indian cartography, it was "very difficult for any one who travels as a trader to ascertain any thing more than the Indian distance from one lake to another." He uses Long's account to claim that, "In his use of Indian maps, La Vérendrye was either less honest or less discerning than the trader and interpreter John Long." In other words, Indian accounts weren't reliable and La Vérendrye, or at least his successors, should have known better than to trust them.

He finishes his tetralogy of articles in response to Barbara Belyea's scathing 1992 historiography. Belyea identifies in the scholarship of the from the 1970s through Lewis's 1991 article as reifying imperial worldviews (Belyea, 1992). Her argument is "that mapping does not represent geographic knowledge in absolute terms, but is instead conventional and culture-specific." In assuming objective omniscience, Lewis and cohort fail to see that their own projects promulgate that part of the colonial project, which devalues indigenous testimony. Lewis's "Metrics, Geometries, Signs, and Language" attempts to rectify his colonial complicity by acknowledging the "need for cross-cultural studies in cartography" and explores ways in which miscommunication between Indian and settler cartographers happened (Lewis, 1993). His analysis adds new information to the conversation, especially the importance of linguistic regions. In a look at the Chickasaw Deerskin Map, he observes that the Chickasaw language constituted "one of the main components" of the Mobilian trade jargon. As such, the Chickasaw were in a prime place to map their communal space.

In 1997, W. J. Eccles wrote his own history of French cartography in the search of a water route to the Pacific (Eccles, 1997). His account is derivative of what has gone on before in all but his level of dismissiveness towards Indian contributors to the emerging North American cartography. Like Lewis, Eccles attributes French misinformation to their indigenous sources. He describes the process:

> The knowledge of the royal officials at Quebec…was based on the vague reports of *illiterate* voyageurs whose personal experience had been expanded by the information they gleaned from the Crees and the Sioux. Those Indian descriptions, filtered through the language barrier, and *their crude maps, sometimes merely drawn in the sand at a beach or on a piece of birchbark with a charred stick*, fed the conceptions and misconceptions of the geography of North America in the minds of the French.

The emphases are mine. Eccles' inclusion of the adjective "illiterate" as well as emphasizing the ephemerality of Cree and Sioux maps with the modifiers "crude"

WAYLON LENK

and "merely" serves to indicate the voyageur and Indian distance from the archive. That distance indicates unreliability, which for Eccles constitutes the root of the Frenchmen's fictive maps.

George Malcolm Lewis returned to the scene to bring it all together in his *Cartographical Encounters* (Lewis, 1998). He inauspiciously introduces his collection of essays by clarifying that "from the very beginning whites needed to know about terrestrial space." His first, self-authored chapter, is a survey of indigenous cartography from 1511 to 1925. While he's clear with his readers that his sources are entirely white, he does acknowledge that there are "white-educated and -trained indigenous specialists" working on petroglyphic maps, the existence of which he's uncertain. He also identifies an empty space in the scholarship on the subject: a "systematic study of...the acquisition of geographic information by alien cultures from the indigenous peoples whose territories they were invading." He includes Mesoamerica – the first time Mesoamerica has been considered side-by-side with what's north of it in this historiography – by way of Elizabeth Hill Boone's chapter on maps in Aztec Mexico (Boone, 1998). She begins her narrative with a look at the painters, then a look at the maps, and finally a discussion of their function. She emphasizes that the human relations central to Aztec cartography imply human movement. Since movement exists at the intersection of space and time, Aztec cartography maps history. To make this leap, she has to clarify that maps, like any other document, have a temporal tense: past, present or future. Maps in present or future tense are prescriptive: this is the lay of the land, and this is what the reader ought to do about it. Maps in the past tense tell history. Gregory A. Waselkov emphasizes that Indian maps existed more in the repertoire than the archive: "Traditional Southeastern Indian maps of the seventeenth and eighteenth centuries were often ephemeral things, sketched in the ground with sticks or, somewhat more permanently, drawn on bark or painted on skins as visual aids to complement a recitation of tribal history, or describe the locations of allies and enemies, or simply to plot a route" (Waselkov, 1998). His goal is to push these maps into the archaeological archive. He categorizes indigenous maps in the colonial southeast into two sets: those made to reflect landscapes in a way understandable to European cartographic conventions, and those like the Catawba Deerskin Map that illustrate "social and political relationships." From phrasing Indian cartography as an event that can exist independent of European intervention to a function of that intervention, and from Quebec to Mexico, *Cartographic Encounters* is a sampler of the historiography thus far.

In his other collection that year, Lewis seeks to categorize the range of scholarship. He begins with the relationship between indigenous people and settlers in cartography:

> ...it is possible to recognize three broad categories of Amerindian cartography, all associated with the concept of contact with Europeans and Euro-Americans. The first stage, precontact, predates even indirect European influence and is

38

rooted in antiquity...The second stage, comprising maps made at the time of first contact...dates from the mid-sixteenth century to the late nineteenth, depending on region...The third stage dates from the establishment of the first permanent Euro-American settlements, the development of regular trade and communications networks, and the beginnings of resource exploitation. (Lewis & Woodward, 1998)

He begins with petroglyphic cartography, or, rather, how he's not sure that it exists. Key to his apprehension is the question of authorial intent. If we can't know that the artist meant to draw a map, then we aren't sure that they meant not to. If an artist draws something meaning it not to be a map, is it still a map? Finally, and this constitutes the bulk of the American section, he looks at "maps made for Europeans." This survey includes land sale maps between Indians and English in New England and wampum maps. Barbara Mundy contributed on "Mesoamerican Cartography" (Mundy, 1998). She introduces the idea that "...cultures of Mesoamerica took the production and use of maps to a level unparalleled elsewhere in the New World." She backs her claim by looking at the independence of Mesoamerican cartographic development, and at its "sophistication." That "sophistication" refutes Eccles' "crude" and insists on Mesoamericans as a civilized people as good as anyone else in "European, Asian, and African traditions."

And then the historiography took a break. Diana Taylor wrote her book, which made waves in the Performance Studies and Theater disciplines, waves from which the early Americanist coves of History were sublimely sheltered. Paul Mapp, in his geographically expansive *Elusive West*, returned the conversation to publication in 2011 (Mapp, 2011). Mapp's project is to "address the issues raised by these imperial actions, and to comprehend more fully the [Seven Years War], we need to look more closely at the ideas about American geography people of Washington and Rogers's century held." By placing his focus firmly on the imperial projects of the French, English and Spanish, Mapp moves away from the breakthroughs in the late 1990s towards studying indigenous maps on their own terms. That, however, is not his project: even though he writes about North America, his scholarship is centered in western Europe.

THE CARTOGRAPHIC SCENARIO

In *The Archive and the Repertoire*, Taylor describes Richard Flores' project mapping "out the way *pastorelas* or shepherds' plays moved from Spain, to central Mexico, to Mexico's northwest, and then to what is now the southwest of the United States. The different versions permit him to distinguish among various routes" (Taylor, 2003). What are the differences between Flores' research and the above historiography? Of course, maps and dance use space differently. While dance inhabits space, maps describe it, except for sometimes when they're sketched in the dust to help communicate how to get from the present location to a location in the distance.

WAYLON LENK

Use of space, then, isn't a fundamental difference. A more critical difference is that Flores begins with human bodies and the historians above start with documents. Yet many of the documents under consideration are in fact mnemonic devices meant to aid embodied activity. This presents a fundamental challenge to the cartographic epistemology from whence most of these historians write. If maps are not primarily archivable documents, but instead tools for embodied action (such as the above example of a map sketched in the dust), then the students of those maps have two choices. First, they can withhold the designation "map" from the documents/events under consideration, thereby maintaining a familiar cartographic ontology. This choice reifies, unfortunately, the barriers established by settlers to dismiss indigenous epistemologies as part of an ongoing project of cultural supremacy. The second choice, with which the above historiography fitfully wrestles, is to validate Indian epistemologies by expanding the definition of what is a map. Specifically, the second choice entails allowing that maps are not only aids for embodied action but are themselves the products of embodied action. Difficulties making that choice of course have to do with racist epistemologies, but they could also have to do with linguistics: historians and geographers simply don't have the vocabulary to speak about embodied cartographies. Taylor's notion of the repertoire, then, may be a useful addition to the discourse on early North American Indian cartography. Writing practically, Taylor posits a shift of focus from "*texts* and *narratives*" (emphases hers) to "scenarios." Scenarios, in her definition, have six aspects: (1) scenarios exist in space; (2) they involve bodies; (3) they're formulaic; (4) they're transmitted in ways that may involve speech, documentation, gesture, etc., but are reducible to none of these; (5) it is necessary for the audience to "situate ourselves in relationship to it"; and (6) they aren't necessarily mimetic, that is, it's not necessary that an actor pretends to be someone else.

"First," writes Taylor, "to recall, recount, or reactivate a scenario we need to conjure up the physical location..." One of the most compelling features of the La Vérendrye map, for the scholars cited above, is its inaccuracy. That is, La Vérendrye mosaicked a variety of geographic impressions resulting in an illustration of a place that does not exist. Since its physical location is fantastic, its mapness is in question. Stefan Ekman's discussion of the ontology of fantasy maps is useful for shedding light on the problem of the physical location of the La Vérendrye map:

> ...the maplike illustrations found in a vast number of fantasy works present a problem. Although they undeniably '[result] from the creative effort of [their authors'] execution of choices,' an overwhelming majority of them are *not* representations of 'geographic reality.' Their 'features or characteristics' bear little or no relation to anything in the actual world. They are simply not maps, as they violate the deeply ingrained notion that a map must in some way represent the world of the cartographer. (Ekman, 2013, p. 19, citing the International Cartographic Association Mission)

EARLY INDIGENOUS NORTH AMERICAN CARTOGRAPHY AS PERFORMANCE TEXTS

Ekman's specification of "the world of the cartographer" is useful in applying mapness and physical location to the La Vérendrye map. The world of the cartographers of this map was *terra semicognita* – a borderland or "middle ground." The collaborators on the map came from French and Cree geographic worldviews which, in the wake of the Iroquoian shatter-zone, created a series of social systems unique from preceding Cree and French cultures (White, 1991). These worldviews both prized arable, fishable and huntable lands to the west: for the French, to extract wealth for their burgeoning empire; for Cree and other Algonquian refugees, to escape hunger. This fictional map reflects a physical geography distorted by mutual Cree and French yearning for accessible resources to the west.

"Second," Taylor writes, "in scenarios, viewers need to deal with the embodiment of the social actors." Social activity in this historiography is constructed around racial edifices of "Indian" and "white," and the writers are whites talking about Indians. Within this paradigm, whites are cast as protagonists, scholars, literate, and experts. Indians, alternatively, are cast as deuteragonists, illiterate, unintellectual, and as objects of study. White audiences of this historiography, therefore, find themselves written *to*. Indians find ourselves written *about*. Even while we are included, necessarily, in the story, we find our presence erased. Belyea's intervention is the exception that proves the rule: that she had to write so forcefully for her colleagues to reconsider, and that, after reconsideration, they largely fell back towards Burpee's racial casting, bespeaks the difficulties for the scholars heretofore contributing to this historiography to lay aside its use of race.

My position as an Indian scholar contributing to this historiography fulfills Taylor's third point about scenarios: that they are "formulaic structures that predispose certain outcomes and ye allow for reversal, parody, and change." While I reverse the trend in this historiography by virtue of my Indian-ness, I reify it by engaging with the archive separate from the Franco-Cree culture from which it began. In other words, in spite of my race, I still approach the work primarily archivally and from an outsider's perspective.

The white and archival dominance of the historiography likewise fulfills Taylor's fourth point: that "the transmission of a scenario reflects the multifaceted systems at work in the scenario itself." The scenario is one of whites protagonizing themselves in their study of a middle ground cartographic encounter.

"Fifth, the scenario forces us to situate ourselves in relationship to it…" writes Taylor. I am an Indian studying what white people have to say about Indians. That archive, however, is only partly theirs. The La Vérendrye map in question is one of many examples of cultural events jointly created by Indians and white. Our project should be to protagonize ourselves, and yet, that project presents certain problems. I feel free to write and talk about this map, and the other less-studied maps in this historiography, because it has such a significant position in the historiography of indigenous North American maps. Since old-time maps in my culture, so far as I've experienced them, all connect to our Religion, I do not feel free to talk or write about them.

Finally, the scenario I'm trying to create to consider the La Vérendrye map and, by extension, all pre-1800s North American Indian maps, is not mimetic. That means that the white geographers and historians are not in some way filling La Vérendrye's role, nor are we filling the roles of the Indian collaborators. Rather, as Taylor puts it, this scenario "conjure[s] up past situations, at times so profoundly internalized by a society that no one remembers the precedence." The racial categories, with whites situated as protagonists, runs through our society in general, and the historiography of North American Native maps from before 1800). If we are to engage with the maps with the sort of dignity that I think we'd like to, I believe the key is insisting on ourselves acting as co-creators of the discourse around our maps. In other words, if we follow Belyea's thesis "that mapping does not represent geographic knowledge in absolute terms, but is instead conventional and culture-specific," and the fact that the so-called La Vérendrye map reflects cultural values as opposed to an absolute reality, our job becomes insisting on defining our historic geographies in the ways that best suit our communities and the cultures from whence we come.

REFERENCES

Belyea, B. (1992). Amerindian maps: The explorer as translator. *Journal of Historical Geography, 18*, 267–277.

Boone, E. H. (1998). Maps of territory, history, and community in Aztec Mexico. In G. M. Lewis (Ed.), *Cartographic encounters: Perspectives on native American mapmaking and map use* (pp. 111–133). Chicago, IL: University of Chicago Press.

Burpee, L. J. (1935). *The search for the Western Sea: The story of the exploration of North-Western America*. Toronto: MacMillan.

Eccles, W. J. (1997). French exploration in North America, 1700–1800. In J. L. Allen (Ed.), *North American exploration, volume 2: A continent defined*. Lincoln, NE: University of Nebraska Press.

Ekman, S. (2013). *Here be dragons: Exploring fantasy maps and settings*. Middletown, CT: Wesleyan University Press.

International Cartographic Association Mission. Retrieved from http://icaci.org/mission

Lewis, G. M. (1986). Indicators of unacknowledged assimilations from Amerindian 'maps' on Euro-American maps of North America: Some general principles arising from a study of la vérendrye's composite map, 1728–1729. *Imago Mundi, 38*(1), 9–34.

Lewis, G. M. (1987). Misinterpretation of Amerindian information as a source of error on Euro-American maps. *Annals of the Association of American Geographers, 77*(4), 542–563.

Lewis, G. M. (1991). La grande rivière et fleuve de l'Ouest/the realities and reasons behind a major mistake in the 18th century geography of North America. *Cartographica, 28*, 54–87.

Lewis, G. M. (1993). Metrics, geometries, signs, and language: sources of cartographic miscommunication between native and Euro-American cultures in North America. *Cartographica, 30*, 98–106.

Lewis, G. M. (Ed.). (1998). *Cartographical encounters: Perspectives on native American mapmaking and map use*. Chicago, IL: The University of Chicago Press.

Lewis, G. M., & David, W. (Eds.). (1998). *Cartography in the traditional African, American, Arctic, Australian, and Pacific societies*. Chicago, IL: The University of Chicago Press.

Mapp, P. (2011). *The elusive west and the contest for empire, 1713–1763*. Chapel Hill, NC: The University of North Carolina Press.

Mundy, B. (1998). Mesoamerican cartography. In G. M. Lewis & D. Woodward (Eds.), *Cartography in the traditional African, American, Arctic, Australian, and Pacific societies* (pp. 183–256). Chicago, IL: The University of Chicago Press.

EARLY INDIGENOUS NORTH AMERICAN CARTOGRAPHY AS PERFORMANCE TEXTS

Taylor, D. (2003). *The archive and the repertoire: Performing cultural memory in the Americas*. Durham, NC: Duke University Press.

Waselkov, G. A. (1998). Indian maps of the colonial southeast: Archaeological implications and prospects. In G. M. Lewis (Ed.), *Cartographic encounters: Perspectives on native American mapmaking and map use* (pp. 205–221). Chicago, IL: The University of Chicago Press.

White, R. (1991). *The middle ground: Indians, empires, and republics in the great lakes region, 1650–1815*. Cambridge: Cambridge University Press.

Waylon Lenk
Department of Theatre
University of Oregon
Eugene, Oregon

VICTORIA GRIMA

5. THE GRADUAL RISE OF MANITOBA'S NORTHERN HYDRO-ELECTRICAL GENERATION PROJECT

INTRODUCTION

There seems to be a general consensus on the concept that *Water* is *Life*. However, notwithstanding this, both Western societies' and Aboriginal cultures' perceptions on the significance of *Water* contrast each other on various forefronts.

Within First Nation cultures, "the importance of inter-relationships among all elements of Creation" (McGregor, 2012, p. 3) constitutes a very predominant belief which emerges from the teachings about the stories of Creation. These teachings describe Earth as a living organism whose sole responsibility is to nourish, cultivate and support all of its life-forms. Moreover, since *Water* is one of the four elements of nature that was bestowed, the Anishinaabe tradition recognises *Water* as being an integral part in the Earth's sustenance of life. Thus, for Indigenous people, *Water* constitutes the blood that flows through the Earth's veins. (McGregor & Whitaker, 2001; McGregor, 2012) In this respect, Aboriginal cultures perceive "waters to be sacred givers of life" (Laidlaw & Passelac-Ross, 2010, p. 2) and therefore, to ensure survival *Water* should be shared wisely and preserved.

On the other hand, Berkes notes that the Western Scientific World developed its dichotomy towards *Water* on the perceptions of *nature:culture* and *subject:object* (Blackstock, 2001). Nature is seen as a commodity which can be exploited in order to cater to the needs that arise (Blackstock, 2001; McGregor & Whitaker, 2001), this frame-of-thought is exhibited when electricity is generated from the natural flow and/ or the sheer force of *Water*. In view of the growing concerns around climate change, hydro-electrical power has become one of the most invested-in, renewable energy resources across the globe. This is because it neither generates air impurities nor leads to an increase in greenhouse emissions. (Canadian Hydropower Association, 2017; International Hydropower Association, 2017) Statistics published by the International Hydropower Association (IHA) indicate that in 2015 the global hydro-electrical generation powered installed amounted to 1,212 gigawatts (GW) (IHA, 2016b).

In 2016, it was observed that the growth in demand for electrical energy and the benefits of being cleaner, consistent and affordable, resulted in an increase in capacity by a further 31.5 GW (IHA, 2017). By 2050, IHA (2016a) is expecting

© KONINKLIJKE BRILL NV, LEIDEN, 2018 | DOI 9789004367418_005

VICTORIA GRIMA

growth in "global demand for energy" by 61 percent. In this respect, it seems that the Earth's *Waters* will continue to be in constant demand to perform and produce at their highest levels. Thus, the observation made by David Laidlaw and Monique Passelac-Ross (2010, p. 2) that "the taking of waters without due regards to the environment and the needs of the current and future generations can only lead to disaster" may become reality after all.

THE SILENCING OF A RIVER

Since its conception in 1961, the Provincial Crown Corporation *Manitoba Hydro* has played, and continues to play, a key strategic role in satisfying the demands for electricity for Manitoba's southern populated urban areas. Manitoba Hydro has a fleet of 15 (six within the southern region, one within the western region, two within the north-western region and six within the northern region) hydroelectric generation stations distributed along four major watercourses. These stations have the capability of generating 5,685 megawatts (MW) of electricity (Manitoba Hydro, 2015a). In fact, the province of Manitoba boasts about being Canada's Hydro Province (Manitoba Hydro, 2015a).

By mid-1950's and late 1960's with the construction of seven hydro-electrical stations and their associative infrastructure, the water-power potential of the western (Saskatchewan river – 472 MW) and southern (Winnipeg river – 560 MW) *Waters* was fully developed (Manitoba Hydro, 1974, 2014). The consideration of the Province's northern *Waters*, in particular, those of the Great River, the *Kache Sipi*,[1] the Nelson, as valuable water-power resource materialized from the geological studies carried out in the early stages of the last century. McInnes (1913, p. 11) observed that out "of the rivers, Nelson, by reason of its great volume and numerous falls, is the most important from the point of view of power development".

In McInnes' 1913 geological and environmental study on the province's northern drainage basins, a measurement of power capacity to the mighty *Waters* of the Nelson was determined to be 6,859,000 horsepower (hp) (approximately 5,114.75[2] MW) (McInnes, 1913, p. 13). From an electrical-power production perspective, such generation capacity was considered to be ground-breaking and of great importance by Manitoba Hydro. In this respect, McInnes' report proved to be crucial in the taming process of the northern Great River which came in the 1960's[3] (which still continues till to date) (Manitoba Hydro, 2014, p. 2–1).

However, when looking back into the Province's northern region past historical events, it seems that the route towards the hydroelectric development of the Nelson's *Waters* has been initiated well before the comprehensive report compiled by McInnes.

The Importance of Waterways

Inglis (1993, p. vi) defines *Traditional Environmental Knowledge* (TEK) as being "the knowledge base" Indigenous communities collected and accumulated throughout

46

millennia of sustaining their lifestyle and cultural traditions by constantly living as one with nature. This knowledge represents a profound understanding of the natural environment's lifecycle together with the diverse ecosystems (terrestrial/land and marine/waterways) that characterise their cultural landscape.[4] It was during the historical era of the fur trade that such land and waterways-based knowledge played a highly significant role in which nation (British vs. French) would gain control over the unspoiled natural resources that the North American wilderness had to offer. For the 200 years from its establishment in 1670, on behalf of the British Empire, the *Hudson Bay Company* with its exclusive privileges over the vast unexplored watershed of the *Hudson Bay drainage basin*[5] did just that (Ruggles, 1984, 1991).

To guarantee a continuous flow of high quality of pelts, the Company utilised maps and charts throughout its years in the trading business to first and foremost keep an eye on their competitors but also to develop a strategic network of trading posts along the northern coastline and within the inland areas (Ruggles, 1984, 1991). The Company immediately recognised the importance of the waterways as mercantile transportation routes. It was for the first forty-three years, between 1670 and 1713, with the aid of coastal cartographic mapping drawn by its explorers, the Company controlled the ports and the shoreline of the Hudson Bay and James Bay areas (Government of Canada, 1973; Ruggles, 1984, 1991). The newly established coastal trading posts were erected at the mouths of the major rivers that drained into these bays (Government of Canada, 1973; Ruggles, 1991).

The post of York Factory which was erected in 1684 on the mouth of the Nelson River, became one of the Company's leading trading hubs for the western inner regions of the *Hudson Bay drainage basin* (Government of Canada, 1973; Ray, 1974). Its location also provided access to the Hayes River which runs almost parallel with the Nelson and the waters of both of the rivers ran through the largest inland fur trading grounds – the whole extent of Manitoba and a substantial section of Saskatchewan (Ray, 1974, p. 54). The Company gained a better understanding of its entire dominion by encouraging its employees to travel back and pass the winter with their Indigenous trading 'allies'. Information on the topographical features and the watercourses characteristics of these rivers were very limited (Ruggles, 1984, 1991).

The first known explorer to venture into the inner regions of the Company's 'territory', between the period of 1690 and 1692, was Henry Kelsey (Ruggles, 1984). With the help of a group of Indigenous trappers that came to trade at York Factory, he travelled back with them into the Nelson River basin and its woodland areas. This led them/him out into the open grasslands and then continued to travel south where the North and South of the Saskatchewan Rivers meet (Government of Canada, 1957; Ruggles, 1991). Unfortunately, Kelsey didn't produce a cartographic representation of the terrain that he travelled into and neither did his journal produce any significant descriptions of the terrain or the hydrological networks (Ruggles, 1991, p. 29). However, doing a brief fast forward into the 20th century, the *Northern Hydro-electrical Generation Project*, the first northern hydro-electrical generation

VICTORIA GRIMA

station to be built within the upper section of the Nelson River was named after him (Manitoba Hydro, 2014). This is the first connection to a historic figure.

Going back to the brief historical accounts of the exploration endeavours of the *Hudson Bay Company*, the waterways of the Nelson-Hayes Rivers from a trading perspective became a major route when the first inland post (Cumberland House) was erected in 1744 in the wooded area of the Saskatchewan River. Transportation of furs towards York Factory increased further through these waterways when the first posts in the "park belt" (Hudson House, North Saskatchewan River proximities) and prairie regions (Chesterfield House, South Saskatchewan River proximities) were erected in 1780 and 1800 (Government of Canada, 1973; Ruggles, 1984, 1991). Thus, the newly built posts provided not only the inner infiltration that the Company had sought for many years but also provided the opportunity to explore further and spatially map its terrain.

In this respect, to fully exploit the navigational routes, the first maps of this region focused on depicting the complex network of its hydrological system. The connections between rivers and lakes, and their associative relationship with falls, rapids, and the location of the boats/canoes portages where then fully illustrated. The Company was able to achieve this monumental cartographic record by encouraging its explorers to collaborate closely with Indigenous people, who were extremely knowledgeable on both survival and navigation within the inner wilderness of the *Hudson Bay drainage basin* (Ruggles, 1984, 1991). The Company's postmaster and surveyor Peter Fidler was one of the few explorers that embraced and respected the native knowledge in his cartographic work (Beattie, 1985–1986). Most of his cartographic mapping of the inner regions occurred between 1795 and 1815 (Ruggles, 1984, p. 160), and according to Beattiee (1985–1986) over two-thirds of the so called 'Indian' maps or sketches can be attributed to him.

To increase his geographical knowledge and at the same time to improve his cartographic skills, he requested detailed descriptions and often sought sketches from travelling fur traders and Indigenous people. In this respect, his work was very precise – for his maps, recorded detailed compass readings of almost every change that he noticed in the profile of the waterways. He also provided measurements that were accompanied by descriptions of vegetation and other landmarks that he observed during his explorative trips. Moreover, on his maps/sketches he meticulously reproduced all information shared by Indigenous people (Ruggles, 1984, 1991). Fidler produced maps/sketches of the Nelson-Hayes routes between 1808 and 1809; sketches of the northern shores of Lake Winnipeg (including the water flow point of entry into the Nelson: Playgreen Lake) and along the Hayes River in 1808 (Ruggles, 1991, pp. 193–236). Fidler finalised his detailed survey of the Nelson in 1809 when he left Cumberland House to travel back to York Fort (Ruggles, 1991, p. 65).

Another surveyor that produced information and descriptions of the Nelson's waterways and its environs was "one of the greatest practical geographers of all time", that is, David Thompson (Ruggles, 1984, p. 154). In some of his early sketches and journal entries in regards to his travels down the Nelson River, Thompson denoted the section of the said watercourse which is above and up to Split Lake and/or even the whole extent of the Nelson, as 'Saskatchewan River' (Tyrrell, 1916, p. xvi). According to the early 20th century geologists, Joseph Burr Tyrrell (1916, p. xvi) Thompson was simply following "the usage of the natives and employees of the Hudson's Bay Company of that time." Thompson within his *Narratives of His Explorations in Western America* between 1784–1812, identifies the Nelson as "a bold, wide rapid River" which "besides it's Rapids has twenty-eight Falls" (Tyrrell, 1916, pp. 435–436).

In these periodicals (the edition edited by Glover, 1962, p. 38), Thompson noted also that "the natural route to the inland country would by the great River", the Nelson, however due to "its immense volume of water, heavy falls and waves make it dangerous for small canoes". It was for these reasons his expeditions preferences took the route by the Hayes River towards York Factory (Glover, 1962, p. 38). Sir John Franklin in his 1819 periodicals provides some information on the colour of the waters of the Nelson. He narrates that the colour of the waters of one of the tributaries of the Nelson River, that is, the Sea River are "muddy white" (Franklin, 1824, p. 65). He further observed that "Play Green [sic] Lake and Nelson River, being the discharges of the Winipeg [sic], are equally opaque, that renders the sunken rocks, so frequent" and thus "very dangerous to boats in a fresh breeze" (Franklin, 1824, p. 66). Franklin enforced this observation by stating that one of the accompanying boats got stuck (Franklin, 1824, p. 66).

Therefore, the exploration of the Nelson-Hayes routes resulted not only significant regarding fur-trading commerce but also a valuable resource for understanding its historical topographical and hydrological features. Moreover, its detailed cartographic descriptions and depictions paved the way for the development of new scientific research on the area in question. These investigations were carried out by the professional geologists that were members of the Geological Survey of Canada.

Water Power Capabilities

The first geological examination on the natural terrain that characterised the Nelson's waterways carried out on behalf of the Geological Survey of Canada, was by Dr. Robert Bell (McInnes, 1913, p. 3; Denis & Challies, 1916, p. 102). His studies were carried out between 1877 and 1880 which produced detailed surveys[6] of the whole extent of the principal waterways route for both the Nelson and Hayes Rivers, that is, from Lake Winnipeg to the point of discharge into the Hudson Bay (McInnes, 1913). These surveys were accompanied by details topographical and geological information within which Bell identified the rapids (particularly on the Nelson) and the flow of the waters (Bell, 1880). Additionally, he also provided descriptions of the aquatic and tree species he observed along the rivers' shorelines during his expeditions, for example, the abundance of "herring white-fish" at the mouths of both rivers (Nelson & Hayes) (Bell, 1880, p. 7), and aspen and white birch around the environs of the Lowest Limestone Rapids (Bell, 1880, pp. 41–44).

VICTORIA GRIMA

A. P. Low in 1885 studied the network of the Berens and Severn rivers and how these interconnect with the route that leads from Lake Winnipeg to Hudson Bay (McInnes, 1913), and McConnell and Cochrane performed geological studies on the countryside during the late 1800's which surrounded the Nelson's environs (McInnes, 1913). J. B. Tyrrell was another member of the Geological Survey of Canada who contributed detailed geological studies for the Nelson River watercourse. He travelled the north-western areas of Manitoba between 1888 and 1891, while his investigations to the sections of northern Manitoba and eastern Saskatchewan were carried out between the period of 1895 and 1899. (McInnes, 1913; Denis & Challies, 1916).

Tyrrell in 1902 produced a very similar detailed geological analysis to the one that Bell provided back in 1878 (Denis & Challies, 1916, p. 102), and mineral deposits and metal compounds were noticed within the area of Pipestone Lake area. Potholes were also noted on an island that falls within the extremities of Playgreen Lake (McInnes, 1913). After the finalisation of these detailed geological studies, the conversation on the *Waters* of the Nelson led to a discussion of their power generation capabilities. William Ogilvie carried out the associative calculations, for the Water Power Branch of the Department of the Interior, on the upper segment of the Nelson in 1910. Subsequently, in 1913 he also calculated the discharges quantities for the rivers that are situated on the eastern and western sides (Denis & Challies, 1916, p. 102). With such studies at one's disposal, in 1911 (Denis & White) the Commission of Conservation (Canada) began a series of publications on the "Water Possibilities of Canada".

The first publication focused on bringing general information and review of each Canadian province's hydro-power opportunities (Denis & White, 1911). For the Province of Manitoba, notwithstanding the listing of possible power sites (11 possible falls and rapids) along the extents of the Nelson River, the discussion concentrated mainly on the hydro-power opportunities of the Winnipeg River (Denis & White, 1911, pp. 283–289). The Commission of Conservation (Canada) produced a much more comprehensive study on the "Water Powers" of the prairie provinces in 1916 (Denis & Challies). One of its chapters provided detailed physical descriptions (including falls/rapids) of the Nelson River, its tributaries together with those of the Hayes River (Denis & Challies, pp. 100–120). However, it seems that the Nelson River's section of this publication was based on a study published three years earlier. William McInnes on behalf of the Department of Mines (Canada) in 1913 published his studies on the "Basins of Nelson and Churchill Rivers". McInnes with the help of his predecessors and with his own additions, he was able to provide climatic, terrain, ecological, geological and hydrological details for both basins. He identified the Nelson and Churchill Rivers as being the largest rivers that drain into the Hudson Bay (McInnes, 1913, p. 5).

The length of the Nelson, which was measured from the Bow (indicated as the longest tributary), was identified as being 1,660 miles (approx. 2,672 kilometres[7]). Its drainage area according to McInnes amounted to 370,800 square miles (approx. 960,368 square kilometre[8]) (McInnes, 1913, p. 5). That is, "its drainage basin embraces all the country, westward to the mountains, lying between the watersheds of Churchill and Athabaska rivers to the north and the Missouri to the south, and eastward to the head-waters of Albany river and to within 50 miles of the head of Lake Superior" (McInnes, 1913, p. 5). Which means it covers four Canadian provinces (AB, SK, MB, ON)[9] and four American states (MN, ND&SD, MT).[10] The basin's water volume was measured to be "118,369 cubic feet per second at extreme low water, measured just below Sipiwesk lake [sic] and above the inflow of the large tributaries, Clearwater, Grass and Burntwood rivers" (McInnes, 1913, p. 5).

The water flows into the Nelson's basin: (a) from the west through the North and South Saskatchewan, which converge into the Saskatchewan River and drains into Lake Winnipeg; (b) from the south through the Red and Assiniboine rivers which ultimately drain into Lake Winnipeg; (c) from the east through Winnipeg River which also drains into Lake Winnipeg, and finally going north from Lake Winnipeg through the series of falls and rapids and then drains into Hudson Bay (McInnes, 1913). McInnes describes the water of the Nelson as being "murky from suspended sediment, but gradually clears as it passes through the numerous lake expansions along its course" (McInnes, 1913, p. 5). The falls and rapids are described as being sharply defined, of steep descent and often they are separated by islands going into narrow channels (McInnes, 1913).

The highest drop according to McInnes observations occurred between the river sections of Cross and Sipiwesk lakes, and also at Gull Land to the foot of Limestone rapid. The latter the drop amounted to 396 feet over 67 miles, while the former the drop constituted of 90 feet within 28 miles (McInnes, 1913, p. 12). With regards to the water-power capabilities, (although McInnes, p. 12, noted that there might be more than fifteen rapids and falls) McInnes identified a measurement of power for the 11 rapids and falls listed in the first "Water Powers" publication of 1911. The said list is hereunder being reproduced:

Table 1. Estimated horse-power for the 11 rapids and falls mentioned in both 1911 and 1913 publications (Denis & White, 1911; McInnes, 1913)

	Estimated horse-power
Limestone rapid	1,140,000
Long Spruce Rapid	1,140,000
Kettle rapid	1,290,000
Gull rapid	900,000
Birthday rapid	320,000
Grand rapid	270,000
Rapids above Sipiwesk lake	416,000
Bladder rapid	147,000
Whitemud fall	403,000
Ebb-and-Flow rapid	148,000
Rapids above Cross Lake	605,000

VICTORIA GRIMA

Thus, the estimated aggregate measurement of power for the waters that pass through the Nelson River amounted to 6,859,000 hp (McInnes, 1913, p. 13).

CONCLUSION

Therefore, the journey that was originally undertaken as a rivalry over who would claim supremacy over North America finest pelt silenced the voice of the mighty *Water* of the *Kache Sipi*, the Nelson River. With the aid of the early explorers' chronicles and the geological surveys produced in the late 1800s and early 1900s (from the likes of Bell, Tyrrell, Ogilvie, etc.), McInnes was able to measure the power of the Great River and so like a wild animal that was domesticated, Manitoba Hydro began its taming regime of the Nelson as early as the 1960s.

During the last half a century, this Crown Corporation controls the natural flow of the water from the construction of dam infrastructure, and also affected the rapids and falls that once characterised the watercourse of the Nelson. Along the length of the Nelson (from Lake Winnipeg to Hudson Bay), a total of six hydro-electric generation stations have been built. A new facility (Keeyask) is currently being constructed between Gull Lake and Stephens Lake, and is envisaged to generate 695 MW of hydroelectricity. To ensure efficiency for production of hydroelectric power, the Churchill River (between 1970 and 1976) was diverted into the Nelson. Thus, the outlet of Southern Indian Lake into the Churchill River was blocked, and through a new channel located in its southern end, diverts water into the Rat and Burntwood rivers, ultimately flowing into the Nelson (Manitoba Hydro, 2015b).

Other regulatory infrastructure (channels and control structures) were built specifically to control water flows/levels and regulate the enormous natural hydrological potential of the Nelson (Manitoba Hydro, 2014). Additionally, to transfer the generated electricity from their respective stations towards the required urban centres, converter stations and High Voltage Direct Current (HVDC) transmission lines were also constructed (Manitoba Hydro, 2014, 2015b). Due to these factors, a substantial amount of boreal forest has been destroyed and more is still being lost since a new transmission line (Bipole III) is currently being built due to the new hydro-generation station under-construction (Manitoba Hydro, 2015b).

Even in our modern day 21st century, the magnitude of the design and implementation of these man-made disturbances have not yet been fully understood, nor have substantive changes to the natural physical composition and biodiversity of the environment of the Nelson's watercourse been fully comprehended. This is quite a remarkable planning shortcoming, in view of the fact that the Manitoba Hydro-electrical generation projects have impacted a very substantial area of the Province's North and an entire river-system's flows.

52

THE GRADUAL RISE OF MANITOBA'S NORTHERN HYDRO-ELECTRICAL GENERATION

ACKNOWLEDGEMENT

NSERC CREATE H2O Program for First Nations Water and Sanitation Security Wa Ni Ska Tan: An Alliance of Hydro Impacted Communities: Research Funding.

NOTES

[1] The Cree name for the Nelson River (Manitoba Conservation, 2000, p, 189).

[2] Conversion 1 horsepower (hp) = 0.00075 megawatts.

[3] The Northern Manitoba Hydro-electrical Generation Project constitutes the construction of hydro generation stations (1957–2020); installation of HVDC Transmission System (1968–1985); the implementation of Lake Winnipeg Regulation Projects (1970–1976); the implementation of the Churchill River Diversion Project (1973–1976) and the installation of Bipole III Transmission System (2013–2018) (Manitoba Hydro, 2015b).

[4] Davidson-Hunt et al. (2010) define cultural landscape as "an area which a particular people have transcribed their culture through their intimate use and understanding of the land".

[5] The extent of this basin was depicted on the 1857 J. Arrowsmith's *Map of North America* (David Rumsey Historical Map Collection). The surface area covers 3,861,400 square kilometers of Canadian land and 180,000 square kilometers of American land (Government of Canada, 1985).

[6] Bell's 1878 survey of the Nelson can be viewed from the Government of Canada's Natural Resources Canada online database. https://doi.org/10.4095/213700

[7] Conversion 1 mile = 1.609344 kilometer.

[8] Conversion 1 square mile = 2.58998811 square kilometre.

[9] AB = Alberta; SK = Saskatchewan; MB = Manitoba and ON = Ontario.

[10] MN = Minnesota; ND&SD = North and South Dakota; MT = Montana.

REFERENCES

Beattie, J. D. (1985/1986). Indian maps in the Hudson's Bay company archives: A comparison of five area maps recorded by Peter Fidler, 1801–1802. *Archivaria, 21,* 166–175. Retrieved from http://archivaria.ca/index.php/archivaria/article/viewFile/11246/12185

Bell, R. (1880). *Report on explorations of the Churchill and Nelson rivers and around God's and Island Lakes, 1879.* Montreal: Dawson Brothers.

Blackstock, M. (2001). Water: A first nations' spiritual and ecological perspective. *B.C. Journal of Ecosystems and Management, 1*(1), 54–66. Retrieved from http://www.jem-online.org/index.php/jem/article/view/216/135

Canadian Hydropower Association. (2017). *Benefits.* Retrieved from https://canadahydro.ca/benefits/

David Rumsey Historical Map Collection. (1857). *Facsimile: Arrowsmith's North America.* Washington, DC: Government Printing Office. Retrieved from http://www.davidrumsey.com/luna/servlet/detail/RUMSEY~8~1~204933~3002214:-Facsimile---Map-of-North-America--

Davidson-Hunt, I., & O'Flaherty, R. M. (2010). *Pikanigikum cultural landscape documentation guide.* Winnipeg: Aboriginal Issues Press.

Denis, L. G., & White, A. V. (1911). *Water-powers of Canada.* Ottawa: Commission of Conservation.

Denis, L. G., & Challies, J. B. (1916). *Water-powers of Manitoba, Saskatchewan and Alberta.* Toronto: Commission of Conservation.

Franklin, J. (1824). *Narrative of a journey to the shores of the Polar sea, in the years 1819-20-21-22* (Vol. 1, 2nd ed.). London: J. Murray.

Glover, R. (Ed.). (1962). *David Thompson's narrative 1784–1812.* Toronto: The Champlain Society.

Government of Canada. (1957). *Routes of explorers* (Atlas of Canada, 3rd ed.). Retrieved from http://open.canada.ca/data/en/dataset/274dc154-4a5d-5257-a47a-81a49c58133b

53

Government of Canada. (1973). *Posts of the Canadian fur trade* (Atlas of Canada, 4th ed.). Retrieved from http://geogratis.gc.ca/api/en/nrcan-rncan/ess-sst/96e248e8-f422-5d69-a085-cce12b04e11a.html

Government of Canada. (1985). *Drainage basins* (Atlas of Canada, 5th ed.). Retrieved from http://geogratis.gc.ca/api/en/nrcan-rncan/ess-sst/7b309ad9-9398-51d4-89d2-32b3871ec3ab.html

Inglis, J. T. (Ed.). (1992). *Traditional ecological knowledge: Concepts and cases*. Ottawa: IDRC Books/ Les Éditions du CRDI.

International Hydropower Association (IHA). (2016a). *Our vision*. Retrieved from https://www.hydropower.org/our-vision

International Hydropower Association (IHA). (2016b). *2016 hydropower status report*. Retrieved from https://www.hydropower.org/2016-hydropower-status-report

International Hydropower Association (IHA). (2017). *2017 key trends in hydropower*. Retrieved April, 2017, from https://www.hydropower.org/2017-key-trends-in-hydropower

Laidlaw, D., & Passelac-Ross, M. (2010, July 8). *Water rights and water stewardship: What about aboriginal peoples?* [Web log post]. Retrieved from https://ablawg.ca/2010/07/08/water-rights-and-water-stewardship-what-about-aboriginal-peoples/

Manitoba Conservation. (2000). *Geographical names of Manitoba*. Winnipeg: Manitoba Conservation.

Manitoba Hydro. (1974). *Power from the Nelson*. Winnipeg: Manitoba Hydro.

Manitoba Hydro. (2014). *Regional cumulative effects assessment for hydroelectric developments on the Churchill, Burntwood and Nelson River systems: Phase I report*. Retrieved from https://www.hydro.mb.ca/regulatory_affairs/rcea/

Manitoba Hydro. (2015a). *The hydro province*. Retrieved from https://www.hydro.mb.ca/corporate/facilities/gi_the_hydro_province.shtml

Manitoba Hydro. (2015b). *Regional cumulative effects assessment for hydroelectric developments on the Churchill, Burntwood and Nelson River systems: Phase II hydroelectric development project description in the region of interest*. Retrieved from https://www.hydro.mb.ca/-regulatory_affairs/rcea/

McGregor, D. (2012). Traditional knowledge: Considerations for protecting water in Ontario. *International Indigenous Policy Journal, 3*(3). doi:10.18584/iipj.2012.3.3.11

McGregor, D., & Whitaker, S. (2001). *Water quality in the province of Ontario: An aboriginal knowledge perspective*. Toronto: Chiefs of Ontario.

McInnes, W. (1913). *The basins of Nelson and Churchill Rivers* (Memoir No. 30). Ottawa: Government Printing Bureau.

Ray, A. J. (1974). *Indians in the fur trade: Their roles as trappers, hunters, and middlemen in the lands southwest of Hudson Bay 1660–1870*. Toronto: University of Toronto Press.

Ruggles, R. I. (1984). Mapping the interior plains of Rupert's Land by The Hudson's Bay company to 1870. *Great Plains Quarterly, 4*(3), 152–164. Retrieved from http://digitalcommons.unl.edu/-greatplainsquarterly/1806

Ruggles, R. I. (1991). *A country so interesting: The Hudson's Bay company and two centuries of mapping, 1670–1870*. Montreal: McGill-Queens University Press.

Tyrrell, J. B. (Ed.). (1916). *David Thompson's narrative of his explorations in Western America, 1784–1812*. Toronto: The Champlain Society.

Victoria Grima
Department of Environment and Geography
Clayton H. Riddell Faculty of Environment, Earth, and Resources
University of Manitoba
Winnipeg, Manitoba

CHARLOTTE BEZAMAT-MANTES

6. FIRST NATIONS, MUNICIPALITIES, AND URBAN RESERVES

Shifting Intergovernmental Power Balance in Urban Settings?

INTRODUCTION

The intentional erasure of Indigenous peoples from urban spaces by the settler society has been a hallmark of the post-contact period. It has been achieved through the relocation of First Nations peoples on rural reserves and their confinement on these lands via a pass system (Barron, 1988); through the displacement of Nations and reserve lands considered too close to towns (Burrows, 2009); and through the imposition of the colonizers' names on places and landscapes. The result is that "much of the "materiality" (i.e., physical quality, presence, structure) and "memory" (i.e., recall of experience, or even existence) of local Indigenous communities" has been erased from urban territories (Fawcett, Walker, & Greene, 2015, p. 162). The erasure from the urban space has fed the dual spatial dichotomy between White/urban and Indigenous/rural; and thus, progressively, "The idea of an urban Aboriginal person became incompatible with the images of Aboriginal peoples that had developed over the last century. Consequently, Aboriginal people who chose to live in cities were seen as an anomaly" (Newhouse & Peters, 2003, p. 6). That idea of incompatibility is reflected in academic literature about urban Indigenous peoples where they are often "viewed through the lens of urbanization, where the focus is on *their* adjustment to the city" (Walker et al., 2017, p. 2, emphasis added). If adjustment is needed, it implies that Indigenous peoples' primary place is not in cities.

After 1951, changes made to the *Indian Act* and the end of the enforcement of the pass system contributed immensely to the migration of Indigenous peoples from rural reserves to urban centres. Between 1951 and 2001, the percentage of the Indigenous population living in cities jumped from 6.7 percent to close to 50 percent (Newhouse & Peters, 2003, p. 5). It represented a migration of Indigenous *peoples*, while in most cases First Nations' *governments* and *reserve lands* remained in rural areas. This started to change when the Treaty Land Entitlement (TLE) process was formalized, allowing for the creation of urban reserves.

The creation of new reserves in cities has the potential to deeply challenge the idea that Indigenous peoples and all that pertains to them belong in rural environments. The establishment of these urban reserves also means the expansion of the physical space where Treaty rights apply and where the sovereignty of a First

© KONINKLIJKE BRILL NV, LEIDEN, 2018 | DOI 9789004367418_006

Nation's government can be exercised. In addition, urban reserves and their potential for the generation of own-source revenues offer First Nations a means to decrease their dependency on federal funding and to increase economic self-sufficiency and political self-determination.

Another critical aspect, on which this paper focuses, is the (re)creation of a relationship between two levels of government that historically had little to do with each other: the First Nation creating the new reserve and the municipality where it is located. In other words, what we witness with the establishment of urban reserves is the creation of a new contact zone which, as Porter and Barry (2015) note, represents a space of interaction that does not exist naturally but rather is constructed and maintained through social relations of power that are often asymmetrical (p. 24). Because Indigenous and Northern Affairs Canada (INAC) requires that the band negotiate an agreement with the municipality before reserve status can be granted to the land (INAC, 2017), the nature and quality of the First Nation-municipal relations are paramount to the success of such an initiative. Since the establishment and development of an urban reserve mean the arrival of a new economic and political player – the First Nation's government – on the urban scene, these reserves can be perceived as a threat to the municipality's sovereignty. The relations between these two governments are inherently political and laden with power rivalries to determine who will have what type of control over the land. This observation has led me to ask: How do the power relations between First Nations and municipalities influence what and where urban reserves can and cannot be?

I look at three aspects of this new contact zone to try and understand how it is constructed and how it shapes the possibilities for urban reserves: the convergence of interests between the First Nation and the municipality; a working relationship between them; and the willingness to respect each other's jurisdiction. I conclude by questioning whether urban reserves actually challenge the exclusion of Indigenous lands and economic activities from cities. I focus primarily on urban reserves in Treaty One Territory (particularly the Winnipeg region) and Long Plain First Nation's urban reserve in Winnipeg. Long Plain First Nation signed Treaty One in 1871 and, like many other First Nations, did not receive the amount of land it was entitled to under Treaty. In 1994, Long Plain signed an individual TLE agreement with Canada to address this land shortfall. The band received $16.5 million to acquire a minimum of 4,169 acres and a maximum of 26,437 acres (Long Plain First Nation Trust, n.d.). As part of its TLE, Long Plain purchased a former Manitoba Hydro building in Winnipeg, which became reserve in 2013.

A NECESSARY CONVERGENCE OF INTERESTS?

Although, theoretically, municipal governments cannot veto urban reserve initiatives, the outcome heavily depends on how they perceive the projects affect their interests (Barron & Garcea, 1999, p. 32). Indeed, the urban reserve creation process puts a lot of power into the municipalities' hands, creating or accentuating asymmetrical relations of power between the First Nation and the municipality. INAC will not consider an addition to reserve in an urban area unless the First Nation has negotiated an agreement with the municipality (INAC, 2017). If the municipality dislikes, for whatever reason, the plans the First Nation is proposing for the land , it can in practice stall negotiations on the agreement, and thus delay the conversion to reserve for an indefinite period of time. In that context, urban reserve projects usually have a higher chance of succeeding if they also serve the municipality's interests in one way or another (Barron & Garcea, 1999, p. 30). This can mean for instance preserving the aspect and use of an area or protecting its tax base, both of which could theoretically be affected by the creation of what amounts to an enclave of First Nations sovereignty within the city. This is not to say that municipalities necessarily feel threatened by or oppose the creation of urban reserves in their midst, but merely to highlight that the *process* of urban reserve creation tips the scales in their favour from the start, which affects the balance of power between them and the First Nation government with whom they negotiate.

Long Plain First Nation's purpose in converting their property to reserve was to create an economic development zone where businesses, band-owned and other, could locate and generate wealth for the First Nation in the form of benefits accrued from sales and rents from tenants. Long Plain came forward with plans for light industrial activities: a gas station, a convenience store, and office space for rental. These plans allowed for a smooth integration of the new urban reserve in the already existing economic fabric of the area. Indeed, the property is located in the St. James-Brooklands-Weston ward. The area is mostly a site for economic activities with businesses, big box stores, and the busy Polo Park shopping mall. Thus, the First Nation's plans did not disrupt the status quo. In fact, one of the original projects for the property was to build a 10-story building to use as a governance house for the Assembly of Manitoba Chiefs (AMC). The City of Winnipeg did not support this idea; apparently, the size of the building would have affected the ability of surrounding businesses to access their properties. After a change in Long Plain's leadership in 2009, it was felt the AMC's project did not serve the First Nation's economic development objectives (Paul, 2012). They removed that component from their proposal and a municipal agreement was signed in 2010. It appears that the interest of the municipality (ensuring the businesses could access their properties) influenced in part what Long Plain proposed in their plans; only when the interests of the two levels of government seemed to converge did the conversion to reserve progress.

A second important point regarding the convergence of interests is that the creation of the urban reserve would lead to the redevelopment of vacant lands in a very dense area, which would be beneficial to the City in two ways. First, it would provide the City with a source of revenues from the sale of services to Long Plain, which the First Nation needs to be able to operate the property. Reserve lands are exempt from taxation, according to sections 87 and 90 of the *Indian Act*, so a mechanism has to be defined to allow the municipality to collect money otherwise to pay for the services it provides to the property. Because the federal government requires an agreement with the First Nation, the City can ensure its interests related to the payment of services will be protected and it will not be affected negatively by the conversion of the property to reserve status. Second, the redevelopment would bring new buildings and upgraded infrastructure which would improve the general aspect of that block, located in a rather old neighbourhood, without costing the City a penny.

It is true that these two benefits (the revenues and the redevelopment) would likely have accrued to the City had the owner of the land been a private individual or company. Saying that the urban reserve project was in the City's interest does not necessarily mean that Winnipeg gains more with it than with a private-led project. It simply means in this case that the City does not lose anything compared to a situation where the landowner is a private one; as such, its interests are preserved.

BUILDING A WORKING RELATIONSHIP

A working relationship between the two levels of government appears to be a necessary condition for an urban reserve to be created and developed. This is a direct consequence of the municipal services agreement (MSA).[1] Reserve lands are under federal jurisdiction so municipal bylaws do not apply, which could theoretically compromise the implementation of zoning and safety regulations. This issue and the payment for services are addressed under the MSA, the purpose of which is to define mechanisms to compensate for the loss of tax revenues and to address the question of bylaw application. In other words, the MSA is the cornerstone that defines the fiscal and planning relationships between the two governments and shapes the possibilities for the First Nation on that piece of land.

First, the nature, amount, and price of services have to be agreed upon by the First Nation and the municipality, provided by the City, and paid for by the First Nation (which pays a 'fee for services' in lieu of taxes). It may seem like a trivial, administrative detail but it is fundamental. Even if the federal government agreed to convert the land to reserve without a signed agreement, the First Nation would have to operate its urban reserve without fire services, waste disposal, snow removal, garbage collection, etc., or would have to put in place the logistics and infrastructure to provide them, which would likely be more costly.

Second, the relationship does not stop when the agreement is signed and the reserve is created; rather, it is an ongoing relationship. Indeed, for any development following the reserve creation, the First Nation usually needs to get permits granted by the municipality and to abide by the city's safety regulations and zoning bylaws, inside and outside of the buildings. It is easy to imagine a situation where the relations between the municipality and the First Nation are strained, for whatever reason, and the municipality delays the issuance of permits as a form of retaliation. That would considerably slow down the development of economic activities on the urban reserve and would likely result in a loss of revenues for the First Nation, thus jeopardizing the whole purpose of the project. These intergovernmental relations vary in nature and frequency depending on the jurisdiction. In Saskatoon, for instance, the municipal

FIRST NATIONS, MUNICIPALITIES, AND URBAN RESERVES

council and the representatives of the First Nations that have an urban reserve in the city have a Christmas gathering every year to maintain their ongoing relationship; whereas in Winnipeg and Headingley, the practice seems to be to meet when needed only. Whichever form it takes, a relationship that is devoid of conflict – or at least one where the participants agree to work together and compromise – appears to be a significant factor influencing the outcome of an urban reserve project positively.

RESPECTING EACH OTHER'S JURISDICTION, IN THEORY AND PRACTICE

As Dust (1995) points out, the *Indian Act* gives First Nations governments "much the same power to make local legislation over reserve lands as Urban Councils have over urban land" (p. 6). When they operate very close to each other, as when an urban reserve is created, this can create the potential for conflict. On the one hand, a fear widespread among municipal governments is that when the reserve is created, they will lose the ability to administer, regulate, and tax that land. In other words, they might see the creation of an urban reserve as an infringement on their sovereignty. On the other hand, the First Nation might be fearful of the involvement on the municipality in its bylaw-making decisions, given that the control and use of land can be seen as "fundamental to First Nation concepts of self-government and self-determination" (Dust, 1998).

Where urban reserves were created, recognition of the other government's jurisdiction and willingness to respect it have usually been made explicit. This is one of the issues that the municipal agreement is meant to address. Often, the two governments have chosen to resort to the concept of bylaw compatibility. The phrasing may seem unimportant but it is actually very significant because it is one of the major components of the contact zone the two governments have defined between them. 'Bylaw compatibility' does not mean that municipal bylaws take precedence over the First Nation's, which could be seen as an encroachment on its sovereignty; it means that the First Nation retains its right to enact bylaws but that those bylaws will be compatible with the ones in place in the municipality. In theory, this allows for the harmonious development and administration of the lands without infringing on the right of any of the two governments to exercise their decision-making powers. Some First Nations have welcomed that arrangement as protecting their sovereignty, sparing them the laborious task of developing a whole new set of bylaws suitable for an urban context, and providing 'certainty' to potential investors. Other First Nations have expressed the view that the notion of bylaw compatibility represents a *de facto* restriction of their sovereignty.

ENDING THE EXCLUSION OF INDIGENOUS LANDS AND ECONOMIC ACTIVITIES FROM URBAN AREAS?

The location of urban reserves in relation to their 'host' urban areas appears to depend heavily on the local context. At one end of the spectrum, Saskatoon has been

59

showcased as a trailblazer with five urban reserves within its city limits as of 2017, while Winnipeg only has one. There are however several urban reserves *around* Winnipeg: Swan Lake First Nation's in the rural municipality (RM) of Headingley, Roseau River Anishinabe First Nation's in the RM of Rosser, and Brokenhead Ojibway Nation's in the RM of East St Paul. Their being called *urban* reserves despite their location in *rural* municipalities finds its origins in the federal government's definition: an urban reserve "is defined as a reserve within or *adjacent to* an urban centre" (INAC, 2017, emphasis added). Out of the five urban reserve in Treaty One Territory, only one is within a city (Long Plain First Nation's in Winnipeg) while the other four are located on the margins, very near the city's limits but not within them. Two hypotheses can be proposed to explain this rurban location of urban reserves. First, there could simply be little or no interest on the part of TLE First Nations in creating reserves within cities. Second, there could be some resistance to the idea of urban reserves on the part of local governments and populations.

Though seven First Nations signed Treaty One in 1871, five only had TLE claims validated by Canada; all of these five Treaty One First Nations have attempted or succeeded at creating an urban reserve in the Winnipeg area. In approximately the last decade, at least ten urban reserve projects in the Winnipeg region were proposed by six First Nations, including those five Treaty One First Nations. Out of these ten projects, four succeeded, two were abandoned, and four are underway. Six of those ten projects aim(ed) for an urban reserve within the City of Winnipeg, and the other four are located in RMs adjacent to the provincial capital. Whether the projects have been successful or not, the mere fact that these initiatives exist shows that there is an interest on the part of some TLE First Nations to acquire and develop urban reserves as close as possible to or within cities. Interestingly, the two projects that were abandoned would have been in a much more central location in Winnipeg than their successful counterparts (at the old Canada Packers site in St. Boniface, and at Portage Avenue and Smith Street). In addition, a project to redevelop the former army base (the Kapyong Barracks) in the affluent Tuxedo neighbourhood as an urban reserve was in and out of the courts between 2008 and 2015, in a legal battle that has seen the federal government appeal every decision issued in favour of the First Nations involved. The scarcity and location of urban reserves in Treaty One Territory clearly cannot be explained away by invoking a lack of interest from TLE First Nations.

In the three last projects mentioned, there has been the suspicion that racism and/or the undue intervention of one or more elected officials or senior bureaucrats opposed to the project have played a role in the delay or failure of the initiative. But apart from the rare cases where there is an explicit opposition to an urban reserve project from local populations or governments (e.g., through a referendum), it is difficult to prove that there is an intentional exclusion of Indigenous lands and economic activities from cities – a difficulty which Barron and Garcea highlight (1999, p. 286). Opposition on racist grounds can be disguised as concerns regarding safety regulations on the new reserve, or loss of revenues, or can be backed by a

FIRST NATIONS, MUNICIPALITIES, AND URBAN RESERVES

narrow interpretation of the duty to consult. Opposition usually remains hidden or implicit. But because of the unequal balance of power between the municipality and the proponent First Nation – a consequence of the process of urban reserve creation itself – an adversarial municipal council would have means at their disposal to delay the process.

It is true that other factors can explain the rurban location of urban reserves in Treaty One (e.g., the location ideally fit the First Nations' plans; the land was more affordable; the First Nations anticipated the conversion to reserve process would be more difficult and lengthy in an urban location, etc.). What should be stressed though is that because INAC's definition of 'urban reserve' is so imprecise, it could be easy to conclude from the existence of a few urban reserves that the exclusion of Indigenous lands and economies from the urban space is history. If we want to critically look at the transformative potential of urban reserves, it would be wiser to ask if First Nations are able to create urban reserves where they wish, and if not, who or what is preventing them from doing so.

CONCLUSION

It is neither possible nor desirable to try and design a "one-size-fits-all" model for the study of urban reserves that could be uniformly applied throughout Canada. The creation and development of these reserves rest on a myriad of factors, some of which this paper has explored. Though some general trends may be identified, they always combine with factors of a more local and contingent nature. Indeed, whether we consider the content of the TLE agreement, the size and nature of the urban reserve project, its location within the city or town, the governments' previous experiences with urban reserve creation, or the level of familiarity of city staff with treaty rights, TLE, and the powers of First Nations governments, all play a role in the process of urban reserve creation and vary from one case to the other.

In any case, a relationship will be (re)created between the proponent First Nation and the 'host' municipality. The creation and development of urban reserves provide an exciting opportunity to analyze the nature and scope of the contact zone that is created in the process, to identify how much of it is predetermined by the system in place (e.g., the TLE agreements, INAC's supervision, the MSA requirement...) and how much rests on the attitudes, interests, strategies, and efforts of the First Nations and local governments. Understanding the nature and scope of these intergovernmental relationships is necessary to assess how they can impact First Nations' efforts at developing economic activities in cities – both an exercise of and a path to self-determination – and how they can challenge the historical exclusion of Indigenous lands and economies from the urban space.

The study of urban reserves is relatively new, and much remains to be done to fully understand their impacts on Indigenous and non-Indigenous communities, economies, and relations. Further research on urban reserves could include an analysis of First Nations-provincial/federal relations; an assessment of the impact of previous experiences on the creation of new reserves in a given jurisdiction; and a study of residential urban reserves. In addition, urban reserves are not progressing uniformly across the country. A comparative analysis between several provinces would help to assess the impact of the local context on the creation and development of urban reserves.

NOTE

[1] The name, content, and number of these agreements depend on the jurisdiction. In Saskatoon for example, a municipal services agreement, a police services agreement, and a school board agreement have to be negotiated. In Winnipeg, the practice seems to be the negotiation of one document, a municipal and development services agreement.

REFERENCES

Barron, F. (1988). The Indian pass system in the Canadian West, 1882–1935. *Prairie Forum, 13*(1), 25–42.

Barron, F., & Garcea, J. (Eds.). (1999). *Urban Indian reserves: Forging new relationships in Saskatchewan.* Saskatoon: Purich Publishing Ltd.

Burrows, P. (2009). *As she shall deem just: Treaty one and the ethnic cleansing of the St. Peter's reserve, 1871–1934* (MA thesis). University of Manitoba, Winnipeg.

Dust, T. (1995). *The impact of aboriginal land claims and self-government on Canadian municipalities: The local government perspective.* Toronto: ICURR Press.

Dust, T. (1998). *Economic development on aboriginal lands and land use compatibility.* Retrieved from http://www.tdust.com/res/econ_dev.pdf

Fawcett, R. B., Walker, R., & Greene, J. (2015). Indigenizing city planning processes in Saskatoon, Canada. *Canadian Journal of Urban Research, 24*(2), 158–175.

Indigenous and Northern Affairs Canada. (2017, April 11). *Urban reserves.* Retrieved from https://www.aadnc-aandc.gc.ca/eng/1100100016331/1100100016332

Long Plain First Nation Trust. (n.d.). *Home page.* Retrieved from http://www.lptrust.ca/MainLPTrust.html

Newhouse, D., & Peters, E. (Eds.). (2003). *Not strangers in these parts: Urban aboriginal people.* Ottawa: Policy Research Initiative.

Paul, A. (2012, October 1). City's first urban reserve open. *Winnipeg Free Press.* Retrieved from http://www.winnipegfreepress.com/local/citys-first-urban-reserve-open-136997393.html

Porter, L., & Barry, J. (2015). Bounded recognition: Urban planning and the textual mediation of Indigenous rights in Canada and Australia. *Critical Policy Studies, 9*(1), 22–40.

Walker, R., Berdahl, L., Lashta, E., Newhouse, D., & Belanger, Y. (2017). Public attitudes towards indigeneity in Canadian prairie urbanism. *The Canadian Geographer, 61*(1), 1–12.

Charlotte Bezamat-Mantes
Institut Français de Géopolitique
Université Paris 8 Vincennes
Saint-Denis, France

CARLY WELHAM

7. INDIGENOUS FOOD SOVEREIGNTY IS A PUBLIC HEALTH PRIORITY

INTRODUCTION

Food sovereignty is the right of communities to define their own agricultural, labour, fishing, food and land systems and policies which are ecologically, socially, economically, and culturally appropriate (B.C. Food Systems Network, 2008). The concept was originally developed by the global farmers' organization Via Campesina, and in the settler-colonial context of Canada food sovereignty has come to be synonymous with Indigenous Food Sovereignty (IFS) as Indigenous activists further defined the term with a focus on decolonization and self-determination of food policies (Desmarais & Wittman, 2014). Speaking from within the discipline of public health, this paper will argue that IFS is a priority for public health research and action due to its potential to positively impact numerous proximal, intermediate, and distal determinants of health as defined by Loppie Reading and Wein (2009).

Food systems have been recognized as a colonial frontier. Colonial policies have forcibly disconnected Indigenous people from land and food systems, and this continues to effect the health inequities demonstrated in high rates of dietary illness among Indigenous populations compared to the Canadian population as a whole (Rotenberg, 2016). The Truth and Reconciliation Commission of Canada found that "this process of culinary acculturation was a key feature of colonialism," as children in Indian Residential Schools were separated from their traditional diet, denied food, or subjected to nutritional experiments (Bagelman, Devereaux, & Hartley, 2016, p. 7). Action to support IFS could help address the ongoing detrimental health impacts of such policies in a contemporary context, while aligning with current Indigenous land protection movements and cultural resurgence.

Despite these challenges, it's estimated the 40–50% of the Indigenous communities in B.C. currently obtain over 200 different types of traditional foods through local harvesting (Desmarais & Wittman, 2014). As IFS is rooted in each community's right to control the direction of their food systems from the land to the table, the policy and program approaches taken to advance IFS are as diverse as the communities themselves. In this paper, the terms "IFS" and "IFS programs" will be used to refer to the diverse breadth of such approaches, which include community gardens, greenhouses and kitchens, harvesting activities, fruit gleaning projects, conferences,

© KONINKLIJKE BRILL NV, LEIDEN, 2018 | DOI 9789004367418_007

CARLY WELHAM

forums, coalitions, feasts, language and cultural programs, environmental research, mapping, and more (B.C. Food Systems Network, 2008).

IFS activists push for a fundamental social change and transformation of society through food systems (Desmarais & Wittman, 2014). This involves addressing many social determinants of health influencing Indigenous communities' abilities to meet their own food needs. In turn, IFS has a reciprocal relationship with its own impacts on many of these determinants, as explored below. This paper will explore the overlap between public health objectives and recommendations from key IFS organizations (including the B.C. Working Group on Indigenous Food Sovereignty and the Food Secure Canada Indigenous Circle) to demonstrate that the scope of public health involves supporting IFS programs and policies.

PROXIMAL DETERMINANTS

Health Behaviours

Perhaps the most obvious benefit of encouraging IFS is the nutritional superiority of traditional Indigenous foods compared to store-bought alternatives, in terms of lower levels of fat, sugar, and carbohydrates and higher levels of vitamins and minerals (Kuhnlein, Receveur, Soueida, & Egeland, 2004). This is encouraging given that the 2012 Aboriginal People's Survey (APS) found that 34% of Indigenous people are overweight, a risk factor for chronic conditions such as diabetes, cardiovascular disease, and hypertension (Rotenberg, 2016). The active lifestyle encouraged by traditional harvesting is also a positive health behaviour implicated in IFS. As well as being of "vital symbolic and spiritual value, essential to the cultural identity of many Indigenous people," there are many health benefits in improving access to Indigenous foods through IFS programs (People's Food Policy, 2011, p. 4).

Employment & Income

Displacement from the land has increased the number of families reliant on the industrial food system (B.C. Food Systems Network, 2008), and many Indigenous communities face high rates of unemployment, poor housing, and scarce educational opportunities (Loppie Reading & Wein, 2009). Poverty can contribute to poor nutritional health, social exclusion, and low social cohesion (Loppie Reading & Wein, 2009), which is significant as societies with more social support tend to have better health (Richmond, 2009). Today, the ability to provide healthy, culturally appropriate foods is situated in a capitalist context with the added challenge of finding the time and energy to balance harvesting with work in the market economy (B.C. Food Systems Network, 2008). This also occurs with less of the communal social structures that historically shared the workload of traditional harvesting. IFS seeks to revitalize social cohesion and community support structures which help insulate individuals from the health effects of poverty, as "tribal values of giving, sharing and trading are at the heart of land care and food sovereignty" (People's Food Policy, 2011, p. 2). By fostering alternatives to capitalist, industrial food systems, IFS aims to reduce the health inequities of dietary-related illness. IFS posits foods not as a commodity, but a sacred, freely gifted source of life (People's Food Policy, 2011).

Food Insecurity

Food insecurity is associated with a range of negative health outcomes, and can be defined simply as not having enough money to buy sufficient food (Rotenberg, 2016). The 2012 APS found that food insecurity rates for Indigenous people living off reserve were 20%, compared to the national average of 8% (Rotenberg, 2016). Store food availability and quality is a major barrier to food security in Northern and remote communities, where food insecurity rates can reach 75% (Kuhnlein et al., 2004). Increasing access to healthy foods is a key component of IFS, exemplified in programs that increase access to Indigenous foods in urban areas through Indigenous community gardens, groceries, and trading networks (People's Food Policy, 2011). Addressing food insecurity will require a coordinated policy effort, and IFS activists have recommended the creation of provincial and federal budgets to finance food programs in urban, rural and remote communities (People's Food Policy, 2011).

However, IFS goes beyond food security. While food security is primarily concerned with food access as measured by production and consumption, IFS centres food citizenship, cultural resurgence, and the authority over how and where food is produced (Food Secure Canada, 2015). While food security can obscure processes of land dispossession, IFS is a radical project that asserts sovereignty over such lands through embodied action (Jarosz, 2014). In this way, IFS transcends proximal determinants related to diet to effect change on the many intermediate and distal determinants of health.

INTERMEDIATE DETERMINANTS

Community Infrastructure, Resources & Capabilities

Community health is associated with community and economic development, and IFS seeks to strengthen both economies and communities. IFS offers a socially and environmentally sustainable form of development that is culturally rooted and inclusive. This is a crucial alternative to resource-intensive industrial economic development options, which decrease access to harvesting areas and degrade the health and abundance of Indigenous foods. Establishing a system that ensures healthy, culturally adapted foods requires re-establishing community based food economies that combine traditional harvesting with ecological agricultural practices (B.C. Food Systems Network, 2008). Many communities are undertaking activities that increase their access to healthy foods while also contributing to the community infrastructure. For example, Indigenous-led community farms have been identified as a way to

CARLY WELHAM

build social networks while reconnecting with the land and supplementing hunted foods (B.C. Food Systems Network, 2008).

Environmental Stewardship

Intimate relationships with the environment have been a major health resource for Indigenous people, which colonialism has sought to slowly transform into a relationship of dispossession and disempowerment (Loppie Reading & Wein, 2009). This is one factor contributing to the current global context of food and environmental crises caused by industrial agriculture. Industrial agriculture is not only incredibly environmentally damaging, especially when compared to the low impact of Indigenous food systems, but it also feeds the constant demand for energy and fuels which are disproportionately extracted from Indigenous lands (Food Secure Canada, 2015). Indigenous people inequitably bear the burden of these environmental costs from colonial society due to environmental racism, the tendency to distribute environmental harm unequally along the lines of class and race.

Key aspects of IFS are developing less resource-intensive harvesting practices, as well as defending Indigenous lands from further destruction. In addition to the numerous individuals working on the land to ensure this, several policy approaches have been suggested to ensure that Indigenous people are able to practice environmental stewardship. One recommendation is to incorporate Indigenous environmental law into Canadian legislation in order to have legal mechanisms ensuring environmental protection (Food Secure Canada, 2015). Another favoured solution is the designation of food reserves on Crown Land for Indigenous harvesting (People's Food Policy, 2011).

Cultural Continuity

The level of social and cultural cohesion in a community, as expressed through the maintenance of traditional activities, intergenerational connectedness, language, spirituality, and social support, is an important component of Indigenous health (Rotenberg, 2016). The role of food in supporting culture is clear from the first pillar of IFS as defined by the BC Food Systems Network Working Group on IFS: food is a sacred gift we have a responsibility to nurture (B.C. Food Systems Network, 2008). Food activists argue that food is an accessible entry point into cultural organizing, linking the rural to urban, and traditional to contemporary (People's Food Policy, 2011).

An impact of affirming local food systems is preserving cultures and the diversity of foods, crops, and ecosystems that are foundational to cultures. There is a wealth of ecological, culinary, linguistic, and social knowledge specific to food, so food systems can play a key role in cultural and language revitalization. Food distribution networks also contribute to supporting some Indigenous nations' social structures, such as seal distribution patterns in Inuit communities contributing to maintaining and honouring familial and social relationships (Kuhnlein et al., 2004). The impacts of food on the social determinants of health, as well as the proven health benefits of cultural continuity, make food policies founded in traditional knowledge a powerful pathway to addressing health inequities (People's Food Policy, 2011).

DISTAL DETERMINANTS

Colonialism

Generations of colonial policy have sought to damage Indigenous peoples' relationships to the environment, and continue today in a federal disregard for treaty rights, intergenerational trauma, and a lack of respect for Indigenous lands and waters on the part of policymakers. First Nations people were forced into reserves while their food systems were treated with contempt as detrimental to progress and development. Bagelman, Devereaux and Hartley argue that the separation from food and medicine on the lands left First Nations undefended against colonial encroachment and disease (2016), so IFS has the potential to be a useful tool in the ongoing defence of Indigenous lands, which seeks to prevent future colonial harms.

As a way of healing the damage done by colonialism, traditional harvesting is connected to a greater rapport with the land, a greater sense of self-reliance, and overall improved health (Loppie Reading & Wein, 2009). One of the four pillars IFS (as defined by the BC Food Systems Network Working Group on IFS) is policy, and reconciling cultural values with colonial laws to influence the wide range of policies negatively impacting land and food systems (B.C. Food Systems Network, 2008). Echoing the national call for reconciliation, a priority recommendation for implementing IFS is healing relationships between settlers and Indigenous peoples who can share the responsibilities for fostering healthy food systems (Food Secure Canada, 2015).

Self-Determination

Self-determination is cited as the most important determinant of health for Aboriginal people (Loppie Reading & Wein, 2009). Self-determination is itself a key principle of IFS, embodied in freedom from dependence on the market economy and the ability to make decisions on the amount and quality of food harvested (B.C. Food Systems Network, 2008). Self-determination requires active and equal participation in decision-making over Indigenous lands and economies. One of the BC Food Systems Network Working Group of IFS's four pillars of IFS is that it is participatory, being practiced everyday at the individual, family, and community levels. The U.N. Declaration of the Rights of Indigenous Peoples declared that self-determination is a right for all Indigenous people, which when paired with the positive impacts on social determinants of health, makes a compelling case for the development of IFS policies and programs.

CARLY WELHAM

Given the key role of self-determination in IFS, most IFS policy recommendations prioritize self-determination through radical shifts in how power and land are shared within Canada. Short-term solutions "to restore and enhance access to traditional Indigenous foods in the forests, fields and waterways continue to be linked to the historic claims to the hunting, fishing and gathering grounds in their respective traditional territories" (People's Food Policy, 2011, p. 2). Although these short-term solutions are needed to combat food insecurity, IFS activists believe that permanent solutions lie within inherent Indigenous sovereignty, and that sovereignty should be recognized as it was at the time of Treaty signing (People's Food Policy, 2011). Land reform through nation-to-nation agreements and adequate land allocation is thus a key IFS policy recommendation (Food Secure Canada, 2015).

CONCLUSION

By strengthening communities, ecosystems, and economies, IFS programs have impacts across a broad range of proximal, intermediate and distal determinants of health. IFS has relevance in contemporary contexts by mediating the impacts of colonization that manifest in ongoing barriers to food access and disconnection from food sources. IFS is a holistic concept with interventions centring on strengthening families and communities, and "such holistic models are important for unifying communities and building on the innate resources of our First Nation and Inuit communities- the spirit of its people" (Richmond, 2009, p. 70). The demonstrated health benefits of Indigenous foods, environmental stewardship, cultural continuity, and self-determination confirm that the scope of public health should align to act in solidarity with food sovereignty movements.

REFERENCES

Bagelman, J., Devereaux, F., & Hartley, R. (2016). Feasting for change: Reconnecting with food, place & culture. *International Journal of Indigenous Health, 11*(1), 6–17. doi:10.18357ijih111201616016

B.C. Food Systems Network. (2008). *Working group on indigenous food sovereignty: Final activity report*. Retrieved from http://www.indigenousfoodsystems.org/sites/default/files/resources/WGIFS_Final_Report_March_08.pdf

Desmarais, A., & Wittman, H. (2014). Farmers, foodies and first nations: Getting to food sovereignty in Canada. *Journal of Peasant Studies, 41*(6), 1153–1173. doi:10.1080/03066150.2013.876623

Food Secure Canada. (2015). *Resetting the table: A people's food policy for Canada*. Retrieved from http://foodsecurecanada.org/people-food-policy

Grey, S., & Patel, R. (2015). Food sovereignty as decolonization: Some contributions from indigenous movements to food system and development politics. *Agriculture and Human Values, 32*(3), 431–444. doi:10.1007/s10460-014-9548-9

Jarosz, L. (2014). Comparing food security and food sovereignty discourses. *Dialogues in Human Geography, 4*(2), 168–181.

Kuhnlein, H. V., Receveur, O., Soueida, R., & Egeland, G. M. (2004). Arctic indigenous peoples experience the nutrition transition with changing dietary patterns and obesity. *The Journal of Nutrition, 134*(6), 1447.

Loppie Reading, C., & Wein, F. (2009). *Health inequalities and social determinants of aboriginal peoples health*. Prince George, BC: National Collaborating Centre for Aboriginal Health.

People's Food Policy Project. (2011). *Discussion paper on indigenous food sovereignty.* Retrieved from http://foodsecurecanada.org/sites/foodsecurecanada.org/files/sites/foodsecurecanada.org/files/DP1_ Indigenous_Food_Sovereignty.pdf

Richmond, C. (2009). Explaining the paradox of health and social support among aboriginal Canadians. *Canadian Issues, Winter*, 65–71.

Rotenberg, C. (2016). *Social determinants of health for the off-reserve first nations population 15 and older, 2012.* Ottawa: Statistics Canada.

Carly Welham
School of Public Health and Social Policy
University of Victoria
Victoria, British Columbia

PART 2

SHARING INTERGENERATIONAL TEACHINGS: LANGUAGE AND STORIES

KĀSHĀ JULIE A. MORRIS (TAHLTAN NATION)

8. USING LANGUAGE NESTS TO PROMOTE THE INTERGENERATIONAL TRANSMISSION OF TĀŁTĀN

INTRODUCTION

In this chapter, I present a summary of my research, which reports on using the language nest model to promote the intergenerational transmission of Tāłtān.[1] I begin by situating myself, my people, and K'asba'e T'oh.[2] After that I recommend some language nest resources, next I present a brief overview of my thesis entitled *K'asba'e T'oh: Sustaining the intergenerational transmission of Tāłtān* (Kāshā, 2017), and I close with readings from the esdahūhedech[3] of four co-researchers.[4] These readings illustrate the representative learnings of this study.

Situating Myself, My People, and K'asba'e T'oh

As an Indigenous[5] person, it is important for me to share the identity of my maternal Ancestral territory (Absolon, 2011; Edōsdi, 2012; Smith, 2012). My traditional Tahltan name is Kāshā – I was named after my grandmother Julia, and my English name is Julie (Thompson) Morris. I am a member of the Tahltan Nation, a Dene-speaking First Nation. Our territories are located along the Stikine River in northern British Columbia (BC), Canada. There are about 3000 members with 1600 who make their homes in the present-day communities of Łuwechōn,[6] Tātl'ah[7] and Tlēgo'īn[8] (TCG, 2015). My people are from Łuwechōn and Tlēgo'īn. I belong to the Tsesk'iye[9] Clan and the Tehkahche[10] is our crest. We are from the Tl'abanot'īne territory. My parents are Tṣi' Tṣa Cathryn (Callbreath) and the late Wallace Thompson, who was a member of the Gitx̱san First Nation of Gitwangak in northwestern BC. My mother is the daughter of the late Kāshā Julia (Vance) and Eyakta' Charley Callbreath. My maternal grandparents were not fluent Tāłtān speakers and chose not to teach what they knew to their children. However, in 1991 they began teaching the language to my sister Edōsdi after she had shown an interest in learning about our language and culture. Many years after my grandmother Elizabeth (Lowrie) Webb passed away, I discovered that she was a Gitx̱an speaker. Sadly, my mom and dad were not taught to speak their mother tongue, and therefore neither was I as a child.

Growing up my teachings were the colonized ways of my people. I was born and raised in the south and make my home in Lax̱ Keen,[11] which is located within the traditional territories of the Nine Allied Tribes of the Ts'msyen First Nation

© KONINKLIJKE BRILL NV, LEIDEN, 2018 | DOI 9789004367418_008

KĀSHĀ JULIE A. MORRIS

on the north coast of BC. I was born and raised in the south, so I am an urban Tahltan. I thought, at one time, that if I had been raised on traditional territory, I would be a fluent Tāłtān speaker. It saddened me to learn that living on traditional territory does not guarantee being brought up knowing one's Ancestral language and culture. There are now fewer than 30 fluent Tāłtān speakers; however, in our nation there is a growing movement toward retaining and promoting our language and culture. We are implementing different ways to pass on our language to our younger generations.

One of the ways Tāłtān is being rejuvenated is through language nests for young children, where small groups of children ages six months to four years old are nurtured in a no-English policy 'Didenek'eh hodinde'[12] environment. The video clip entitled *Tahltan Language Nests 2* https://vimeo.com/187371286 (Edōsdi & Bourquin, 2016a) is from our documentary entitled *Dah dẕāhge nodeṣidē: We are speaking our language again* (Edōsdi & Bourquin, 2016b); it shows our Dzimēs Chō T'oh[13] and K'asba'e T'oh programs in action. All of our language nests are family-like settings where children spend quality time with language mentors and communicate only in Tāłtān. With a one-to-three ratio of language mentors to children, it is like visiting with estsū[14] and estsiye.[15]

My research reports on the K'asba'e T'oh, the second of three language nest programs established by the Tahltan Central Government's Socio-Cultural Working Group and Dah Dẕāhge Nodeṣidē (DDN).[16] K'asba'e T'oh opened on December 18, 2014. The nest is operated out of a house and is the only Tahltan language nest not on reserve land. The Dzimēs Chō T'oh opened in May 2014. The Meska'ā T'oh[17] briefly opened in June 2016. There are plans to reopen it once language coordinator and language mentor positions can be filled.

Language Nest Media Resources

One of the best ways to learn about language nests is to visit one, but since that is not always possible, listed in Table 1 are three informative language nest media resources.

Table 1. Language nest documentation resources

Author	Title of media	Publication
First Peoples' Cultural Council	*The language nest story: As told by Kathy Michel* https://www.youtube.com/watch?v=ffUTiwsRlag	2014 (21:03)
Edōsdi & Bourquin, M.	*Dah dẕāhge nodeṣidē: We are speaking our language again* http://vimeo.com/217095185	2016 (1:04:06)
First Peoples' Cultural Council	Language/Programs/Language Nest http://www.fpcc.ca/ language/Programs/Language-nest.aspx AND Language nest handbook online companion toolkit	2016

74

The first two media resources are online documentaries: *The language nest story: As told by Kathy Michel* (First Peoples' Cultural Council, 2014, September 16) and *Dah dẕāhge nodeṣidē: We are speaking our language again* (Edōsdi & Bourquin, 2016, October 18). Both are introductory and give voice to the challenges and successes of language immersion programs and are told by the people doing the work. The other is a website specific to the operation of language nests, ranging from how to obtain funding to language-learning activities. The First Peoples' Cultural Council's website (2016) has information about funding opportunities along with several helpful resources, such as the "Language immersion handbook" and the "Language Nest handbook online companion toolkit."

OVERVIEW OF THESIS

It was important for me to do research that would be beneficial for my people, so with guidance and in consultation with the DDN, I received permission to do a case study with the people involved in the K'asba'e T'oh program. The values and principles guiding my study are grounded in 'Tahltan Voiceability,' an Indigenous methodology based upon our Tahltan worldview (Edōsdi, 2012). Tahltan Voiceability set the tone for not only how I carried out my research, but also how I presented the voices of my co-researchers. Edōsdi defined this Indigenous methodology in her doctoral dissertation:

> In regards to Tahltan Voiceability, I define "voiceability" in a similar way to "readability," with readability (n.d.) being defined as, "the quality of written language that makes it easy to read and understand." In terms of Voiceability, I came up with this term when trying to find a way to portray the Tahltan voice – including that of the co-researchers, my Elders and Ancestors, and myself – in such a way that readers would be able to "hear" our voices on paper. However, I also wanted to extend it to mean how a people can find their voice and find strength in their voice, in order to heal and become a stronger healthier nation. (p. 90)

The style of writing used in this study has a conversational tone to it, as I wanted to use words that were less "high language" so my work would be accessible to both non-academic and academic audiences (see also Edōsdi, 2012, p. 22). Take for example the sharing of the learnings in the form of esdahūhedech. In honouring Indigenous oral storytelling traditions, I re-presented the voices of my co-researchers in the form of esdahūhedech to not only acknowledge them but also to enrich readers' experiences with an authentic understanding of the challenges and successes of bringing our languages back into everyday use through immersion programming for young children.

Overall, I made 14 visits with eight co-researchers – two administrators (the director and language nest coordinator), two language mentors, and four language nest parents – to hear about their perspectives and experiences regarding how the K'asba'e T'oh got started, how things are progressing, and what motivated

KĀSHĀ JULIE A. MORRIS

and continues to motivate them to be involved. Throughout the analysis process, co-researchers approved his or her own transcript, shortened transcript, and endodēsdił.[18] Through a thematic reduction of original transcripts, one main theme of chitlesidēdli[19] and three subthemes of collaboration, nation-building, and identity and belonging, rose to the fore as most significant. Chitlesidēdli is when everyone gathers for social, cultural, and language-learning activities; it is a time for kinship, teaching, and passing down esdahūhedech that has been practiced for time immemorial. I re-created an endodēsdił for each of the co-researchers' shortened transcript to illustrate the thematic connections. Each endodēsdił is an edited version of its shortened transcript but stays true to the authentic voice and words of the co-researcher and exemplifies the thematic connections.

ESDAHŪHEDECH OF THE CO-RESEARCHERS

The wisdom and knowledge of my co-researchers are the heart of this study as they are the experts; they are the ones telling the endodēsdił I am documenting. The voices of my co-researchers have helped me to articulate Tahltan Voiceability. "Giving voice to our Ancestors and Elders, as well as to all of our people, sets the stage for research that is useful, relational, and transformative" (Edōsdi, 2017, p. 21). I will close with excerpts from four esdahūhedech, which reflect the co-researchers' unique personal experiences in the language nest, and include a theme-based postscript after each endodēsdił.

Edōsdi: Director, Tahltan Language and Culture Program

Edōsdi is Tahltan from the Tl'abanot'īne territory. Her English name is Dr. Judy Thompson. She is a member of the Tsesk'iye Clan and is esdedze.[20] She has been involved in learning Tāłtān for 26 years and has been the director of the Tahltan Language and Culture Program since 2012.

This first reading is from the endodēsdił entitled "Beginning with the roots."

I first started learning the language from Granny and Grandpa back in 1991. I didn't learn to speak the language fluently and still haven't, but going through that process of finding out, learning songs, learning stories, meeting our relatives, meeting more Elders, that definitely changed who I was and who I am. I feel really proud of what we've done as a people. With the documentary we did, we were able to get footage of the babies and adults speaking. And I feel as though I'm a key part of the work we're doing, so I feel a part of our community, our people. Even though I'm not physically up there all the time – I don't live up there, and I don't think I ever will – but just being involved in this, it connects me to our people.

I see the language nests as being the foundation of the revitalization of our language. It's sort of like getting to the roots, teaching the babies, so I see

76

USING LANGUAGE NESTS TO PROMOTE THE TRANSMISSION OF TĀŁTĀN

everything going from there. We still need to work with the parents. We all learn to speak our first language as babies, as toddlers, as newborns by just hearing language and just being around the language, and so this is where I see us doing it as naturally as we can. Obviously, it's not, if it were really natural, parents would be speaking it at home to their babies. But it's not happening yet, so I see this as working toward that. Maybe down the road we will have babies learning Tāłtān at home. If I had to only work on one program and get rid of all the other ones, I'd stick with the language nests. That's to me the number one, most important one, and so from there, everything flows from that with our language revitalization work.

Postscript

Edōsdi spoke about how she identified with being an urban Tahltan, yet has developed close bonds with her people. She touched on nation-building along with the collaborative efforts to revitalize Tāłtān. Further, she emphasized the value in language nests as being central to a language revitalization plan.

This next reading also highlighted collaboration, nation-building, and identity and belonging.

Odelia Dennis: Language Nest Coordinator

Odelia Dennis is Tahltan from the Tl'abanot'īne territory. She is a member of the Chi'yōne[21] Clan. She has been involved in learning Tāłtān for four years. Odelia is a researcher on the Tāłtān Language Revitalization Team and is the language nest coordinator.

This second reading is from the endodēsdił entitled "Learning our language."

Learning my Tahltan language has really put me at ease with my identity issues, which started in early adulthood. It seems like whatever anyone says about Iskut, it doesn't really bother me because I know my language, no one can take that away from me. They can talk about where I'm from, they can talk, they can say my grandpa wasn't Tahltan, or they can say anything about that, but they could not say that I don't even know my language. They couldn't say that because that's something that I have that can't be taken. So, I definitely identify myself as a Tahltan woman. I strongly identify with being Tahltan now, whereas before, it was people causing me to question that.

I started learning the Tahltan language in 2012, and my son Arden was two years old, so he barely even spoke English. I remember feeling so fulfilled in my life when he could understand me. And I would be alone in that, right? And then when Dzimēs Chō T'oh opened, it was it was all five little kids, including my son. It was starting to happen all over again, all these children were understanding Tāłtān and were responding to my Tāłtān commands, and I was just so thrilled.

77

KĀSHĀ JULIE A. MORRIS

Postscript

Odelia spoke about her personal identity issues, which she has resolved, attributing that resolution to learning her language. She also provided a glimpse into the rewards of learning and teaching our language. As the result of her dedication, Odelia has helped to establish two Tahltan language nests.

This next reading is from a language nest parent's perspective. It is evident that her child is picking up the language and is happy at the nest.

Carmen Dennis: Language nest parent

Carmen is Tahltan and is a member of the Tsesk'iye Clan. Her daughter Myra had just completed her first year in the language nest.

This third reading is from the endodēsdił entitled "Singing Tāłtān."

Myra's singing took me by surprise this year, and for her to memorize it! The singing of it. I was like, holy man! I didn't expect my daughter to memorize that and getting so many compliments from the instructors and from the Elders. And when they have other students that are in the language program, every now and then they come over to the language nest here in Dease Lake like from Telegraph or from Iskut to build up their hours, and then they would come up and compliment me and be like, "Hey you know your daughter, she catches on to this really good. You know we've heard she's a star pupil." And that makes me really proud.

Postscript

In terms of satisfaction, Carmen spoke about the success of the nest as she described her daughter's language-learning abilities. Also, the connection and identity and belonging from having other people recognize her daughter as a 'star' brought her joy. Hearing the young ones speaking our language helps to strengthen and create new relationships in our communities.

This next reading is also about connection, nation-building, and identity and belonging.

Pat Etzerza: Language Mentor

Pat is a Tahltan Elder and a member of the Tsesk'iye Clan. He was born and raised in Tlēgo'īn. Pat has been involved in Tahltan language revitalization programs for several decades. He is a language mentor in the nest.

This final reading is from the endodēsdił entitled "Starting with the tots."

It is very important that we revitalize our language. It's our identity. It defines who we are as people. You know we have our own language, our own history.

USING LANGUAGE NESTS TO PROMOTE THE TRANSMISSION OF TĀŁTĀN

We're different people. Your identity, you must know your language to know who you are and where you come from 'cause it's very important that you know your history, your language, your customs. It's so important that we start with the tots because I've witnessed, I see it happening right in front of my eyes, these kids are picking it up so quickly and that's an awesome feeling!

I will tell you another story about when that Lieutenant Governor[22] came to Dease Lake. She came to visit our nest and everything worked out perfectly. Those kids were asking for what they wanted to drink, and in what cup – like we have green, red – all kinds of different coloured cups. They went to Odelia and said, "Desbet,"[23] and she gave them something to eat. And "Enla' ghatān ots"[24] that's all you say "Enla' ghatān ots"; they run to the bathroom. And then as the Lieutenant Governor was leaving, she turned around, and my little granddaughter said, "Nanustī."[25] That took her heart with her. "I'll see you," she said. It was so awesome for her to say.

Postscript

Pat recalled how collaboration with Canadian governments is not new; however, these arrangements have only provided support for short-term language programming. The language nest children are inspiring a return to traditional language-learning roles, as they pick up and learn the language and use it, inside and outside of the language nest.

CONCLUSION

Research to assess and evaluate our language nest programs should be a priority. This would provide us with valuable insight and help inform the direction of our immersion language planning. This research could also examine better ways to support the people in the nest. While this study focused on the K'asba'e T'oh, I need to stress that language nests can be established in all Indigenous languages and communities. We need to create fluent speakers and help others improve their fluencies and proficiencies in their languages. Speaking our Ancestral languages is important and can be achieved by creating space in our lives for language-learning. Mēduh.[26]

NOTES

[1] Tahltan language.
[2] Dease Lake Language Nest.
[3] I have used this Tāłtān word in place of the term stories to refer to plural of story and also for the collection of co-researchers' tellings.
[4] These are the people involved in the language nest whom I visited and who helped me address the research questions. This research was community-led with the co-researchers' influence in the shaping and the meaning making process of this study.
[5] I have capitalized Indigenous, Ancestral, Ancestor, and Elder to show respect and acknowledgement.

KĀSHĀ JULIE A. MORRIS

[6] Iskut.
[7] Dease Lake.
[8] Telegraph Creek.
[9] Crow.
[10] Frog.
[11] Prince Rupert.
[12] Speak our people's way.
[13] Iskut Language Nest.
[14] Grandma.
[15] Grandpa.
[16] Tahltan Language and Culture Council.
[17] Telegraph Creek Language Nest.
[18] I have used this Tāłtān word in place of the term story.
[19] We come together.
[20] My younger sister.
[21] Wolf.
[22] The Honourable Judith Guichon, Lieutenant Governor of BC visited K'asba'e T'oh on September 18, 2015.
[23] I'm hungry.
[24] Wash your hands.
[25] I will see you.
[26] Thanks.

REFERENCES

Absolon, K. (Minogiizhigokwe). (2011). *Kaandossiwin: How we come to know*. Halifax: Fernwood.

Edōsdi/Thompson, J. C. (2012). *Hedekeyeh hots'ih kāhidi–"Our ancestors are in us": Strengthening our voices through language revitalization from a Tahltan worldview* (Unpublished doctoral dissertation). University of Victoria, Victoria. Retrieved from http://dspace.library.uvic.ca

Edōsdi/Thompson, J. C. (2017). The artistry of research: The strength and stability of voice. In K. Staikidis & C. Ballengee-Morris (Eds.), *Transforming our practices: Indigenous art, pedagogies, and philosophies*. Reston, VA: National Art Education Association Press.

Edōsdi/Thompson, J. C., Bourquin, M. (Producers) & Bourquin, M. (Director). (2016b, October 18). *Dah dẕāhge nodeṣidē: We are speaking our language again* [Video file]. Retrieved from https://vimeo.com/217095185

Edōsdi/Thompson, J. C., Bourquin, M. (Producers) & Bourquin, M. (Director). (2016a, October 18). *Tahltan language nests 2* [Video file]. Retrieved from https://vimeo.com/187371286

First Peoples' Cultural Council. (2014, September 16). *The language nest story* [Video file]. Retrieved from https://www.youtube.com/watch?v=ffUTiwsRlag

First Peoples' Cultural Council. (2016). *Language program*. Retrieved October 12, 2016, from http://www.fpcc.ca/language/

Kāshā/Morris, J. A. (2017). *K'asba'e T'oh: Sustaining the intergenerational transmission of Tāłtān* (Unpublished master's thesis). University of Victoria, Victoria. Retrieved from http://dspace.library.uvic.ca

Smith, L. T. (2012). *Decolonizing methodologies: Research and indigenous peoples* (2nd ed.). New York, NY: Zed Books.

Tahltan Central Government. (2015). *Tahltan quarterly/Tatl'ā*. Retrieved from http://tahltan.org/newsletters-2/

Kāshā Julie A. Morris (Tahltan Nation)
Indigenous Education
University of Victoria
Victoria, British Columbia

ISAAC MURDOCH[1] (NARRATOR) AND JASON BONE[2] (EDITOR)

9. BIBOONIIWININII: MIIGAAZOO-DIBAAJIMOWIN
WINTER SPIRIT: FIGHT STORY

BIOGRAPHY

Jason Bone Ndizinikaaz, Mikinaak Doodem, Giizhigoowining Doonji, bangi eta Anishinaabem, ni noonde nitaa Anishnaabem onjida ginistodan Aadisookaanag – My name is Jason Bone, I'm Turtle Clan from the Anishinaabe-Ojibway community of Giizhigoowining – Keeseekoowenin, Manitoba. I speak a little Ojibway but I want to get better to understand the sacred stories and beings to this continent. Foundationally, what inspired my studies was my dad's insistence, as I expressed my uncertainty about undertaking the task not being a fluent speaker, that the most important aspects of Ojibway language are concepts that go far beyond the day to day language of communication. It took me a while to learn and understand that Spirit loves Anishinaabeg people so much, she will always send message to someone who still listens to the "voice of nature."[3] It would be an honor to share this Anishinaabe – Ojibway Story and Language research within this book.

My Masters of Arts Thesis was titled Baagak Aadisookewin: Legends of History and Memory. My research interests are to explore what Anishinaabe-Ojibway stories about Anangokwaan (The Star World) and Miish'akomoo (Sasquatch/Bigfoot) can tell us about our human history under the academic advise of Dr. Niigaanwewidam James Sinclair.

THE SPIRIT OF STORY

Concepts from Walter Benjamin's *The Storyteller* begin with the claim that the present-day storyteller is by no means a present force. He addresses the decline of the role of which storytelling plays in not just households in Europe, but all humanity. This aligns with the same challenge in Anishinaabe-Ojibwe communities today – the art of storytelling is coming to an end. Benjamin attributes this to experience, which is the source from where the tales come from – mouth to mouth, oral transmission – has fallen in value.[4] The process of assimilation, which takes place in depth, requires a state of relaxation, which is becoming rarer and rarer. Likewise, the gift for listening is lost, along with community of listeners.[5] Benjamin argues that in the process the great writers were those whose narratives differed least from the speech of the storyteller.[6]

© KONINKLIJKE BRILL NV, LEIDEN, 2018 | DOI 9789004367418_009

ISAAC MURDOCH AND JASON BONE

There are two quotes from this article that will be foundational to building my PhD research proposal:

Actually, it is half the art of storytelling to keep a story free from explanation, as one reproduces it. Leskov is a master at this. The most extraordinary things, marvellous things, are related with the greatest accuracy, but the psychological connection to the events is not forced on the reader. It is left up to him to interpret things the way he understands them, and thus the narrative achieves an amplitude that information lacks.[7]

And,

That is why this story from ancient Egypt is still capable, after thousands of years of arousing astonishment and thoughtfulness. It resembles the seeds of grain which have laid for centuries in the chambers of the pyramids shut up air tight and retained their germative power to this day.[8]

BIBOONIIWININII: MIIGAAZOO-DIBAAJIMOWIN
WINTER SPIRIT: FIGHT STORY

Isaac Murdoch

I want to thank everyone for coming and for being here this morning. I want to thank our host. She is very pregnant so we commend her strength and resilience because I believe she is having her baby today or tomorrow. Let's give her around of applause.

I have no idea what I am going to say. The conference is rising, rising up. And what does that mean, "Rising Up," in terms of research? When I think of research, I think about trying to understand or gain knowledge about something. The only reason why someone would research something is to try to learn something. And right now, I think that is really critical. When I think of our own research, I think it is so valuable because our ancient ancestors had the code; they had the ancient map on how to live on these lands.

As we all know Canada is gearing up to celebrate Canada 150. I want to celebrate the thousands and thousands of years our Indigenous people kept this land in pristine condition. The year was 1867. Canada became a country. And when Canada became a country, there was something called the Indian problem. Of course, that was free roaming Indigenous people. That was the Indian problem. And so of course, the Indian Act was put in place to contain and dissolve the Indian problem. And so that was basically to ensure Indigenous people were on reserves, where they could be colonized, where they could be contained. So the glorious free for all in resource extraction could take place. And it did.

For 150 years this country this country has had the most incredible run with resource extraction, let me tell you. And there has been a consequence of this blasphemy; I learned that on 300, the lands and waters have been polluted catastrophically. All over the earth this is taking place to Indigenous people. All over the earth we are

82

BIBOONIIWININII: MIIGAAZOO-DIBAAJIMOWIN – WINTER SPIRIT: FIGHT STORY

seeing something called micro plastics; climate change; decrease in trees; half of the worlds trees have been cut down; the polar ice caps are melting; polar bears are turning into brown bears. We are in a great, great, time of change.

The two legged are on a quest to destroy the earth. There is no question. We are in that time now. So how do we figure out what's the right path to move forward? What do we do? Because everything seems so big. Like, how do you stop polar ice caps from melting? It seems huge.

The Great Lakes have been polluted. I come from there. They don't have the technology to take the cancer-causing agents out of my tap water. How is it even possible to pollute Great Lakes? But it's happening. I believe a thousand years from now, they are going to look back in history when the two-legged tried to destroy everything. And they are going to tell this story. And what's really incredible about this story, this Aadisookaan, is we are the characters in it; and everything that we do from this very second on is going to be the next part of the story.

And so, I ask myself, 'how do we move forward'? – What do we have to learn? And the very first thing that comes to my mind is we have to go back to the ancient teachings that sustained these lands for thousands and thousands of years. We must go back to the sacred stories of our people. Because that's where we are going to learn the code, the map, the thing. Where is that going to be found? In a university class, possibly? Is it going to be found in the bush? Sure. Could be found with grandma and grandpa, could be found with a little kid. Just rambling on how they do, they say amazing things.

I think in this story, in this time, because we are dealing with something serious, we can't confine where we get our knowledge from. We can't put rules and regulations on it. There shouldn't be a right or a wrong. I think that discussion should happen after we save the planet. I think right now we are at a point in history where we really, really, need change. And so, I think, what do we do? And so, I am going to tell you a story. A little story of when the two-legged tried to destroy the earth. And maybe from this story, there might be something there to help us to decide what to do now.

I have a four-year-old daughter. In the last 40 years, half of the world tress have been cut down. The climate has risen two per cent. In forty years if it sustains that rate that means the climate will be at four per cent, and, there are going to be hardly any trees left. That's basically something we all don't want. Chances are in 40 years I am going to still be kicking around. I'll be like this old elder, but its coming quick. It just seems like yesterday I was four years old. I don't think we can wait to fool around anymore. The scientific community has said this, 'That our voices are not strong enough. And that the only hope this world has, lies in the Indigenous resistance.' That's what there are saying. I sat there with David Suzuki and that's what he told me. 'The only hope we have is with the indigenous resistance.' So, he supports it, the scientific community supports the resistance. The resistance is always fuelled with art, songs, and stories. So here is a revolutionary story I heard a long time ago:

ISAAC MURDOCH AND JASON BONE

The two legged were on a quest to destroy the earth. They were greedy with everything that they had. They wanted to take more fat than was needed out of the moose. They wanted to make that zaasiganag, and they wanted to waste it. They took more berries, they took more fish, they took lots of everything and they just let it go to waste. This is what happened long ago.

And when this happened, it started to create a fear amongst the animals. They didn't even want to be around the Anishinabek because of the way they were acting; but there was an old man in the sky, Biboon-Inini, who would watch the earth from way up in the stars, in the north and see what the Anishinaabe were doing. They were trying to ruin everything. So of course, the old man had a plan. His plan was to blow his sacred breath down on the earth and freeze it, and kill the people so that they wouldn't spread their greediness all over everything. So that's what the old man started to do. He started to blow his breath on the earth from the stars, this very powerful spirit.

But there is a power here on earth that was just as strong as that old man's breath, and maybe even stronger, and that was the birds. When the birds sang their sacred songs, they cast their medicine all over the earth, even the hard to reach places those songs went to. And it pushed that old mans breath back into his mouth. So, the old man was kind of grumpy and mad, he thought these birds are ruining everything. Their songs are to powerful. I am going to go down there and get all those birds, and put them in a bag, and store them in my wigwam. Then I am going to blow my breath, those birds won't be able to do nothing. Then I will freeze the earth and kill those greedy two legged.

So that's what the old man did, went down to earth, Shkaagamik Kwe, grabbed all those birds, put them in a great big bag and stored them in his wigwam in the stars and then he blew his breath. And when he blew his breath, everything started to freeze, the wind and snow was a lot like it is here in Winnipeg, gusting in all different directions, from upwards and downwards. Of course, everything started to freeze. Everything started to perish. Only the strong were surviving. And so, the old man just kept on blowing.

The Anishinabek, they were already being greedy with everything, at the very moment in time, when all they had to do was share what they had. They went the other way. They became greedier, because times were tougher, they were supposed to share during the tough times, but they decided not too. So, the old man said, 'I'm going to kill all of them.'

But it was the animals. It was a cold winters night, blowing like mad, and those animals, they got together, they made a small fire. And they sat around this fire and they had a sacred council meeting to discuss how are they going to save this earth, from this old mans cold, and very powerful breath, and they talked about it. And they all went around talking about what they could do to help. And it was agreed, at that very meeting, on that cold night that four of them would go on a warrior's quest to save the earth. The four that agreed to go was Gaag the porcupine. Gaag is a very unlikely hero because Gaag, can't even jump over this, like, it has no, you know, its an unlikely hero. But it said, I have a strong back, look at my quills. They're sacred. The next animal that decided to go was Nigig the Otter. Very fast, a strong warrior defends its family with integrity and courage. The next animal was Bizhiw the lynx. Strong back legs, a good jumper, smart. Can think 155 moves ahead, no problem. And the last animal was Ojiig the fisher. Which is, if you don't know what a fisher is, is like a small wolverine, its like a smaller version. Bushy tail, eats squirrels, can climb. Can cruise on the ground fast; jump from tree to tree. Those were the four animals that wanted to go on this mission.

What they decided to do, there plan was to climb this mountain and once they are on there, jump up into the stars, zig zag across to where that old man was, get those birds and bring them back down to earth so they could sing their songs. And maybe kill that old man. At least that was their plan. Or at least have a good talk with him.

You know what they did, because porcupine is not a jumper, they grabbed porcupine by the arms and legs and when they climbed up that mountain, they threw porcupine up. But when he was spiralling up into the stars it hit something. It hit a power that covers the earth, the Anishinaabe call that Giizhigdong, a very invisible power that circles it. And of course, porcupine came down, crashing onto that mountain. And when he landed, he landed on his hands and feet, and it busted them. That's why they wobble around, and their feet and hands are all puffy and you'll see them walking, look at their feet, its like their busted. It to remind us of what happened, so long ago, when the two-legged tried to ruin everything by being greedy.

The next animal to try to make this jump now, through this incredible thing that we call Giizhigdong, was Nigig the otter. Nigig jumped, whoosh, and when it was going towards Giizhigdong, it tightened its head up, and bam, it came down too. And when it hit that mountain, it slid on its stomach all the way down. That's why they slide around today. It's to remind us of what happened not so long ago when we started to waste our fat, and our berries. Of course, the third animal, Bizhiw the lynx, stood there and took that jump. Bam, and when Bizhiw came crashing down on that mountain, it busted its tail off. And it squished its face when it hit Giizhigdong, that's why it looks like that. It's to remind us of what happened, when the two legged, when they refused to give what they had away.

The only that was left was Ojiig the fisher, the smallest of the animals. But Ojiig was raised right. Ojiig knew from the fasting, and from the songs, that were learned from the grandma's and grandma's, that if it was going to do something, and ask for something, it had to give something. And so Ojiig didn't have nothing so fisher dug in the ice and the snow and found six bearberries. Bearberries are those little red berries. They will keep. That's why they are called bearberries, because they hibernate in that snow. Ojiig found six of them. And Ojiig grabbed those six bearberries, and held them up to the sky, and said, I offer these to the great spirit of everything so that I can go on this warrior mission, and Ojiig casted those berries to the earth.

And when Ojiig looked up, that's when everything changed, because there was a crack in Giizhigdong. The other animals made a crack but didn't know it. So, Ojiig knew that it could bust through. And Ojiig jumped and was able to bust through Giizhigdong, one good solid jump. And when it got on top and started to look across the sky to the stars and seen that old man's wigwam.

But he saw something standing in front of it. There was a great big Ojijaak, a crane, sitting there guarding it. Ojiig the fisher knew that Ojijaak the crane has a big mouth. You should hear them when they scream. They're loud, scary, when they scream. All he had to do was scream once and that old man would know something was after those birds. So, Ojiig had an idea. He thought well I can't go there now, I got to try figure out what am I going to do about this bird, and he had a plan; to crawl back down to earth, to go through Pagano Giizhig, that hole in the sky, to go back down to the earth and gather a bunch of Gaaga'aanduk begew – spruce gum; and then sneak back up through that hole; through Pagano Giizhig; and across the sky; and to sneak behind crane; and when crane turns around and opens his big mouth; he would shove that Gaaga'aanduk begew – spruce gum right in there. Big job. Actually, a really huge job.

But that's what Ojiig did. Went down and got some spruce gum. Crawled up through that hole; went across the stars; snuck behind that Ojijaak the crane and when Ojijaak turned around and opened its big mouth; he shoved that Gaaga'aanduk begew – spruce gum right in its mouth. Well of course, as that spruce gum was going down, Ojijaak was able to make a little noise, 'whooo,' Just enough for the old man for the old man to know something was wrong. Just enough for the old man to reach over for his bow and arrows. But Ojiig is quick, fast. Ojiig, the name suggests it's like this going on the ground, that's what Ojiig means.

So, Ojiig the fisher ran into that wigwam and grabbed that bag of birds and ran outside really quick, and started running for that hole. Of course, that old man was running behind with his bow and arrow, "You bring those birds back!"

Ojiig the fisher started to pour those birds down that hole. Well of course the birds started to flutter all over the earth, they started to sing their sacred

BIBOONIIWININII: MIIGAAZOO-DIBAAJIMOWIN – WINTER SPIRIT: FIGHT STORY

songs, medicine was going everywhere it knew where to go. And it started to heal the earth from the old man's breath. But things weren't too good for fisher. Because as fisher was pouring those birds down, that's when he heard it, it was a snapping of a bowstring.

That old man had him lined up as he was pouring those birds down and shot an arrow at him. And of course, that old man is a very powerful spirit, Biboon-Inini, his arrow's can go to the end of the earth no problem. They always hit their mark. That's when Ojiig the fisher got it, got struck by the old mans arrow, right in its tail. But those arrows are very powerful. And it killed odjick the fisher, right there. And fisher went upside down on its back and it lay there. Of course, at this point, the birds are singing their songs all over the earth. But they have a lot of work to do, because everything is frozen. So, the Old Man in the sky knows, that all he has to do is go down collect all those birds one more time, and keep blowing his breath because there is going to be no more hero's. And for sure he would be able to kill all the Anishinabek.

So that's what he was readying to do, to leave his wigwam to go do this. When six lights entered through the top of his wigwam, and they lowered themselves, and as they were lowering themselves, they turned into Anishinaabe form, those six lights. And each one of them had a red berry in their hand. And they told the old man, 'We seen everything. We seen the greedy people. We seen the birds, the animals. We seen everything freeze. And we also seen how you are going to go down there and finish them off, but what you are doing isn't right.'

They said it wasn't fair to take the birds hostage and kill all the animals. But they said it was fair to freeze the humans. But because they were still good humans left, that they had to interject, they had to go in there and stop they said. They said it wasn't right to freeze good people, and so they told the old man,

'We made a decision, for half the year, you can blow your sacred breath on the earth, to remind the two legged they have to be generous with what they have. They have to give what they have away.'

So, he can freeze them with his sacred breath; and for the other half of the year, we will let the sacred birds sing their songs. So that life could flourish, so that their medicines could be cast over everything and that life can flourish.

And they said for Ojiig the fisher, for doing that they are going to turn Ojiig into stars. And of course, they turned Ojiig into what we know as the big dipper. Ojiiginaan is what I heard it being called. And in the springtime, you will see Ojiig on its arms and legs, travelling across the sky. Of course, water gushes to the earth and everything casts its sacred voice and life flourishes. And in the fall time, Ojiig is on its back. It's dead. It got shot by that arrow. And blood drips from its tail down to the earth. And it paints all of the trees red when the old man blows his breath when winter comes. Then in the springtime, it's back in its four legs.

When I think about that. The very first thing I think about is my mother, when I was a baby my mother's water broke. Water came gushing to the earth – I came out and sounded my sacred voice to the world. Of course, there was growth. There was life. 2017 – the humans have polluted almost everything on the planet. We are in a sacred story. They will tell this story. We are the characters in this story. This is spiritual. So, what are we going to do? Do we make up frameworks? Policy? What do we do? What's the answer? Because right now as we speak. We are the story.

I had two groups of people. Adults, they were actual teachers, and I had little kids, six-year old's. And I had to work with these two groups. I didn't know what to do. So, what I did was I told the adults, I said, you're going to sit over here and you're going to make a chief and council, and your going to discuss how to bring clean water to baby birds, because they don't have a clean water plant. And I grabbed the kids, I told them the same thing. You have to figure out how to bring clean water to baby birds. Go!

Well the adults. Oh my goodness. Like, I wanted a Chief and council meeting and you should have seen the flip charts, like they were just going hard. Veins were just popping out of their foreheads. Policy discussion and analyst, they had all these frameworks, it got political. It got heated. Finally, this leader emerged, but he was the worst one, he was mad. Flip chart, after flip chart. Ok. Great. When I looked at the little children they were all singing songs in a circle, so I thought that was kind of neat.

So, the moment came when we had to figure out how are we going to do this, how they were going to get water to birds. So, ask the adults if they could explain. Sure enough, the leader, flip chart after flip chart, ratifications. Old parties. New parties. You name it. Government this. Government that. And they had somehow completely taken apart the system, and recreated it with the very system that they were taking apart. But, that's what they are going to do. They had doctorates, Masters degrees, they were some of the smartest people that we have in this country. And that's what they decided to do.

So, then I asked the little children. How are we going to get clean water to baby birds? And they said, easy. And in the centre of their circle, they had a clay pot. And in the clay pot was clean fresh drinking water. And what they said was they are going to go out into the forest into the back and give them water.

And so of course, they stood up, and we started to follow them, and these little kids were carrying this water, this clean drinking water, through the hallway, singing their songs, out the back door, through the playground, into the ravine, in the back. And they laid that bowl of water at that tree, and we are sitting there. I was completely blown away. This is the part that gets me every time. Then the group was disrupted. There was commotion on the left side. A group of mallards with baby birds had interrupted the group. So we took off. I said let's go. So, we started to go walk away.

BIBOONIIWININII: MIIGAAZOO-DIBAAJIMOWIN – WINTER SPIRIT: FIGHT STORY

Go back up that trail. And I kid you not, when we turned around, those birds were drinking out of that bowl. Those six-year-old children, in twenty minutes how to bring clean water to baby birds, and not only did they figure out how to do it. But they actually did it.

The superior genius adults were blown away. It was one of the most spectacular things that I seen in my life. And so, when I think about what to do, the adults made their decisions based on this, their big powerful brains; and the children, they made their decision from their heart, they knew what to do.

Right now, I am here to tell you, that every act of rising up for these lands is going to make a difference. Use your heart as a guide. Its not impossible it just seems that way. Because if it wasn't for the strong back of porcupine. If it wasn't for the strong-willed ways of otter, and the strong everything of bizhoo, lynx fisher wouldn't have made it through. So, take that jump; do it, because you are going to make a difference. Research your heart, that's my message, thank you. Miigwetch. I wish I could tell you part two of the story, but maybe next year.[9]

NOTES

[1] Ojibway Storyteller and Activist.
[2] Graduate Student in Native Studies.
[3] Walter Benjamin, The Storyteller, p. 369.
[4] Ibid., p. 362.
[5] Ibid., p. 367.
[6] Ibid., pp. 362, 363.
[7] Ibid., p. 366.
[8] Ibid.
[9] Isaac Murdoch was the keynote speaker at the University of Manitoba's Native Studies Department second annual international graduate studies conference, "Rising Up: A Graduate Students Conference on Indigenous Knowledge and Research in Indigenous Studies." "Rising Up" attracts scholars in all forms of Indigenous research with approximately 60 representatives from around the world to showcase their work. Also, the Ojibway spelling for this story followed the double system established by Pat Ningewance's *Talking Gookoms Language: Learning Ojibwe* (2004).

REFERENCES

Benjamin, W. (2006). The storyteller. In D. J. Hale (Ed.), *The novel: An anthology of criticism and theory 1900–2000.* Malden, MA: Blackwell Publishing.
Ningewance, P. (2004). *Talking Gookom's language: Learning Ojibwe.* Lac Seul: Mazinaate Press.

Isaac Murdoch
Onaman Collective
Cutler, Ontario

Jason Bone
Department of Native Studies
University of Manitoba
Winnipeg, Manitoba

MICHELLE LIETZ

10. IN DEFENSE OF THE ORAL TRADITION

The Embodiment of Indigenous Literature and the Storytelling Styles of Dovie Thomason and Louis Bird

Those of us who study texts, or literature more specifically, have all had a moment where we recognize that the fiction is mirroring the reality. We understand that our realities help shape the worlds we create but what we do not often discuss is the way our fictions shape our reality and the influence our stories have on who we are as individuals. All that we read has the power to shape us in some way if the experience permits such intimacy, and the texts that speak to us become embodied within us.

For Indigenous writers and storytellers, this is natural and automatic, as stories carry not only teachings, but histories, culture, and traditions as well. Some of us see the whole world as an accumulation of stories, and the historical, political, and literary are always also personal. To demonstrate this entwined nature of stories and storytelling, I will explore the storytelling practices and styles of Dovie Thomason[1] and Louis Bird,[2] beginning with Thomason. Lakota/Kiowa Apache storyteller Dovie Thomason is, herself, a remarkable illustration of the embodiment of indigenous literature. She flawlessly blends Indigenous history with traditional stories and personal narrative to create a literary experience that is simultaneously unique and familiar.

While performing "How the West Was Spun" in Winnipeg, Manitoba on November 28th, 2016 Dovie sits in front of a relatively small gathering in a traditional buckskin dress with elk teeth sewn in and her hair is in leather-wrapped braids. She begins by telling the audience that Buffalo Bill never called his Wild West a show. "He called it his 'Wild West: A History Lesson,'" she says, "And so I created my Wild West, A History Lesson" (2:27–40). Dovie's history lesson is transfixing: she reshapes the popular narrative and reveals aspects of the men behind history's icons the world does not often see. She connects moments in time across different decades and centuries to reveal the patterns of colonization and the burdens of the past that Indigenous people continue to carry. Not far into her history lesson, when describing the international debut of the original "Wild West history lesson," Dovie tells the audience that among these animals and Indians (Black Elk among them) Cody took Soldiers with him for his Wild West show in England. These soldiers were the newly re-established seventh cavalry, re-established because Crazy Horse and his many warriors defeated the old seventh cavalry when Custer was leading the cavalry in the Battle of the Greasy Grass. Dovie says, "survivors," corrects herself and says "not, there were none –" and she laughs. In her short moment of laughter, Dovie illustrates

© KONINKLIJKE BRILL NV, LEIDEN, 2018 | DOI 9789004367418_010

MICHELLE LIETZ

the memory alive within her, as well as the memory of most of her audience, who chuckles with her. Her laughter in this moment demonstrates the ability to connect in a shared moment of celebration across time of a day when the Indians claimed victory over the invaders of their land; it's the same memory we recall at the mention of Crazy Horse, or the utterance of "Hokahe." Dovie says instead:

> Members of the newly resurrected seventh cavalry. The seventh cavalry, you can't get rid of them. They just keep getting wiped out and they keep coming back. Right now, the seventh cavalry is serving in Afghanistan, they call themselves the Crazy Horse Company. You can't beat history when it comes to fiction, folks…you know? It's just impossible to believe. It was only fifteen years since the Little Bighorn, or the Greasy Grass, whichever you prefer to call it. (22:22–23:07)

She's right, of course, that history is stranger than fiction. By including this ghastly example of misusing the name of a man turned legend, Dovie reminds her audience that these myths and legends continue to have profound impact on people in the present. The seventh cavalry has taken the name of an Indigenous hero and repurposed it to promote *their* survival and the erasure of contemporary Indigenous identity. Such use of his name by the current seventh cavalry implies that Crazy Horse was the last true fighter of the Indigenous people and, in the end, they went the way of the buffalo – an American myth that allows human rights abuses to be continuously ignored when perpetrated against Indigenous people. And, of course, Dovie talks about the buffalo, too. She mentions, when discussing Cody's collection of animals and Indians, that at a time when there were roughly two hundred buffalo left, Cody bought ten of them to bring with him to England. Indigenous people have long been associated with buffalo in the American narrative. It is an animal sacred to many Indigenous people but, for the purposes of the American narrative, it was always important to connect the "disappearance" of the buffalo with the "disappearance" of Indigenous people. To hear people speak of buffalo today, they often say things like, "well, they're bison though. Real buffalo are extinct." They say the same thing about Indigenous people. Questions of blood quantum and degree of "Indian-ness" are constantly used in attempts to justify colonization; if Indigenous people are simply a relic of the past, there is no need to address the contemporary effects of colonization on Indigenous people, today. It's as true now as it was when Black Elk travelled to England with Buffalo Bill.

Dovie retells Black Elk's descriptions of crossing the ocean and seeing such things for the first time. She speaks of Black Elk's voyage across that sea and says, "'if I die here, my spirit will never find its way home' – it's the only thing he said that kept him alive" (24:04–14). Dovie tells the audience that when their ship finally landed, they landed in Grave's End. She briefly mentions how ominous this place must have been, this English town where Pocahontas is buried:

> It wasn't the first time Indians had been brought to meet the queen. Something that had been done since the days of another person. The curse of the C's

92

I call it. Columbus. There's quite a curse around the C. Columbus and Cody and Conquistadors and Cavalry. And they were taken, as Pocahontas had been taken, to meet a queen. They were taken, as Pocahontas was taken to the Globe theatre to see some Shakespeare because it's a civilizing thing to see Shakespeare, everyone should have it happen to them, you know, you should go see Shakespeare, and Shakespeare at the Globe theatre when Pocahontas was there at the Globe theatre when the Wild West was there, the show they were performing was *The Tempest.* (24:19–25:28)

Dovie goes on to explain *The Tempest* as a play about revenge, magic, and great forces of nature. A violent stormy sea sets the revenge plot into action, and keeping in mind Dovie's theory about the curse of the C, I think once again of Caliban. Caliban, of course, is the primitive original inhabitant of the island of which Prospero has taken control. Dovie tells her audience that Shakespeare wrote this play just after the Americas were discovered. It's difficult not to get distracted here, as an academic who has been forced through the traditions of the literary canon to study Shakespeare many times. Immediately my mind starts filling in blanks. I remember that *The Tempest* is first performed in 1611, just four short years after Jamestown was founded. Dovie says this is the play Pocahontas saw when she was taken to the Globe, and I wonder what Pocahontas thought when she heard Caliban utter the words, "you taught me language, and my profit on't / Is I know how to curse. The red plague rid you / For learning me your language!" (I.II. 366–368). While the lens of history has made Caliban into an embodiment of the exploitation of colonized peoples through European imperialism, I always found this statement from him to be full of brave, stubborn resistance. I found myself and my history in these words from Caliban in the only Shakespeare play I ever felt compelled to discuss in truly passionate debate. I wonder if Black Elk and his fellow Indigenous travellers saw Caliban as like them, exploited for the sake of the colonial narrative.

And while these lessons are not to be discounted, as they are remarkable in their depth, the most moving parts of this narrative are not, in fact, the reshaping of historical narratives to reveal truths behind myths. Rather, the most powerful parts of Dovie's history lesson are the personal elements embedded within the story. Dovie purposes the possibilities of individuals not often considered, and at the same time makes herself inextricable from the history behind the myth. Such action reveals in stunning clarity the liveness of history and its constant impact on people both then and now. She wonders aloud at how Buffalo Bill's show took the enemies of a nation and transformed them into America's favourite entertainment by re-enacting battles when the Indian Wars were declared over. Once America decided that Indigenous people were extinct in their nation, people didn't hesitate to pay to see the novelty of Indians.

A while later, Dovie talks about the rarely acknowledged moment in history of when Cody and Custer first met. Dovie tells her audience that Custer had accepted an assignment from Sheridan that was essentially babysitting the Grand Duke Alexis of Russia, at a time in his career when Custer was in and out of military exploits.

MICHELLE LIETZ

"Grand Duke Alexis heard that America was running out of buffalo – and he couldn't let that happen without killing one" says Dovie (37:30–41). Custer was assigned to protect the Grand Duke Alexei while he made his way through the west in his luxury train-car full of champagne, searching for buffalo to shoot (or have someone shoot for him) from the window of the train. "But when he got there," Dovie says, "there was already somebody there, Buffalo Bill Cody was there in his buckskins, Buffalo Bill Cody, the man who had already killed five thousand buffalo" (38:50–57). Custer, of course, wanted the glory of assisting in the Duke's buffalo hunt all to himself, as did Cody, which naturally would lead to some kind of tense interaction. That is, Dovie notes, until they noticed "they both wore red sashes" (39:18–23).

"I'm imagining the conversation," Dovie says. "They found that they both shared a deep abiding passion for 'Wild Bill' Hickok" (39:30–42). Dovie goes on to describe Custer's obsession of wearing black velvet with gold braid and "d'Artagnan boots" and Cody's obsession with buckskin, beadwork and fringe, both with red sashes. "They had some sort of bromance," Dovie interjects with this thought, temporarily grounding her audience into the present once again with modern slang and reinforcing the understanding that although she's talking about back then, she's also talking about now. Dovie laughs while she says, "I have this fantasy that they traded sashes before they went their ways" (39:45–40:40:56). The genocide of the buffalo Custer and Cody were there to participate in is almost obscured by this fantasy and strange history, if not for the heavy pauses Dovie uses when explaining that, although this is why Cody was committed to keeping Custer in the show, Custer still had to go have his own adventures, of course referring to killing more buffalo and more Indians. It is Custer's defeat at the Battle of the Greasy Grass that Cody later recreates for thousands to see. It is a defeat that Cody frames as a horrific massacre of an American hero, and the creation of this history has far outlived both Cody and Custer. She doesn't need to mention the curse of the C's again for me to understand these men as curses, perpetuating the erasure of Indigenous people through genocide and propaganda. Dovie says of Custer, "maybe he learned something from Cody about PR," and reminds the audience that "Myths could be manufactured," describing the self-made celebrity status that both Cody and Custer created for themselves.

"Now Custer had been building his own myth," Dovie says, "he was the boy general and he also was the journalist who reported back on his own activities in the field. He wrote the reports of himself and sent them back over the wires. Now who would manipulate the media in such a way, it's hard to imagine now isn't it?" (35:41–36:24). Dovie laughs at her suggestive question, and the audience laughs with her, knowing without needing her to say that she's alluding to the Twitter-addicted current President of the United States. Once again, Dovie quietly pulls the audience through history and into the present moment. In this way, Dovie reminds her audience that we have seen this myth-making before. I imagine there's an exasperated sigh hanging over this story, perhaps the kind of sigh that accompanies the unspoken wish that society would have learned by now to recognize these people through the obfuscating narratives they create. Custer's myth-making, of course led to an excuse to fight for the land

IN DEFENSE OF THE ORAL TRADITION

of the Plains tribes. Certainly, his descriptions of Lakota territory suggest the same kind of belief in a divine right to the West that made the idea of Manifest Destiny so popular. This manufactured divine right to Indian land shaped the demonizing of Indigenous people, allowing genocide and oppression to continue. Very recently, I watched livestreaming video of hundreds of Indigenous people during a non-violent action to promote the protection of water. They were being sprayed with fire hoses in sub-freezing temperatures by police clad in riot gear. In the aftermath, as the police officers spun their narratives of dangerous, violent Indians attacking innocent police officers in riot gear, I witnessed far too many people buy into the familiar story and dismiss what their own eyes were telling them. They make claims of Indigenous people once again being a hindrance to "civilized" progress.

Dovie tells this story as a history lesson, filling in pieces of often overlooked moments, people and purposeful acts. She, like many other Indigenous writers and storytellers, understands that history is inextricably entwined with the embodiment of stories. History itself is a narrative, a story, and who tells the story has everything to do with how we understand the world. For all of his myth making, we can still tell stories about Custer clad in black velvet, scenting his hair with cinnamon oil, because our memories are long when we tell stories. And we can tell new stories to explain the realities of the world those before us could not have foreseen.

To recognize, honour, and participate in the stories and histories we embody is perhaps the best means of stripping down these myths, as Dovie displays at the end of her story "How the West was Spun" when, thinking out loud about her next show and the next plane ride, she stands, strips off her buckskin, and discards the myth of the ideal, traditional Indian storyteller of a bygone era. Her story is personal again, another jarring reminder of where and when we are, listening to her history lesson. This last action reminds the audience that beneath their preconceived notions of what an Indian is supposed to be there exists a real person, with a smartphone in her pocket and a long memory, full of stories that make us and shape us. Dovie said it best: stories are survivance. Stories are our survival, our continued existence, our resistance and the histories of where we've been.

For Omushkego Cree storyteller Louis Bird from the Winisk First Nation, it is not so much any combination of story, words, or phrases that gives Louis Bird the sense of living and embodied story. Rather, it comes along gradually while listening to him talk. My first exposure to Louis Bird's storytelling was in Dr. Warren Cariou's "Oral Traditions and Indigenous Performance" class at the University of Manitoba in the Fall of 2016. The following February, Dr. Cariou brought Louis Bird to the University of Manitoba to perform his stories. From February 13th–16th, Louis Bird performed his stories in Winnipeg both at the University of Manitoba as well as the Millennium Library. During this visit, I had the opportunity to both see him perform publicly as well as sit and visit with him over coffee and tea. From these interactions, I realized that it doesn't matter what setting he's in – whether it's a performance in front of dozens of people, or a couple of people having tea – Louis Bird cannot help but tell stories. It's automatic for him, like breathing – powerful stories flow

95

MICHELLE LIETZ

effortlessly out of him as he talks, given life through his gestures and the way he changes his cadence of speaking when conveying dialogue.

Often, these characters in his stories blend so well with the telling that it seems almost like channelling – as if these characters are speaking through Louis, instead of his speaking for or about them. But mostly, it is his humour that provides the listener a sense that these stories are living within Louis – his entire face lights up, and he will laugh before ever revealing to his listeners what the joke actually is. It's as if he's listening to the stories speaking within him, laughing as they reveal themselves to him even before he can share them with the rest of us. And, like Dovie, Louis's stories contain a unique blend of specificity of people, places, customs, and time that are nearly impossible to replicate in text and are, therefore, rarely found outside of the oral tradition. To keep these stories is to be entrusted with the lifeblood of a people and a culture, and to participate in their telling is to become a part of their history. Louis uniquely demonstrated this phenomenon when, sitting down to some fried pickerel, he told a story about when he first told Dr. Warren Cariou the story of the "wild woman," inspired by the voice emanating from Dr. Cariou's GPS directions while they were driving one day. Louis invited a table of students into this story both by sharing the story of the "wild woman" with us, and by sharing a new story about modern technology and the still-relevant lessons of old stories. By listening to storytellers, and by telling stories, we share in a rich tradition of transmission through relationship – the human element necessary to engage in oral traditions is perhaps the most important aspect, as it reinforces the fact that living memory is necessary to truly understand the rippling effects of history, and it reminds us that stories too, require a relationship of reciprocity; that, in order to remember who we are and how we came to be, we must listen.

NOTES

[1] Permission to use specific examples from Dovie Thomason's performance was given by Dovie Thomason. More information about Dovie Thomason can be found on her website at https://doviethomason.com/

[2] Audio versions of Louis Bird's storytelling can be found at ourvoices.ca

REFERENCES

Shakespeare, W. (1997). The tempest. In S. Greenblatt, W. Cohen, J. E. Howard, K. E. Maus, & A. Gurr (Eds.), *The Norton Shakespeare*. New York, NY: W.W. Norton.

Thomason, D. (2016, November 28). *How the west was spun. An evening of storytelling with Dovie Thomason* [Audio recording]. Winnipeg: Ralph Connor House.

Michelle Lietz
Department of English, Film and Theatre
University of Manitoba
Winnipeg, Manitoba

PAUL M. R. MURPHY

11. AN ELABORATE EDUCATIONAL ENDEAVOUR

The Writing of Basil H. Johnston

It is disingenuous to say that the late Anishinaabe writer Basil Johnston suffers from a lack of recognition. By my own count, he has been referenced or cited mainly as a primary resource hundreds of times, but the questioned remains – why? Why is Johnston continually referenced and cited? Put another way, what explains Johnston's enduring appeal, his relevance? One answer centers on the idea of education in its broadest sense. With that in mind, it is possible to consider what Johnston does, to consider what he writes, as an elaborate educational endeavour.

Indeed, in the "Preface" to his first book *Ojibway Heritage: The ceremonies, rituals, songs, dances, prayers and legends of the Ojibway* published in 1976, Johnston writes that in order to understand Indigenous heritage and peoples, it is the "beliefs, insights, concepts, ideals, values, attitudes, and codes" of the Indigenous peoples themselves that "must be studied" (7). Johnston's concern is diverse, and he submits that there is "no better way of gaining that understanding than by examining native ceremonies, rituals, songs, dances, prayers, and stories." However, Johnston's educational exercise can be looked at differently, in a way more reflective of an Indigenous perspective.

The philosophy of holism comes to mind when trying to understand what holds Johnston's work together, what can help explain or define his tradition. For my purposes, I understand holism to mean "attention to the whole person in their total environment" (The Institute On Governance, "Summary of the Final Report of the Royal Commission on Aboriginal Peoples: Implications for Canada's Healthcare System" 5). In addition, Volume 3 of the *Royal Commission on Aboriginal Peoples* entitled "Gathering Strength" briefly expands on the concept of holism in relation to health and social services. The authors write that Indigenous peoples have "advised … that the health of body, mind, emotions, and spirit must be understood holistically" (3). They equate "supporting and enhancing whole health" with "a state of well-being in the individual and harmony with social and environmental systems that are themselves functioning in a balanced way."

The idea of the "whole person in their total environment" striving for "harmony" and "balance […]" very much resonates with Johnston's literary output. Without romanticising or an undue reliance on victimhood, Johnston presents from an Indigenous perspective a holistic way of looking at the world that allows us the opportunity to think about and understand our place in it, our personal responsibilities,

© KONINKLIJKE BRILL NV, LEIDEN, 2018 | DOI 9789004367418_011

PAUL M. R. MURPHY

and the conduct of others. I use a holistic approach to explain Johnston's enduring relevancy by demonstrating how he establishes with the writing of *Ojibway Heritage*, what I refer to as the Anishinaabeg school of literary expression. Through this tradition, Johnston reworks and re-presents his concerns over many years through his numerous writings and genres, thereby sharing his concerns with subsequent generations. Before exploring further the relationship between a holistic approach and Johnston's relevancy, some commentary on his audience, major concerns, and method is necessary, and an old Canadian political adage serves as a point of departure.

Although the principles and situations are different in terms of the adage's original use and my use here, the sentiments it expresses move us further toward understanding Johnston's method. In using the adage as a means of appreciating his method, two different, but related goals appear. On the one hand, Johnston does not want Indigenous peoples "pushed out" or relegated to the sidelines of society because of ignorance on the part of the non-Indigenous population. And on the other hand, he also does not want Indigenous peoples remaining or becoming "separate" or isolated from the mainstream because of their own intransigence. So if the adage is applicable, and I think it is, Johnston's audience is comprised of both Indigenous and non-Indigenous peoples. Supporting this assertion, in the "Preface" to *Ojibway Heritage* Johnston writes, "It is in the hope that the heritage of the Ojibway peoples and their Algonkian brothers and sisters will be a little better understood that this book was written" (7). He likens the "unwritten traditions" he explores as the sharing of a gift "with those whose culture and heritage may be very different but who wish to enlarge their understanding."

Johnston's concern about enlarging "understanding" between non-Indigenous and Indigenous peoples is an enduring feature of his work. In "Is There A Place On This Blanket? The Place of the Indian in the Multi-Cultural Fabric of Canada," from *Think Indian: languages are beyond price* published in 2010, he writes about a possible unity or "coming together" if non-Indigenous peoples were to allow "Indian values and modes" into their own cultures (232). As an example of the way in which Johnston reworks and re-presents his concerns across time, he writes, "Our understanding of certain common fundamental matters would be increased. We would discover, in our differences and similarities, merit and worth and begin to compose our mistrust and our enmities that divide our hearts and poison our minds." Here, understanding Johnston desires is not a one-sided exchange. Rather, it is more accurately described as a mutual exchange of understanding or simply mutual understanding. However, another story moves us even closer to appreciating the essential method of Johnston's literary output.

On one level, "They Don't Want No Indians" from his 1978 short story collection *Moose Meat and Wild Rice: Rollicking tales about life on a modern day Indian reserve* humorously recounts Sudbury Indian Centre employee Xavier McMac's repeated attempts to arrange for the burial of friend and former band member Dan Pine Cone. To put it mildly, we learn about issues of mistaken identity when Sergeant Goodenough of the Sudbury Police Service is unable to identify a body at the city morgue. In conversation with Xavier, Goodenough says, "Hard to tell whether he's

98

AN ELABORATE EDUCATIONAL ENDEAVOUR

Indian, Chinese, Japanese, or Korean, but he could be one of your people" (130). But as the story unfolds, a deeper, more critical examination occurs, one that draws our attention to issues of race, racism, ignorance, stereotype, government incompetence and irresponsibility, as well as Indigenous frustration, anger, and resilience; all of which are central concerns found throughout much of Johnston's writing.

The "unidentified body" does not remain so for long. The "corpse" is not a nameless "Indian" person nor is it an unknown Asian Canadian. Rather, as Xavier indicates, it is a person possessing an identity, family, community, and personal history, "Why, it's Dan Pine Cone ... from Moose Meat Point but now registered on the Ishpiming Reservation" ("They Don't Want No Indians" 131). We learn that Dan had a wife from whom he was separated, and because of financial hardship she is unable to arrange for his burial, and the task then falls to Xavier. The rest of the story follows Xavier's plight; he needs one-hundred dollars to have Dan's body released so that it can be buried. Indian Affairs won't help, and the Provincial Department of Health and Welfare is no better (133–134).

Although Xavier's response is one of frustration, it is completely justified and understandable, "Oh, Dammit! ... You guys are just like Indian Affairs, making all kinds of excuses, giving no help, hiding behind jurisdiction. You want Indians to integrate, then you don't want them to. Nobody wants them; nobody wants us" (134). Xavier eventually obtains the release of Dan's body by arranging a personal bank loan. But because he has not given much thought to what he is going to do upon arriving at his destination he does not have any place to deposit Dan before finalizing burial arrangements. He tries the local Ontario Provincial Police detachment where he is told, "We aren't set up to handle bodies" (137). He then approaches the priest's residence, but when he asks if he can "leave the body here for the night," the housekeeper replies, "No!" (138).

In many ways, "They Don't Want No Indians" is prototypical of Johnston's overall method because even when faced with seemingly overwhelming forces and misunderstandings, the Sudbury Police, the federal government, the provincial government, the OPP, and the Catholic church are all against Xavier, he is determined and perseveres with his task, eventually arriving at a place of mutual understanding, and more importantly, he arrives at a place of mutual understanding and respect with someone who would not normally be considered an ally. Xavier and his companions finally check in with the Anglican minister who initially expresses misgivings about putting Dan up because he is Catholic. But the minister's wife intervenes, and because of her prompting, he relents, "Very well. Bring the body in" (139). Once Xavier and the minister settle Dan in, Xavier feels the "burden lift" and stays for coffee with Oscar and his wife (139–140). As a sign of his resilience, Xavier tells his traveling companions, "You see? ... Just keep at a thing and by God you get it done one way or another" (140).

Johnston repeats a similar pattern in his autobiographical novel *Crazy Dave* (1999) that tells about the life of his Grandmother Rosa and her son, Johnston's uncle, David McLeod (311, 320). The pattern, and by that I mean the appearance or possibility of an Indigenous/non-indigenous relationship founded on mutual

99

PAUL M. R. MURPHY

understanding and respect in the light of seemingly insurmountable obstacles, also appears in a general way in the memoir *Indian School Days* (1988) where Johnston recounts his experiences while incarcerated at residential school in Spanish, Ontario during the 1930s and 40s (66).

That the three stories referenced above are all human-centric does not mean that "Man's World" represents the extent of Johnston's purview. As previously mentioned, Johnston's range is all-encompassing including not only the human world, but also the physical, plant, and animal worlds. He describes the relationships between the various "orders of creation" in the following way, "All four orders are so entwined that they make up life and one whole existence" (*Ojibway Heritage* 21). In a move that endorses a holistic approach to his work, Johnston writes, "With less than four orders, life and being are incomplete and unintelligible. No one portion is self-sufficient or complete, rather each derives its meaning from and fulfills its function and purpose within the context of the whole creation." What's more, Johnston's conception of creation is such that he appreciates the existence in the world of realities other than the physical; that is, he acknowledges the existence in the world of the corporeal and the incorporeal simultaneously.

Johnston's human-centric stories demonstrate the essential method of his literary output and his animal-centric stories perform a similar function. The "Man's Dependence on Animals" section from *Ojibway Heritage* contains such a story. We learn that the animals served the Anishinaabeg and continued to do so even after more and more was demanded of them. At this time the Anishinaabeg also "understood the utterances of the animals" and "the animals understood" the Anishinaabeg (50). But this was a negative understanding, different in type from the understanding explored earlier, "this mutual understanding ... enabled man to impose greater burdens upon his brothers." It was a "mutual understanding" lacking respect. The Anishinaabeg "commanded" the animals and the animals in turn "served" the Anishinaabeg. Eventually the animals held a "great meeting" and decided to make it "difficult" for the Anishinaabeg to "enslave" them again, "no longer will we speak the same language. Instead we shall speak in different languages. From now on we shall live to ourselves, for ourselves. Let men learn to fend for themselves without our help" (52). And thus, Man remained "dependent upon the animals for his food, clothing, and tools." He was also "dependent upon animals for knowledge of the world, life, and himself." But Johnston also tells about an animal/Anishinaabeg relationship that ultimately, more closely resembles the human-centric stories characterized by mutual understanding and respect explored earlier.

In this story, Johnston tells about a time when the deer, moose, and caribou "vanish" from the land of the Anishinaabeg (56). Following the disappearance, the Anishinaabeg go in search of the missing animals and owl discovers that the deer and others are apparently "imprisoned" by the crows. The Anishinaabe attempt to free the deer, moose, and caribou, but following a few inconclusive skirmishes, the Anishinaabeg seek a "truce" during which they ask the deer why they are so indifferent to the Anishinaabeg's "rescue" attempts? The deer chief responds, "You have assumed wrongly that we are here against our wishes. On the contrary, we choose

100

to remain here and are quite content. The crows have treated us better than you have ever treated us when we shared the same country with you." The Anishinaabe chief then asks, "How did we offend you?" (57). The deer chief accuses the Anishinaabeg of "despoil[ing]" deer haunts, "desecrate[ing]" deer bones, and "dishonour[ing]" the deer and themselves (57). When the Anishinaabe Chief asks what he can do to "make amends?" the deer chief responds, "Honour and respect our lives, our beings, in life and death. Do what you have not done before. Cease doing what offends our spirits." The Anishinaabe chief agrees and the crows release the deer, moose and caribou who then voluntarily follow the Anishinaabeg "back to their homeland."

I now turn to an individual component of the holistic approach and establish the ways in which the oral tradition helps Johnston advance his myriad concerns as he examines the "life of the Anishnabeg and their outlook" (*Ojibway Heritage* 57). In describing his choice of source material, Johnston writes, "I have turned more to the legends, myths, stories, ceremonies, songs, and languages of my people" ("Looking Back From Writing To Publication," *Think Indian: Languages are Beyond Price* 197). He explains why this is so by referencing and acknowledging his oral forebears and sources, "It is in the old legends, myths and stories that I have found my inspiration and direction" (198–199).

I next consider a familiar subject of Johnston's "diverse forms" with reference to the "Nebaunaubaewuk and Nebaunaubaequaewuk" or Mermen and Mermaids stories. Mermaid stories figure prominently in Johnston's oeuvre. He shares them in *Ojibway Heritage* (1976), *Tales of the Anishinaubaek* (1993) later retitled and published as *Mermaids and Medicine Women: Native Myths and Legends* in 1998, *The Bear-Walker and Other Stories* published in 1995, *The Manitous: The Spiritual World of the Ojibway* published in 1995, and *The Star-Man and Other Tales* published in 1997. They are all taken from "the ancient oral tradition and recorded by ... the world's leading native expert" Basil Johnston (*The Manitous* back cover). With the exception of the "Mer-Man: Nebaunaubae" from *The Bear-Walker and Other Stories*, which lists Johnston as both storyteller and translator, all of the stories are primarily indebted to "the eminent Ojibway narrator Sam Ozawamik, of the Wikwemikong First Nation, in Ontario" (*Mermaids and Medicine Women* front cover). Contrary to what some have said recently about the attribution or lack of attribution of oral story sources, Johnston acknowledges the sources of the oral stories he shares beginning with *Ojibway Heritage* where he writes, "For the stories I have recorded I am indebted to innumerable storytellers in Ontario" (8). He then lists numerous individuals, including family members and "acknowledges" their "understandings" and "guidance."

Many of these stories share a number of characteristics. For example, the setting of several presents young Anishinaabe protagonists either fishing or camping or both (*Ojibway Heritage* 169, *Mermaids and Medicine Women* 75, *The Manitous* 134, *The Bear-Walker* 22). The stories also involve the failure to heed a warning or respect protocol, "How many times have I warned you that this would happen" (*Ojibway Heritage* 170), "You really shouldn't eat that" (*The Bear-Walker* 22), "When I left to go fishing, I didn't offer tobacco as you told me to do, because I didn't believe in those

PAUL M. R. MURPHY

practices and ... I thought they were just superstitious fairy tales" (*The Manitous* 134). And often, a protagonist is ultimately trapped by a mermaid and transformed into a merman (*Ojibway Heritage* 169, *Mermaids and Medicine Women* 77, *The Manitous* 135). But what I find most interesting about the mermaid and merman stories is the idea of disappearance as a trope that Johnston repeats across time and the possible affect, if any, it has on those familiar with Johnston's and other similar stories. The disappearance trope helps explain Johnston's contemporary relevance.

Disappearances, vanishings, and missing individuals are ubiquitous in Johnston's writing. In the five mermaid stories referred to above, all but one share this feature. This is also true for the deer, moose, and caribou story referenced earlier. Without putting too fine a point on it, I believe that the disappearance stories serve a specific function. They desensitize the reader to the fear and sorrow normally associated with such experiences. That is not to say that those emotions are unacceptable responses to such occurrences. Rather, it suggests that in addition to those responses, others responses such as anticipating possible transformation, change, and rebirth are equally valid. Viewed another way, the ubiquity of the disappearance trope quite possibly makes the unpleasant less so. It makes it familiar so that when confronted with it, the reaction is not necessarily one of fear and sadness, but more along the lines of, perhaps, resigned acceptance. Although it is probably impossible to qualify or quantify how or why this is so, I think such a hypothesis remains valid in terms of responses to Johnston's literary disappearances and also in terms of responses to actual disappearances. Such an understanding also goes some distance in demonstrating Johnston's education in action.

He is an exemplar of endurance in that he does not waver in his commitment to sharing an Anishinaabe understanding of the world through his storytelling. Johnston remains relevant today because he reworks and re-presents his stories over time in a way that helps us make sense of contemporary society. Although appreciative of the past, he understands the need to revisit and revise where and if necessary. About his commitment and technique, Johnston writes, "It is for you and me to take the legacy conferred upon us by the past, give it new and fresh expression in the present, and if our talents permit, for the benefit of the future" (*Think Indian* 198). As an example of one possible new expression of a past story, at the end of the "Mermaid" story from *Mermaids and Medicine Women*, Johnston writes, "One time, the old man and woman were down at the shore. Their thoughts were about their son who had lost his life in that water. Just then he surfaced. They surfaced" and the old woman said to her husband, "Sam, look! ... Little mermen and mermaids" (79). Those surfacing included the son as a merman and his family. In other words, the son was not lost, he was now transformed as half-fish and half-human or a merman, with a mermaid wife, and many "mer-children." The tone here is much more positive when compared to the story's earlier iteration, the "Nebaunaube or Nebaunaubaequae" section in *Ojibway Heritage*. There, the merman Mizaun's meeting with his parents is bitter sweet. They lament that they will never see their son again and although Mizaun promises to visit, his parents remain "inconsolable," "No matter what he said, they refused with a shudder" (170). Unlike the more recent version, there is nothing promising about this encounter between the merman and his parents. The latter mermaid story reflects what I believe to be modern day realities, which, in this instance, include a non-traditional family configuration, a reality not uncommon to a great many people, Indigenous, or not.

This last area considers Johnston's non-fiction, another component of a holistic appreciation of his body of work, which I examine through the lens of social realism. As literary theorist Robert Warrior puts it, Indigenous non-fiction authors "speak more directly to the situations and conditions Native people face" (*The People and the Word: Reading Native Nonfiction* xx–xxi). He continues: "Native nonfiction authors have not only produced literary texts but have become a source for critical models for critics" (xxi). Once it has been elucidated, Johnson's vast body of non-fiction will be an invaluable resource for Indigenous scholars, especially its discourse on Indigenous languages, cultural practices, and storytelling.

More directly, social realism means a conscious appreciation of the realities in Indigenous communities. Johnston possesses such an understanding and this is one possible reason why his work has been critically neglected: some people don't want to hear what he has to say. As writer and theorist Craig Womack sees it, a social realist "cannot simply walk away from those things that are killing us in Native communities" (*American Indian Literary Nationalism* 170). He continues, we all "know the statistics," adding "thinking must save us, and this is where critics come in." He expands on this idea by writing "A major strategy" for such writers "is commenting on social policy and articulating community strategies for increased health, in one's art, while keeping it artful." Johnston shares these concerns and, besides the debilitating effects of spiritual and cultural thirst, he might very well say that lifestyle choices and destructive behaviours are major impediments to Indigenous fulfilment. For example, when ostensibly describing a dance and fight at his Grandmother Rosa's reserve some time in the past, he writes, "Deeper down was the age-old inborn trait of the Anishinaubae to beat the hell out of one another," a behaviour that, if we read between the lines, was not as uncommon as we might think nor as simple a matter as a jilted suitor getting even (*Crazy Dave* 162). He also speaks out about the scourge of child abuse, "Our people love to proclaim their affection for children. Most of them have this love. But children were beaten, whipped, struck, booted, yelled at, neglected, uncared for often enough that our story-tellers recounted it in their stories" (*The Gift of the Stars* 16, *Honour Earth Mother* 121–122). He reminds us that it is important to remember that personal conduct is "nurtured in the home" with "credit or blame assigned as deserved" (*Honour Earth Mother* 147).

With reference to a healthier lifestyle, he writes, "In former days tribes counselled their youth to 'Do something for your people,' and they had their means and methods of training and instruction to prepare their youth to fulfil tribal obligations" ("Do Something For Your People," *Think Indian: Languages are Beyond Price* 56). And although Johnston's realizes that it is not possible to serve in the "old way, you must, if you are to help your people, take courses and programs, risks and opportunities

103

PAUL M. R. MURPHY

that render you discerning in judgement, fit in body, and mindful of the well-being of your tribe" ("Do Something For Your People" 56). Johnston advocates for an intense program of education, what I earlier called an "elaborate educational endeavour." He wants all of us to increase our understanding of Indigenous peoples and cultures. Those equipped with such knowledge then have a duty to share what they have learned in a meaningful way. Nothing could make Johnston's writing more relevant. It is what he does and it is also a matter of fulfilling one's responsibility to self and community.

REFERENCES

Johnston, B. H. (1976). *Ojibway heritage: The ceremonies, rituals, songs, dances, prayers and legends of the Ojibway.* Toronto: McClelland & Stewart.

Johnston, B. H. (1978). *Moose meat and wild rice: Rollicking tales about life on a modern day Indian reserve.* Toronto: McClelland & Stewart.

Johnston, B. H. (1986). Do something for your people. In B. H. Johnston (Ed.), *Think Indian: Languages are beyond price* (pp. 55–62). Wiarton: Kegedonce.

Johnston, B. H. (1993). *Tales of the anishinaubaek.* Toronto: Royal Ontario Museum.

Johnston, B. H. (1995a). *The Bear-Walker and other stories.* Toronto: Royal Ontario Museum.

Johnston, B. H. (1995b). *The Manitous: The spiritual world of the Ojibway.* Toronto: Key Porter.

Johnston, B. H. (1997). *The star-man and other tales.* Toronto: Royal Ontario Museum.

Johnston, B. H. (1998). *Indian school days.* Toronto: Key Porter.

Johnston, B. H. (1998a). *Mermaids and medicine women: Native myths and legends.* Toronto: Royal Ontario Museum.

Johnston, B. H. (1998b). They don't want no Indians. In B. H. Johnston (Ed.), *Moose meat and wild rice: Rollicking tales about life on a modern day Indian reserve* (pp. 130–140). Toronto: McClelland & Stewart.

Johnston, B. H. (1999). *Crazy Dave.* Toronto: Key Porter.

Johnston, B. H. (2000). Looking back from writing to publication. In B. H. Johnston (Ed.), *Think Indian: Languages are beyond price* (pp. 190–198). Wiarton: Kegedonce.

Johnston, B. H. (2003). *Honour earth mother.* Wiarton: Kegedonce.

Johnston, B. H. (2010). *The gift of the stars.* Wiarton: Kegedonce.

Johnston, B. H. (2011a). Is there a place for me on this blanket? (The place of the Indian in the multicultural fabric of Canada). In B. H. Johnston (Ed.), *Think Indian: Languages are beyond price* (pp. 229–234). Wiarton: Kegedonce.

Johnston, B. H. (2011b). *Think Indian: Languages are beyond price.* Wiarton: Kegedonce.

Report of the Royal Commission on Aboriginal Peoples. (1996). *Volume 3: Gathering strength: 1. New directions in social policy: 3. Looking ahead* (p. 3). Retrieved from http://www.caid.ca/Vol_3_RepRoyCommAborig.html

The Institute on Governance. (1997, October 5). *Summary of the final report of the royal commission on aboriginal peoples: Implications for Canada's healthcare system.* Ottawa: The Institute on Governance. Retrieved from http://www.1997_October_healthrcap.pdf

Warrior, R. (2005). *The people and the word: Reading native nonfiction.* Minneapolis & London: University of Minnesota Press.

Weaver, J., Womack, C. S., & Warrior, R. (2005). *American Indian literary nationalism.* Albuquerque, NM: University New Mexico Press.

Paul M. R. Murphy
Department of Native Studies
University of Manitoba
Winnipeg, Manitoba

JUSUNG KIM

12. KOREAN INDIGENOUS EPISTEMOLOGIES WITH NOTES ON THE CORRESPONDING EPISTEMOLOGIES OF INDIGENOUS SCHOLARSHIP

INTRODUCTION

Our journey of comparing Korean Indigenous epistemologies alongside Indigenous ones begins with: defining and understanding the importance of epistemology; raising historical consciousness and awakening from the Euro-Western hegemony and paradigm; connecting Korean Indigenous epistemologies; and enacting a scissor, rock, paper game as an example of Korean ways of knowing. Let us go on our exploration together!

Defining and Understanding the Importance of Epistemologies

Epistemologies are understood as multiple and complex knowledge systems and ways of knowing. What counts as knowledges, how and where to gain them, who is involved, and why knowledges are needed for what purpose are the main concerns of epistemologies. No doubt, epistemology matters (An, 1996; Hart, 2010; Kovach, 2012; Wilson, 2008). Rarely do we live without embodying cultural knowledges. According to Linda Smith (2012), "discovering our indigenous knowledge…and making our knowledge systems work for indigenous development" (p. 161) are important projects. The reason is that epistemologies and their innate spirits have the potential to shape our feelings, thoughts, and actions from which our being, living, and becoming arise.

Epistemology reflects an *atma* (i.e., true character, genuine personality/ self, vitality) of its worldview – ways of living, knowing, and doing. That is, epistemologies represent spirits of people, communities, and nations across history, so that history and ancestors are considered living spirits (Kang, 2015) deeply melted in our knowledges, bodies, and daily practices. Our ancestors have passed their spirits on to live with us over time-space, and such spirits are imbued with sharing knowledges and cultural practices. These epistemologies, built up through a long history, guide our particular ways of cultural knowings (Chilisa, 2012; Meyer, 2008; Wilson, 2008). As long as we keep our epistemologies alive, we can survive, transmit our knowledges to the next generations, and thrive in any historical circumstances.

© KONINKLIJKE BRILL NV, LEIDEN, 2018 | DOI 9789004367418_012

JUSUNG KIM

Smith (2012) shows how Indigenous people survive and thrive by using imaginative spirit and creative thinking during colonization.

Imperialism and colonization reproduce colonial ideology and epistemology of the Euro-Western paradigm at the expense of Indigenous philosophies and epistemologies. The colonial project aims to colonize the mind, body, and spirit of Indigenous people. Education and educational institutions have been used as powerful weapons to construct the colonial ideology, knowledge, and practice by oppressing voices and epistemologies of the colonized (Cote, 2009). Likewise, Chilisa (2012) also argues that current academic scholarship is based on philosophy, history, and culture of the Euro-Western paradigm, and many nations in the world still follow Euro-Western models of social sciences that were constituted by empire (Pascale, 2011).

Colonial epistemology can be depicted as: being dichotomous (i.e., separation between object/subject, human/nature, and mind/body) linear, hierarchical concrete decontextualized, neutral ahistorical, and apolitical (Darder, 2015); problem-focused, argumentative, and competitive (Meyer, 2008); and individualistic and cognitive (Hart, 2010). This colonial epistemology being considered legitimate, civilized, and universal knowledge (Smith, 2012) excludes Indigenous ways of knowings through: cosmic, interpersonal, intrapersonal, and environmental relations (Wilson, 2008); folktales, proverbs, languages, myths, and clothes (Chilisa, 2012); stories/conversations, walking in nature, silence, fasting, ancestors, and community forums (Kovach, 2012); stories, metaphors, ceremony, pray, vision, dream, and insight (Hart, 2010; Wilson, 2008); breathing/meditation, pilgrimage, music/dance/song, poetry, play/game, and exercise/martial arts (An, 1996; Choi, 2012; Ha & Mangan, 1998; Lee, 2008; Tara, 2011). In effect, epistemologies align with particular philosophies of history and historical consciousness (Chilisa, 2012; Pascale, 2011; Smith, 2012; Wilson, 2008).

HISTORICAL CONSCIOUSNESS AND AWAKENING FROM EURO-WESTERN HEGEMONY AND PARADIGM

Many Indigenous researchers from around the globe have expressed the importance of raising historical consciousness and awakening from the Euro-Western paradigm to decolonize from a Western academic dominance. Park and Jeong (2014) note that trusting systems, having confidence of Korean thoughts, and removing fear of foreign thoughts should be a starting step for decolonization. Similarly, Linda Smith (2012) focuses on critical consciousness, awakening from a Western hegemony and culture, and liberating the captive mind from the oppressive conditions that exclude the voices of the colonized. Kovach (2012) also emphasizes the importance of decolonizing one's mind and heart along with uncovering whiteness, social structure, and power relations.

To counter a global colonization in scholarship, Indigenous people have brought with them historical consciousness of how they unearth their ancient Indigenous

106

KOREAN INDIGENOUS EPISTEMOLOGIES WITH NOTES

epistemologies and worldviews that continue to be relevant today (An, 1996; Kang, 2015; Kovach, 2012; Wilson, 2008). These worldviews can be understood as being: whole, contemplative, intuitive, metaphoric, joyful, or liberating beyond being rational/intelligent, objective, or empirical (Meyer, 2008). Reclaiming Indigenous knowledges and philosophies harmonizes and balances with the colonization process of Euro-North American-centered scholarship. To change the culture of colonizing research, we need to encompass "all *three* categories" of body, mind, and spirit which are all connected to each other (Meyer, 2008). The spirit category within this triangulation (e.g., culture, intuition, contemplation) beyond cognition and reason alludes to Indigenous worldviews and epistemologies, but the realm of spirit in Western academic scholarship has been neglected due to the focus on empiricism of colonial thoughts (Meyer, 2008). Voicing traditional Indigenous epistemologies is part of the decolonizing journey, and it can be a pathway of sharing diverse knowledges and worldviews for the common good.

KOREAN INDIGENOUS EPISTEMOLOGIES

The starting place for conceptualizing Indigenous research frameworks is the knowledges. (Kovach, 2012, p. 54)

Samjae: From Start to Finish of Korean Indigenous Epistemologies

Korean Indigenous epistemologies refer to the study of knowledge systems and ways of knowing based on Korean philosophy, language, and culture. Above all, Korean epistemology views knowledges as *life* to be nourished (Kang, 2015). Likewise, Simonds and Christopher (2013) have the same idea that Indigenous knowledges are depicted as *being alive*. That is, knowledges themselves are considered having life and spirits as they are born, grow, and die, and these journeys keep repeating across time-space. Based on Hawaiian epistemology, Meyer (2008) asserts that, "knowledge that endures is spirit driven. It is a life force connected to all other life forces. It is more than an extension than it is a thing to accumulate" (p. 218). If knowing something implies life, then the pursuit of knowledges would be attributed to be respectful and sacred of life. Given this logic, knowledges should be created, used, and modified for social and ecological justices (Kovach, 2012) or for the benefit of all elements of *samjae* (Jeong & Kang, 2013; Park & Jeong, 2014; Seo & Sim, 2007). Samjae symbolizes the three elements of the heaven, the earth, and the humans.

This Korean trinity of samjae is the foundational concept of Korean philosophy (An, 1996; Lee, 2008). All living and nonliving things in samjae are interrelated and intermingled as *one*, so they are all equal and come from the same foundation, the cosmos (An, 1996). Any knowledge against life-centred philosophies runs into the trap of how knowledges can serve as lethal weapons to destroy life-ecosystems including inter-human relationships, humans and nature harmony/balance (e.g., animal, plants,

JUSUNG KIM

resources), and inter-nation relationships. Such poisonous knowledges tend to arise out of philosophy in which the value of life and living is not so much appreciated and prioritized. Thus, inevitable are the results of dehumanization, degradation of environments, and colonization around the world.

Spiritual Knowings

Korean epistemologies develop a principle of spiritual knowing to life. Such epistemologies play an important role in vitalizing the value of life-centred philosophy to live interdependently within the samjae system (An, 1996; Kang, 2015; Park & Jeong, 2014). Seen through this lens, a substantial nature of knowledges can be understood differently from a human-centred and individual-focused knowledge gained through an empirical way of knowing practiced in Western thoughts (Darder, 2015; Hart, 2010; Kovach, 2012). Transcending the fact that we are more than simply body and mind enables us to expand the boundaries of knowing and being (Meyer, 2008). Intuition, fasting, vision, dream, prayer, and spiritual insights via living experiences can be the pathways of obtaining life-oriented knowledges and becoming a saint (Ha & Mangan, 1998; Kovach, 2012; Loppie, 2007). Likewise, Smith (2012) supports this idea that Indigenous traditional epistemologies are concerned with the virtues of ecological biodiversity systems, climate change, and human rights. Furthermore, Stewart (2009) applies these knowledge systems into her research by incorporating an Indigenous wholistic concept of the universe into research methodology regarding the values of caring and sharing. This is called a "spirit-centered truth that is older than time...all about the purpose and reason of our lives" (Meyer, 2008, p. 229). Spiritual knowings are underrepresented in Western academia, but they have the potential to be explored.

Saint/Wise Person/Good Citizen: The Goal of Korean Epistemologies

In Korean epistemology, the purpose of knowledge seeking is to become a saint/ wise person or a good citizen rather than knowledge gain and accumulation (Choi, 2012; Kang, 2015; Seo & Sim, 2007). Such a goal of becoming a saint or good person can be accomplished by attaining heightened knowledges of the virtue of life through music/song/dance (Choi, 2012) and exercise/martial arts (Ha & Mangan, 1998). Simply put, our heightened knowledges and consciousness enable us to reach the substantial nature of the cosmos that alludes to vital life and living (Kang, 2015). Similarly, Wilson (2008) notes that if our research does not change us as person, then our research project is not done right. That is, if we know, realize, and act in line with the universal law of the cosmos (respect for life), we live in and accomplish a beautiful, peaceful, and happy life. Commonly known as Do, Tao acts as a catalyst to realize teachings of the heavenly path of samjae. The ultimate purpose of Korean knowledge systems is to know the natural flows of samjae and practice them. In this manner, Korean epistemologies go beyond mere humanism because their ultimate

108

vision is to reach cosmic teachings of samjae and to realize the importance of vital life by ongoing practices in everyday life.

Knowing/Teaching/Practicing as One

Knowing, teaching, and practicing of Korean Indigenous philosophies and epistemologies are interconnected entities (Choi, 2012; Kang, 2015; Lee, 2008). If we understand 'knowing', then we can understand 'teaching' and 'practicing' at the same time because they are related to each other. A modified proverb 'Catch three birds with one stone' arises to better explain the trinity in unity of knowing, teaching, and practicing. Yes, knowledges are not knowledges and are dead without taking actions towards realities, and this harmony concept among which knowing, teaching, and doing coexist ubiquitously is compatible with a oneness assumption of Korean philosophy (An, 1996). Prioritizing human development in leisure culture can help people enhance life satisfaction and self-esteem, because knowing and learning lead us to satisfy higher human needs for self-development and fulfillment (Kim & Iwasaki, 2016). This notion of human development and growth by learning and knowing something new is particularly congruent with the values of Korean society, which hold a strong belief that ancient education serves as a tool to become a saint or good citizen (An, 1996; Choi, 2012; Ha & Mangan, 1998). It is also important to remind us that human completion through repetitive performances contributes to social completion (e.g., social justice) as we humans are interconnected and intermingled to our communities and environments (An, 1996; Madison, 2012).

Wholistic Knowledge Systems

Korean epistemologies are concerned with wholistic knowledge systems (An, 1996; Lee, 2008). That is, while Korean epistemologies emphasize interrelational knowledges among samjae in a harmonious way, Western espistemology argues that knowledge and truth are constructed separately between subjects and objects in a struggle mode (Darder, 2015; Meyer, 2008). The former are called relational epistemologies, collective knowing, and decolonizing knowledges (Chilisa, 2012; Kovach, 2012; Smith, 2012; Wilson, 2008). A variety of Korean knowledges come from samjae where a combination of humans, the heaven, and the earth interact to know, teach, and perform reciprocally in myriad ways. For example, we can come to know an interconnection between the heaven/sky and our body as we practice meditation/yoga through breathing techniques. Yes, the possibilities of ways of knowing are unlimited (Chilisa, 2012), as we make connections with the cosmos, the interpersonal, the intrapersonal, the spiritual, and the environment (Wilson, 2008). Teachers can be any living and non-living entities.

No knowledge arises out of nothing in Korean epistemologies. Knowledges originate from interacting with samjae reciprocally, because knowledges themselves have vital life that needs nourishment to grow (Kang, 2015). Similarly, knowledge

JUSUNG KIM

systems represent how the social shapes certain ideologies and discourses (e.g., the ruling class) (Martin, 2012; Pascale, 2012; Smith, 2012). To better understand social knowledges, we need critical consciousness that is skeptical of mainstream expectations, leading to a wake-up call in the service of the common good (Meyer, 2008). Having said that, the process of knowledge attainment or meaning-making is transactional and intersubjective as we cannot detach ourselves from what we know and who we are in a given society. The realities, contexts, and knowledges Korean epistemology is based on are socially and culturally constructed through shared meanings and understandings of realities unlike a fixed or rigid entity of a positivistic grand truth and law. In other words, knowledge is communicated, shared, and formed with social actors through continuous social interactions among samjae. Meyer (2008) notes that "we are heading into the field of hermeneutics-interpretation-via epistemology…To realize that *all* ideas, *all* histories, *all* laws, *all* facts, and *all* theories are simply *interpretations*" (p. 230). This interpretational knowledge system has brought us to possibilities for unshackling colonizing knowledges and facilitating liberation spirits. Knowledge creation needs to be a reciprocal and dialogical venture of research interactions of-, by-, and for- the people, as a part of everyday life.

Knowledges exist and can be created everywhere beyond classrooms, textbooks, and schools. Naturally, ways of knowing can be unlimited and embedded in every aspect of our life including: language and history (Kang, 2015); practices, rituals, and revered traditions (Chilisa, 2012); and commonsense beliefs, ancient wisdoms, and mystical knowings of life through intuitive experiences (i.e., spirit) (Meyer, 2008). These spiritual ways of knowing cultivate contemplative consciousness that brings us to insight, steadiness, and interconnection along with "the joy or truthful insights of your lessons and the rigor found in your discipline and focus" (Meyer, 2008, p. 229). Knowledge creation is not limited to the cognitive process from which an individual gains meaning and information. This kind of knowledge creation tends to ignore other sources of obtaining knowledge including intuition, dreams/fantasies, corporeal personal experiences, or artistic experiences common in Indigenous cultures (Hart, 2010; Lee, 2008; Smith, 2012; Wilson, 2008).

Focusing on Indigenous relational wholistic knowledges, Meyer (2008) shows that "knowledge was the by-product of slow and deliberate dialogues with an idea, with others' knowing, or with one's own experience with the world" (p. 221). Likewise, Kovach (2012) points out that "Tribal knowledge systems are holistic. They move beyond the cognitive to the kinetic, affective, and spiritual. They are fluid. Tribal knowledge systems are born of self-in-relation, and within that social nesting silent self-knowledge is valued" (p. 176). For this reason, the chasm between the knowers and the known is blurred because any element of samjae is tightly interconnected to one another. For instance, humans can learn something meaningful from the sun that teaches us a circular philosophy. Chilisa (2012) also supports this idea that "Knowers are seen as beings with connection to other beings, the spirits of the ancestors, and the world around them that inform what they know and how they can know it" (p. 116). As such, knowledges and knowings are performed with living interrelationships through which every element of samjae constantly interacts with one another.

Embodying Knowings

The ways of gaining knowledges in Korean philosophy are better understood in the light of being behavioural/personal/internal via embodied experiences. Genuine knowledges must be experienced directly through our body, mind, and spirit (Fremantle, 2001 as cited in Meyer, 2008). Similarly, Liu (2013) highlights that "Asian traditions do not privilege scientific methods of observation above the intuitive illumination of the original mind but rather see these as complementary forms of knowing" (p. 453). Cultivated are the spirits of harmony with nature, self-reflexivity, and spiritual insight, and a sense of unity among body, mind, and spirit through living experiences (Lee, 2008). Moreover, Kovach (2012) explains that "Indigenous ways of knowing are internal, personal, and experiential" (p. 43) so that unidimensional standard research for Indigenous groups is impossible and heartbreaking for Indigenous people.

According to principles of samjae, Korean epistemology focuses on the values of self-awareness and reflexive thinking. We move our body/mind/spirit within any element of samjae to learn something through internal/personal experiences in our daily life. Meyer (2008) furthers that "true intelligence *is* self knowledge" (p. 224). For Meyer, smells have a wide range of diversities and knowledges if we slow down and really smell something. In addition, Kovach (2012) accentuates an importance of embodied learning for Indigenous people saying, "inward knowing that arises from personal experience...attention to inward knowing is not optional... all we know for sure is our own experience" (p. 49). Only when we self-reflect and delve into knowing a deeper inner world of existence instead of lingering at outer surface levels of samjae, can a better understanding of Korean epistemologies be highly possible. From both Korean and Indigenous perspectives, every knowledge counts irrespective of any element of samjae because no knowledge can be regarded as invaluable from Korean epistemology. One of the pathways to keep traditional Indigenous epistemology alive is to play a game, such as a simple scissor, rock, paper game in a Korean context.

SCISSOR, ROCK, PAPER GAME: AN EXAMPLE OF KOREAN WAYS OF KNOWING

A scissor, rock, paper game (note: this order reflects a Korean cultural practice) shows how Koreans teach, know, and practice Korean philosophies. Let us play this game together to help us better understand Korean ways of knowing, learning, and practicing. Knowledge in action!

First, an underlying philosophy of this game is spiritual, relational, and wholistic because it teaches how each element of samjae is interconnected to each other. To

JUSUNG KIM

illustrate, a rock in the shape of fist from this game symbolizes the sun/heaven/ sky that looks like a circle, scissors represent the humans as a triangle, and a paper shows the earth as a square. This wholistic way of knowing and practicing, based on Korean philosophy, is different from Euro-Western philosophy that focuses on a specialized, fragmented, and individualized knowing (Darder, 2015; Hart, 2010). If we go deeper into Korean philosophy through this simple game, we can ultimately encounter the issues of peace, green movement, human rights, and social justice that intersect with one another. Our ancestors teach the difficult and wholistic Korean philosophy via a scissor, rock, paper game in our daily life.

Second, this Korean game teaches collective knowings and teachings as the game requires at least two people to play and can be enacted 'anywhere' and 'anytime'. That is, ways of knowing and teaching are practiced in a collective manner rather than an individual activity. Ways of knowing and teaching are dialogical and reciprocal as we perform collective teachings and knowings ubiquitously. Koreans believe that teaching/knowing/doing can be possible at any time-space in everyday life, so everything and everyone in life can be a teacher. We can learn something important from plants, animal, humans, and even inanimate objects. For example, a round soccer ball teaches how we play soccer and how to live life because the soccer ball teaches us lessons of hard work, harmony, and honesty.

Third, a primary goal of teaching, knowing, and practicing through this Korean game is to become a wise person/saint. It does not mean that the knowledge acquisition and accumulation that is valued in Euro-Western culture is not important. Equally valuable are both knowing knowledge and becoming a saint in Korean philosophy. Korean ancestors have played this game to teach Koreans the philosophy of samjae so that they try to live in accordance with the Tao of the cosmos (e.g., life-centred principle). Our parents teach us the value of unconditional love and devotion. As if like the cosmos, mom and dad raise offspring and embody continuous practices of sincere care. This is why teachers/masters/parents are respected in Korean culture, because they are responsible for cultivating the human completion of our children. Thus, the ultimate vision of knowing and teaching in Korean philosophies is to balance both knowledge gain and the pursuit of becoming a saint/good citizen. A scissor, rock, paper game serves as a catalyst to know, teach, and practice Korean philosophies.

REFERENCES

An. C. B. (1996). *The lost Bae-Dal thought and the origin of eastern thoughts*. Seoul: The Guk-Hak Archive Council.

Chilisa, B. (2012). *Indigenous research methodologies*. Los Angeles, CA: Sage.

Choi, J. M. (2012). *The aesthetic thought of Korean traditional music. Korean traditional music and rhythm study 2*. Seoul, Korea. Unpublished paper.

Coté, J. (2009). Education and the colonial construction of Whiteness. *Australian Critical Race and Whiteness Studies Association Journal, 5*(1), 1–14.

Darder, A. (2015). Decolonizing interpretive research: A critical bicultural methodology for social change. *The International Education Journal: Comparative Perspectives, 14*(2), 63–77.

KOREAN INDIGENOUS EPISTEMOLOGIES WITH NOTES

Ha, N. G., & Mangan, J. A. (1998). The knights of Korea: The Hwarangdo, militarism and nationalism. *The International Journal of the History of Sport, 15*(2), 77–102.

Hart, M. A. (2010). Indigenous worldviews, knowledge, and research: The development of an indigenous research paradigm. *Journal of Indigenous Voices in Social Work, 1*(1), 1–16.

Jeong, Y. H., & Kang, J. M. (2013). Hongiginkan humanitarian and the development model of creative economy. *Humanity Policy Journal, 17*, 7–134.

Kang, S. W. (2015). *The heavenly manu's light sutra & Dhanuraja authentic politics.* Seoul: Diyo-Sun Myung-Ryun Royal Academy.

Kim, J. S., & Iwasaki, Y. (2016). Role of leisure-generated meanings in adaptation to acculturation stress of Korean immigrants in Canada. *Loisir Et Société/Society and Leisure, 39*(2), 177–194.

Kovach, M. (2012). *Indigenous methodologies: Characteristics, conversations, and contexts.* Toronto: University of Toronto Press.

Lee, K. M. (2008). *A study of taekwondo spirit.* Seoul: Taekwon Maru.

Liu, J. H. (2013). Asian epistemologies and contemporary social psychological research. In N. K. Denzin & Y. S. Lincoln (Eds.), *The landscape of qualitative research: Theories and issues* (4th ed., pp. 443–474). Thousand Oaks, CA: Sage.

Loppie, C. (2007). Learning from the grandmothers: Incorporating indigenous principles into qualitative research. *Qualitative Health Research, 17*(2), 276–284.

Madison, D. S. (2012). *Critical ethnography: Method, ethnics, and performance.* Los Angeles, CA: Sage.

Martin, D. H. (2012). Two-eyed seeing: A framework for understanding indigenous and non-indigenous approaches to indigenous health research. *Canadian Journal of Nursing Research, 44*(2), 20–42.

Meyer, M. (2008). Indigenous and authentic: Hawaiian epistemology and the triangulation of meaning. In N. K. Denzin, Y. S. Lincoln, & L. T. Smith (Eds.), *Handbook of critical and indigenous methodologies* (pp. 217–232). Los Angeles, CA: Sage.

Park, S. J., & Jeong, K. H. (2014). A study on the contents and directions of the uniqueness of Korean thought. *Korean Association of National Thought, 8*(4), 37–62.

Pascale, C. (2011). *Cartographies of knowledge: Exploring qualitative epistemologies.* London: Sage.

Seo, G. Y., & Sim, B. S. (2007). The study of life consciousness of Dangun legend. *Eastern Philosophy Studies, 50*, 129–158.

Simonds, V. W., & Christopher, S. (2013). Adapting western research methods to indigenous ways of knowing. *American Journal of Public Health, 103*(12), 2185–2192.

Smith, T. L. (2012). *Decolonizing methodologies: Research and indigenous peoples.* London: Zed Press.

Tara. (2011). *Yuch (戎): Embedding the principle of the universe.* Seoul: Tara.

Wilson, S. (2008). *Research is ceremony: Indigenous research methods.* Winnipeg: Fernwood Publishing.

JuSung Kim
Applied Health Sciences & Kinesiology and Recreation Management
University of Manitoba
Winnipeg, Manitoba

MELANIE BELMORE AND MELANIE BRAITH

13. CHANNELLING INDIGENOUS KNOWLEDGE THROUGH DIGITAL TRANSMISSION

The Opportunities and Limitations of Indigenous Computer Games

INTRODUCTION

The idea of this collaborative essay is to analyze the workings of computer games by Indigenous game designers to point out the opportunities but also the limitations of those games when it comes to cultural learning. In doing so, we intend to offer the reader two different perspectives grounded in two different cultural and academic backgrounds. Melanie Braith is a non-Indigenous scholar from the South of Germany working on Indigenous literature. Currently, she is a Ph.D. student in the English Department at the University of Manitoba. Melanie Belmore is an Anishinaabe from Whites and First Nation, ON and a Ph.D. student in the Native Studies Department at the University of Manitoba. Over the course of the essay, we will both offer our insights by discussing an Indigenous game each. Melanie Braith will discuss how Never Alone facilitates intercultural learning and offers lessons about the values of allyship and Melanie Belmore draws from Honour Water to stimulate a conversation that centers the learning and passing on of Indigenous knowledge through technology. In the end, we will offer a joint conclusion.

CULTURE, STORY, AND ALLYSHIP: THE LEARNING EXPERIENCE
OF *NEVER ALONE*

Never Alone (Kisima Inŋitchuŋa) is a video game released in 2014 that was developed in corporation with the Iñupiat, an Indigenous people whose traditional territories stretch over parts of the Alaskan Arctic. For the creation of the game, its designers worked together with Iñupiat storytellers, Elders, and community members. The company behind the game, Upper One Games, was founded in 2012 and was, by its own admission, the first Indigenous-owned commercial game company in the United States (Neveralonegame.com). Upper One Games' *Never Alone* offers its players an intriguing mixture of learning and entertainment. I argue that there are various levels of intercultural learning that the game offers its players and that these levels operate in an interconnected way.[1] On the first level, *Never Alone* offers teachings about Iñupiat culture in a rather straightforward manner by including short movies called 'cultural insights.' Through these videos, which are unlocked successively as the

© KONINKLIJKE BRILL NV, LEIDEN, 2018 | DOI 9789004367418_013

game progresses, the player learns about the community's culture, history, territory, and about the fact that, according to Amy Freeden, in Iñupiat culture "there is this extreme value of interconnectedness and interdependence" (Walkthrough Videos: Cultural Insights 1, 00:22–00:27). As Métis scholar Warren Cariou puts it: "As [the player is] taught about the culture and the land, one might say that they become more "related" to the people and the place" (Cariou "Performance").

On a second level, the game teaches the player about Iñupiat culture through storytelling. The plot of the game is based on a traditional Iñupiat story entitled "Kunuuksayuka," as it was told by Robert (Nasruk) Cleveland, an Iñupiat storyteller born at the end of the 19th century (*Unipchaaŋich* i). As they make their way through the game, the player gets to hear a version of this traditional story being told in the Iñupiat language while they are offered the English subtitles to read along. However, the player not only gets to hear and read the story but by playing the game, they contribute to a performance of the story. Moving within the Arctic landscape of *Never Alone*, the player performs the story together with the game's protagonists Nuna and Fox. The player enters the game's story world and performs the story by navigating the characters through ice and snow and helping them to find the source of a blizzard that is threatening their community.

Over the course of the game, the player learns to interact not only with the characters but also with the natural world around them. The strong Arctic winds can either help or work against the player. The player needs to listen closely to wind's howling and study the pattern of the falling snow so as to work together with the natural forces. This teaches the player about Iñupiat interactions with the land. As Ishmael Angaluuk explains in one of the cultural insights entitled "Everything Is Alive":

> We spend all our time out in nature. You get very intimate with the world, and over time, if you're living that life, you start to sense that everything has a spirit, there is a consciousness in everything. Everything is alive. If everything is alive then we want to respect it. And if we're going to use it, we want to use it respectfully. (Cultural Insights 1, 19:53–20:23)

The third level on which the game imparts its teachings is less straightforward. I argue that *Never Alone* teaches its players not only about Iñupiat culture but also about the values of allyship. Rather than immersing the player by letting them adopt the identity of Nuna or Fox, the player is encouraged to be aware of their own identity (as a player) and to act as an ally to the two characters.

In order to put the player in the position of an ally, the game's design includes various components that prevent the player from overly identifying with the characters. I will identify and analyse these components of the game over the remainder of my part of this essay. The first component is the game's visual perspective: The game is not designed to offer its players a first-person perspective. Therefore, the player is not able to adopt Nuna or Fox' point of view and to identify with the characters. Instead, the game is designed as a so-called "side-scrolling game." The omniscient point of view and the limited options for moving in the world of the game create a distance between characters and player. The design furthermore, limits the player's movement through the Iñupiat territory. Instead of roaming and exploring the territory freely by navigating the characters through an open world game, the player of *Never Alone* has to follow Nuna and Fox on their way forward. While the side-scrolling-perspective imposes certain limits on the player's freedom, it also offers them a better overview that helps them in enabling the characters to perform the required actions. The player can see both characters at the same time and can switch more easily between playing Nuna and playing Fox. In the two-player mode, the side-scrolling-perspective allows for both players to equally follow the game and to figure out how to best work together as the game teaches about the reciprocal relationship between Nuna and Fox.

During the game, players will encounter places that Nuna alone is unable to reach and that she needs Fox' help for and vice versa. The game's perspectival design, therefore, foregrounds the way in which the characters interact and depend on each other and thereby emphasizes relationships. This interconnectedness is a key value in Inupiat culture, which is, to quote Ishmael Angaluuk, built on "that special relationship between humans and the natural world, and the animals" (Cultural Insights 1, 00:38–00:46). While playing *Never Alone*, the player enacts an embodied relationship with the characters and thereby performs the role of an ally. Tessa Blaikie Whitecloud, who identifies as an ally to Indigenous people, states that "[b]eing an ally means recognizing that oppression exists and affects people that are not yourself, so as an ally you are trying to align yourself with actions, ideas, and movements that serve to undermine the systems that perpetuate that oppression and strive for liberation" (Whitecloud "FAQ"). Whitecloud's definition of an ally adequately describes the role of the player in relation to the world and the characters of *Never Alone*: While not affected by the blizzard and the problems of the Iñupiat community themselves, the player nevertheless helps Nuna and Fox with actions, ideas, and movements to fight against those problems.

The player feels included in a community without appropriating an Inupiat identity. Lynn Gehl, Anishinaabe scholar and activist, states that responsible allies are "fully grounded in their own ancestral history and culture" in order to avoid what she calls 'wannabe syndrome' (Gehl "Ally Bill of Responsibilities"). *Never Alone* not only prevents the player from adopting the identity of the characters, it also makes the player aware of their own identity as a player and as an ally. For example, the game constantly instructs the player which keys to press or suggests positions to which they should move the characters. These instructions are on an ontological level that is different from that of the game's story, but they are nevertheless part of the game. The same is true for the position of the player: They are on a different ontological level but nevertheless part of the performance of the story. The instructions that the game gives, remind the player of the fact that they are operating on a different ontological level. Being aware that it is her or his actions that help Nuna and Fox navigate the difficult arctic environment, the gamer self-consciously enacts the role of an ally: they participate in a community, take on responsibilities for this community but are also aware of their own place.

The question that remains is, however, what happens to the player's position as an ally when they have successfully finished the game? Activist Harsha Walia argues that an ally's "commitment should be made for long-term support. This means not just being present [...] in moments of crisis, but developing an ongoing commitment to the well-being of Indigenous peoples and communities" (Walia 46). The ally position that the player adopts in relation to Nuna and Fox is, at first appearance, not designed for this kind of long-term support. Whether the player translates the values of allyship that the game has taught them into further actions is a question to which there is no universal answer. This, however, does not take away from the possibilities for further action that the game opens up. The virtual relationships that have been established between the player and the Iñupiat community might inspire the player's further self-education about the issues encountered in the game as well as their sharing of these issues with others. It might even foster further political action because as Stephanie Irlbacher-Fox argues: "[r]elationship is fundamental to meaningful co-existence, and an antecedent to motivating change within settler society over the long term" (IrlbacherFox 223). *Never Alone* therefore constitutes a starting point for potential allyship and establishes relationships that might be translated into further actions in the non-virtual world.

As I hope to have shown, *Never Alone* allows for the non-Indigenous player's intercultural learning of Inupiat knowledge and it teaches them the values of allyship on different levels that work together and reinforce each other. Eventually, these teachings potentially have a transformative effect on the player that causes them to translate what they learned into actions performed in the world outside the game.

DIGITAL MEDIA AND THE ELDER'S ROLE: A DISCUSSION OF THE GAME *HONOUR WATER*

Honour Water, created by Elizabeth LaPensée, is an interactive iPad game, which can be downloaded, for free, from the app store. Through the game-making process, LaPensée takes on a collaborative approach by working with the songwriter Sharon Day, listening to the voices of the Elders, and "water carriers, singers, women, and allies" (July 2016). The game includes three songs: Miigwech Nibi (Thank You Water), Gii Bimoseyaan (I Walked), and Gizaagi'igonan Gimaamaanan Aki (We Are All Loved by Mother Earth). LaPensée says that "[p]eople from all over are welcome to sing these songs with good intentions for the water. The hope is to pass on these songs through fun gameplay that encourages comfort with singing and learning Anishinaabemowin [the Ojibway language]" (5 Mar 2016) and that she "was asked by Elders to record water songs that are allowed to be shared digitally so that they could [be learned and passed on]" (4 Aug 16). The player follows along with the words in Anishinaabemowin and fluent and nonfluent speakers can engage in the game. For the nonfluent speakers, there are features that allow time for practice and pronunciation; the Anishinaabemowin words translate into English allowing the player(s) to understand what they are singing.

There are features that that the player(s) can explore, they are: "Play," "Practice," "Record," "Lyrics," "Song Info," and "Artist Info" that the player(s) can explore, The "Play" tab is the main area that offers the player(s) to play the game; the "Record" section takes the player(s) into fun activity allowing them to record their own singing. The "Lyrics" offer a breakdown of each song allowing the player(s) to study and to learn the words. The areas "Song Info" and "Artist Info" provide information on the meaning of the songs and the artist's background. The website, www.honourwater.com offers the songs, but not the additional features that are included in the game.

Although the game teaches players how to sing the water songs and what the words mean, a significant aspect that is vital to Indigenous culture, that is not possible to achieve through gameplay, is the connection and relationship to the Elder. Even though LaPensée has achieved this connection and relationship with the Elders through the collaborative approach she undertook throughout the game-making process, it is physically impossible for her to pass this on to future players. In Indigenous communities, from time immemorial and to present, the Elders have been and still are the knowledge holders, because they have the most life experience; it is their responsibility to the community to pass on their knowledge to the next generation. The passing on of knowledge entails a reciprocal relationship, to which a connection between the learner and the Elder is vital. To best, explain the meaning of a reciprocity relationship, I will turn to the Grandmothers.

In the article, "Carriers of Water: Aboriginal Women's Experiences, Relationships, and Reflections" by Kim Anderson, Barbara Clow, and Margaret Haworth-Brockman, eleven Grandmothers, from different Indigenous communities, shared their knowledge about the teachings and the relationship with water that was passed down to them by their Elders. The article lists the Grandmothers shared knowledge into three themes, which are, *water is life, water is sentiment, and water can heal.* The article opens up the discourse with the fundamental relationship between Aboriginal women and water, in which the Grandmothers state that "the first duty ... to water is simple gratitude, to offer thanks" (15). Because the water has spirit, the gratitude in which the Grandmothers expand on centers offerings such as tobacco and song. The Grandmothers also discuss feeding the spiritual relationship with water by ceremonial practice; one includes the full moon ceremony, which "is about giving thanks for the renewal of life and the life force, as it is connected to water and women's cycle" (15). The Grandmothers that participated in the study "exemplified this relationship and the sense of responsibility that came with it" (16) and that the responsibility is reciprocal. The Grandmothers that hold the water teaching will pass them down and will engage in ceremonial practices that offer thanks and healing of the water.

Having discussed the significance of water and the passing of Indigenous knowledge, as explained by the Grandmothers, I am reminded of the renowned storyteller and Omushkego Elder Louis Bird. In 2010, the Centre for Creative Writing and Oral Culture at the University of Manitoba held a storytelling event inviting Louis Bird to share stories in a live performance; the Centre recorded the event and titled it as, *Louise Bird Cree Stories Event*. Once Bird reached the stage he gave a thanks for the hospitable applause and later stated that, "[f]or the last four years I've been very sick with the old man disease called arthritis" (3:04) [and] I was not able to walk; I was just staying in bed" (3:15). Bird then explains a telephone call he received in which he was asked if he could attend, he responded with "[y]es of course I will come" (3:22). Bird goes on to say how he jumped out of bed and began to feel better. The thought that *he needed to feel wanted* triggered because Elders are the knowledge holders and it is their responsibility to pass on this knowledge, Bird demonstrates the need to feel wanted because, even though feeling arthritic pain, he did not hesitate in accepting the invitation. Bird called this hope, which I interpret as the hope of feeling needed, hope for passing on knowledge, and most importantly, the hope of the continuity of the Indigenous tradition. Bird, of course, pulled off a spectacular performance, sharing his stories, sharing his experience, and passing on Indigenous knowledge. Through storytelling, he fulfilled his Elder role. There is a fear that lingers within me; with the rapid growth of technology and new digital media, is the Elder's role in the community diminishing? *Honour Water* and other media devices appear to be a good way to teach the Indigenous culture; however, if media devices are being used to teach, what position does that put the Elder in? Do they become like Bird, sick with disease lying on the couch, waiting for a phone call that may never come because the teachings are downloadable from the Internet?

The importance of Elders passing on knowledge to the younger generation in a reciprocity relationship manner includes not only a human connection between teacher and learner, but also a connection to the land. In Leanne Simpson's article, "Anticolonial Strategies for Recovery and Maintenance of Indigenous Knowledge" she states that:

> Opportunities for knowledge holders to pass their knowledge down to younger generations become fewer. As people have fewer reasons to go out on the land, there are fewer occasions for children to observe, experience, and learn from the natural world. (Simpson, "Anticolonial" 379)

Simpson argues that because of land separation, the younger generations are not learning Indigenous knowledge through a land-based approach by their Elders. Although Simpson is discussing the destruction of land brought on by large 'multinational corporations' in and around Indigenous communities, it is fitting that the statement is also applied to the technology age. The technology age has seen an increase in the general population's usage of games and apps. Although culture preservation and accessibility are at play, there is a potential risk that surfaces. The danger in Indigenous knowledge being passed on through media abates the Elder's role in the community, in which they may not be as needed as they once were.

Simpson goes on to say that, "we must … teach children how to learn from the land and how to understand the knowledge of the land. From the perspective of Indigenous Peoples, how you learn is as important or perhaps more important than what you learn" (Simpson, "Anticolonial" 380). The game *Honour Water* teaches players, in a fun-engaging method, the water healing songs. However, it does not teach the 'how,' which is the connection and relationship with the land, this can be done with the Elders. The Elder's role as a teacher is necessary for learning Indigenous knowledge because they can teach the how to the next generation about the land and build that connection and relationship that is vital in an Indigenous perspective. The intention is not to dismiss the game, but rather, to give caution. Although the game reaches a wide audience, especially with those who are not in touch with their Indigenous roots, the relationship between Elder and learner is lost through game-play.

To dismiss both the digital media and the Elder's role in teaching as a means of passing on Indigenous knowledge is to put Indigenous knowledge continuity at risk. *CBC News* reporter Priscilla Hwang captures the story of youth and Elders working together in a program called "Reel Youth." The article titled, "Youth and Elders Team up to Make Northern Films" illustrates the brilliance of young strategic minds that intertwine digital media and the Elder's role as teacher to demonstrate that the two can act as the continuity to learn and to pass on Indigenous knowledge. Through this program, a team of youth recorded Elder Edward Oudzi's life in the Northwest Territories from "his life on the land, from mushing dogs to hunting and fishing" (*CBC News*). One youth, named Migwi stated that, "[i]t made me feel like I was a part of a culture," and that it "made me feel pretty good because I haven't really been with the culture as much because I lived out in the city for a long time" (*CBC News*). Digital media can act as a bridge for Indigenous people that have not been able to connect with their roots, whether it is because they are living in urban areas, or because through over 500 years of colonization, cultural roots may have been lost. With the technology age that has fast approached modern times, and as I am still sitting here in the dark asking what happened to the ol' traditional way, it is hard to ignore the fact that digital media is here to stay. Since European contact, Indigenous peoples have proven the ability and skills of adapting to modern technologies on their own terms. Digital media is, just, another tool that Indigenous peoples can utilize for their own practices and traditions that will ensure the continuity of Indigenous knowledge.

CONCLUSION

Even though the two perspectives come from different cultural and academic backgrounds, the essay discusses gameplay from an Indigenous-centered viewpoint by either including personal experience or privileging Indigenous thinkers and theorists and their allies. Despite the different arguments raised, we both agree that video-games can offer support in cultural learning, but they should never replace the lived relationships. As the technology age is here to stay and the enhancement of video-games keeps advancing, this tool should be at the disposal of the Indigenous communities. The technology era brings about a time where the utilization of video-games can serve as a means for the preservation and continuity of Indigenous

MELANIE BELMORE AND MELANIE BRAITH

knowledge. Taking advantage of exercising both new and old traditional ways can work in favor of passing on Indigenous knowledge.

NOTE

[1] I am writing my part of this essay from my position as a non-Indigenous scholar from Germany – the position, which also shaped my experience of playing *Never Alone*. My analysis emerges from my own experience and therefore focuses on the way in which the game imparts Indigenous knowledge by creating intercultural rather than cultural learning: I reflect on the ways in which non-Indigenous players interact with *Never Alone*.

REFERENCES

Anderson, K., Clow, B., & Margaret Haworth-Brockman. (2013). Carriers of water: Aboriginal women's experience, relationships, and reflections. *Journal of Cleaner Production, 60*, 11–17.

Cariou, W. (2016, May 26). Performance, (Kin)aesthetic memory, and oral traditions in never alone [Blog Post]. *Never alone: Resources and reflections: Composed for ILSA 2016*. Retrieved 4 December, 2016, from https://ilsaneveralone.wordpress.com/2016/05/26/performance-kinaesthetic-memory-and-oral-traditions-in-never-alone/

Cleveland, R. (1980). *Unipchaaŋich imagluktugmiut: Stories of the Black river people*. Anchorage, AK: National Bilingual Materials Development Center.

"Game." (2016). *Never alone*. E-line media/Upper one games. Web. 03 June 2017.

Gehl, L. (2017). *Ally bill of responsibilities*. Retrieved 18 January, 2017, from *Lynngehl.com*

Honour Water. (n.d.). Retrieved from http://www.honourwater.com/#intro

Honour Water. (2016). Elizabeth Lapensee. Pinnguaq. Videogame.

Hwang, P. (2016, December 29). Youth and elders team up to make northern films. *CBC News.*

Irlbacher-Fox. (2014). #IdleNoMore: Settler responsibility for relationship. In Kino-nda-niimi Collective (Eds), *The winter we danced* (pp. 222–223). Winnipeg: Arbeiter Ring.

Louis Bird Cree Stories event, August, 2010. Perf. Louis Bird. Centre for Creative Writing and Oral Culture. 2010. Vimeo Class Folder. Web.

Never Alone: Kisima Inŋitchuŋa. Upper One Games. 2015. Video Game.

Simpson, L. (2004). Anticolonial strategies for the recovery and maintenance of indigenous knowledge. *The American Indian Quarterly, 28*, 373–384.

Walia, H. (2014). Decolonizing together: Moving beyond a politics of solidarity toward a practice of decolonization. In Kino-nda-niimi Collective (Eds.), *The winter we danced* (pp. 44–50). Winnipeg: Arbeiter Ring.

"Walkthrough videos of the Game: Cultural Insights 1." *Never Alone: Resources and Reflections: Composed for ILSA 2016*. 16 Apr. 2016. Web. 27 May 2016.

Whitecloud, T. B. (2015, September 21). FAQ on being an indigenous ally. *Red Rising Magazine.*

Melanie Belmore
Department of Native Studies
University of Manitoba
Winnipeg, Manitoba

Melanie Braith
Department of English, Film, and Theatre
University of Manitoba
Winnipeg, Manitoba

MONICA MORALES-GOOD

14. KNOWLEDGE AND PRACTICES IN CONFLICT

Indigenous Voice and Oral Traditions in the Legal System

INTRODUCTION

In his influential essay, *Listening for a Change: the Courts and Oral Tradition*, John Borrows introduced a not uncommon position endured by many Indigenous peoples all across the Americas – the struggle to present facts in a courtroom (5–11). Indeed, this situation is not a new one, but one faced by Indigenous peoples for centuries.

Following Borrows' articulation of the complicated position of Indigenous cultures within the courtroom, this essay maps the following discussions as challenges for oral tradition and cultural components in the courtroom.

We begin by problematizing the role of authenticity through a colonized lens. Then we move to consider the challenges of oral history in courts, thus giving appropriate importance to evidence presented as oral traditions. Next, we discuss some study cases performed in Southeast Mexico, where comparison and contrast are made between the State court system and Indigenous judges.

This essay advances the idea that oral tradition, Indigenous language, and cultural messages constitute an important piece of information as a testimony of prior events and thus should be considered carefully. Finally, this essay argues that indigenizing the courtroom can lessen this challenge. When bringing two cultures under the same judge, Indigenous experts can act as mediators and cultural brokers in order to achieve a fairer outcome for all parties.

THE COLONIZING LENS

Since colonial times, it has been important to establish a sense of hierarchy. Very quickly, Indigenous peoples learned that they needed to follow orders, and they learned that the special characters written on paper shared an important meaning, even if they distorted the truth. Thus, the chronicles written during the colonization process, with the help of Indigenous informants, have prevailed as important testimonies of the conquest. As a reference, in Mexico, we have the testimonies of Bartolomé de las Casas, Diego De Landa, and Bermardino de Sahagún. But what then happened to the Indigenous Council and oral traditions?

With this Indigenous-versus-colonizer frame of mind, we turn to Gregorio Lopez y Fuentes' influential Nobel piece, *El Indio*. From this thought-provoking novel,

© KONINKLIJKE BRILL NV, LEIDEN, 2018 | DOI 9789004367418_014

I would like for us to focus on the very realistic portrayal of disrespect shown to the Indigenous Council by the colonizers. When presenting "proper evidence" to obtain an Indigenous guide, the Indigenous authority fell into oblivion. For example, when the expedition leader requested a guide – with the help of an interpreter – he presented a paper before the Indigenous elder and insisted that the law compelled them to obey. The Indigenous elder looked at the order knowingly; despite the other elders' resistance to letting the foreigners into their lands, the paper had imposed the order, and therefore won. The oldest council member then told the tales of their past sufferings, their wanderings in the mountains, their experiences with hunger and famine – all because the tribe had disobeyed the whites and provoked their anger. So it was decided to obey the conqueror's request, even if the paper had been empty and no actual legal order had been given. As exemplified by Lopez y Fuentes, the Indigenous Council had little to no power over what was "officially enforced." Although the foreigners' demand was dubious, the Indigenous elder, conscious of their longsuffering and hardship, reacted in a way that would be more beneficial for his people (33–35).

With their own knowledge, testimonies, and limited writings, Indigenous peoples have intensely fought to demonstrate the legitimacy of their oral histories and ownership of their lands. Their stories were rewritten and reinterpreted by the colonizers. These accounts prevail today as historical "facts" while the Aboriginals' oral traditions are reduced to hearsay or myth. Moreover, Latin America's long history of repression and military movements has made Indigenous peoples believe that justice was not made for them. Hence, many Indigenous cultures in the South have opted to avoid legal prosecution against the State; as a result, many have lost their homes or been pushed to remote lands. There they have been able to establish at least some sort of resistance against the never-ending problems with colonization and modernization. Nevertheless, Indigenous peoples in Canada are an important example to look at when bringing land claims against the court. Such is the case of *Delgamuukw vs. British Columbia*, in which the Indigenous people were able to present oral traditions in order to sustain their arguments for land ownership.

ORAL HISTORY IN TRIAL

Just as in *El Indio*, the "official paper" became a valid testimony giving much less weight to oral traditions. The same development occurred in the Canadian Supreme Court during the Delgamuukw case, when the presiding judge seemed to favor Western ideologies of evidence. Many people who don't acknowledge the worth of the Indigenous oral histories have rejected them. When explaining the difficulties of oral traditions, Borrows cites historians and anthropologists, such as Nicolas Perrot and Robert Lowie, who express very negative opinions of oral traditions, discrediting them as ridiculous and fabulous notions with no historical account (6–7). Given the nature of oral traditions and their customary deliverance, Borrows explains that some people see the passage of oral traditions as the "telephone game," thus diminishing

KNOWLEDGE AND PRACTICES IN CONFLICT

their importance and validity as the message is passed on through generations and changes meaning or fact (7–10). In this fashion, a major issue concerning miscomprehension and misinterpretation of oral traditions is that some people might deem them as hearsay. Val Napoleon makes this point in her essay *Delgamuukw: A Legal Straightjacket for Oral Histories?* She explains how Judge McEachern allowed Indigenous oral history under the hearsay rule only to later dismiss them as being of dubious value. McEachern recognized that while Indigenous oral histories could be accepted as testimony for the Indigenous Gitksan's and Wet'suwet'en's claims, they could not be relied upon unless they were confirmed and supported by what he considered "admissible evidence" (131). With this opinion, he dismissed the elders' testimony.

Lawyers, historians, anthropologists, and ultimately judges are all trained in different intellectual fields. They each work with different intellectual cultures, and consequently, their approaches to facts are different. The belief in absolute judicial neutrality, then, depends heavily upon an open mind, free of prejudice and preconception, as well as on the judge's ability to reason correctly.

Indeed, Napoleon argues that it was McEachern's own refusal to give appropriate weight to oral traditions that influenced his conclusion that the Gitksan and Wet'suwet'en people could not properly demonstrate ownership of their land (132). To Judge McEachern, the written documents "speak for themselves" while oral history lacks evidentiary support (Cruikshank 32). He did not see the evidence with an open mind, refused to hear the testimony and the messages embedded in the oral tradition, and failed to consider the possibility that the courtroom setting had altered the significance of the testimony.

WHEN WORDS BECOME MEANINGFUL

As we have seen, the problem resides not just in what the judge rules as fact. Another important aspect to consider is the linguistic issue involved in the trials, especially at times when the people who have decision-making power do not have knowledge of oral traditions and Indigenous knowledge. Given the descriptive nature of Indigenous languages, an Indigenous testimony cannot be reduced to a simple reading of the translation or interpretation. Indigenous languages require explanation and cultural background to understand the messages they convey fully.

One of the beauties of Aboriginal languages lies in their deep meaning and complicated relationship with translation. Edward Chamberlin refers to this as "untranslatability." He sustains this terminology by citing Plato's philosophy that states, "... if we change the forms of story and song ... we change something fundamental in the moral and political constitution of a society" (14). In the first chapter of *If This is Your Land, Where Are Your Stories?* Chamberlin does an outstanding job of discussing the mythological, anthropological, linguistic, and cultural aspects of language, including the differences between oral and written cultures, and the problem of misinterpretation.

125

He, also, refers to Judge McEachern's refusal to listen to Gitksan's Elder Mary Johnson's song as part of her *ada'ox* (spelled variously), the oral tradition of the Gitksan. The judge said he felt uncomfortable and embarrassed when Mary offered to sing and asked the Gitksan's attorney if having the lyrics written down would be sufficient to avoid the performance (20). Attorneys work to transform their clients' narratives and messages in a way that they believe will work in the legal system and would be the best for delivering meaning across cultures, but having a song written down? Would writing the words on paper demonstrate the song's proper value? What convinces people? The lyrics, the words, or the paper? Finally, how would the reading of a song's lyrics convey the same significance as the voice, intonation, rhythm, melody, and overall feeling?

Val Napoleon and anthropologist Julie Cruikshank argue that knowledge is inherently bound to culture. In this fashion, language cannot be treated separately from culture. The attempt to transfer knowledge from one culture to another decontextualizes and fragments the native meaning when being heard in the courtroom (Napoleon 51). As such, and because of their historical and cultural content, oral traditions become inherently controversial. This is without mention of the limited timeframe of a trial and the lack of context and cultural aids that may otherwise ease the connection between the Indigenous knowledge and the Western lens. Thus, misinterpretation could be very costly to Indigenous peoples. For the Gitksan peoples of British Columbia, it cost them their ownership rights, though the decision was later overturned. For people in Latin America, it has cost their lands, autonomy, and freedom.

When talking about English or Spanish as dominant languages, an effort must be made to try to indigenize them. Home is a place where language is developed. Hence, it becomes a symbol for the power of stories and culture. More recently, Indigenous cultures continue to be endangered by globalization and neoliberalism. Indigenous oral traditions continue to be dismissed because little credibility is assigned to them or because they are not engraved on paper.

Chamberlin says, "Culture is always threatened by anarchy, as belief is to doubt. That's the essential nature of both culture and belief, and it is protected by the ceremony ... The real power of ceremony is not in achieving peace ... but in embracing contradiction" (25). I suggest that reconciliation between language and culture cannot be magically achieved. Instead, it requires an ongoing process of mediation and acceptance of others' worldviews.

At its core, the dilemma of misunderstanding arises from two worlds coming together on common ground with very uncommon ideologies and backgrounds. I suggest looking back at the Indigenous Tribal Council, learning from their problem-solving skills, and having elders present for court cases as experts and counsel for federal matters. Different subjects like law, history, and anthropology need to be understood in conjunction. The voices of Borrows, Cruikshank, Chamberlin and Napoleon, among many others, argue for a constructive and incorporative way to bring Indigenous culture into the context of litigation.

OUR LANGUAGE SPEAKS ABOUT OUR KNOWLEDGE, BELIEFS, AND WAYS OF LIVING

A process of inclusive understanding demands to acknowledge the existence of multiple ways of acquiring knowledge. As Margaret Kovach states "Knowledge is neither acultural nor apolitical" (30); without our language, we are not quite ourselves simply because Indigenous culture, education, religion, and the relationship with the world around us, is deeply embedded within our languages and ways of knowing. The descriptive nature of Indigenous languages express all those elements, as well as a position of power or marginalization. To speak of communication in the Indigenous sense goes far beyond comprehending what we hear; thus, to interpret Indigenous speech requires the inclusion of cultural, social, spiritual and anticolonial parameters that will help break cultural barriers.

With this idea of knowledge and language, I'd like to consider the Latin American sphere now. Specifically referencing Mexico's Indigenous peoples, I move to analyze some of the problems that emanate from Indigenous interactions within the judiciary system. Considering Mexico's Indigenous population, it is evident that cultural and linguistic factors play a significant role during judicial processes. Today, in Mexico alone, *thousands* of Indigenous peoples are in jail, not knowing the charges they face due to a language barrier. The State's failure to accommodate the Indigenous population and provide appropriate interpretation has been cited as one of the primary reasons for the imprisonment of Indigenous peoples (Berk-Seligson 11–6; García 82–5). The present inability of the judicial system to cope with linguistic and cultural diversity must serve as an anchor to explain the disproportionate numbers of Indigenous speakers in the legal system. The existence of community-based programs aimed to help Indigenous peoples legally demonstrates the difficulty in accessing the legal system, resulting in constant discrimination (Sieder 103). This situation is more noticeable in countries with a considerably high fraction of Indigenous peoples, such as Guatemala, Bolivia, and Ecuador.

The Zapatista movement in the early 1990's made evident the situation shared by Indigenous communities in Chiapas and Guatemala. The dawning of the passage of the North American Free Trade Agreement unveiled the poor living conditions concealed by the romantic idea of tourism in Mexico. In his seminal work, Bill Weinberg publicized an interview with Subcommander Marcos. Striving to present the obvious, Marcos said:

> ...Indian people face very complex structures of exploitation. I've implicated the federal government, the big farmers, the *coyotes*, the municipal government, the police, the army. There are a lot of people living with the blood of Indian people. People don't understand this in other countries. They think that Mexico is Acapulco ... They think that Indians just make pretty clothes, they are curiosities. They cannot even imagine that these people are dying. (Weinberg 130)

Sadly, the Zapatista movement failed to hold on to the media and news feeds, thus reducing global attention given to the Mayas of Chiapas. But not all was lost. Because of this, there has been a revival of Indigenous tribal councils. In the southern Mexican states, Indigenous communities have sought to revitalize their justice practices. In *The Challenge of Indigenous Legal Systems,* Rachel Seider touches on pluralistic reforms that have allowed for the revival of Indigenous law. Although Mexico and Guatemala have always experienced relatively low support for legal pluralism, the change has been slow but steady. Before the 1990 reforms affecting various countries in Latin America, the legacy of colonialism kept Indigenous law marginalized. Over the last couple of decades, jurisprudence has allowed for Indigenous peoples to exercise their own forms of law to some extent. In this fashion, Guatemala has developed what Seider defines as "alcaldía indígena" which is a group of Indigenous communal authorities. Similarly, in Chiapas, some municipalities have worked hard to create "consejos de honor" (honor councils). In both cases, they continuously seek to reduce lynching, robbery, and crime, all while maintaining the paradigm of human rights (Seider 106). In the case of Oaxaca, Mexico, some cases are better solved with the intervention of the Indigenous council (CEPIADET).

The questions that keep outside communities interested are: how does Indigenous law work, and how is it more effective than the State government? There has been some contention about whether the Indigenous law is carried out under "due process" and if it provides enough protection to people accused of wrongdoing. Another controversy is the severity, punishments, and the interpretation of sanction applied by the Indigenous authorities. This system strives to solve community issues locally. Crime at the federal level cannot be solved by the Indigenous council because of its legal complexity. The penalties range from monetary fines to communal work and labor and periods of detention, although some judges are against detention since it imposes a double penalty to the family, as many families' sustenance comes directly from agricultural work. For these people, missing a day of work represents the loss of day's worth of food for their family (Rios Zamudio 295–96).

Indigenous projects encourage participation of all members of the community; women hold strong decision-making power and are highly respected among Indigenous peoples. Finally, it is worthwhile to say that, while the national judicial system cannot guarantee the justice and security of the population, incidents of violence and robbery have decreased considerably where Indigenous justice systems are strong (Rios Zamudio 108).

In Mexico, some states guarantee that in cases involving an Indigenous defendant, the authorities will make sure that preference is given to judges and authorities who are Indigenous speakers or, in their absence, they will have an Indigenous interpreter. Besides language, the constitution states that Indigenous customs, practices, and laws should be considered before delivering a sentence (Oaxaca's Political Constitution). In reality, the exercise of this fundamental human right is filtered through bureaucratic layers, often including dominant language bias, linguistic and cultural misconceptions, the use of inadequate interpreters and notions of anti-Indigenous prejudice.

Indeed, there are many advantages to consider when juxtaposing the State and the Indigenous system. First, the cultural gap would be significantly reduced, since the Indigenous authorities are fully aware of the tribe's cultural aspects. Secondly, language misunderstanding and misappropriation would be lesser issues. Finally, the elders always work together to decide what is best for the community. Just as in Gregorio Lopez y Fuente's novel, the community's well-being is essential. However, this Indigenous authority is at times harmed by prejudice and is strongly challenged by a constant political opposition that restricts their jurisdiction. Seider concludes that although Latin America has recognized Indigenous forms of justice systems, their biggest obstacle continues to be the corrupt government that promotes the development of programs that seek to extract resources from Indigenous lands and is highly injurious to the Indigenous community and identity (106).

Along those lines, Jane F. Collier's *Models of Indigenous Justice in Chiapas, Mexico* is a comparison of visions of judicial systems between the state of Oaxaca and Zinanteco. In this article, Collier gives credit to the Indigenous courts of peace and conciliation. Her main objective, however, is to shed some light on the way justice is delivered across the two judiciary systems; for example, reference is made to the court building erected by the State specifically for the Indigenous judges to exercise and practice law. Although the courtroom was provided with a podium and enough space to hold audiences, the judges prefer to use small meeting rooms where the disputants and judges fit tightly, but also where the judge sits among them without establishing distance and hierarchies (94–95). It shows a very Indigenous way of looking at tribal issues, as the elders look for the parties' collaboration to solve conflicts.

Zinanteco, and most Indigenous judges strive to resolve the problem and any hard feelings between the parties. In many cases, the audience with the Zinanteco judges continues until the issue is resolved. Collier also analyzes the legal process and how the judges adhere to their culture and beliefs in order to issue a judgment. For example, Indigenous judges solve the cases according to their traditions and customs, even if they are not in accordance with the Mexican constitution (97). Ultimately, the Indigenous judges strive to handle the issues in such a way that will promote reconciliation and avoid violence.

When the cases are solved by the community, the issue of misinterpretation is considerably reduced, as Indigenous judges bring the parties and the other judges into the same office. After the matter is presented, the judge seeks the active participation of everyone involved in the dilemma by asking what they want to do about it, and conjunctively they look for the best resolution. The Zinanteco judges encourage the parties to come up with solutions that will "calm their angry hearts" (96). If one of them remains angry, the case continues until both sides agree on a solution, as opposed to the traditional state system, in which the judgment is given and must be enforced.

There are municipalities in Mexico where the elected officials are not Indigenous, even though the majority of the population is Indigenous. In order to solve cases, such authorities require the help of traditional authorities to help fill in cultural gaps. Following the example of Chiapas and Oaxaca, other states have also started to follow the Indigenous justice system. The elected judges in those municipalities are full members of Indigenous communities and have held many positions within the community system; their main focus is on relationships rather than on individuals. The task of Indigenous leaders is not one of judging, but rather one to "fix quarrels" (Collier 98), thus acting as a mediator.

The fact that Latin American countries are allowing for Indigenous people to reconcile and revive their law as Indigenous judicial systems represent a movement towards decolonization of their judicial system. However, many issues prevail that are considered unfair toward Indigenous authorities. For example, some states hold prejudice and negative views toward them, and to a point, the state authority limits their problem-solving capacity. The judges' practices and decisions are challenged and questioned by the State. Most importantly, their pay is merely symbolic; hence, they combine their daily jobs with their roles as judges. Rios Zamudio observes that the Indigenous judges provide a service to society regardless of the pay; nonetheless, they have sacrificed their own crops in order to aid society (210). Thus, a fair hourly wage should be considered by the State.

CONCLUSION

Finally, we return to our opening argument. We have seen how proper evidence with Western historical validity plays an important role during trials. Indigenous oral traditions are frequently rejected under a Western lens because these stories are not documents. However, for Indigenous cultures, they certainly are. With the excuse that Indigenous languages are redundant and vague, some people have taken the liberty to reinterpret their oral histories and instruct about the challenges of dealing with oral histories. The time has come to stop this, and the revival of Indigenous cultures is palpable today. Today, Mexican communities and civil actors continue to fight for fairer representation of Indigenous peoples when facing the legal system. In a legal setting that was imposed for the colonizer denying Indigenous processes and autonomy, an indigenization and acculturation process of the legal institutions is deemed essential. More than anything, the acceptance of Indigenous language, traditions, and cultural elements as "fact" should be recognized as an inherent right to all people. If judges were to seek training on Indigenous matters, or even if they sought experts' opinions with an open mind, many of the cultural messages would make perfect sense. Had Judge McEachern seen evidence under a different scope, the Gitksan evidence would have been sufficient. It was his prejudice against Indigenous peoples that blinded him and prevented him from seeing and listening *"for a change."*

REFERENCES

Berk-Seligson, S. (2008). Judicial systems in contact access to justice and the right to interpreting/ translating services among the Quichua of Ecuador. *Interpreting, 10*(1), 9–33.

Borrows, J. (2001). Listening for a change: The courts and oral tradition. *Osgoode Hall Law Journal, 39*(1), 1–38.

Chamberlin, J. E. (2003). *If this is your land, where are your stories? Finding common ground.* Toronto: A.A. Knopf Canada.

Collier, J. F. (1999). Models of indigenous justice in Chiapas, Mexico: A comparison of state and Zinacanteco visions. *PoLAR: Political and Legal Anthropology Review, 22*(1), 94–100.

Cruikshank, J. (1992). Invention of anthropology in British Columbia's supreme court: Oral tradition as evidence in Delgamuukw v. B.C. *BC Studies, 95*, 25–42.

García, C. O. (2002). *Derecho consuetudinario y pluralismo jurídico.* Guatemala: Cholsamaj Fundacion.

CEPIADET. (2010, December). *Informe sobre el estado que guardan los derechos lingüísticos de los pueblos y comunidades indígenas en el Sistema de procuración y administración de justicia en Oaxaca.* Retrieved 3 March, 2017, from http://fundar.org.mx/mexico/pdf/informecepiadet.pdf

Kovach, M. (2009). *Indigenous methodologies: Characteristics, conversations, and context.* Toronto: University of Toronto Press.

López y Fuentes, Gregorio. (1991). *El Indio.* Mexico: Porrua.

Napoleon, V. (2005). Delgamuukw: A legal straightjacket for oral histories? *Canadian Journal of Law and Society, 20*(2), 123–55.

Sieder, R. (2012). The challenge of indigenous legal systems: Beyond paradigms of recognition. *The Brown Journal of World Affairs, 18*(2), 103.

Weinberg, B. (2000). *Homage to Chiapas: The new indigenous struggles in Mexico.* New York, NY: VERSO.

Zamudio, R., & Lucia, R. (2011). Indigenous Mayan justice in the Southeast of Mexico. *Revista de Derecho, 35*, 180–219.

Monica Morales-Good
Faculty of Creative and Critical Studies
University of British Columbia – Okanagan
Kelowna, British Columbia

PART 3

RE-DRESSING COLONIAL LEGACIES: COUNTER-NARRATIVES OF RESISTANCE

LAURA FORSYTHE

15. SELF-DETERMINATION UNDERMINED

Education and Self-government

In the past, the Canadian governments' education policy has been a tool of oppression, but it can be a tool of liberation founded on First Nation control over education. First Nations view education as a means to achieving self-determination and redressing the negative impacts of colonial practices.[1]

INTRODUCTION

Enshrined in the Indian Act and Treaties is the Federal Governments' legal responsibility for Indian Education. Joint agreements between Provincial school jurisdictions, First Nations and the Federal Government have created unmatched failure in educational delivery to Indigenous learners for over one hundred years. The deplorable state of minority education in Canada has been documented thoroughly in the Royal Commission on Aboriginal Peoples (RCAP), the Truth and Reconciliation Commission and countless other studies.[2] Our current educational system is failing Indigenous learners with graduation levels, and fundamental skills of Indigenous learners continuing to fall well below the national average non-Indigenous learners achieve. According to the Assembly of First Nations, the National Secondary school data identifies the graduation rate of Indigenous learners to be approximately 36% compared to 72% for non-Indigenous learners.[3] In the previous generation, while 61% of individuals aged 20–24 years had completed high-school nationally, only 13% of Indigenous students in the same age range achieved a high-school diploma.[4]

Since the late nineteenth century, the Federal government has gradually "allowed" Indigenous people more control and authority over education K-12 plus post secondary education through various types of governing agreements. That said, arguably all Final Agreements, Self-Government agreements, Comprehensive Land Claim Agreements and Government to Government Agreements education clauses retain degrees of Federal and Provincial oversight and interference, which prevent the freedom necessary for effective Indigenous educational reform. Indigenous leadership negotiating for the future education of its members have been forced to adhere to flawed education delivery

© KONINKLIJKE BRILL NV, LEIDEN, 2018 | DOI 9789004367418_015

systems that have repeatedly failed for generations. Clauses incorporated into Self-Government and Final Agreements with First Nations and Metis groups reflect a Federal refusal to relinquish control over Indigenous education under the guise of granting self-determination.

Scholars and community members have asserted that the success of Indigenous learners is directly related to the amount of involvement and control in their community has on the delivery of its education.[5] However, the agreements with Indigenous Nations have not reflected the call for control of Indigenous Education envisioned by the National Native Brotherhood as early as 1972.[6] In their policy paper *Indian Control over Indian Education* they speak to the jurisdictional issues surrounding Indigenous education and the "unusual school services" provided by joint agreements with the Provincial and Federal Government and the "Master agreements" which violated local control.[7]

Forty-two years ago, the Assembly of First Nations demanded a review of existing documents to establish the current level of First Nations local control.[8] This paper will survey the educational clauses included in thirty-seven self-government agreements between First Nations and the Federal Government from 1975 to 2014 across Canada to identify the amount of local jurisdiction the following Nations have gained over community education through their negotiations.

The following First Nations have been included in the survey:

Carcross Tagish First Nation	Champagne and Aishihik First Nation
Gwich'in Council	Inuvialuit
James Bay Cree and Inuit	Kluane First Nation
Kwanlin Dun First Nation	Little Salmon Carmacks First Nation
Maa-nulth First Nation	Miawpukek First Nation
Nacho Nyak Dun First Nation	Nisga'a Lisims Government
Sahtu Dene and Metis	Sechelt Indian Band
Selkirk First Nation	Sioux Valley Dakota Nation
Ta'an Kwach'an Council	Teslin Tlingit Council
Tłıchǫ	Tr'ondëk Hwëch'in
Tsawwassen First Nation	Vuntut Gwitchen First Nation
Westbank First Nation	

Thirty-seven agreements between respective First Nations, Her Majesty the Queen in Right of Canada (represented by the Minister of Indigenous Affairs and Northern Development) and The Provincial Government (represented by the Government Leader of the Province) will assess their ability to empower or disempower the First Nations in obtaining governance over their own education. These documents include Agreements in Principle, Self-Government Agreements, Final Agreements, Government to Government Agreements, Self-Government Acts and Comprehensive Land Claim Agreements spanning numerous communities. The survey compares the agreements for the following clauses; jurisdiction, transferability and the power to enact laws regarding education.

JURISDICTION

Jurisdiction is the formal recognition by both the Federal and Provincial government of the inherent right of power, authority, and control for First Nations to make decisions about the education of their members and the control over the foundation of their education system. First Nations throughout Canada have sought this critical component of Aboriginal rights through negotiation including the provincial effort of sixty-eight British Columbian First Nations negotiating a Canada-First Nations Education Jurisdiction Agreement.[9] Their efforts brought forth Bill C-34, First Nations Jurisdiction over Education in British Columbia Act. This Act provided the First Nations in British Columbia with the First Nations Education Authority as a governing body for education with the jurisdiction to co-manage curriculum and examinations for courses necessary to meet graduation requirements.[10] Unfortunately the jurisdiction is only a co-management arrangement. All decisions made are subject to consult with the Ministry of Education in British Columbia.[11] This language and stipulation undermines the British Columbian First Nations jurisdiction over the education of their members and their ability to create curriculum that meets their learners' needs due to oversight intended to ensure a reflection of the standards seen in the Provincial Public schools.

Throughout the creation of the additional Nation to Nation agreements with Canada, Indigenous leaders expect that power and authority to control education should increase. An examination of the education clauses in the final agreements of the fourteen First Nations under the Yukon Umbrella agreement, reveals that the Canadian Government utilized templates for negotiation during negotiations for efficiency and consistent control of the First Nations' education. In fact, eleven of the fourteen agreements contain identical language defining permitted funded activities for settlement corporations under taxation.[12] However, no mention of jurisdiction over these programs is mentioned in the clauses under education for any of these eleven First Nations.

Only four Nation to Nation agreements grant jurisdiction of education. The Westbank First Nations agreement outlines their jurisdiction for kindergarten, elementary and secondary education on Westbank Lands for Members with no elaboration of other responsibilities pertaining to educators or language.[13] The James Bay and Northern Quebec Agreement states the Cree and Kativik school Board shall have jurisdiction and responsibility for elementary and secondary education and adult education.[14] The Miawpukek First Nation has jurisdiction of its' own members on their land with respect to education.[15] Finally the Sioux Valley Dakota Nation Governance Agreement in 2014 grants jurisdiction in relation to education.[16]

With only four of the thirty-seven agreements granting educational jurisdiction in some capacity to the First Nations there is a need for an investigation of the clauses that empower the First Nations to enact laws regarding education. A survey of jurisdictions demonstrates that only four of thirty-seven varying from Final Agreements, Self-Government Agreements, Comprehensive Land Claims, Government to Government Agreements have included clauses that outline the specific jurisdiction of education under their control.

The Sechelt Indian Band Self-Government Agreement, Nisga'a Final Agreement, the Tsawwassen First Nations Final Agreement, the Maa-nulth First Nation Final Agreement, and the Tłıchǫ Land Claims and Self-Government Agreement do not indicate the First Nations educational jurisdiction, but rather their ability to enact education laws. The ability to enact laws is not exclusive to these First Nations but no accompanying clauses outline their jurisdiction. This ambiguity can provide or limit opportunity. An examination of the capacity to enact laws concerning education is needed to determine the degree of self-determination that the First Nations have over their members' education.

POWER TO ENACT LAWS

Within their agreements, the Nisga'a, Tsawwassen, Maa-nulth, Tłıchǫ and Sioux Dakota may make laws with respect to preschool or kindergarten through grade 12 education on their respective lands.[17] Slight variations exist between the agreements. The Tsawwassen may only make laws for their Tsawwassen educational institutions. In contrast, the Maa-nulth agreement extends First Nations jurisdiction concerning education to near-by public institutions as well so that any educational laws the Maa-nulth First Nation passes will also be applicable to non-members.

Eleven First Nations under the Umbrella Agreement in the Yukon have negotiated in their respective Self-Government Agreements a single clause regarding enacting educational laws for the provision of education programs and services for Citizens choosing to participate, except licensing and regulation of facility-based services off Settlement Land.[18] The power to enact laws only remains dominant if they prevail when in conflict with a Provincial or Federal law clause stating that in the event of an inconsistency the First Nations law will prevail. Unfortunately, none of the eleven First Nations whose agreements contain the ability to enact educational laws contain such a prevailing clause that protects their bylaws. Similarly, there is no inclusion of a prevailing clause in the Sechelt Indian Band Self-Government Act, Sahtu Dene and Metis Comprehensive Land Claim, and the Tłıchǫ Land Claim and Self-Government Agreement.[19] The James Bay and Northern Quebec Agreement stipulates that for all other applicable laws of general application in the Province, if these laws are inconsistent with the section on education, then the provisions of the agreement shall prevail. Interestingly, there is an additional clause that states that bylaws created by those under the James Bay and Northern Quebec Agreement require the approval of the Minister of Education and can be disallowed.[20]

Regarding post-secondary education, only the Nisga'a and Sioux Dakota Nation have the power to enact laws for post-secondary stipulated in their agreements whereas the Tłıchǫ are explicitly denied ability to make laws for post-secondary.[21] The Sioux Dakota have the most extensive authority of all communities included in this study. Their agreement includes a clause which states they have jurisdiction over education and may make laws about pre-school education; elementary and secondary education; technical and vocational education and training; post-secondary education; education about Dakota culture and language; curriculum; entities, structures or mechanisms, for delivering education services; and accrediting individuals to teach Dakota culture and language on their lands.[22]

In contrast, several nations with a more limited scope of jurisdiction over education of their members have secured a prevailing clause concerning conflicts between provincial or federal educational laws and signatory tribes including the Miawpukek First Nation, Nisga'a, Westbank First Nation, Tsawwassen First Nation, Maa-Nulth First Nation, Sioux Valley Dakota Nation, Inuvialuit law. For these nations, in conflicts between First Nation law and a federal or provincial law, the First Nation law prevails.[23] Following this survey it is concluded that not all First Nations and Councils who have entered into an Agreement have negotiated the power to enact laws or that those laws prevail.

TRANSFERABILITY

In instances in which the First Nation is granted the jurisdiction over education, agreements contain a clause like the Maa-nulth First Nation Final Agreement law is making with respect to kindergarten to grade twelve education clauses:

a) establish curriculum, examination, and other standards that permit transfers of students between school systems in British Columbia at a similar level of achievement and permit entry of students to the provincial post-secondary education systems[24]

which negate that jurisdiction by requiring that the First Nation educational institutions permit transfer between Provincial school systems and the First Nation School.

The Miawpukek First Nation, and Westbank First Nations which have been afforded the jurisdiction over early childhood development, primary, elementary and secondary education and curriculum development are subject to a clause stating their curriculum, examination and other standards must transfer between Provincial schools, and admission to post-secondary institutions considerably limiting the scope of the initial educational jurisdiction.[25]

Of those agreements already identified as lacking jurisdiction but having the ability to enact law, they also share the subsequent clauses that require transferability. The Nisga'a and Tsawwassen have only been granted the ability to make laws for pre-school to grade twelve education including teaching Nisga'a language and culture but are subject to transfers of students between school systems at a similar level of achievement and grade 12 achievement guidelines that will permit admission of students to provincial post-secondary education systems.[26]

In the Maa-nulth First Nation Final Agreement, control is lacking even though they have been afforded the ability to make laws regarding K-12 education. Their curriculum, examination, and other standards must permit transfers of students between school systems in British Columbia and permit entry of students to the provincial post-secondary education systems.[27]

LAURA FORSYTHE

The Sioux Valley Dakota Governance Agreement provides them with the ability to create laws for pre-school, elementary, secondary and post-secondary education regarding Dakota language and culture, curriculum, and delivery including the accreditation of their teachers. Underminingly the subsequent clause enforcing transferability to all curriculum impacts the actualization of control when adhering to standards under provincial laws.[28]

Although the Tłįchǫ have gained the ability through the Tłįchǫ Agreement to enact laws for all education except post-secondary for its citizens and community including language and culture they have not secured the ability to accredit teachers. Further, their agreement also contains a transfer and matriculation clause so that they must design curriculum, examinations and other standards with the objective of permitting transfers of students between and within a provincial and territorial school and to gain admission to provincial and territorial post-secondary education systems.[29]

The Inuvialuit Self-Government Agreement in Principle does grant the ability to enact laws concerning early childhood, and kindergarten to grade twelve, however, two subsequent clauses indicate that they must establish standards compatible with NWT core principles and objectives for early childhood education and they must permit institutional transfer.[30] In contrast, The James Bay and Northern Quebec Agreement does not contain a clause that indicates curriculum and achievement benchmarks must be transferable. It also appears to contain language that empowers the Cree and Kativik School Boards through committee or council to develop curriculum involving culture and language. Since both school boards are overseen by a Minister of Education, once again changes to the curriculum are subject to external provincial and federal evaluation and eventual approval.[31]

The Sechelt Indian Band Self-Government Act, the Sahtu Dene and Metis Comprehensive Land Claim and the twelve of the Yukon Umbrella Final Agreements and Self-Government Agreements do not indicate a mandatory transferability clause.[32] Nonetheless, this is not an indication of increase control but perhaps more importantly the consequence of no documented ability to develop, deliver or manage curriculum within any of their agreements.

CONCLUSION

After a comprehensive survey of thirty-seven agreements made between respective First Nations, the Minister of Indigenous Affairs and Northern Development and the appropriate provincial representative concerning educational jurisdiction, the power to enact laws and independence of control over their education the self-governing agreements have been found ineffective in allowing Nations the authority necessary to operate and regulate their own educational institutions. These agreements have not provided the Nations with the autonomy and freedom to develop curriculum from an Indigenous pedagogy or worldview. They do not empower Nations to identify an educational delivery system that fits their members. Nor do they provide Nations the opportunity to attempt alternative traditional or innovative methods to educate their members that may have resulted in higher achievement and engagement levels.

Even where Nations have managed to negotiate relatively broad powers to develop curriculum and certify teachers. The direct impact of transferability and lack of prevailing clauses provided in the Agreements prevent the First Nations from obtaining true jurisdiction over their own members education. Further, the power to enact laws which prevail over Provincial and Federal laws, and the ability to develop curriculum apart from the Ministry of Education provincial mandates is unknown. Additional research into the actualization and effects of the transferability clauses would be needed to comment on their impact due to these negotiations. In any case, this survey demonstrates federal and or provincial imposition of a series of templates when negotiating self-governance education clauses that aim to limit the powers to First Nations. As a result, there is a demonstrated need for continued negotiation. Research into the individual communities' educational outcomes is needed to fully understand the direct correlation between educational self-determination and, Indigenous educational achievement. From this additional research there is an opportunity to respond to the Assembly of First Nations' call for action to review all existing governance documents for making recommendations for the continuance, revision, termination of education clauses in existing agreements, or to influence the ninety agreements that are currently under negotiation in Canada.

NOTES

[1] Assembly of First Nations, and Canadian Electronic Library. First Nations Control of First Nations Education: It's our Vision. It's our time/Assembly of First Nations. DesLibris Document Collection. Ottawa, Ont. Assembly of First Nations. 2010.

[2] Marlene Brant Castellano, Lynne Davis, Louise Lahache, & Canadian Electronic Library (Firm). (2000). *Aboriginal education: Fulfilling the promise*. Vancouver, BC: UBC Press, p. xi.

[3] Assembly of First Nations. (2012). Chief Assembly on Education; A portrait of First Nations and Education, 1.

[4] Ibid.

[5] Wilman, David., Farrow, Malcolm. (1987). Self-Determination in Native Education in the circumpolar North: proceedings of the seminar Inuit Control of Inuit Education: Inqaluit, 24.

[6] Assembly of First Nations. (2012). *Chief assembly on education: A portrait of first nations and Education* (p. 5).

[7] Ibid.

[8] National Indian Brotherhood. Indian Control of Indian Education; Policy Paper (1972).

[9] First Nations Education Steering Committee. Jurisdiction over Education in British Columbia (2006).

[10] First Nations Jurisdiction over Education in British Columbia Act (S.C.2006, c.10).

[11] First Nations Jurisdiction over Education in British Columbia Act (S.C.2006, c.10).

[12] Teslin Tlingit Council Final Agreement (2013), 195; Champagne & Aishihik First Nations Final Agreement (2013); Nacho Nyak Dun First Nation Final Agreement (2013), 289; Little Salmon Carmacks First Nation Final Agreement (2013), 210; Selkirk First Nations Final Agreement (2013), 321; Tr'ondek Hwech'in First Nation Final Agreement (2013), 329; Kluane First Nation Final Agreement (2013), 328; The Carcross/Tagish First Nation Final Agreement (2013), 356; Kwanlin Dun First Nations Final Agreement (2017), 332; Vuntut Gwitchin First Nations Final Agreement (2017); Ta'an Kwach'an Council Final Agreement (13 January 2002), 264.

LAURA FORSYTHE

[13] Westbank First Nations Self Government Agreement (October 2003), 45.
[14] Ibid.
[15] Miawpukek First Nation Self Government agreement in-principle (8 November 2013), 33.
[16] Sioux Valley Dakota Nation Governance Agreement (2013), 29.
[17] Nisga'a Lisims Government. The Nisga'a Final Agreement (2000), 176; Tsawwassen First Nation Final Agreement (15 September 2010) 150, Maa-nulth First Nations Final Agreement (2 July 2008), 169; Justice Laws Website Sechelt Indian Band Self-Government Act (S.C. 1986, c. 27) (19 December 2016), 6; Tłįchǫ As long as this Land Shall Last. Tłįchǫ Land Claims and Self-Government Agreement (25 August 2003), 28.
[18] Teslin Council Self-Government Agreement (2013), 17; Champagne and Aishihik Self-Government Agreement (May, 1993), 16; Little Salmon Carmacks First Nation Self Government Agreement (2013), 9; Selkirk First Nations Self-government Agreement (2013), 8; Tr'ondek Hwech'in First Nation Self-government Agreement (2013), 16.; Kluane First Nation Self-Government Agreement (2013), 13; Carcross/Tagish First Nation Self-Government Agreement (2005), 13; Kwanlin Dun First Nations Self-Government Agreement (2017), 13; Vuntut Gwich'in First Nations Self-Government Agreement (2017); Ta'an Kwach'an Council Self-Government Agreement (13 January 2002); Nacho Nyak Dun First Nation Self Government Agreement (2013), 13.
[19] Justice Laws Website Sechelt Indian Band Self-Government Act (S.C. 1986, c. 27) (19 December 2016); Tłįchǫ As long as this Land Shall Last. Tłįchǫ Land Claims and Self-Government Agreement (25 August 2003); Sahtu Dene and Metis Comprehensive Land Claims (1993).
[20] The James Bay and Northern Quebec Agreement (JBNQA) c 16.0.11, 16.0.2, 17.0.11, 17.0.2 (1975).
[21] Nisga'a Lisims Government. The Nisga'a Final Agreement (2000), 176; Tłįchǫ As long as this Land Shall Last. Tłįchǫ Land Claims and Self-Government Agreement (25 August 2003), 28; Sioux Valley Dakota Nation Governance Agreement (2013), 28.
[22] Sioux Valley Dakota Nation Governance Agreement (2013), 28.
[23] Nisga'a Lisims Government. The Nisga'a Final Agreement (2000), 177; WestBank First Nations Self Government Agreement (October 2003), 46; Miawpukek First Nation Self Government agreement in-principle (8 November 2013) 32; Tsawwassen First Nation Final Agreement (15 September 2010) 150; Maa-nulth First Nations Final Agreement (2 July 2008), 169; Sioux Valley Dakota Nation Governance Agreement (2013) 29; Inuvialuit Regional Corporation Inuvialuit Self-Government Agreement (15 July 2015), 48.
[24] Maa-nulth First Nations Final Agreement (2 July 2008), 169.
[25] Miawpukek First Nation Self Government agreement in-principle (8 November 2013), 33; WestBank First Nations Self Government agreement (October 2003), 45.
[26] Nisga'a Lisims Government (2000), Final Agreement 176; Tsawwassen First Nation Final Agreement (15 September 2010), 150.
[27] Maa-nulth First Nations Final Agreement (2 July 2008), 169.
[28] Sioux Valley Dakota Nation Governance Agreement (2013), 28.
[29] Tłįchǫ Land Claims and Self-Government Agreement (25 August 2003), 54.
[30] Inuvialuit Self-Government Agreement in Principle (15 July 2015), 48.
[31] The James Bay and Northern Quebec Agreement (JBNQA) (1975).
[32] Telsin Tlingit Final Agreement (2013); Champagne & Aishihik First Nations Final Agreement (2013); Little Salmon Carmacks First Nation Final Agreement (2013); Selkirk First Nations Final Agreement (2013); Tr'ondek Hwech'in First Nation Final Agreement (2013); Kluane First Nation Final Agreement (2013); The Carcross/Tagish First Nation Final Agreement (2013); Kwanlin Dun First Nations Final Agreement (2017); Vuntut Gwitchin First Nations Final Agreement (2017); Ta'an Kwach'an Council Final Agreement (13 January 2002); Nacho Nyak Dun First Nation Final Agreement (2013).

REFERENCES

Assembly of First Nations. Chief Assembly on Education; A portrait of First Nations and Education. http://www.afn.ca/uploads/files/events/fact_sheet-ccoe-3.pdf. 2012

SELF-DETERMINATION UNDERMINED

Aboriginal and Territorial Relations. Gwich'in Self-Government Agreement Negotiations Process and Schedule. https://www.aadnc-aandc.gc.ca/eng/1100100025062/1100100025067. January, 2008.

Castellano, Marlene Brant, Lynne Davis, Louise Lahache, and Canadian Electronic Library (Firm). *Aboriginal education: Fulfilling the promise*. Vancouver, B.C: UBC Press.2000

Council of Yukon First Nations. Champagne & Aishihik First Nations Final Agreement. http://cyfn.ca/wp-content/uploads/2013/08/champ-aish-fa.pdf. 2013

—. Kluane First Nation Self-Government Agreement. http://cyfn.ca/wpcontent/uploads/2013/08/kluane-sga.pdf .2013

—. Kluane First Nation Final Agreement. http://cyfn.ca/wp-content/uploads/2013/08/kluane-fa.pdf. 2013

—. Little Salmon Carmacks First Nation Final Agreement. http://cyfn.ca/wpcontent/uploads/2013-/08/little-salmon-fa.pdf. 2013.

—. Little Salmon Carmacks First Nation Self Government Agreement. http://cyfn.ca/wpcontent-/uploads/2013/08/little-salmon-sga.pdf. 2013.

—. Nacho Nyak Dun First Nation Final Agreement. http://cyfn.ca/wp-content/uploads/2013/08/nacho-nyak-dun-fa.pdf. 2013.

—. Nacho Nyak Dun First Nation Self Government Agreement. http://cyfn.ca/wpcontent-/uploads/2013/08/nacho-nyak-dun-sga.pdf. 2013.

—. Selkirk First Nations Final Agreement. http://cyfn.ca/wp-content/uploads/2013/08/selkirk-fa.pdf. 2013.

—. Selkirk First Nations Self-government agreement. http://cyfn.ca/wpcontent/uploads/2013/08/selkirk-sga.pdf. 2013.

—. The Carcross/Tagish First Nation Final Agreement. http://cyfn.ca/wpcontent/uploads/2013/08-/carcross-tagish-fa.pdf. 2013.

—. Tr'ondek Hwech'in First Nation Final Agreement. http://cyfn.ca/wpcontent/uploads/2013/08/-trondek-hwechin-fa.pdf. 2013.

—. Tr'ondek Hwech'in First Nation Self-government Agreement. http://cyfn.ca/wpcontent-/uploads/2013-/08/trondek-hwechin-sga.pdf. 2013.

—. Umbrella Final Agreement. http://cyfn.ca/agreements/umbrella-final-agreement/. 2013.

—. Teslin Tlingit Council Final Agreement. http://cyfn.ca/wp-content/uploads/2013/08/teslin-tlingit-council-fa.pdf. 2013.

—. Teslin Council Self-Government Agreement. http://cyfn.ca/wp-content/uploads/2013/08/teslin-tlingit-council-sga.pdf. 2013.

First Nations Education Steering Committee. Jurisdiction over Education in British Columbia (2006) www.fnesc.ca/.../Overview%20of%20First%20Nations%20Education%20Jurisdiction

Indigenous and Northern Affairs Canada. Sahtu Dene and Metis Comprehensive Land Claims. https://www.aadnc-aandc.gc.ca/eng/1100100031147/1100100031164. 1993

—.Ta'an Kwach'an Council Self-Government Agreement. https://www.aadnc-aandc.gc.ca/DAM/DAM-INTER-HQ/STAGING/texte-text/sga_1100100030782_eng.pdf. 13, January, 2002.

—.Ta'an Kwach'an Council Final Agreement. https://www.aadnc-aandc.gc.ca/DAM/DAM-INTER-HQ/STAGING/texte-text/al_ldc_ccl_fagr_ykn_taan_kwa_1330361309025_eng.pdf. 13, January, 2002b.

—. WestBank First Nations Self Government agreement. https://www.aadnc-aandc.gc.ca/DAM/DAM-INTER-HQ/STAGING/texte-text/wfn_1100100031767_eng.pdf. October, 2003.

—.The Carcross/Tagish First Nation Self-Government Agreement. https://www.aadnc-aandc.gc.ca/DAM/DAM-INTER-HQ/STAGING/texte-text/cta_1100100030665_eng.pdf. 22, October, 2005.

—.Carcross/Tagish First Nation Self-Government Agreement https://www.aadnc-aandc.gc.ca/eng/1100100030664/1100100030681. 2005.

—. Maa-nulth First Nations Final Agreement. https://www.aadnc-aandc.gc.ca/DAM/DAM-INTER-BC/STAGING/texte-text/mna_fa_mnafa_1335899212893_eng.pdf. July 2, 2008.

—.Sioux Valley Dakota Nation Governance Agreement. https://www.aadnc-aandc.gc.ca/DAM/DAM-INTER-HQ-LDC/STAGING/textetext/sioux_valley_dakota_governance_agree_1385740747357_eng.pdf. 2013.

—.Miawpukek First Nation Self Government agreement in-principle. https://www.aadnc-aandc.gc.ca/DAM/DAM-INTER-HQ-LDC/STAGING/texte-text/ldc_ccl_sgb_miaw_1402323649082_eng.pdf. 8, November, 2013

143

LAURA FORSYTHE

—. (September, 15, 2010) Tsawwassen First Nation Final Agreement. https://www.aadnc-aandc.gc.ca/DAM/DAM-INTER-BC/STAGING/texte-text/tfnfa_1100100022707_eng.pdf

—. Archived- Bill C-33 First Nations Control over First Nations Education. (2014) https://www.aadnc-aandc.gc.ca/eng/1358798070439/1358798420982

Inuvialuit Regional Corporation. Inuvialuit Self-Government Agreement in Principle http://www.irc.inuvialuit.com/publications/pdf/INUVIALUIT_SELF-GOVERNMENT_AIP-Signed.pdf. July 15, 2015

Justice Laws Website. Sechelt Indian Band Self-Government Act (S.C. 1986, c. 27) http://laws-lois.justice.gc.ca/PDF/S-6.6.pdf. December 19, 2016.

—.First Nations Jurisdiction over Education in British Columbia Act (S.C.2006, c.10) http://laws-lois.justice.gc.ca/eng/acts/F-11.75/page-1.html

Nisga'a Lisims Government. The Nisga'a Final Agreement. http://nisgaalisims.ca/the-nisgaa-final-agreement. 2000.

The James Bay and Northern Quebec Agreement (JBNQA) http://www.gcc.ca/pdf/LEG000000006.pdf. 1975.

Tłı̨chǫ As long as this Land Shall Last. Tłı̨chǫ Land Claims and Self-Government Agreement http://www.tlicho.ca/sites/default/files/documents/communities/T%C5%82%C4%B1%CC%A8ch%C7%AB%20Agreement%20-%20English.pdf. August 25th, 2003.

Wilman, David., Farrow, Malcolm. Self-Determination in Native Education in the circumpolar North: proceedings of the seminar Inuit Control of Inuit Education: Inqaluit, North West Territories, Canada, June 27-July1, 1987

Yukon Government. Kwanlin Dun First Nations Final Agreement. Aboriginal Relations. http://www.eco.gov.yk.ca/aboriginalrelations/pdf/kdfn_final_agreement.pdf. 2017

—. Kwanlin Dun First Nations Self-Government Agreement. Aboriginal Relations. http://www.eco.gov.yk.ca/aboriginalrelations/pdf/kdfn_sga.pdf .2017

—. Vuntut Gwich'in First Nations Self-Government Agreement. *Aboriginal Relations.* http://www.eco.gov.yk.ca/aboriginalrelations/pdf/vg_sga.pdf . 2017

—. Vuntut Gwitchin First Nations Final Agreement. *Aboriginal Relations.* http://www.eco.gov.yk.ca/aboriginalrelations/pdf/vuntut_gwitchin_fa.pdf . 2017

—. Gwich'in First Nations Comprehensive Land Claims Agreement. *Aboriginal Relations.* http://www.eco.gov.yk.ca/aboriginalrelations/pdf/gwichin_comprehensive_land_claim_agreement.pdf .2017

—. Kaska Framework for Government to Government Agreement. *Aboriginal Relations.* http://www.eco.gov.yk.ca/aboriginalrelations/pdf/Framework_Agreement.pdf. 2017

Laura Forsythe
Department of Native Studies
University of Manitoba
Winnipeg, Manitoba

KARINE MARTEL

16. DANIELS V. CANADA

*The Supreme Court's Racialized Understanding
of the Métis and Section 91(24)*

In 1999, Harry Daniels, a prominent Métis leader and president of the Congress of Aboriginal Peoples, began an action that sought a long and overdue clarification for the Métis: whether they fall under the jurisdiction of the provincial or federal government. Prior to this action, this question was left unanswered and to the interpretation of both levels of government. As a result, the Métis have been treated as "political footballs," bounced between the provincial and federal governments who have both denied having responsibility for the Métis (*Daniels v. Canada*, 2013). This has created a situation where the Métis have suffered under the same detrimental policies towards Canada's Indigenous peoples, but have been denied the participation into programs to remediate such discriminations. As Justice Phelan noted, this has made the Métis the "most disadvantaged of all Canadian citizens" (*Daniels*, 2013, para. 84).

On April 14th, 2016, the Supreme Court of Canada (SCC) finally put an end to this "jurisdictional tug-of-war" (*Daniels v. Canada*, 2016, para. 15). It ruled in *Daniels v. Canada* that the Métis are considered to be "Indian" under section 91(24) of the Constitution Act, 1867 and thus, fall under the exclusive jurisdiction of the federal government (Daniels, 2016). The decision was seen as a victory by many for it ended the long controversy over which level of government has jurisdiction over the Métis. However, many scholars have cautioned that perhaps the *Daniels* case would not usher in the level of change it was expected to bring. For example, Leroux and Vowel (2016) stated that the "[*Daniels*] decision is quite narrow, and simply clarifies which level of government non-status Indians and Métis must turn to when seeking legislative action" but that "asserting Aboriginal rights remains as difficult as always" (p. 33). Larry Chartrand (2013) too, has said that while the government now possesses the jurisdiction to act, it does not necessarily mean it will act. Before we can even begin to look at what will come from the *Daniels* case we must be critical of the Supreme Court's decision itself.

PROBLEM #1: OPERATING IN A WESTERN LEGAL SYSTEM

Before delving into the Supreme Court's *Daniels* opinion, it is important to explore the problems associated with pursuing this matter through the Canadian legal

© KONINKLIJKE BRILL NV, LEIDEN, 2018 | DOI 9789004367418_016

system. The first problem with attempting to redress this issue has to do with the constitutional provision in question. It was created in 1867 to provide the federal government with the exclusive jurisdiction over "Indians and lands reserved for the Indians", which until the *Daniels* decision, has usually been interpreted to mean First Nations and Inuit people. This has denied the Métis the opportunity to be included in important negotiations, discussions, and programs and policies for Indigenous peoples. However, section 91(24) was originally created with purposes to control and assimilate Indigenous peoples. As Stevenson (2004) points out, section 91(24) has had a colonial history regarding Aboriginal peoples in Canada, as under such powers, the Crown has asserted its sovereignty over every aspect of Indigenous peoples' lives and Indigenous peoples' lands. Under section 91(24) the government has enacted legislation such as the Indian Act, which has a long history of attempting to control and assimilate Indigenous peoples and estrange them from their lands, spirituality and traditions (see Chapter 9 of the RCAP titled "Indian Act"). It is no surprise then, that many Métis individuals today worry that being included under section 91(24) and under federal jurisdiction will translate into Indian Act-like government control and discrimination over the Métis (Adese, 2016).

This power thus characterizes the Indigenous-Crown relationship in paternalistic manner. Larry Chartrand (2013) has suggested that, by bringing this action forward, the plaintiffs have stated that they are willing to give up their self-determination by allowing the federal government to exercise its unilateral governance over the Métis and Non-Status Indians. Chartrand (2013) adds that believing the federal government can legislate unilaterally for Indigenous peoples is itself colonial thinking. Thus, one wonders whether this legal action will help the Métis pursue self-determination and develop a nation-to-nation relationship with the state, or will it simply incorporate the Métis into a long-standing, paternalistic relationship that exists between the government and Indigenous peoples. Some scholars have pointed out that even when the Métis were not included in s. 91(24), many Métis organizations already did engage in self-determination by offering similar programs for the betterment of their people (Dubois & Saunders, 2013). Alternatively, Catherine Bell has suggested that the Métis can be better served if they pursue their agenda through the international arena (Stevenson, 2002).

Section 91(24) also comes with its own set of problems as a constitutional provision. Larry Chartrand (2013) cautions that the idea of "lumping all Indigenous nations into one category of 'Indians' is also problematic because such a definition forces a unification of distinct societies and essentializes multiple nations and cultures into one uniform and artificial ethnic class" (p. 186). Moreover, unlike section 35 of the Constitution Act, 1982, s. 91(24) does not differentiate between different Aboriginal groups, therefore there is no incentive for the government to tailor its programs to specifically address each Indigenous group's unique needs (Chartrand, 2013).

While section 91(24) may be fraught with flaws, the *Daniels* case may still remove a significant obstacle for the Métis – that of being heard by the federal

DANIELS V. CANADA

government – which could then allow the Métis to pursue greater recognition and greater rights. However, even before we can begin to think of such possibilities, we must analyze the *Daniels* opinion as a foundation from which to build on. Unfortunately, as I will show, the *Daniels* case provides an unstable foundation from which to build greater recognition and promote Métis rights, as it puts forth a racialized understanding of the Métis and s. 91(24).

PROBLEM #2: LOOKING FOR SIMILARITIES BETWEEN MÉTIS AND NON-STATUS INDIANS

The first indication of the racialization of the Métis in the *Daniels* case is the inclusion of both the Métis and non-status Indians (NSI) together as plaintiffs in this action (Daniels, 2013). As Jean and Carly Teillet (2016) highlight, the very first mistake was made on behalf of the Congress of Aboriginal Peoples who brought this case forward with NSI and Métis together as plaintiffs. Having both the Métis and NSI together as plaintiffs in this action required the courts to reflect on the similarities between these two groups. The Federal Court then found a similarity between the NSI and the Métis, saying that "Non-status Indians and Métis were differentiated from others in Canadian society, particularly Euro-Canadians, because of their connection to this racial classification" (*Daniels*, 2013, para. 532). To say that the Métis and NSI are similar in that they are both connected to the notion of the Indian race is backwards and wrong because race should not be the sole determinant factor in measuring Indigenous identity and should then be rejected as the basis for determining inclusion under s. 91(24) (Teillet & Teillet, 2016).

Another common feature between these two groups, the federal court found, was their "strong affinity for their Indian heritage without possessing Indian status" (Daniels, 2013, para. 117). By linking these two Indigenous groups together through their shared exclusion from s. 91(24), the *Daniels* case also inadvertently refers to race. It is clear that the common denominator or shared characteristic between these two groups' which has prevented them from inclusion under s. 91(24) has been their "mixing" with Europeans, or their smaller percentage of "Indian blood." In other words, the Court reflects that both the Métis and NSI still have some Indian ancestry but, due to their "mixedness" with whites, have been historically excluded under s. 91(24). This then marked the entire *Daniels* case with a conversation around the Métis and NSI's "mixed" identity, as I will later show.

The SCC's connection between Métis and NSI went so far that they decided they did not need to distinguish these two groups from one another, saying that "there is no need to delineate which mixed-ancestry communities are Métis and which are NSI. They are all 'Indians' under s. 91(24) by virtue of the fact that they are all Aboriginal peoples" (Daniels, 2016, para. 46). This further proves that s. 91(24) promotes a "lumping" of all Aboriginal peoples into one ethnic class as it disregards all other aspects of their identity. By making such a statement, the courts

KARINE MARTEL

blatantly ignored both the Métis and NSI's unique political, social, and cultural differences and instead, chose race as the primary denominator of their indigenous identity.

The Court even uses the terms NSI and Métis interchangeably in its opinion. For instance, when speaking about Non-status Indians, the Supreme Court stated that "some [NSI] closely identify with their Indian heritage while others feel that the term Métis is more reflective of their mixed origins" (Daniels, 2016, para. 18). According to Brenda Macdougall (2016), this comparison between the Métis and NSI is "frustratingly simplistic when historically contextualized" as a focus on these groups' mixed ancestry largely ignores any history embedded within both of these groups' identities which make them who they are (p. 2). The Métis and NSI possess their own unique histories and identities and have experienced, though perhaps similar, their own varying histories of marginalization and disenfranchisement by the Canadian government though different colonial policies and procedures. By highlighting the similarity between the Métis and NSI –that both groups are mixed and both have a connection to the racial category of "Indian"– the Métis get reduced to nothing more than a mixed-people and their unique history and identity is erased. To further problematize the *Daniels* decision, the courts have also reduced section 91(24) to nothing more than a racial classification among Canadians.

PROBLEM #3: VIEWING SECTION 91(24) AS A RACIAL CLASSIFICATION

Not only did the *Daniels* courts understand the Métis primarily as a "mixed" people, the courts also articulated that s. 91(24) serves as a racial classification among Canadians. This began in the Federal Court where Justice Phelan quoted *Attorney General of Canada et al. v. Canard* saying that in the *Canard* decision, Justice Beetz recognized that s. 91(24) "creates a racial classification and refers to a racial group" (Daniels, 2013, para. 114). The Supreme Court further supported this understanding of s. 91(24) when it too cites *Canard* saying that "*Canard* shows that intermarriage and mixed-ancestry do not preclude groups from inclusion under s. 91(24)" (Daniels, 2016, para. 41). As the federal court then noted, "Non-status and Métis were differentiated from others in Canadians society, particularly to Euro-Canadians, because of their connection to this racial classification" which the court notes was done by "way of marriage, filiation and most clearly intermarriage" (Daniels, 2013, para. 531–532). Therefore, the underlying logic for including the Métis under a racial classification of "Indian" is that the Métis can still be included under this category because they have "mixed" with Indians. Therefore, their amount of "Indian blood" is inadvertently highlighted so as to allow the Métis to find comfort in this racial classification.

The problem with viewing s. 91(24) as creating a racial classification among Canadians is that it is perpetuating a long-established history of race being used as a tool to subjugate one group of people while elevating another. In his book, *'Métis':*

Race, Recognition and the Struggle for Indigenous Peoplehood, Chris Andersen (2014) explains the detriment of the use of race and blood in thinking about Indigenous identity, especially for the Métis. He begins by showing how, from the very beginning of their arrival to Canada newcomers relied on race to make sense of the differences that existed between themselves and the Indigenous peoples they observed. Colonizers soon realized they could rely on race to create social classifications where Euro-Canadians were viewed to be more superior than Indigenous peoples, therefore justifying the atrocities that would follow as a result of colonization (Andersen, 2014). Over the years, race has become the primary way to neatly organize society into hierarchical classifications. Eventually, the idea of racial classifications became permanently ingrained in the minds of Canadian officials, citizens, and even in the minds of Indigenous Peoples themselves that we often forget such classifications were first invented and imposed by the colonial state to create a structure that would give itself power to thrive off the backs of the racialized and instead, we view such classifications as something "natural" or as "just the way things are" (Andersen, 2014, p. 32).

PROBLEM #4: DEFINING THE MÉTIS AS "MIXED"

There are many linguistic references in the SCC's opinion to the Métis being considered "mixed". For example, the SCC's *Daniels* opinion (2016) is full of references to Métis' "mixedness," with words such as "half breed" (para. Intro), "mixed communities" (para. 17), and "mixed people" (para. 18). A quick search for the word "mixed" in the federal court opinion reveals that this word was used 47 times in Justice Phellan's opinion to describe Métis history and Métis identity. When the Supreme Court made the final ruling in *Daniels* it put forth that "Métis" can refer to two different peoples, one of which reduces the Métis to nothing more than "mixed", or part Indian, part white. In Justice Abella's opinion, she wrote that "there is no consensus on who is Métis or a non-status Indian, nor need there be... 'Métis' can refer to the historic Métis community in Manitoba's Red River Settlement or it can be used as a general term for anyone with mixed European and Aboriginal heritage. Some mixed-ancestry communities identify as Métis, others as Indian" (Daniels, 2016, para. 17). As Brenda Macdougall points out, "mixing" happened in every indigenous community, but what happened to mixed-blooded individuals depended on the social, political and economic landscape (Macdougall, 2016). Here however, the Supreme Court failed to understand that "'mixed blood' does not equal Métis any more than 'full blood' equals Indian" (Macdougall, 2016).

For the Métis, the use of "mixed" or "half-breed" is especially problematic as the Métis have to constantly battle the idea that they are less Indigenous than other Indigenous peoples. Just ask any Métis person and they likely have had to defend their indigeneity to others. In fact, the *Daniels* case is a testimony to the fact that Métis people have tirelessly argued for decades that they too are just as Indigenous as others and therefore, deserve as place at the table of Indigenous affairs. While this case aims to finally correct this by articulating that the Métis are equals to their indigenous brothers and sisters, the Supreme Court's understanding of Métis as mixed has only hurt the Métis cause. As Chris Andersen (2014) points out, by defining the Métis as mixed or hybrid, Métis people are viewed as less Indigenous than other Indigenous peoples who are not primarily referred to as a mixed people. This is because under a racial definition of indigeneity the Métis are perceived as a "mixed" or "hybrid" people, or as individuals who are one part Indian, one part white (Andersen, 2016). Under this racial definition, the Métis are inevitably seen as less Indigenous than other Indigenous groups as only the Métis' Indian part is what allows them a way into this racial definition of Indigenous identity. Therefore, the Métis appear to be a lot less Indigenous than other Indians who are not primarily defined as a mixed-race people (Andersen, 2016). Hence, by speaking of the Métis as "mixed" in its *Daniels* opinion, the SCC is furthering ideas of the Métis as not wholly indigenous but rather as part Indigenous.

To further prove that the Supreme Court's definition of Métis is flawed, one just needs to look at how society has already understood and responded to the *Daniels* decision. By stating that the Métis could include all those with mixed blood, the court has legitimized many peoples' claims to Métis identity, many of which have no genuine tie to a historic Métis community or modern Métis nation (Gaudry & Andersen, 2016; Vowel & Leroux, 2016). In 1978, the federal government established the Consultative Group on Métis and Non-status Indians' Socioeconomic Development, which found in its report that if we were to equate Métis and NSI to all Canadians with some degree of Aboriginal ancestry, the number of Métis and NSI would be in the millions (Taylor, 1979). In fact, since the release of the *Daniels* opinion the number of Métis people is growing as many people with distant indigenous relatives are now self-identifying as Indigenous, or Métis. The newly formed Minikak nation of Quebec exemplifies this trend. The group was founded in December 2015 and provides membership to anyone who can prove a genealogical connection to at least one Aboriginal ancestor in their past, though individual members' ancestors may have come from various different Indigenous nations and have no relation at all to one another (Andersen & Gaudry, 2016). Groups such as the Minikak nation are echoing the courts' findings in which "Métis" or "Indigenous" can mean as little as being "mixed", namely having some level of Indian ancestry mixed with European ancestry. Jean and Carly Teillet (2016) worry that "in defining Métis in a manner that would include anyone with a drop of Indian blood, Phelan J potentially creates a Métis out of a person who may not self-identify as Métis, may not be considered Métis by a Métis community, and may have no ancestral ties to a Métis community" (p. 18). The Supreme Court's *Daniels* opinion seems to have reduced Métis identity to something the Métis work hard to combat: the idea that Métis can mean as little as having mixed ancestry. Moreover, by thinking of the Métis as mixed, the Supreme Court disregarded one of the most crucial aspects of Métis identity: community acceptance.

PROBLEM #5: REJECTION OF COMMUNITY ACCEPTANCE AS A FACTOR IN DETERMINING MÉTIS IDENTITY

Instead of viewing Aboriginal people as a race, Jean and Carly Teillet (2016) suggest that we should consider them as a collective. In fact, community is at the heart of what founded the Métis nation. It is what made them different from their First Nations and European ancestors, as they formed a community, which bridged together certain aspects of Indian culture, language, practices, as well as certain aspects of European life, to create their own communities and eventually, their own political organizations. Andersen (2014) too rejects a racial definition of the Métis. Instead defines Métis "peoplehood" through an event-based approach, where he demonstrates the formation of Métis nationalism and Métis political identity over time by highlighting important events where the Métis have had to band together and define their own communal boundaries in resistance against colonial oppression such as the Battle of Seven Oaks or the establishment of Riel's provisional Métis government (Andersen, 2014). In fact, belonging to a nation continues to play a critical role in defining Métis identity, both in terms of legal definitions and in Métis nations' membership criteria. For instance, in the courts the SCC has listed community acceptance as a criterion in determining who is Métis for the purposes of establishing s. 35 rights (*R. v. Powley*, 2013). As for Métis nations, the Manitoba Métis Federation (MMF) defines "Métis" as "a person who self-identifies as Métis, is of historic Métis Nation Ancestry, is distinct from other Aboriginal Peoples, and is accepted by the Métis Nation" ("Citizenship/ Membership", 2017). In this definition, we see community acceptance playing a role in determining Métis identity, both in the past and in the present. Namely, a Métis person must show an ancestral connection to a Métis nation, thus showing that the individuals' ancestors were part of a historic Métis community in the past. Moreover, a Métis individual must be accepted by the Métis Nation today.

However, the Supreme Court chose a different approach in defining Métis identity in its *Daniels* opinion. The court opined that community acceptance, a criterion for defining the Métis in the *Powley* case, will play no role in determining who are section 91(24) Métis. Instead, the Supreme Court ruled that s. 91(24) "membership should be broader" (Daniels, 2016, para. 47–49). Therefore, not only did the SCC make it clear that it viewed Métis identity as a racial identity, but it further rejected the fact that Métis identity is a collective identity, where someone belongs to a Métis community or Métis organization. While the Supreme Court was likely trying to be inclusive of all Métis by rejecting the Powley criterion of community acceptance, (Daniels, 2016, para. 49), in doing so, Andersen and Gaudry (2016) point out that the Court has "dismissed generations of Indigenous political practice" where Métis people have continuously defined their own communal boundaries (p. 28). In thinking about who are the Métis, the SCC could have consulted the United Nations Declarations on the Rights of Indigenous Peoples (UNDRIP) and gathered that Indigenous identity is a political, national, economic, and cultural identity (UNDRIP, 2007). More importantly however, the SCC should have also consulted the UNDRIP and gathered

KARINE MARTEL

that it is best practice to leave it up to an Indigenous nation to determine their own community parameters (UNDRIP, 2007, art. 33). As Gaudry and Anderson point out, likely the biggest mistake the court made in its *Daniels* opinion was ignoring the fundamental fact that "determining who belongs to Indigenous political communities is the purview of those political communities" (Gaudry & Andersen, p. 28).

PROBLEM #6: LOOKING FOR MÉTIS' "INDIANNESS"

Due to its understanding of the Métis as mixed and of section 91(24) as a racial classification, the Court needed to find ways to allow the Métis to fit within this definition. The most logical way to do so was to highlight the "part" of the Métis that is "Indian", and therefore allows them to fit within the racial classification of "Indians". Thus, instead of being an evaluation of the Métis' unique aspects that make them Indigenous, the court began to highlight ways in which the Métis resembled the conventional image of an "Indian". The Supreme Court was successful in this endeavor, as it found plenty of evidence where the Métis were treated as "Indians". For example, the Supreme Court highlights how many Métis individuals were sent to residential schools like the Indians, as there would have been a need to assimilate them into greater Canadian society (Daniels, 2016, para. 28–30). Moreover, the SCC relied on the fact that, like the "Indians", many Métis people lived on reserves (Daniels, 2016, para. 29). Some Métis even lived on a reserve specifically created for the Métis, called St-Paul de Métis (Daniels, 2016, para. 31).

The problem with highlighting this as evidence is that it is looking for the interdependence of the definition of Métis and Indian. Brenda Gunn (2015) explains that "continued emphasis on Métis culture in opposition to Indian culture limits understanding Métis as a people because the gaze is not turned inward (p. 439)". While the court may not have been thinking of Métis in opposition to, but rather similar to Indian, the gaze is still not turned inward to the Métis. Here the courts are still focusing on what is Indian and not what is uniquely Métis. She adds that "the problem with the use of 'Métis not Indian' reiterates that one cannot know who is Métis without knowing who is Indian" (Gunn, 2015, p. 436). Here the courts demonstrate their difficulty knowing who is Métis without having to rely on their conventional understanding of what is an Indian.

The examples cited above are also telling of the court's understanding of an "Indian". By highlighting instances throughout history where the Métis were sent to residential school and put on a reserve, the courts have evaluated the Métis against the idea of an "Indian" as someone needing to be assimilated or controlled (Daniels, 2016, para. 25–27). With this, the court has shown how it understands "Indian" to be synonymous with backwards and in need to civilization. Another example of such evidence presented in Daniels is when the court suggests that the Crown would have needed to prevent any Métis rebellions as it expanded further west, and therefore, would have wanted to have jurisdiction over the Métis (Daniels, 2016, para. 25–26). The court also emphasized the Métis' inclusion in a statute from the Indian Act, which

152

meant to prevent sales of intoxicating liquors to Indians, as the Métis, like "Indians" were believed to cause problems while intoxicated (Daniels, 2016, para. 27). By citing historical examples like these where government officials would have wanted to exert jurisdiction over the Métis, the courts have reiterated the idea of the "savage Indian", and have highlighted ways in which the Métis match this description.

Métis scholar Emma Larocque has coined a term called the "civ/sav dichotomy", short for civilized/savage, which she describes as "an ideological container for the systematic construction of self-confirming 'evidence' that Natives were savages who 'inevitably' had to yield to the superior powers of civilization as carried forward by Euro-Canadian civilizers" (LaRocque, 37–38). By highlighting such evidence listed above, the Supreme Court has demonstrated that it cannot move past this "civ/sav" binary as it has chosen to put forward an understanding of "Indian" that is in line with backwardness and savagery. In fact, as Jean and Carly Teillet (2016) point out, the courts have created the legal construct of "Indianess" in order to verify Indigenous peoples' claims to Indigenous rights. In conclusion, the courts have evaluated the Métis' request to be included under s. 91(24) against an understanding of "Indianness" that is synonymous to "savage", which is not only a wrong representation of "Métis", it is also in fact, not a correct representation of any "Indian" or Indigenous person.

Instead of viewing s. 91(24) as a racial classification and viewing the Métis as mixed the Supreme Court could have echoed Métis organizations' own definitions of themselves. For instance, the Métis National Council says the Métis are a unique people who emerged out of historical and political reasons (Stevenson, 2002). However, because the SCC relied on an originalist legal interpretation of the *Daniels* question it is no wonder its opinion contained so many references to the Métis as mixed and to section 91(24) as a racial classification, as an originalist approach requires the question to be asked from the perspective of the framers of the Constitution.

A SOLUTION FORWARD?

Some scholars like John Borrows argue that the best way forward for Indigenous peoples' interaction with Canadian law is to have Indigenous legal traditions operate alongside Common law and Droit Civile in Canada. While we should work tirelessly to have our own Indigenous legal traditions and Indigenous ways of knowing be accepted in Canadian law, even the smallest steps that continuously force the western legal system to finally accommodate Indigenous peoples, their traditions, their histories, and their ways of knowing are crucial towards achieving such goals. For one, if we are to continue operating in the western legal parameters, it is important that our judges and justices stop interpreting the law from an originalist perspective, meaning from the perspective of the framers of the constitution at the time they were writing such provisions. In the *Daniels* case, the courts interpreted the legal question before them from an originalist position, which required judges and justices to think of the Métis and the purposes of section 91(24) as the framers would have in 1867. It is no surprise then that the courts considered Indigenous identity as a racial identity and viewed s. 91(24)

KARINE MARTEL

as a racial classification, as this would have been true in 1867. However, as this paper has shown, it is inconsistent and problematic to rely on a colonial mindset from the year 1867 as the basis from which to interpret the law and to then create a decision which is meant to serve as the foundation on which Métis people will negotiate claims with the federal government and further clarify their section 35 rights. If we are hoping to start somewhere, it is time we allow ourselves to move away from colonial understandings of Indigenous identity and colonial understandings of Canada's Constitution.

REFERENCES

Adese, J. (2016). A tale of two constitutions: Métis nationhood and section 35's impact on interpretations of Daniels. *TOPIA: Canadian Journal of Cultural Studies, 36*, 7–19.

Anderson, C. (2014). *'Métis': Race, recognition, and the struggle for indigenous peoplehood.* Vancouver: University of British Columbia Press.

Chartrand, L. (2013). The failure of the Daniels case: Blindly entrenching a colonial legacy. *Alberta Law Review, 51*, 181–189.

Citizenship/Membership. (2017). Retrieved from http://www.mmf.mb.ca/membership.php

Daniels v. Canada. 2013 FC 6. (2013). Retrieved from The Canadian Legal Information Institute.

Daniels v. Canada. 2014 FCA 101. (2014). Retrieved from The Canadian Legal Information Institute.

Daniels v. Canada. 2016 SC 12. (2016). Retrieved from Lexum.

Dubois, J., & Saunders, K. (2013). 'Just do it!': Carving out a space for the Métis in Canadian federalism. *Canadian Journal of Political Science, 46*(1), 187–214.

Gaudry, A., & Andersen, C. (2016). Daniels v. Canada: Racialized legacies, settler self-indigenization and the denial of indigenous peoplehood. *TOPIA: Canadian Journal of Cultural Studies, 6*, 19–30.

Gunn, B. (2015). Defining Métis people as a people: Moving beyond the Indian/Métis dichotomy. *Dalhousie Law Journal, 38*(1), 414–446.

Macdougall, B. (2016). The power of legal and historical fiction(s): The Daniels decision and the enduring influence of colonial ideology. *International Indigenous Policy Journal, 7*(3), 1–6.

R. v. Powley. 2003 SCC 43. (2003). Retrieved from Lexum.

Stevenson, M. (2002). Sec. 91(24) and Canada's legislative jurisdiction with respect to the Métis. *Indigenous Law Journal, 1*, 237–262.

Stevenson, M. L. (2004). Métis aboriginal rights and the 'core of Indianess.' *Saskatchewan Law Review, 67*, 301–313.

Taylor, E. C. (1979). *The Métis and non-status Indian population: Numbers and characteristics.* Retrieved from http://publications.gc.ca/collections/collection_2017/aanc-inac/R5-166-1979-eng.pdf

Teillet, J., & Teillet, C. (2016). Devoid of principle, the federal court determination that sec. 91(24) of the constitution Act, 1867 is a race-based provision. *Indigenous Law Journal, 13*(1), 1–20.

The Constitution Act, 1867, 30 & 31 Vict, c 3, 12. Retrieved from The Canadian Legal Information Institute.

The Constitution Act, 1982, Schedule B to the Canada Act 1982 (UK), 1982, c 11. 12. Retrieved from The Canadian Legal Information Institute.

The Indian Act. (1996). *Report of the royal commission on aboriginal peoples* (Chapter 9, pp. 234–308).

United Nations Declaration on the Rights of Indigenous Peoples. (2008). Retrieved from http://www.un.org/esa/socdev/unpfii/documents/DRIPS_en.pdf.

Vowel, C., & Leroux, D. (2016). White settler antipathy and the Daniels decision. *TOPIA: Canadian Journal of Cultural Studies, 36*, 30–42.

Karine Martel
Department of Native Studies
University of Manitoba
Winnipeg, Manitoba

BELINDA NICHOLSON

17. CANADIAN CYBER STORIES ON INDIGENOUS TOPICS AND WHITE FRAGILITY

Why is the Online Comment Section So Volatile and Divisive?

We all donate enough money to the government to keep thier [Indigenous people's] sorry assess on welfare, so shut the f**k up and don't ask me for another handout! (sic)

– Lorrie Steeves (Facebook, CBC News)

INTRODUCTION

When online media intersects with the topic of Indigenous people, a frightening trend can be found. The online comments sections often become volatile and heated, with malicious and racist statements overriding any constructive comments. What makes the responses to Indigenous stories so explosive? What causes this knee-jerk reaction of vitriol and rage? Through Robin DiAngelo's (2011) theory "White Fragility" the inappropriate reaction of white commenters who encounter race-based news stories can be explored. This issue of prejudicial remarks inundating the online comment sections had become so rampant, that on November 30, 2015, the Canadian Broadcasting Corporation (CBC) had to close their comments forum until they could find a way to mitigate the harm that these often-anonymous commenters were causing. This step by CBC calls into question another facet of online commentary, how would the removal of anonymity help stop racist internet attacks? Through John Suler's (2004) theories, the "Online Disinhibition Effect" and "Dissociative Anonymity" a breakdown of the psychological mechanism of online spaces and anonymity resulting in cyber racism can be analyzed.

WHITENESS, RACISM AND WHITE FRAGILITY

A cursory examination of news stories in Canadian media discussing Indigenous people quickly demonstrates a disheartening proclivity of online commenters toward the outpouring of racist and sometimes violent comments aimed at Native Canadians. Throughout online media, the comments section affords readers the ability to add their perspective to most news stories. These forums are platforms that create a space for diverse viewpoints to be shared, and at times, debates to be waged as opinions clash. Despite the positive aspects of having a comment section, this

© KONINKLIJKE BRILL NV, LEIDEN, 2018 | DOI 9789004367418_017

BELINDA NICHOLSON

forum has provided a voice for a different type of commenter, the discriminatory, biased, racist individual to have their voice amplified. This 'keyboard racist' enters the comment section and quickly unleashes an array of prejudiced, ignorant and ill-informed worldviews. Who are these individuals? Are they always blatantly racist, publicly making their harmful views known to all? Not always. Often these "keyboard racists" are people who do not think they are racist, people who may start a sentence with "I'm not racist but...", people we interact with every day.

Socially, white citizens are taught to see their worldview as objective. Whiteness is viewed as race-less and normative. Whites carry an "invisible knapsack" of privileges that often blind them to the realities for People of Colour (PoC) (McIntosh, 1989, p. 1). Peggy McIntosh details how white people inherently create conflict for PoC through their Whiteness and ignorance of their white privilege:

> as my racial group was being made confident, comfortable, and oblivious, other groups were likely being made unconfident, uncomfortable, and alienated. Whiteness protected me from many kinds of hostility, distress, and violence, which I was being subtly trained to visit in turn upon people of color [...] Power from unearned privilege can look like strength when it is in fact permission to escape or to dominate. (p. 3)

This unearned power of white privilege is entrenched in our society. In media, white people are often not labelled, while People of Colour are. This tendency is not only othering, but the listing of a racial descriptor other than "Caucasian" in a news story can act as the catalyst for whites to start their racist diatribe. Unfortunately, the online world creates the perfect platform for individuals to share their antipathy concerning racially focussed discussions.

One theory of why white people respond negatively to race-based conversations can be found in Dr. Robin DiAngelo's (2011) paper "White Fragility." White Fragility looks at white people and their discomfort with discussions on race. When a white person is confronted with a racially based conversation or issue, they often react harshly, with an abrupt loss of self-censorship. DiAngelo explores this internal tension provided by conversations about/with People of Colour, and the extreme reactions that can occur when white people's "fragility" has been initiated. DiAngelo asseverates:

> White people in North America live in a social environment that protects and insulates them from race-based stress. This insulated environment of racial protection builds white expectations for racial comfort while at the same time lowering the ability to tolerate racial stress, leading to [...] White Fragility. White Fragility is a state in which even a minimum amount of racial stress becomes intolerable, triggering a range of defensive moves. [...] Whites have not had to build tolerance for racial discomfort and thus when racial discomfort arises, whites typically respond as if something is "wrong," and blame the person or event that triggered the discomfort (usually a person of color). (2011, pp. 54, 61)

The defensive moves that DiAngelo refers to includes "anger, withdrawal, emotional incapacitation, guilt, argumentation, and cognitive dissonance" (2011, p. 55). These reflexive responses, when applied to an online forum, can manifest in hostile, malevolent and discriminatory statements. White Fragility acts to shut down any progress or learning that could have been achieved through conversations about race, as well as allows white individuals to harm PoC through their racist tirades.

For readers perusing the online news forum, when they encounter an Indigenous report they are confronted by the media's othering and labelling of the individual's indigeneity. When faced with the terms "Aboriginal", "Indigenous" "First Nations" and so on, some white Canadians' White Fragility is activated. Whites desire to insulate themselves from race-based stress can result in the "keyboard racist" releasing their (misplaced) blame/guilt/anger/rage upon the online comments section. As DiAngelo states 'this blame results in a socially-sanctioned array of counter-moves against the perceived source of the discomfort, including: penalization; retaliation; isolation; ostracization; and refusal to continue engagement" (2011, p. 61). One such retaliatory comment was posted on Facebook, and noted in the Macleans' article: *Welcome to Winnipeg: Where Canada's racism problem is at its worst* (Macdonald, 2015). Macdonald's article scrutinizes the pervasive racism problem in Winnipeg, including the racist post made by Winnipeg teacher Brad Badiuk:

> Oh Goddd how long are aboriginal people going to use what happened as a crutch to suck more money out of Canadians? They have contributed NOTHING to the development of Canada. Just standing with their hand out. The benefits the aboriginals enjoy from the white man/europeans far outweigh any wrong doings that were done to a concured people. Get to work, tear the treaties and shut the FK up already. Why am I on the hook for their cultural support? [sic] (Macdonald, 2015)

This comment, posted under Badiuk's real name on Facebook, quickly gained notoriety. Badiuk's comment unleashed fury from not only Winnipeggers, but many Canadians, horrified by his overt racism. Due to the backlash against Badiuk's racist comment he was suspended from his job as a high school teacher at Kelvin High School. Badiuk also had a court case filed against him by Manitoba Grand Chief Derek Nepinak. Grand Chief Nepinak's case was later dropped after Badiuk apologized during a mediation ceremony they both attended (Lambert, 2016). Badiuk's racist rant is a demonstration of White Fragility and the impetuous reaction of a white individual encountering a story about Indigenous people.

Recently, another Winnipeg individual shared their sentiments about the Indigenous population in cyber space. On June 6, 2017, Corina Myhaluk (Robinson-Desjarlais, 2017) posted on Facebook:

> People like that are the reason people like me turn rasist and bitter !! Every time I see another missing and murdered person in winnipeg I think … awesome they won't be ripping off anyone else. There still is a lot more room red

BELINDA NICHOLSON

> River !!! They aren't going missing because they are good people it's because they are bottom feeders. [sic] (June 8 2017, APTN)

Myhaluk's White Fragility was activated when she encountered a news story about Indigenous people. She quickly attacked, using anger, argumentation and racist "defensive moves" to alleviate her cognitive dissonance and re-establish internal "white racial equilibrium" (DiAngelo, 2011, p. 57).

Despite the harm caused by Myhaluk's racist comment, there was an interesting development from other online commenters. Putting supportive comments from "Fragile" whites aside, other members of the cyber community promptly shared Corina Myhaluk's statements and proceeded to contact the purported businesses which she worked; and the Manitoba Dental Assistants Association (MDAA) where she listed herself as a board member. As a result of Myhaluk's violent posts being shared prolifically, outrage at her comments gained widespread attention and news stations such as Aboriginal Peoples Television Network (APTN) picked up the story. MDAA began to distance themselves from Myhaluk as the organization launched an investigation into her actions. With all her alleged former employers expressing concern with her actions it was becoming clear that Myhaluk's online racist comments had initiated personal "real life" consequences. Encouragingly, both Badiuk's and Myhaluk's harmful comments had quick and sweeping blowback, creating scenarios for learning and investigations into why such racially charged statements were shared publicly.

This phenomenon of "keyboard racists" has brought an issue to the forefront for news media, how to allow their readers the ability to engage in discussions or make comments, without giving a platform to share racist commentaries. For the Canadian Broadcasting Corporation (CBC) this issue had come to a head on November 30, 2015. Attempting to gain control of their comments section, CBC shut down the ability to make comments on stories discussing Indigenous topics. This decision was deemed necessary to mitigate harm to the readers affected by these vicious remarks and to determine how the Canadian Broadcasting Corporation would move forward. Subsequently, CBC released a statement that same day, stating "[t]oday we made the difficult decision to temporarily close comments on stories about indigenous people. We hope to reopen them in mid-January after we've had some time to review how these comments are moderated and to provide more detailed guidance to our moderators" (McGuire, 2015). CBC then went on to clarify their stance:

> We've seen thoughtful, insightful and moving comments on our pages. We've seen ignorant, ill-informed and objectionable comments as well. All of it is acceptable, in our view, in a marketplace of ideas where the issues of the day are freely debated and tested. For that to work, the debate must be respectful, even if it's vigorous and pointed.

> But as our guidelines make clear, we draw the line on hate speech and personal attacks.

While there are a number of subjects and groups of people who seem to bring out higher-than-average numbers of worrisome comments, we find ourselves with a unique situation when it comes to indigenous-related stories.

We've noticed over many months that these stories draw a disproportionate number of comments that cross the line and violate our guidelines. (McGuire, 2015)

As CBC admitted that some of the posts in their comment section involved hate speech, their open-ended Editor's Blog press release did not specify how this issue would be remedied until the following year.

On June 13, 2016, CBC News released a statement detailing one of their approaches to help control the issue of "keyboard racists". This countermeasure was aimed at the individuals holding accounts used to make comments on CBC online forums. After much anticipation, CBC finally announced, "[y]ou will not have access to your original account after June 13. All accounts will be frozen. […] On June 13, all our CBC.ca community members will be asked to use their real names when engaging on our sites." Although other media platforms also had a "real-name" policy, this was a bold move for CBC. Interestingly this change was not implemented solely due to the racists on Indigenous stories, but also due to an outcry by the New Brunswick Francophone community. In the Canadian Broadcasting Corporation's article: *CBC announces end to anonymous online comments*; they explained that the "policy change comes in the wake of a complaint by a group of prominent New Brunswick francophones over what they considered hateful attacks on the province's French-speaking community" (CBC News). Despite some vocal commenters decrying this change as expensive, invasive and unnecessary, the "real-name" policy was formally implemented in June 2016.

This transition by the Canadian Broadcasting Corporation brought about questions of why? Why does using one's "real name" change the online dynamic? As one of the individuals that spearheaded the request for CBC to make this change, University of Moncton law professor Michel Doucet rationalized, "I think people, when you have to put your name, it's easy to hide behind a pseudonym and say anything you want, but when you have to put your name, people will think twice" (CBC News). Why people "think twice" was explored by John Suler, Professor of Psychology at Rider University.

Dr. John Suler, a specialist in the psychology of cyberspace describes in his paper, *The Online Disinhibition Effect*, how anonymity can encourage users of internet to speak freely, even when sharing prejudicial views,

Everyday users on the Internet – as well as clinicians and researchers – have noted how people say and do things in cyberspace that they wouldn't ordinarily say and do in the face-to-face world. They loosen up, feel less restrained, and express themselves more openly. So pervasive is the phenomenon that a term has surfaced for it: the online disinhibition effect. (Suler, 2004, p. 321)

BELINDA NICHOLSON

The online disinhibition effect gives the individual posting online the fearlessness to post their racist opinions and the (cyber)space to do so. The poster, while sharing their biased and xenophobic views, feels they are untouchable due to their online persona. They are spurred by an article discussing race, then proceed to unleash their views on the online forum.

If this distance from one's in-person identity meant that prejudiced individuals felt they could share racist views with impunity, could other factors contribute to this situation? Within his essay, Suler breaks down the various components that make up the online disinhibition effect. In the section: "Dissociative Anonymity" Suler asserts,

> [a]s people move around the Internet, others they encounter can't easily determine who they are. Usernames and e-mail addresses may be visible, but this information may not reveal much about a person, especially if the username is contrived and the e-mail address derives from a large Internet service provider [...] In the case of expressed hostilities or other deviant actions, the person can avert responsibility for those behaviors, almost as if superego restrictions and moral cognitive processes have been temporarily suspended from the online psyche. (2004, p. 322)

This cloak of anonymity gives the commenter the misplaced "courage" to speak out on their discriminatory beliefs. "This anonymity is one of the principle factors that creates the Online Disinhibition Effect. When people are given the opportunity to separate their actions online from their in-person lifestyle and identity, they feel less vulnerable about self-disclosing and acting out" (Suler, 2004, p. 322). This perceived lack of vulnerability means a "keyboard racist" feels they have the freedom to share their biased view without recourse.

When exploring why individuals lash out while engaging in online race-based discussions, it is imperative to understand the varied components that are initiated. Through White Fragility, whites not only feel they are not racist, they react in such a manner to avoid any conversations involving race. This creates a harmful space in which much-needed learning or growth is impeded. When pairing White Fragility/ Privilege with the Online Disinhibition Effect, where anonymity creates false security for racists to lash out, the results can be disastrous. Despite this, there is a shift towards finding online solutions with real-life impacts, which can help to create positive cyber-sociological paradigm shifts.

Some individuals, despite the possibility of societal backlash and reprisal, continue to post racist responses to news reports and stories on Indigenous topics. A few theories can be used to gain an understanding as to why some (often white) individuals react with such venom to online accounts about People of Colour. Through a detailed look at McIntosh's (1989) study of "White Privilege", DiAngelo's (2011) thesis "White Fragility" and Suler's (2004) theories of "Online Distribution Effect and Perceived Anonymity" the interplay of internet identities and anonymity coupled with a Euro-centric, white supremacist psyche can help to explain why

160

whites react violently when faced with racial discussions. This theoretical breakdown may be used to provide some insight into the minds of those who perpetuate racism. Hopefully, this understanding may be used to create future reconciliation, instead of division.

REFERENCES

CBC Help Center. (2016, June 6). Changes to your account and commenting effective June 13, 2016. *CBC News.*

DiAngelo, R. (2011). White fragility. *International Journal of Critical Pedagogy, 3*(3), 54–70.

Lambert, S. (2014, August 8.). Wife of Winnipeg mayoral candidate apologizes for 'drunken native' remarks. *The Globe and Mail.* (Winnipeg: The Canadian Press.)

Lambert, S. (2016, January 5). Indigenous leader drops lawsuit against Winnipeg teacher over Facebook comments. *CBC News.*

MacDonald, N. (2015, January 30). Welcome to Winnipeg, where Canada's racism problem is at its worst. *Macleans.ca.*

McGuire, J. (2015, November 30). Uncivil dialogue: Commenting and stories about indigenous people. *CBC News.*

McIntosh, P. (1989). White privilege: Unpacking the invisible knapsack. *Peace and Freedom Magazine,* 10–12.

News, CBC. (2014, August 12). Steeves explains wife's racist comments. *CBC News.*

News, CBC. (2016, March 17). No more anonymous online comments, CBC announces. *CBC News.*

Poitras, J. (2016, March 18). CBC ban on anonymous comments will be complicated, expensive, expert says. *CBC News.*

Robinson-Desjarlais, S. (2017, June 8). Facebook posts target missing and murdered indigenous women. *APTN News.*

Suler, J. (2004). The online disinhibition effect. *CyberPsychology & Behavior, 7*(3), 321–326.

Belinda D. M. Nicholson
Native Studies Graduate Studies Program
University of Manitoba
Winnipeg, Manitoba

TIMOTHY MATON

18. HOW IMPERIAL IMAGES DEMONIZE INDIGENOUS SPIRITUALITIES

INTRODUCTION

Even though it happened more than 500 years ago, the Protestant Reformation continues to affect how Anglo-Saxon people use pictures to demonize Indigenous spiritualities today. Consider, when reading this article, how demonizing images, like those that circulated during the Protestant Reformation, continue to be used to equate Indigenous spirituality with 'idolatry'. When doing this, let's think about how to resist that visual rhetoric, and how to strategize against it, and, how to repel its aesthetic message; by learning to identify what they look like and how it works. In endeavouring to do this, the work will articulate how the philosophical aesthetics of the Reformation have been constructed, aesthetically and philosophically, as a demonizing strategy, and, how it continues to propagate its demonizing rhetorics today.

My claim is that the philosophical precepts of the Reformation have been used to attack *pharmakon* (a term used to denote witches and magicians generally) by defining them in a manner that's evolved out of the Divine hermeneutics forwarded by St. Thomas Aquinas and St. Augustine. The philosophical aesthetics these two authors produced demonstrate why the Catholic worldview can be seen as syncretic to newer Protestant dogmas; and, show how they religiously justified Christian attacks against autochthonous peoples by portraying the Indigenous peoples as 'demon-worshippers' and terrorists. The rhetorical aesthetics of these Divines continue to be the most popular aesthetics weaponized against demonized peoples spirituality today; and, like other strategies of war, I believe these philosophical and aesthetic roots must be understood if their visual targets, the Indigenous peoples of Turtle Island, are to resist the attacks of their followers.

Resisting demonization means understanding how the philosophical precept called the "philosophy of history" has operated as a means to war synonymous with the timeless crusade against what the church deems 'evil'. It is essential to understand how the demonic Reformation prints thought about 'evil', ideologically, in a manner that it conceived as an imperial warfare engine useful for the genocidal war it fought against autochthonous peoples spiritual and physical health.

Christianity has traditionally antagonized worldly or earth-based spirituality because of how it sees itself as the spiritual antithesis to earth-based cultures. So, when St. Augustine of Hippo (354–450 AD) sets up the Christian dichotomy articulated

© KONINKLIJKE BRILL NV, LEIDEN, 2018 | DOI 9789004367418_018

TIMOTHY MATON

The City of God Against the Pagans, where he calls for a "philosophy of history", he puts forward the idea that there is an essential ideological conflict characterizing every interaction between any earth-based peoples and those who are spiritually Christian. There-in, the Christian 'Godly city' that Augustine puts forward within his book is eternally always at war with everything pagan and earthly. Therefore, he claims that the religion of Christ will never be reconciled with what he deems the Earthly City of the pagan.

Figure 1. A plate from Rev. Father Gallonio's Tortures and Torments of the Christian Martyrs *shows the Christian Martyrs being tortured by pagans and being forced to commit idolatry. In a metaphysical yet pictorial manner, this book was written as a how-to manual, demonstrating how, if the depicted situation got reversed, a Christian might go about torturing pagan people.*

Augustine's *dualism* is the root of an ideologically "religious doctrine that the universe contains opposed powers of good and evil" (NOAD, definition of "dualism"). Wherein, only "spiritual" Christian peoples can have spirit, and exist in "relation to, or affect... (of) the human spirit or soul (being)... opposed to material or physical things" (NOAD, "spiritual", parenthesis added).

Likewise to that, the English language has come to qualify 'spirituality' ideologically, in a manner that's both anti-autochthonous and antagonistically opposed to the ideal conception of 'things' being 'spiritual'. Hereby, in consideration of English and Eurocentric religious frameworks, the dualistic word 'spiritual', contains a Christian ultimatum; and requires that an English Christian should either deny the Earthly city and become spiritual, or otherwise, be damned to the earthly worship of material or physical things.

The word spiritual does not easily syncretize itself with the animist religion, where; "attribution of a soul to plants, inanimate objects, and natural phenomena" exists in a physical or material world. The English notion of spirit ideologically demonizes any "belief in a supernatural power that organizes and animates the material universe" (NOAD, "animism"). The English language religiously clarifies that, in accord to etymology; having faith in the power of objects brings the believer outside of the spiritual world, and, puts them in a relationship to the earth.

Likewise, during the English war against the *pharmakon*, King James expresses that same conceptual dualism, where he declares war upon all forms of magic by issuing his *Daemonologie* in order to legally support that war, while, in 1604, also authorizing the beginning of the work that would become the King James Bible. Thus, the creation story initiating the English translation of the Bible happens in context of a war that's waged against autochthonous relationships to the earth.

In ascending to his various thrones, James issues the *Daemonologie* twice. Once upon ascent to Scotland's throne (1597), and again upon ascent to the English (1603). In doing that, he makes his earnest intent clear; he will not offer mercy to those of his people whose faith makes them citizens of an Earthly city. And, when issuing the Bible in 1611; he shows in unambiguous terms that he intends to use this war to further his imperial interests.

His tract legally condones terrorizing soil-based healing practitioners. It wages war by circulating new visual definitions of magic, sorcery, necromancy, and witchcraft, and, he uses the worship of pictures to denounce people who practice soil-based healing traditions. He sets out to alienate Indigenous peoples from their land in a manner synchromeshed to existing print conventions – which are similar and comparable – and circulating in Reformation Germany. For example, Baldung's "Witches Sabbath" (1510) and Francisco Ugo Carp's "Diogenes" (1520–1530) very clearly articulate the philosophical manners of thinking found spoken in the picture-conventions affirmed by James in his 1597 + 1603 chronicles, like, for example, the earlier Witch-hunt Act (1542).

The definition of magic that's being circulated in Reformation prints, both Catholic and Protestant, are formulations of the way that pharmacologists, who were

Figure 2. Hans Baldung's "Witches' Sabbath"

Figure 3. Franciscus Ugo Carp's "Diogenes".

primarily women with knowledge of herbs or earthly medicine, could be accused of demon-worship (see Harrison's "The Two Reformations" for more about this). While the verbiage of the tract applies equally to both men and women, it also gives special attention to the evils of women. And, it blames them with extra force. In practice, it would be primarily women who would be targeted by it. Customary medicine people, or *pharmakon,* were, up until that time, heavily reliant upon earthly remedies or wisdom, and being an earth-healer gave women a central importance in the community. This had previously been tolerated by the ancient Catholic church. But under the new Reformation laws, a *pharmakon* could be easily convicted of devil-worship; leading to her being tortured and murdered.

That new situation was a result of a Reformation revision coming about after St. Augustine's work gained greater circulation. Augustine himself did not believe that magic and devil worship existed as literal powers of conjuration, so, *pharmakon* were allowed to work for the well-being of their community. James, however, sat in opposition to the denials provided by Augustine, and, he believed that devil-worship bestowed magical powers that were absolutely real and absolutely evil.

HOW THE REFORMATION WAS SYNCHROMESH WITH THE AUGUSTINIAN PHILOSOPHY OF HISTORY

The original thrust of Christians opposing pagans translated itself many times in Christian history. Shortly after the discovery of the New World, Christianity was thought to be opposed on the one hand to the societies of the New World and on the other to the heretics of Europe. The peoples of the New World were virtually destroyed by European invaders at the same time that Europe was being decimated by witch-hunts, the Inquisition, and religious wars. (Vine Deloria, *God is Red*)

During the witch-hunts of the Reformation, the old philosophy of history and the aforementioned dualism put forward by Augustine had been reinvented and retranslated to remake it into a new kind of Christianity useful for that particular imperial era. James Shotwell articulates an important understanding of what that meant in his *Encyclopedia Britannica* article "History" (1911). In that definitional record, Shotwell articulates the idea that Augustine's philosophical "idea... has underlain all Christian philosophy of history" (p. 529), and he writes that it was essential to their spiritual conviction that evil is real, that Christian empire building is good, and that history tells the ongoing story of a war between the transcendental city of God and the Earthly cities of the devil. In this ideological purview of history, all of the atrocities committed against Indigenous peoples, according to the Christian church, have been approbated by God. Thus, the "Philosophy of History" articulates an absolute dogma where all sins against the devil are supposedly forgiven by the Christian God, and any domestic act of war could be justified if it was an act against earthly 'evil'.

TIMOTHY MATON

When making these claims, the Church of England was not accepting the international bulls that had been decreed by the Pope. It is also questionable whether the Crown intended to abide by the Pope's *inter catera* decree, where the Pope granted Spain and Portugal's claims to areas of America.[1] The British Crown's primary religious endeavour was to dethrone that papal order, because England claimed the Pope was responsible for maintaining the devilish customs it saw magically inhabiting the lands it was annexing in Ireland, Scotland, and France.

In order to do this, England accused the papists of being pagans who believed in the devil. It rejected the ancient tenements of the ancient medieval church, saying, for example, that the papists must reject the notion of Divinity and their belief that "Natural objects, understood literally, pertain to the body of man... (including how they) pertain to his soul...". England questioned that old idea that any *pharmakia* had been "given to mankind to provide for his physical needs..." (Harrison, 1998, p. 20, quoting origen). Instead, it attacked traditional folk practitioners who care for people's earthly yet essential needs.

By calling for the eradication of all earthly Divinities and *pharmakia* in the isles, the Protestant church was critiquing and modifying the hermeneutics that had been put forward by St. Thomas Aquinas. It was also rejecting some aspects of the ancient Greek classical humanists- and retaining or modifying other aspects of the antique metaphysical system. Aquinas' claims that Divine powers are Godly and not inherently evil (having been given to people by God at creation), whereby, "Divine power extends over matter, as produced by God, it can be reduced to act by the Divine power... by matter being moved to a form... the act of matter" (Aquinas, 1225–1274). Thus, the ancient customs of acknowledging the Divine powers of matter and form, that had been permissibly useful before the Reformation (although never seen as spiritual substitute for the Worship of God), were no longer allowed.

King James, in *Daemonologie,* had explicatively interrogated the evils of the Greek system of learning, and deplored the Christian notion of the Divine. In this book, he seems to reject earth-based pharmacology at its root; in the soil.

He legalizes putting those who use soil-based processes of healing on trial, and advocates for the use of torture as a means to punish them. King James' explanation of why the war on the earth is legal and rational was derived from the story of Deuteronomy,[2] and specifically, from the story of King Saul. Whereby, James correlates the way Divines use pictures to soil-based healing practices. In it, he claims that anyone who deals in earthly substance (for ill or healing) "denies the power of the Deuill, denies the power of God, and are guiltie of the errour of the Sadduces" (King James, 1603, p. 53).[3]

King James's tract articulates the notion that, with the fall of King Saul, God has shown that he gives the right to sovereignty, only to those Kings who follow the Old Testament's (OT) laws, statutes, and ordinances. Any King who does not follow that rule was, for James, forfeit of their right to rule if they do not follow the OT rules of the Bible. That foremost rule, according to the story of Saul, means God

168

HOW THE IDOLATROUS REFORMATION DEFINED MAGIC USING PHILOSOPHICAL IMAGES

unequivocally bans the Divinations (and the Divines) who consult pictures. Because of King Saul's fall, King James felt empowered to declare that all non-Protestant States are in *diffidatio* to his Protestant faith, and, that the rule of any non-Protestant ruler was invalid. This, therefore, meant that their territory could be legally annexed to his.

It was for this reason that he did style himself the King of France, Ireland (and beyond), despite not actually having the physical power to control the people in those Kingdoms (also see Deloria, 1973).

HOW THE IDOLATROUS REFORMATION DEFINED MAGIC USING PHILOSOPHICAL IMAGES

James' claim to sovereignty has been built using an OT Biblical account of King Saul's consultation with a Divine named "The Witch of Endor". In it, King Saul lost his throne because of his consultation with a Divine who conjured a picture of his future. Having thus lost the support of God, Saul dies in battle with the Philistines, and the King's Temple is ransacked. The Temple's sacralised devices, which are described throughout the OT, are then rendered profane by nature of having engaged in the wrong kind of worship (Kings 24:4).

HOW IDOLATROUS IMAGERY ARTICULATES REFORMATION IDEOLOGY IN CORRESPONDENCE TO NOTIONS OF THE SACRAL AND THE PROFANE

Baldung's "Witches Sabbath" and Franciscus Parmen Ugo Carp's "Diogenes" are excellent exemplars of the way printed pictures get used to define magic, necromancy, sorcery, and witchcraft during the early Reformation. In accord to the idea of evil they demonstrate; the picture becomes a conventional way to fallaciously claim that a non-Christian 'evil' is 'real'. The picture, being synonymous to evil, would be used to vilify Indigenous peoples in the Red River region of Turtle Island by picturing them in a manner that demonstrated their *diffidatio* to the rule of law, and the Christian God.

For example, in the "Witches' Sabbath" (1510), it clearly demonstrates what the basic witch archetype looks like. In "Diogenes", by Ugo Carp (1524–7), the idea of evil is complicated, and the image goes beyond the literal depiction of sorcery or necromancy, and becomes an exceptional trope that appears similar to sorcery and necromancy, but is vague though conclusive with regard to its pronunciation of 'evil'. The image of Diogenes has a different target audience, which gives it a distinct purpose, as it is aimed at *intelligentsia*, and depicts how the act of identifying a sorcerer or necromancer can be a cryptic exercise. Thus, according to that nuance, it complicates the process of recognizing demon-worship among learned and educated people.

Both images portray visual conventions that can be used to identify paganism and *diffidatio* to the OT God of the Bible. At the time, prints had become reproducible,

TIMOTHY MATON

and Baldung's work had contributed to the creation of new print technologies. Thus, his work could be circulated among churches where they would be used as teaching tools that helped clergy identify the demon-worshippers in their community. The prints were designed to help people recognize *pharmakon* , with the aim of putting them on trial, torturing, and killing.

In those images, the symbolic presence of poultry and the grindstone was much rehearsed, and can be imagined as an analogy to an essence of humanity, aka, its soul. The sacral object of the image was an animated object, ritualistically repeating old conventions in new ways analogous to the common, generic, or concrete experience of peoples whose correlation to the sacral objects of the world. It could be seen as something that had been redefined in accord to both Biblical and Reformation philosophical conventions (like those established in the works embodied in King James' Bible, St. Augustine, or St. Aquinas) (see Figures 18.2 and 18.3).

The image called "Diogenes" is a depiction of a learned Greek pagan and rebel who is posed like a Greek Heracles. His devilry is expressed in his characteristically ascetic and rebellious visual nature. In the story of Diogenes, he is said to live in a barrel that is located close to the Greek Agora (or marketplace). Hence, Diogenes' residence is ambiguously somewhere between the natural world (or Earthly city) and the Godly.

This treacherous learned man, who is satanic because he has rejected his father's religion, was probably seen with revulsion (see Harrison's chapter "The Two Reformations"). This personage's sorcery was probably also tropic, in that, he might be seen as demonic, since he is pagan, but also as a potentially redeemable pagan, as he lived before Christ's coming and could have been 'raked' from hell by Christ's raking of the pagans. The image demonstrates the conventions of the sorcerer's religion by physically posturing him to resemble a demon-worshipper. Because he is Greek, he is from a society that predates Christianity, and it is uncertain whether he could be saved from hell by the coming of Christ, but his *diffidatio* to his father makes this seem unlikely. In Diogenes arms, he holds a chicken that also looks a lot like grindstone (but it may or may not be one), but may instead be an animistic and transformational object.

Diogenes' appearance is both learned and wild; he is a syncretic and analogous representation of magic. His factitious satanism is embedded in his being a rebel who has rejected his nation and his father, and that's why he lives in a barrel. The evil of Diogenes is thus arguably analogously real; it exists is an implied state revealed by having correspondence to an ideological convention that's visually absolute, but also, cognitively ambiguous and conceptually challenging.

Beside Diogenes, a plucked chicken demonstrates the presence of an animistic system of logic; the imaged thing is not a representation of animism in itself, but is an embodiment of a conventional sorcery that's also debatable. The animated chicken dancing beside him is a trope, because it parodies Plato's absurd oral statement that humans are categorically "featherless bipeds" (British Museum). That oral allusion, however, when comparing the human being to a plucked chicken, is

170

from oral culture and Reformation folk-lore; it's never been proven by any written ancient manuscript. The witticism of that damning oral relay portrays Diogenes as a trickster, and attacks how, in Socratic humanism, a person was anecdotally chicken. It is, of itself, an illustration of how the sorcerous image only represents one fraction of the whole story, but is probably none-the-less 'evil' by OT standards.

When I encountered Robert Brown's encyclopedic *The Countries of the World...*, I saw that its supposedly objective and factual representations of Indigenous peoples in Canada repeated the religiously contrived aesthetic conventions of the Sixteenth century. This "popular account" is an atlas of the world, and is rich in maps and illustrations that claim to scientifically document the entire world's races, landscapes, countries, etc. The publication was printed for popular audiences, and many of its images visually repeat the old Reformation conventions perceptible in "Diogenes" and "Witches Sabbath".

Figure 4. Robert Brown's "An Old Squaw Pounding Cherries"

TIMOTHY MATON

Brown's racist picture, "An old Squaw Pounding Cherries: A Scene in the Red River Country" shows an Aboriginal woman pictorially repeating the old conventions already used by English imperialists when they sought to articulate what earthly animism, witchery, and possibly even sorcery looked like in European religion. Exemplifying those conventions, the woman in the portrait holds a pounding stone, which reminds me of the chickens in the other two images, and, I speculate she has inherited her traditional aesthetics, not specifically from "Diogenes" and "Witches Sabbath" themselves, but from the common, generic, or concrete images developed following the conventions that got set after their time. Beside her, an idyll man smokes what could possibly be a sacred pipe.

Like in "Diogenes" and "Witches Sabbath", the Indigenous characters seated in the Red River Valley are shown factitiously, being homeless, residing in nature (or between it). The woman depicted is metaphorically speaking, within the pagan "Earthly city". Both of the characters in the picture are depicted holding objects that Christians deemed sacral, and there is no Temple depicted nearby to make those objects spiritually obedient to what Christians would see as God's OT law. The two figures presented in the image are made to appear very Earthly and animistic, thus their citizenship in the City of God, or civilization, is very doubtful, and thus, by Protestant standards, their sovereignty appears deposable to the English audience it is meant for.

CONCLUSION

Civilization had created a savage, so to kill him. Idea had begotten image, so to kill it. (Francis Jennings, *The Invasion of America*)

Francis Jennings aptly describes how Europeans transported the "ideas and institutions with which they conquered and colonized at home..." to America. According to Jennings, the Old World devices were used to define Indigenous peoples society in North America in much the same way they had been used in the Old Country (1975, p. 3, parenthesis added).

Europeans first reached Turtle Island four years after King James issued *Daemonologie* in England, and yet, there is no doubt that the British Crown had always intended to make an absolute claim, based on the Divine right of Kings, to the land in North America. The English sovereign intended to extend his sovereignty over everything known to him, using metaphysical forms of law. The Reformation's philosophy of history clearly shows that the Crown saw that imperial Kingdom as an infinite and expandable universe that went way beyond any visible or physical world. When seeking to expand their imperial domain, a common British colonial strategy was to frame things using what seemed to be scientific aesthetically; but what that fundamentally amounted to was very thinly masked religious ideologies that desire an imperially expanded territory. The Crown's aim was to visually

172

misrepresent savagery in a manner that could allow its extirpation of Indigenous sovereignty, world-wide.

When doing this, the imperialistic colonizer transitively fused "'the magic of the primitive'" to colonialism's "'own magic, the magic of primitivism,'…" (Vizener quoting Taussig's *Shamanism, Colonialism and the Wild Man*). Whereby, "The (colonial) contradictor (intentionally depicts) figures of the wild and primitive, (being) 'less than human and more than human', because he wants to transform them into "the fetishized anti-selves made by civilizing histories'" (p. 38, parenthesis added). In that revisioning of Indigeneity, the misrepresented pagan is presented as a thing that's metaphysically a monster incompatible with any kind of religiously civilized society.

When creating these kinds of contemporary misrepresentations, colonials are visually justifying a spiritual war against what they misrepresent as a primitive threat. This is not unlike what Augustine did when he wrote his justifications of war against the earthly. Likewise, the colonizer ideologically reinvents the magic of print to *demonstrably* show that Indigenous peoples are either intellectually less human than the common person, or are a super-human exception to normal standards. Thus, the Anglo-Saxon mind portrays the pagan as a thing visibly incompatible with its status-quo society. In doing this, its pictorial goal is to damn Indigenous peoples, by portraying them as monsters or demons.

For Vizener, the most common imagery produced to represent Indians is not really about 'Indians' at all. He writes that the supposedly objective "simulations (of tribal spirit)… (really) have no referent (to Indigeneity)… in (Indigenous) language and experience…" (p. 98). And therefore, are not accurate or factual or scientific, even if they claim to be objective in that manner. The English simulation of reality, in-itself, has very little or nothing in common with what Indigenous linguistic cultures experience in them self, and is, therefore, a monstrous invention in and of itself.

Likewise, W.J.T. Mitchell provides eye-opening insight into how Christian images have *created* the notion of the pagan by making claims that merely *represent* the pagan. In his book *What Do Pictures Want?* He describes how animistic images, or *imagos,* have been scientifically structured by an imperialistic impulse that wants to make pictures "symptoms of what they signify" working "within a total system" that produces and reproduces simulated notions that go on parade as absolute truths.

The Anishnabe scholar Gerald Vizenor has also observed the way that imperial images are, objectively speaking, ideological fabrications that can only *claim* to be objective representations of Indigeneity. For him, imperial images claim to represent Indigenous peoples, but this is an objectively untruthful claim; because the truth of an imperial image is contrived to convince its audience of something, when really, a truthful image should simply *be the truth,* it need not *convince.*

Exemplifying this, Vizenor writes that "(t)he tribal referent" and an Indigenous notion of self is rarely pictured, by colonial or imperial pictures, because Anishnabe reality is more real than pictures can depict. The 'tribal referent' inside an image cannot be found in the old scientific records because the pictured reality isn't simply

TIMOTHY MATON

pictorial; it actually exists "in the shadows of heard stories... (where) shadows are their own referent" (p. 98). A truly tribal reference given by Christian or western imagery is not a factual or historical truth in any scientific or religious sense, but is a "shadow" found in the "silence and simulations of survivance"(ibid).

When saying this, Vizenor is not presuming that abstract ideas must always be seen as things that are distinct from the living image that communicates their messages. He is not conceding to the Western ban on worshipping images. Instead, he is asking his reader to 'braid' and 'plait' the meaning of the image together with a spiritual outlook that's non-colonized, or, decolonial. For him, learning to recognize the ways that meanings and images are related requires looking at how meaning and objecthood are unified in the thing.

To me, doing this means having a metaphysical understanding of images that's autochthonous, and defies the anti-autochthonous definitions coined by western authors like Aquinas, Augustine, and King James. As Dean Radar writes (when quoting Vizenor, 2015):

> ... the (A)nishnabe did not have a written history"... (but) "The past was a visual memory and oratorical gesture of dreams plaiting an endless woodland identity between the conscious and unconscious worlds of the people. The song poems of the (A)nishnabe are intuitive lyrical images of woodland life. (p. 303, parenthesis added)

NOTES

[1]   The Peace of Westphalia called for equality between Protestant and Catholic peoples and redefined sovereignty in 1648.

[2]   The Second Commandment of the *Decalogue*, proclaims:

> You shall not make for yourself a graven image, or any likeness of anything that is in heaven above, or that is in the water under the earth; you shall not bow down to them or serve them.... (Deuteronomy 5:8)

James himself does not directly refer to this, but his reliance upon 'the law' pointedly goes in that direction.

[3]   James writes:

> ... even as God by his Sacramantes which are erthlie of themselves workes a heavonlie effect... (but unlike clay and spittle, which work with heavenly effect) there was no vertue in that which he outwardlie applied (p. 43)

and therefore works by the devil and magic.

REFERENCES

Aquinas, T. S. (1225–1274). Question 105: The change of creatures by God. *Summa Theologiae*. Canonicus Surmont, Vicarius Generalis. Westmonasterii. Approbatio Ordinis. 1920.

Baldung, H. (1510). Witches' sabbath. British Museum. Retrieved from http://www.britishmuseum.org/research/collection_online/collection_object_details.aspx?objectId=1424213&partId=1

HOW IMPERIAL IMAGES DEMONIZE INDIGENOUS SPIRITUALITIES

Brown, R. (1876). An old squaw pounding wild cherries. In *The countries of the world: Being a popular description of the various continents, islands, rivers, seas, and peoples of the globe* (Vol. 1, p. 205). London, UK: Cassel, Petter, Galpin & Co.

Deloria, Jr., V. (1969). *Custer died for your sins: An Indian manifesto.* Norman, OK: University of Oklahoma Press.

Deloria, Jr., V. (1973). *God is red.* New York, NY: Grosset & Dunlap.

Gallonio, Rev. Father, & Allinson, A. R. (Trans.). (1903). *Tortures and torments of the Christian martyrs: From "De SS Martyrum Cruciatibus".* London, UK: William Brendon and Son.

Harrison, P. (1998). The two reformations. In *The Bible, Protestantism, and the Rise of Natural Science.* Cambridge, UK: Cambridge University Press. 1591.

James. (1603). *Daemonologie, in Forme of a dialogue, divided into three bookes.* London, UK: William Cotton & Will Aspley.

Jennings, F. (1975). *The invasion of America: Indians, colonialism, and the cant of conquest.* Williamsburg, VA: Omohundro Institute of Early American History and Culture.

Mitchell, W. J. T. (2005). *What do pictures want?* Chicago, IL: University of Chicago Press.

New Oxford American Dictionary. (2010). Oxford University Press.

O'Connor, P. (2010). *Derrida: Profanations.* New York, NY: Continuum International Publishing Group.

Rader, D. (2015). Reading the visual, seeing the verbal: Text and image in recent American Indian literature and art. On *The Oxford handbook of Indigenous American literature.* New York, NY: Oxford University Press.

Shotwell, J. (1911). History. In *Encyclopedia Britannica.* Cambridge, UK: Cambridge University Publishing.

Ugo Carp, F. (1520–1530). *Diogenes, a woodcut after Parmigianino.* British Museum. Retrieved June 15, 2017, from http://culturalinstitute.britishmuseum.org/asset-viewer/ugo-da-carpi-diogenes-a-woodcut-after-parmigianino/bgHJLpwNLBqwYg?hl=en

Vizenor, G. (1993). *Manifest manners: Postindian warriors of survivance.* Hanover, NY: Wesleyan University Press.

Timothy Maton
Native Studies
University of Manitoba

MIRIAM MARTENS

19. AN 'INDIAN' INDUSTRY

*Tourism and the Exploitation of Indigenous Cultures
in the Canadian West*

The depiction of Indigenous peoples in both tourist advertisements and events has become one of Canada's strongest branding strategies since Confederation in 1867. As the Canadian Tourism Committee (CTC) notes, Canada has two primary attributes that attract tourists: a vast landscape and, more importantly, the presence of "authentic" Indigenous peoples.[1] This article examines the changing depiction of Indigenous peoples in Western Canada's tourism industry, specifically focusing on tourist advertisements and events since 1867. In the years between Confederation and the Second World War, Canada's tourism industry capitalized upon depictions of Indigenous peoples, with tourists being offered the rare opportunity to see a "race" that was "dying off" because of their "savage" nature and alleged inability to adapt to an increasingly modern society. Since the mid-twentieth century, however, the depiction of Canada's Indigenous peoples in tourism advertisements and events has shifted in an attempt to emphasize the multicultural nature of Canada and its continuing effort to preserve (rather than eradicate) Indigenous traditions.

Prior to the construction of the Canadian Pacific Railway (CPR) tourists were restricted to exploring the eastern half of Canada as "the rocky terrain and fear of large and powerful Indigenous nations that had yet to be dominated by Canada's colonial hand."[2] However, as a condition of confederation for eastern provinces in 1867 and British Columbia in 1881, a transcontinental rail line was constructed. Completed in November 1885, the CPR soon recognized that tourism could aid in subsidizing the costs of running a national rail company. Initially, advertisements capitalized on services offered by the rail company, such as a luxurious seating, food, and beverages.[3] However, Daniel Francis writes that "comfort was not enough: travelers had to be offered spectacle," first provided in the form of Canada's western landscape.[4] It was then brought to the CPR's attention that many photographers were taking pictures of Indigenous peoples during their travels and selling them to tourists wanting a reminder of the "exotic" peoples they had only ever heard about before their travels.[5] The CPR then moved to capitalize on the marketing potential of Indigenous peoples and their cultures, as postcards and pictures featuring "Indians" became one of the company's most effective marketing strategies. As souvenirs, postcards allowed wealthy travelers to return home and share the wonders of Canada

© KONINKLIJKE BRILL NV, LEIDEN, 2018 | DOI 9789004367418_019

with others. One photograph from the 1880s featuring a Cree family and travois was available for sale to travelers as a memento of their journey to Western Canada along the CPR (Figure 1). For tourists, the picture provided a lasting reminder of the "exotic Indian" and his family. Simultaneously, it served as an incentive for those who had not yet had the opportunity to view the dying "Indian" in its "natural habitat" to travel westward. Pictures and postcards bought by tourists served as both advertisements and a form of commemoration – a snapshot of a culture that was soon to become "extinct" because of its inability to become "civilized."

Figure 1. Cree family with travois, near Calgary, Alberta (reprinted with permission from the Glenbow Archives, Calgary, Alberta)

Postcards found in the personal collections of famed Canadian writer Pauline Johnson also demonstrate the use Indigenous peoples for increased tourism. Johnson travelled across North America and England in the late-nineteenth and early-twentieth century performing her work for a wide variety of audiences. She collected postcards from the many places she visited, a significant number of which feature the stereotypical "rare and wild Indian" of Western Canada. A postcard from 1907 titled "Chief Joe Healy and Braves" features a group of Indigenous men on horses, outfitted in traditional garb (Figure 2). With modern town buildings and a water tower in the background, the juxtaposition of traditional and modern civilizations within a single frame emphasizes the "Indian's primitiveness" and inability to adapt to an increasingly industrialized nation. As the central figure in the picture, Chief Joe Healy – whose status is indicated by his white horse and large headdress – embodies the "Noble Savage," an Indian stereotype that remains "a symbol of the natural virtue of the New World."[6] As a Noble Savage, Chief Joe

Healy was viewed as ignorantly leading his people into extinction as they failed to assimilate and become part of the modern Canadian society pictured behind them.

Figure 2. Chief Joe Healy and Braves (reprinted with permission from the William Ready Division of Archives and Research Collections, McMaster University Library)

Johnson's collection also contains a postcard that starkly contrasts the image of the Noble Savage. Instead, the "Ignoble Savage" – who was viewed as violent, unpredictable, and consequently a detriment to settlement in the West – was featured on a postcard entitled "Indian Arrest by Mounted Police, Canadian West."[7] The postcard shows Indigenous men holding rifles as two Mounted Police approach them on horseback (Figure 3). On horseback and in their distinctive uniform, the Mounted Police appear far superior to the "savage" Indians. This superiority is only

Figure 3. Indian arrest by mounted police, front (reprinted with permission from the William Ready Division of Archives and Research Collections, McMaster University Library)

confirmed on the reverse side of the postcard where a short paragraph explains that the dangerous nature of the "Redskins" was no match compared to the patriotic determination of the Northwest Mounted Police (Figure 4). Thus, a confrontation between good and evil is depicted on this souvenir – the redcoat protectors of the nation versus the rabble-rousing "Redskins." As Francis notes, Mounties are the heroes in Canada's nation-building adventure story, offering Indians the possibility of progress and effortlessly subduing those who resist.[8] From the safety of a railcar, tourists could travel through Western Canada and see the increasingly rare Noble Savage or they could travel along the same railway used by Mounties and visit where the Ignoble Savage was defeated and civilized by Canada's quintessential law enforcement.

Figure 4. *Indian arrest by mounted police, reverse (reprinted with permission from the William Ready Division of Archives and Research Collections, McMaster University Library)*

Promotional items nurtured tourists' excitement regarding the possibility of seeing Canada's "exotic Indian." However, travellers did not always encounter the same "Indian" portrayed in advertisements that they hoped to encounter. In his 1891 book *By Track and Trail*, world traveler Edward Roper writes about seeing a group of Blackfoot by a railway station in Saskatchewan. Roper notes that many of the Blackfoot people were "partly civilized in dress… [and] had good faces, but the ideal Red Man was not there."[9] Later, as Roper travelled through Alberta, he saw Indigenous peoples adorned with paint, feathers, and traditional clothing. Consequently, Roper's desire to see the "ideal Red Man" advertised to him as essential to Western Canada's exoticism was fulfilled. Nearing the turn of the century, the reality was that many of

AN 'INDIAN' INDUSTRY

the Indigenous peoples in Canada were becoming part of white, "civilized" society as they were pushed onto reserve lands and forced to assimilate. Initially, tourists did not mind seeing the "civilized Indian" along their journey as it made the "traditional Indians" they encountered appear to be dying off. Travelling to Western Canada was therefore considered one of the final opportunities to view the rare "Red Man."[10]

In the years leading up to the First World War and during the 1920s, Canadian tourism continued to prosper.[11] However, the industry became stagnant with the onset of the Great Depression. In the decades following the Second World War, Canada's tourism industry was renewed and went through a period of intense growth with the development of mass tourism, offering "standardized, packaged tours with 'low levels of involvement.'"[12] Alongside the emergence of mass tourism there developed a change in the depiction of Indigenous peoples in advertisements for Western Canada. Although Indigenous peoples were still situated in the past and not represented as they lived in contemporary society, they were now portrayed as an integral part of Canada's heritage. During the mid-1980s, referencing Indigenous cultures became a core element in promoting Canada as an inherently accepting and multicultural nation.[13] Portraying Canada as a nation that was innately "native" was a way in which the country distinguished itself from other travel destinations. A government poster from the mid-1980s featured in Valda Blundell's research provides an example of how the tourism industry claimed Indigenous artwork as representative of the Canadian West.[14] The poster features a Northwest Coast Totem Pole and the word "Canada" centered below the image, along with a small Canadian flag. The image insinuates that Canada takes pride in its multicultural past and that Indigenous peoples are at the heart of the country's development. Totem poles are particularly representative of British Columbia, as Francis writes that "almost every provincial milestone has been celebrated with the raising of a pole" whether related to Indigenous accomplishments or not.[15] Sociologist Renisa Mawani comments on the presence of totem poles along Canada's Pacific Coast, specifically those found at Brockton Point in Stanley Park that, as of 2017, attract 8 million visitors annually.[16] The irony, however, is that the vast majority of totem poles found in Stanley Park represent the Kwakwaka'wakw and Haida Nations of Northern British Columbia, not the Coast Salish who typically voice ancestral and legal claims to the land on which the park is founded.[17] Carved into the totem poles are stories and histories specific to the Kwakwaka'wakw and Haida Nations, but the intense spiritual meaning of these carvings are lost when not displayed on the land of their respective nations.[18] Mawani writes that totem poles are national art forms that have come to signify "both a Native Otherness and... Canada's national heritage" – a heritage no longer dominated by colonization but by multiculturalism.[19]

Souvenirs bought by tourists have also become an invaluable method of advertising, as they are both a reminder of and promotion for places tourists visit. When touring the Canadian West, there are a plethora of souvenirs available for sale – such as clothing and trinkets – depicting Indigenous cultures. Valda Blundell refers to these as "native-type" souvenirs, the majority of which are not made by Indigenous peoples but are mass produced.[20] Blundell recalls a trip to the Toronto

181

Fall Gift Show in 1990 with over 700 exhibitors at the Canadian National Exhibition Grounds.[21] Amongst all the exhibitors, approximately two-dozen were selling "native-type" souvenirs that were mass-produced by non-Indigenous companies and on the low-end of the price spectrum.[22] Blundell also noticed that the number of booths selling "native-type" souvenirs far outweighed the select few selling authentically Indigenous, handcrafted items.[23] Like the pictures and postcards sold as souvenirs by the CPR, souvenirs sold a century later also failed to portray Indigenous peoples in a contemporary and accurate manner. Native-type souvenirs have become representative of Canada's "native" heritage, as they are not sold to tourists as a reminder of Indigenous peoples they may have encountered, but as "keepsakes of the country" visited.[24] Tourists, therefore, return home with inauthentic, mass-produced mementos that advertise Canada as a multicultural nation trying to preserve the traditions of its Indigenous population.

Regarding actual places and events that tourists have come to see since Confederation, they follow the same trajectory as Canadian tourism advertisements concerning Indigenous peoples, shifting from a narrative of colonization to one of multiculturalism and preservation. However, a constant in the portrayal of Indigenous peoples since Confederation has been the element of spectacle, which requires individuals to act according to societal expectations rather than portraying their culture authentically. Banff Indian Days are an example of the spectacle surrounding the "Indian" in Canada's history. This event developed in 1894 when a flood washed out a portion of the railway tracks in Banff, forcing one of the CPR's tourist trains to stop. The rail company then sent a local guide down to the Stoney reserve at Morley "to invite the Indians back to Banff to entertain the marooned travellers."[25] The guide returned with a group of Indigenous people who performed traditional dances and competed for prizes in rodeo events organized by the CPR. This unplanned performance was so popular that the CPR, in conjunction with local businesses, decided to make Banff Indian Days an annual occurrence every summer until 1978. This event attracted thousands of tourists from both across Canada and the globe as it provided an opportunity for people to see the rare "Indian" in person.

In 1920, the 250th anniversary of the Hudson's Bay Company (HBC) was another grand occasion featuring Indigenous peoples. Writing about the Red River Pageant – one of the many events celebrating the HBC's anniversary – historian Peter Geller examines the commemorative album compiled after the celebration. Within the album, one image is particularly telling in terms of how pageant's organizers wished to portray Indigenous peoples' to tourists. The image shows Chief Kinnewakan passing a filled pipe of peace to Governor Sir Robert Kindersley. Geller notes that this photograph was meant to epitomize the celebration of a "two-hundred-year-old friendship," just as the pageant had been advertised.[26] However, although this image suggests friendship, it is a friendship dominated by colonizers. For example, Geller comments on the positioning of Kindersley in relation to Kinnewakan, as the former towers over the latter while accepting the peace pipe. Geller also notes that Kindersley's top hat and his position on a stage "adds further height to his imposing frame," and consequently is a physical representation of hierarchy in 1920s Canadian society – the "uncivilized Indian" as submissive and dependent on the "civilized" white man.[27] Serving as an advertisement to come and experience Canada's unique heritage, the album of the 1920 Red River Pageant portrayed Indigenous peoples in a "traditional" fashion as organizers strove to present an "idealized view of the 'real Indian.'"[28]

Examining Indigenous representation after the Second World War, the Olympics are a spectacle that attracts worldwide attention. Canada is privileged to have hosted the international sporting event three times, two of which took place in Western Canada. In planning the Opening Ceremony of the 1988 Calgary Olympic Games, organizers wanted to focus on three figures they believed to be the backbone of Calgary's "unique western heritage": the Royal Canadian Mounted Police (RCMP), the "Indian," and the Cowboy.[29] The Opening Ceremony thus began with the entrance of the Calgary Stampede Showband, after which the audience was asked to "please welcome our native Albertans: the tribes of Treaty 7 of 1877, a treaty still in effect and honoured today." Representatives of five prairie nations then rode into the stadium on horseback while wearing traditional garb.[30] Despite the seemingly inclusive nature of the Opening Ceremony thus far, Cath Ellis argues that there is a very prominent possessive narrative to the festivities, particularly the welcoming of Indigenous peoples into the stadium. Ellis notes that by welcoming "*our* native Albertans," the tribes of Treaty 7 were showcased as a possession of past colonial powers and remained so as visitors were awarded the authority to welcome Canada's Indigenous peoples to their own land.[31] Furthermore, the order of performances within the Opening Ceremony contributed to the display of a hierarchy of power. After the Tribes of Treaty 7, performers from the Calgary Stampede entered the stadium followed by the "world –famous Royal Canadian Mounted Police" who performed an abbreviated version of their Musical Ride.[32] In featuring the Musical Ride, Olympic organizers were perpetuating what Jennifer Adese refers to as the "benevolent Mountie myth." Adese argues that Mounties have been romanticized in Canadian public memory as protectors of the Canadian West who ensured that the prairies were safe for settlement.[33] The Mountie is remembered in Canadian history as subduing the "fiery spirit of the Indian," and the order in which performances occurred in Calgary's Opening Ceremony broadcasted this myth to an international audience. Although the Calgary Olympics did not depict Canada's multiculturalism in the same fashion as the aforementioned post-war advertisements – which focused on the nation's innate "nativeness" – the Opening Ceremony did communicate to the world that, thanks to the efforts of the RCMP, "Indians" and settlers were now on peaceful terms and able to co-exist.

The 2010 Vancouver Olympics, however, did see Canada portrayed as a multicultural nation that *embraced* its Indigenous heritage. The 2010 Vancouver Winter Olympics differed substantially from the preceding Olympic Games hosted by Canada as, for the first time in Olympic history, the Four Host First Nations (FHFN) – the Lil'wat, Musqueam, Squamish, and Tseil-Waututh – were considered equal partners of the Vancouver Organizing Committee (VANOC).[34] In the Bid Book

MIRIAM MARTENS

compiled by the Vancouver Olympic bid team, it was argued that Vancouver should host the Olympics because of how the city embraced multiculturalism and because "Canada brings together the cultures of the world, as well as an ancient and rich First Nations culture, in one harmonious society."[35] In total, over 300 Indigenous peoples from across Canada participated in the Olympic Opening Ceremony, which began with representatives from the FHFN welcoming the audience in their vernacular, English, and in French. Next, hundreds of Indigenous peoples entered the stadium performing the traditional dances of their Nation. All stopping to raise their hands, the announcer declared that "... on behalf of all Canadians, the Aboriginal peoples of Canada welcome the athletes of the twenty-first winter games." Ellis notes that the welcome was a particularly important moment in the opening ceremony as it demonstrated to an international audience that "Indigenous sovereignty can co-exist with Canadian sovereignty."[36] Like the souvenirs that can be purchased when travelling to Western Canada, the Indigenous peoples in Vancouver's Opening Ceremony were depicted as emblematic of Canada. This spectacle saw Indigenous peoples portrayed as being at the heart of Canadian heritage – an ironic statement when one considers how Indigenous peoples have suffered at the hands of the Canadian government since Confederation, being cordoned off into reserves and forced to assimilate. Rather, this spectacle should be considered as the heart of a very specific Canadian heritage, one that was constructed by a settle colonial society that maintains its hegemonic authority over "authenticity" in Canada's heritage industry.

In examining the history of Western Canada's tourism industry since Confederation, a trend in the representation of Indigenous peoples in both advertisements and events becomes clear. In its formative years, Canada's tourism industry needed to present travellers with something that made Canada a unique and intriguing place to visit. This pursuit of a "unique quality" was achieved through the promotion of the spectacle of the "real Indians." In the years between Confederation and the 1930s, Indigenous peoples were seen as a race that was soon to be extinct due to their inability to adapt to modern civilization. With Indigenous peoples always depicted in a "traditional" manner, travellers flocked to Canada's West for what was believed to be one of their final chances to view the "Red Man." After the Second World War, Canada was instead promoted to tourists as a nation that embraced its multicultural heritage. Elements of Indigenous cultures were, and still are, advertised as representative of Canada, glossing over the negative interactions between Euro-Canadians and Indigenous peoples throughout the nation's history. With tourism remaining one of the most lucrative industries in Canada's economy, the nation's tourism industry should strive to find a way of presenting Indigenous history in a way that is both interesting and truthful.

NOTES

[1]   Jennifer Adese. (2012). *Aboriginal: Constructing the aboriginal and imagineering the Canadian national brand* (PhD Thesis). McMaster University, Hamilton.

AN 'INDIAN' INDUSTRY

[2] Adese, "Aboriginal," 59.
[3] Daniel Francis, *The Imaginary Indian: The Image of the Indian in Canadian Culture* (Vancouver: Arsenal Pulp Press, 1992), 179.
[4] Francis, *The Imaginary Indian,* 179.
[5] Francis, *The Imaginary Indian,* 179.
[6] Francis, *The Imaginary Indian,* 13.
[7] Francis, *The Imaginary Indian,* 81.
[8] Francis, *The Imaginary Indian,* 81.
[9] Roper, *By Track and Trail,* 119.
[10] Francis, *The Imaginary Indian,* 182.
[11] Adese, "Aboriginal," 63.
[12] Adese, "Aboriginal," 63.
[13] Valda Blundell. (2002). Aboriginal cultural tourism in Canada. In J. Nicks & J. Sloniowski (Eds.), *Slippery pastimes: Reading the popular in Canadian culture* (p. 41). Waterloo: Wilfrid Laurier University Press.
[14] Valda Blundell. (1989). Speaking the Art of Canada's Native Peoples: Anthropological Discourse and the Media. *Australian-Canadian Studies, 7*(1–2), 34.
[15] Francis, *The Imaginary Indian,* 186.
[16] Stanley Park. *TripAdvisor Canada.* https://www.tripadvisor.ca/Attraction_Review-g154943-d155652-Reviews-Stanley_Park-Vancouver_British_Columbia.html (accessed June 1, 2017).
[17] Renisa Mawani, "From Colonialism to Multiculturalism? Totem Poles, Tourism, and National Identity in Vancouver's Stanley Park." *ARIEL: A Review of International English Literature,* 35 (2004): 36. As of 2017, there are nine totem poles at Brockton Point. The only totem pole representative of the Squamish Nation was carved by Robert Yelton, whose late mother was the last surviving resident of the Brockton community. This meaningful carving was not commissioned until almost ninety-years after the first totem poles were collected in Stanley Park. There are other carvings and gateways made by Squamish, Tsleil-Waututh and Musqueam First Nations artists whose traditional territory is Stanley Park, however, the totem poles maintain their status as Stanley Park's greatest tourist attraction.
[18] Mawani, "From Colonialism to Multiculturalism," 31.
[19] Mawani, "From Colonialism to Multiculturalism," 37.
[20] Valda Blundell. (1993, January). Aboriginal empowerment and souvenir trade in Canada. *Annals of Tourism Research, 20*(1), 65.
[21] Blundell, "Aboriginal Empowerment and Souvenir Trade in Canada," 65.
[22] Blundell, "Aboriginal Empowerment and Souvenir Trade in Canada," 68.
[23] Blundell, "Aboriginal Empowerment and Souvenir Trade in Canada," 68.
[24] Blundell, "Aboriginal Empowerment and Souvenir Trade in Canada," 68.
[25] Francis, *The Imaginary Indian,* 179.
[26] Geller, "Hudson's Bay Company Indians," 68.
[27] Geller, "Hudson's Bay Company Indians," 69.
[28] Geller, "Hudson's Bay Company Indians," 72.
[29] Adese, "Aboriginal," 109.
[30] Cath Ellis. (2012, May). The possessive logic of settler-invader nations in olympic ceremonies. *Journal of Tourism and Cultural Change, 10*(2), 112.
[31] Ellis, "The Possessive logic of settler-invader nations in Olympic ceremonies,"112.
[32] CODA, *XV Olympic Winter Games Organizing Committee* (Edmonton: Jasper Printing Group Ltd., 1988), p. 295.
[33] Adese, "Aboriginal," 112.
[34] Gardiner, A. (Ed.). (2010). *With glowing hearts: The official commemorative book of the XXI olympic winter games and the X paralympic winter games.* Mississauga: John Wiley & Sons Canada, Ltd.
[35] VANOC. *Vancouver 2010 Bid Books: Volume 1–3* (Vancouver: Vancouver Olympic Bid Committee, 2002), p. 3.
[36] Ellis, "The Possessive logic of settler-invader nations in Olympic ceremonies," 117.

185

MIRIAM MARTENS

REFERENCES

Adese, J. (2012). *Aboriginal: Constructing the aboriginal and imagineering the Canadian National Brand* (PhD Thesis). McMaster University, Hamilton.

Blundell, V. (1989). Speaking the art of Canada's native peoples: Anthropological discourse and the media. *Australian-Canadian Studies, 7*(1–2), 23–43.

Blundell, V. (1993, January). Aboriginal empowerment and souvenir trade in Canada. *Annals of Tourism Research, 20*(1), 64–87.

Blundell, V. (2002). Aboriginal cultural tourism in Canada. In J. Nicks & J. Sloniowski (Eds.), *Slippery pastimes: Reading the popular in Canadian culture* (pp. 37–60). Waterloo: Wilfrid Laurier University Press.

CODA. (1988). *XV olympic winter games organizing committee.* Edmonton: Jasper Printing Group Ltd.

(n.d.). Cree family with travois, near Calgary, Alberta. *Glenbow Museum Archives* (Image No: NA-4035-87). Retrieved June 1, 2017, from http://ww2.glenbow.org/search/archivesPhotosResults.aspx? XC=/search/archivesPhotosResults.aspx&TN=IMAGEBAN&AC=QBE_QUERY&RF=WebResults& DL=0&RL=0&NP=255&MF=WPEngMsg.ini&MR=10&QB0=AND&QF0=File+number&QI0= NA-4035-87&DF=WebResultsDetails

Ellis, C. (2012, May). The possessive logic of settler-invader nations in olympic ceremonies. *Journal of Tourism and Cultural Change, 10*(2), 105–123.

Forsyth, J. (2002). Teepees and tomahawks: Cultural representation at the 1976 olympic games. In K. B. Wamsley, R. K. Barney, & S. G. Martyn (Eds.), *The global nexus engaged: Past, present, future interdisciplinary olympic studies* (pp. 71–76). London: The University of Western Ontario.

Francis, D. (1992). *The imaginary Indian: The image of the Indian in Canadian culture.* Vancouver: Arsenal Pulp Press.

Francis, D. (1977). *National dreams: Myth, memory, and Canadian history.* Vancouver: Arsenal Pulp Press.

Geller, P. (1996). Hudson's bay company Indians: Images of native people and the red river pageant, 1920. In S. E. Bird (Ed.), *Dressing in feathers: The construction of the Indian in American popular culture* (pp. 65–77). Boulder, CO: Westview Press.

Johnson, E. P. (1907). Chief Joe Healy and Braves. *The William Ready Division of Archives and Research Collections,* McMaster University Library: A.Y. & Co.

Johnson, E. P. (1910). Indian arrest by mounted police, Canadian West. *The William Ready division of archives and research collections, McMaster* University Library: E.G. MacFarlane, c.

Mawani, R. (2004). From colonialism to multiculturalism? Totem poles, tourism, and national identity in Vancouver's Stanley Park. *ARIEL: A Review of International English Literature, 35*, 31–57.

O'Bonsawin, C. M. (2013). Indigenous peoples and Canadian-Hosted olympic games. In J. Forsyth & A. R. Giles (Eds.), *Aboriginal peoples and sport in Canada* (pp. 35–63). Vancouver: UBC Press.

Roper, E. (1891). *By track and trail: A journey through Canada.* London: W.H. Allen & Co.

Stanley Park. *Tripadvisor Canada.* Retrieved June 1, 2017, from https://www.tripadvisor.ca/Attraction_ Review-g154943-d155652-Reviews-Stanley_Park-Vancouver_British_Columbia.html

VANOC. (2002). *Vancouver 2010 bid books: Volume 1–3.* Vancouver: Vancouver Olympic Bid Committee.

Gardiner, A. (Ed.). (2010). *With glowing hearts: The official commemorative book of the XXI olympic winter games and the X paralympic winter games.* Mississauga: John Wiley & Sons Canada, Ltd.

Miriam Martens
Department of Anthropology
McMaster University
Hamilton, Ontario

IRWIN OOSTINDIE

20. CELEBRATING CANADA 150 BY EXPLOITING COAST SALISH CULTURE

> We're a country based on immigration going right back to our quote indigenous people unquote, who were immigrants as well, 10, 12, 14,000 years ago.
> – Governor-General David Johnston, June 16, 2017 (Pedwell, 2017)

Just two weeks before the crescendo of Canada 150, the country's official sesquicentennial celebrations on which the Federal Government was spending a half billion dollars, the head of state made a flippant remark about the Indigenous Peoples of this land. Johnston later walked back and apologized for the turn-of-phrase, but it was nevertheless revealing of the colonial mentality at the heart of the Canadian settler-colonial project. The notion of First Nations as 'immigrants like the rest of us' is one of the rhetorical strategies for denying the fundamental contractions facing the Canadian establishment: Indigenous sovereignty, rights, and title.

Johnston's remarks were awkward for the powers-that-be, because these days the government practices are more sophisticated strategy for denying and obfuscating Indigenous rights. The Canada 150 extravaganza is just one example of how cultural events and celebrations are subtly weaponized to help reaffirm notions of Canada as consensual project, presenting "our Indigenous peoples" as equal partners – the better to deny their fundamental rights to the land. Here on the west coast, the 2010 Winter Olympics also provided a powerful demonstration of the mechanisms for this process.

With dominant society's fixation on dates and anniversaries to justify its occupation, we rely on placeholder anchors of history such as a moment when Captain Cook or George Vancouver sailed nearby, when a whisky bar and township were established (concurrent in Vancouver's case), and ignore the continued and ongoing occupation and use of the lands and waters by the Coast Salish.

Colonial festivals and anniversaries serve the role of reformatting the collective hard drive, to use a contemporary analogy. Cohen would describe this as "cultural repression becom(ing) part of consensual reality: blind spots, shared illusions and zones of tacitly denied information. Collective memory is pressed into shape by being repressed (2001, p. 137).

Conducting the action of celebrating a system designed to annihilate Indigenous culture, languages, and economies require tightly-crafted messaging and unpacking. Over the bombastic noise of anniversary fireworks, and self-congratulatory speeches by white politicians, the language of denial seeps into all of the forcibly vacated

© KONINKLIJKE BRILL NV, LEIDEN, 2018 | DOI 9789004367418_020

spaces and the growing population of settler immigrants is assured that the business of occupation is settled and a unified inclusive plan has been set to be followed.

Celebrations direct the public's gaze to pomp and circumstance instilled with liberal "good intentions" of Prime Minister Justin Trudeau with his hand-over-the-heart theatrics (Hopper, 2015). If the celebration were one of exposing the raw ugliness of domination then the public would become alienated from the charade. Instead, it is made beautiful, and the Indigenous People themselves are invited to perform to "fellow Canadians."

The 20.3 million passengers who arrived at Vancouver International Airport in 2015, besides being treated to a massive exhibition of *Vancouver Aquarium*-branded sea creatures, were introduced to British Columbia with a display of West Coast Indigenous artworks. Riffing off symbols of Vancouver culture and popular myths of an inclusive just society, tourists are sold the cultural notion of an integrated society at peace with itself. In turn, displays at the Vancouver Airport are a sense of pride for British Columbian residents who feel connected to a larger force of equality for all, the Canadian narrative of universal Medicare and a country free of a soiled past or the ills of social injustice.

Living on marginalized reservations, Coast Salish were blocked from their economic resources with which they could broach the communication and information divide, and so, therefore, were silenced through non-participation in mainstream Canadian society. Under the direction of the CRTC, a federalist multiculturalism would emerge using national and regional public and private broadcasters to promote assimilation and cultural erasure. Federal policies were advanced by early Canadian communications scholars who feared the threat of U.S. cultural hegemony. Until decades later, with the establishment of Indigenous media options (via community-access cable, community radio, or eventually the APTN) Coast Salish had no broadcasting options to have their culture reflected back to them. Still today, confronted by hurdles of accessing media production resources, and without economies of scale, Coast Salish continue to be more likely to access Cree, Dene, or Anishnabeg media content over their own west coast realities. Meanwhile the early scholars were partially correct, soon enough, Hollywood and mainstream Canadian culture was pushed through the radio and TV systems into Indigenous homes on and off reservations. (Ironically the biggest Hollywood native star was Chief Dan George of the Tsleil-Waututh).

When Coast Salish truism is not reflected back to its people, then erasure is fast-tracked. Media, arts and culture are of course critical areas of developing and supporting delivery of distinct culture, however language is the other key element of Indigenous People's culture and which was systematically attacked through the assimilative infrastructure of Canada. While a separatist Quebec was seduced to federalism through language and culture investments, divided and (somewhat) conquered Indigenous languages were criminalized for decades. Federal and provincial/territorial cooperation has yielded many benefits for the past thirty-five years and has resulted in (official language) investment of about $5 billion over that period (Government of Canada,

2006, p. 4). It is noteworthy that in recent years, social media has served as a new communications platform for direct self and community Coast Salish representation.

FOUR HOST FIRST NATIONS, 2010 OLYMPICS, AND CANADA 150+

In *Travel, transition and translation – A discussion paper that considers issues related to cultural environments and post-creation support for Aboriginal Artists*, C.C. Wherry writes:

> If a community's cultural vision is clearly defined, authenticity, protocols and artistic excellence will be protected. In turn, these foundational values will inform planning and provide balance for potentially conflicting priorities such as cultural tourism or business strategies that focus only on economics and structural form. (Wherry, 2006, p. 6)

More often than not, Coast Salish culture is seen by dominant settler society only briefly through tokenized Coast Salish protocol work, which disproportionately benefits the settler cultural institution instead of the Coast Salish representatives or artists. Sharing moments of Coast Salish protocol before Vancouver-area events is a notion of cross-cultural inclusion now normalized. However, what is required for the status quo to change is to halt with token gestures, which merely maintain the glass ceiling and structural marginalization, and instead support and place Coast Salish culture at the centre and on the main stages of settler cultural institutions and festivals. Supporting the development and sustenance of Coast Salish culture and language can be done throughout the region by these same settler cultural institutions thru adoption of Coast Salish Protocols and prioritizing the advancement of Coast Salish culture through commissioning and inclusion.

In the past fifteen years, the three levels of colonial government have frequently called upon Coast Salish culture and band council governments to participate and honour neoliberal impacts on the land. Vancouver's restructuring as a city for international elites, marketed to the world as an inclusive society, is often done with Coast Salish iconography and symbolism. In the decades after their cultures were no longer illegal, but still facing effects of intergenerational trauma and ongoing colonial policies, Coast Salish culture has persevered and is in a state of resurgence. I have witnessed this being done through grounding culture to ancient spiritual traditions, and protecting the stories, and family and village networks which hold together the culture.

Strategic investments by settler governments shrewdly recognize that Coast Salish band council governments' cooperation on regional economic megaprojects was necessary in order to avoid lengthy legal battles and title fights. The most prominent project on this front was the Four Host First Nations Secretariat (FHFN), a creation of First Nation band council governments delivering an instrument to endorse the 2010 Olympics & Paralympic Games. The Canadian state and Olympics corporate partners received a concrete benefit by not having the Games Bid boycotted and the Games not awarded to Canada. The participating First Nation governments were Squamish and Lil'Wat, and later joined by Tsleil-Waututh and Musqueam. The FHFN calculated and bartered the value of their Olympics' endorsement in exchange for money and participation. Habermas' theory of social accommodation can be useful here, examining the tenuous delivery of First Nations' collusion with the colonial project, and deriving community benefits for the four governments. At the time, the band councils calculated these short-term investments as beneficial and unlikely to be secured outside of protracted treaty negotiations or legal title fights. To secure the Bid, the 2010 Olympics delivered procurement opportunities, the building of cultural centres, and return of 50 acres of land to the Indigenous communities (whose unceded lands and waters the Games were to take place on).

To ensure public support for the Olympic bid and to bypass any questions of Coast Salish title rights, media partners used *'reasoning devices'* (Gamson & Modigliani, 1987, p. 143) to inform the public on how to judge this issue. Vancouver Sun columnist Daphne Brapham described the process of the FHFN demanding financial compensation for their participation:

> If it sounds like blackmail, it's worth remembering that what the First Nations are asking for – a share of the profits and benefits – is no different than what Intrawest Corp (the owners of Whistler/Blackcomb) will be asking for if Canada gets the Games. It's no different than UBC or SFU striking the best deals they can for hockey and speed skating arenas proposed to be built on their land. Call it blackmail if you will, but in some circles, it's just considered good business. (Bramham, 2002, para. 3)

The question of unceded land title was never on the table, and unfettered rights was equally kept away from the settler population by Olympic sponsoring media business who steered the public away from the fact settler and First Nation governments both desired the appearance of peaceful citizens in front of the global media.

In telling the story of revising historical truths, as CEO of the FHFN, Tewanee Joseph describes to a TEDx audience how he "spearheaded the largest re-brand of Aboriginal people in Canadian history" (Tewanee Joseph, 2016). In Joseph's eyes, the 2010 project brought substantial financial and cultural benefits to First Nations across Canada and advanced their place in Canadian society. Fast-forward from the Olympic Bid of 2002–2004 to planning for the 2017 Canada 150 birthday celebrations, when the City of Vancouver chose to get involved with another marquee event referred to as Canada 150+. The three-pronged celebration included a celebration of west coast canoe culture, a 10-day aboriginal cultural tourism festival (at the FIFA Women's World Cup Live Site), and a redux of the 2012 Walk for Reconciliation, in which tens of thousands took part. (City of Vancouver, 2016). The City's first Indigenous contractor was Tewanee Joseph, advising on protocol and strategy. With just months to go, and despite no community-level discussion, Squamish Council would select a liaison to the Canada 150+ planning exercise.

190

With just weeks to go, the Musqueam and Tsleil-Waututh Councils would formally agree to sign on.

The vast majority of contracted and participating Canada 150+ curators and arts organisations were not Coast Salish. Worth noting, also, none of the participating organisations have internal Coast Salish cultural policies (beyond practicing territorial acknowledgements), and almost none have Coast Salish staff or Board members. The minimal amount of Coast Salish cultural participation, direction and ownership is revealing. Almost all of the professional labour producing the Indigenous-themed festival is from non-Coast Salish planners, curators, and consultants.

The initiative received a $2.3-million grant from the federal government (Smith, 2016) with another $2.4 million from the City of Vancouver, and is operated out of the City Manager's Office (the same City department which led the 2010 Olympic Bid project management for the City). Rather than be managed through a transparent Cultural Services funding system (with peer-assessment), or offering a call for Coast Salish artists, or directly downloading the funding to the Coast Salish communities to self-determine their own priorities, the City Manager's office seconded senior Cultural Services staff and contracted production to BrandLIVE, a high-profile corporate event production company with no role in Indigenous arts and culture in the region.

The dilemma for the Canada 150+ festival was how to put icing on a cake before the cake has been baked. Quantitative data analysis of the state of Coast Salish culture and representation, as well as Canada Council funding levels reveal a cultural sector underdeveloped when compared to non-Coast Salish and settler cultural operations in the Vancouver area. As an active participant in the cultural sector for the past three decades, I have witnessed multiple generations of Squamish, Tsleil-Waututh and Musqueam artists being forced to survive in the marketplace chasing commissions, retail sales and occasional contract work.

Compared to the arts sector as a whole operating in Vancouver, Coast Salish artists receiving funding from any Canada Council program in 2014/15 was an abysmal 0.02% of Canada Council spending in Metro Vancouver. (Low, 2016) An observer might expect equity and targeted Canada Council funding for Indigenous artists in Metro Vancouver in 2014/2015 to be much better then, but only 3% of Indigenous artists or arts groups receiving funding were Coast Salish. With 97% of funding going to migrant or non-Coast Salish artists, Indigenous artists inadvertently advance the colonial goal of liberal pan-nativism and Coast Salish erasure by taking up public space through arts festivals and venues that have no Coast Salish cultural policies. Rather than advancing the culture of the Peoples where they operate, these productions typically limit their Coast Salish protocol action to territorial acknowledgements or occasional short-term hiring. (Noteworthy to readers, while migrant Indigenous have ended up in Vancouver for a variety of historical reasons, and form one of the largest off-reserve populations in Canada, it is nevertheless a contradiction that as migrant Indigenous struggle for a sense of home and identity, this can simultaneously compound the impacts of colonialism on Coast Salish Peoples).

Instead of prioritizing Coast Salish culture's growth and survival, the City of Vancouver participates in an exploitative and colonial exercise. The City (and Canada) benefit from the absence of cultural objectives and work plans which could be set out by the Coast Salish cultural sector. Governments reinforce tokenistic relationships, instead of investing proactively and sharing appropriate cultural planning strategies so that investments can emphasize development and legacy for each participating First Nations partner. By using the absence or limited cultural infrastructure and policies from First Nations, the City reinforces a paternalistic and infantilized relationship which is led by brokers and gatekeepers, many well-intentioned, but nonetheless with an almost complete absence of Coast Salish leadership and accountability. Instead of investing in multi-year reconciliation and redress cultural funding to address the gaps in Coast Salish access and participation in the regional cultural sector, the City proposes a "melting pot" of multiculturalism, and pan-native identity politics in direct competition to the nascent Coast Salish nationhood movement.

Confronting pan-native arts definitions, Charlotte Townsend-Gault observes:

> What is the point of perpetuating a category called "Native art," when the work is irreconcilably diverse and the category restrictive or discriminatory? It is not an art category at all, but the outcome of a socio-political situation constituted by a devastating history, by the shifting demographics of the non-Native population in a pluralist society. (Townsend-Gault, 1998)

By reviewing past exhibition history of the Vancouver Art Gallery, the Coast Salish region's premier public arts institution, it is evident that less than 0.01% of the artists exhibited have been Coast Salish. With the VAG's $17 million annual operating budget, and new plans for a gallery site where the 2017 Canada 150+ celebrations took place, one must question the ethics of such public investments to promote what will likely be an Emily Carr cultural tourism destination – which itself could do more damage than good for Coast Salish cultural resurgence and representation.

> The total amount of taxpayer dollars contributed to a new gallery (is) $200-million, and that doesn't include the amount of money the city of Vancouver is foregoing by donating the prime piece of Vancouver real estate upon which the new gallery would be built. (Mason, 2016)

CONCLUSION

When it is not blended with Indigenous culture from across Canada, the Coast Salish cultural resurgence is therefore hyper-commodified, fetishized and packaged for the notion of aboriginal cultural tourism. This takes place at the arrival gates of the

Vancouver International Airport, to the 2010 Olympics artwork, and Canada 150+ celebrations. Coast Salish culture receives little structural and ongoing funding, yet is being used disproportionately, as the Truth and Reconciliation Commission was used for, to present the notion that all is well and "business as usual." But there is an extreme disconnect between the health and presentation of Coast Salish culture and the number of Coast Salish artists actually employed full-time in their craft, compared to the city as a multi-billion dollar economic zone.

> The collective fictions that everyone is structured by, projects a view of capitalism that is deeply concerned with the empowering of colonialized cultures but the reality that we all know to be the case by virtue of our lived experience is, in fact, the opposite, increased poverty among colonized subjects. "Capitalism's rapacity," Fisher notes, "depends upon various forms of sheathing. The basic contradiction of capitalism is the need for anti-production, the ideological sheathing through PR, branding and advertising. (Hoffman, 2016)

Throughout the branding for Vancouver's celebration of Canada's 150th birthday, Coast Salish and migrant Indigenous Peoples are marketed as a reconciliation device consistent with recent City efforts to promote good relations with the three local First Nation governments. "The modern City of Vancouver was founded on the traditional territories of the Musqueam, Squamish and Tsleil-Waututh First Nations and that these territories were never ceded through treaty, war or surrender" (City of Vancouver, 2014). While a City recognition of Indigenous rights has no legal or jurisdictional basis it does promote the liberal insinuation of a shared partnership with other governments, although the true reality of the relationship is one of obfuscating historical facts and contradictions and marred with complex and competing interests. Many of these are kept from the public as the governments jockey and posture through this so-called reconciliation era.

While marquee events such as the Olympics can deliver the legacy of cultural facilities and investments, it is unclear if the greater net benefit does not accrue to the settler colonial governments and the greater Canadian society as a whole. How then can a structurally disadvantaged community actually influence mass society? Through the Olympics or Canada 150+ initiatives, is mainstream Canada willing to absorb and improve, or simply *accommodate* Indigenous People's needs and realities (McLaughlin, 1993, p. 599).

The motivation to the settler state of Canada to pressure First Nation governments' complicity in reconciliation-themed marquee events can be construed as a structure to scatter opposition. Glen Coulthard states "what is treated in the Canadian discourse of reconciliation as an unhealthy and debilitating incapacity to forgive and move on is actually a sign of critical consciousness, of our sense of unjustice, and of our awareness of and unwillingness to reconcile" (Coulthard, 2014, p. x). At its own peril, the colonial state avoids surrendering Crown lands, and so coerces under-resourced Indigenous communities to accept monies to participate in these elaborate

193

performances of masking and postponing genuine reconciliation. Is there an ability for Coast Salish culture to retain an element of *counter-public sphere* (McLaughlin, 1993, p. 355) within a colonial public sphere? By revising the colonial sphere with the goal of delegitimizing or strengthening Coast Salish First Nation governments, the situation reflects what Glen Coulthard (2014) describes as Indigenous self-government defined by the Canadian state.

While appearing to promote Indigenous cultural resurgence, settler cultural practices instead cherry-pick when and how they use Coast Salish culture to adorn its festivals and events. If Canadian cultural institutions and governments were to invest in Coast Salish culture and language – as is done propping up regional cultural interests in Quebec – the assimilation agenda of the federal governments would be less advanced, but the quality of authentic inclusion would be higher. Settlers hold complex and contradictory beliefs about the nature of their Canadian society, but regardless of intentions, denying Coast Salish culture its rightful place in occupied Coast Salish Territory ensures it will continue to be undermined in the landscape, the schools, museums, arts spaces and places of power. Coast Salish culture instead will be marginalized by dominant society, used as an adornment by institutions, and stand as a symbol of the hypocrisy of the generosity of Canadian multiculturalism. Coast Salish themselves will be used by settlers to deny accountability for a past marred by genocide, and one which is only in the recent era working through the intergenerational experience of violence, trauma, and criminalization.

Until landmarks are returned to their rightful Coast Salish placenames, and settler society moves beyond the liberal instrument of territorial acknowledgements, and colonial governments work for genuine reconciliation and redress, and the Coast Salish are held up by dominant culture as the legitimate cultural heroes of their unceded lands and waters, this place shall be merely the forever colonial wild west.

NOTE TO READER

As a Dutch settler living and learning about the history of the Peoples whose unceded lands and water I am living upon, I am gratefully indebted for the patience and generosity of many Coast Salish individuals who have shared theirs and their ancestors' knowledge with me. I attempt this writing to educate my settler peers on our roles and responsibilities to lift up Coast Salish culture.

For the purposes of this chapter, I concentrate on the geographic area of *Vancouver,* with the shared lands and water of the Musqueam, Squamish, and Tsleil-Waututh. I recognize the area has been simultaneously used by Coast Salish Peoples from surrounding areas since time immemorial.

REFERENCES

Bramham, D. (2002, June 10). First nations stake claim on 2010 Olympics: If the games are held in Vancouver and Whistler, Mount Currie and Squamish natives want a fair share of the economic benefits. *The Vancouver Sun*, p. B3.

CELEBRATING CANADA 150 BY EXPLOITING COAST SALISH CULTURE

City of Vancouver. (2014). *MOTION 6: Protocol to acknowledge first nations unceded traditional territory*. Retrieved from http://council.vancouver.ca/20140625/documents/ptec6.pdf

City of Vancouver. (2016). *Strengthening our relations: Canada 150+*. Retrieved from http://vancouver.ca/people-programs/vancouver-commemorates-canada-150.aspx

Cohen, S. (2001). *States of Denial: Knowing about atrocities and suffering*. Cambridge: Polity Press.

Coulthard, G. (2014). *Red skin, White masks: Rejecting the colonial politics of recognition*. Minneapolis, MN: University of Minnesota Press.

Gamson, W. A., & Modigliani, A. (1987). The changing culture of affirmative action. In R. G. Braungart & M. M. Braungart (Eds.), *Research in political sociology* (Vol. 3, pp. 137–177). Greenwich, CT: JAI Press.

Government of Canada. (2006). *Government response to the sixth report of the standing senate committee on official languages*. Retrieved from http://publications.gc.ca/collections/Collection/CH14-12-2006E.pdf

Habermas, J. (1991). *Philosophical discourse of modernity*. Cambridge: MIT Press.

Hoffman, T. (2016). No exit postmodern style. In M. Fisher (Ed.), *Capitalist realism, is there no alternative?* Winchester: Zero Books. Retrieved from http://ctheory.net/ctheory_wp/no-exit-postmodern-style/

Hopper, T. (2015, October 21). Emoting 101: Decoding the gestures of the touchy-feely Trudeau era. *National Post*. Retrieved from http://news.nationalpost.com/news/canada/canadian-politics/emoting-101-decoding-the-gestures-of-the-touchy-feely-trudeau-era

Low, D. (2016). *Canada council aboriginal arts funding data set* [Data file].

Mason, G. (2016). *Hope builds for new Vancouver art gallery with prospect of federal funds in globe and mail*. Retrieved from http://www.theglobeandmail.com/news/british-columbia/hope-builds-for-new-vancouver-art-gallery/article28662147/

McLaughlin, L. (1993). Feminism, the public sphere, media and democracy. *Media Culture and Society, 15*(4), 599–620.

Pedwell, T. (2017, June 19). Gov. Gen. David Johnston apologizes for referring to indigenous people as immigrants. *Toronto Star*. Retrieved from https://www.thestar.com/news/canada/2017/06/19/governor-general-johnston-apologizes-for-referring-to-indigenous-people-as-immigrants.html

Smith, C. (2016). *City of Vancouver and federal government team up for major celebration of indigenous art, music, and culture*. Retrieved from http://www.straight.com/arts/849766/city-vancouver-and-federal-government-team-major-celebration-indigenous-art-music-and

Tewanee Joseph. (2016). *The power of an invitation at TEDxBCIT*. Retrieved from https://www.youtube.com/watch?v=aIq_tifWbyw

Townsend-Gault, C. (1998). First nations culture: Who knows what? *Canadian Journal of Communications, 23*(1), 31–43. Retrieved from http://www.cjc-online.ca/index.php/journal/article/view/1021/927

Vancouver International Airport. (2015). *YVR connects: 2015 sustainability report*. Retrieved from http://www.yvr.ca/en/about-yvr/leadership-and-accountability/sustainability-report/our-business

Wherry, C. C. (2006). *Government*. Ottawa: Aboriginal Affairs Branch, Department of Canadian Heritage.

Irwin Oostindie
School of Communications
Simon Fraser University
Burnaby, British Columbia

EDUARDO VERGOLINO

21. RECLAIMING INDIGENOUS SCHOOLING PROCESS AGAINST COLONIZATION

Writing about education is a Homeric and an arduous process of questioning our own process of teaching-learning and the fundamental knowledge that most schools have proliferated during centuries. I am not going to solve or presuppose that all my questions will be answered by an instantaneous magic trick. However, I do believe that a consequence of being affected by the post-metaphysical, post-modern and critical thinking turned me into a questioning and anxious person. Since my first visit to Pankara community in Northeast Brazil, more specifically in the countryside of Pernambuco State approximately 450 km from the Capital Recife, I have been focusing my interviews and research on the way schools are built inside the community and what is the purpose of schooling process inside those Indigenous communities in the area called Sertao pernambucano. However, we are going to focus on three fundamental questions about schools inside Indigenous communities. How can we think a schooling process that respects the Indigenous knowledge? Is it possible to see the Western knowledge in an Indigenous perspective? Is it right to fragment the Indigenous knowledge to a Western framework? These three questions cannot be answered in one article or book, not even in a course. These are the kind of questions, which try to open our minds to something else more important, the actual language and thinking used in Indigenous schools.

First of all, it is important to notice that orality and storytelling are the principal methods of teaching and learning about the world, about the relationship between members of the community and about most contents inside the group. Walter Benjamin affirms, "For storytelling is always the art of repeating stories, and this art is lost when the stories are no longer retained. It is lost because there is no more weaving and spinning to go on while they are being listened to" (p. 367). Indicating the relationship of methods of teaching and learning is probably the most powerful difference between Western schools and Indigenous schools, even though most Indigenous schools are incapable of changing the structure of teaching.

Mobile groups as gathered and hunters consolidate relationships in a mere of what is good to the members of the group and how it can turn life better, there are no needs of standardization or imposition of thoughts (Kulchyski, 2000; Sahlins, 1972). Although the point seems more political than educational, there are similarities and behaviors practiced among the political realm that influence directly in schooling process and how should we work to improve the Indigenous knowledge inside the

© KONINKLIJKE BRILL NV, LEIDEN, 2018 | DOI 9789004367418_021

EDUARDO VERGOLINO

schools. Politically, schooling process is the perfect machine to alienate and put together as many individuals as possible and manipulate what, when and how they will think. Fredric Jameson (1991) points that, "This is, however, precisely why it seems to me essential to grasp Postmodernism not as a style but rather as a cultural dominant: a conception which allows for the presence and coexistence of a range of very different, yet subordinate, features" (p. 3). The schools currently bring inside itself the obscure ritual of annihilate the subjectivity of human beings and shape their minds to a subordinate position inside the mainstream society. Jameson shows the cultural logic of late capitalism in a path to lead to the hyperspace, although the same reasoning or at least some of his thoughts can be attached to schooling process as a reflex of a multiplicity of humans subjectivity living in coexistence, changed to be underestimated to society as empty machines.

Schools are the colonial heritage being practiced every day inside Indigenous communities in Northeast Brazil and also in some places in Canada. Nevertheless, there are many different movements of teachers, communities, and intellectuals looking to this relation between school and colonialism there is an important question: What is the purpose of schools inside Indigenous communities. What is the importance of ways of knowing to a particular community? How can the structure of schools affect the process of keeping the Indigenous knowledge?

The Indigenous communities in Brazil and Canada follow in a certain way specific laws that create the opportunity to community self-governance, even though laws have a very strict hierarchy. Schools, Community, Provincial, State, Federal Government, it seems that every part of the State influences Indigenous schools. Curriculum, language, schedule, children age, contents, books, writing system, alphabet and many others rules that schools have to strictly follow as a manner to keep the community out of the schools and unable to take care of the children inside the school. The possibility to change the actual system of education or, at least, the method of ways of knowing is getting harder every day. The Indigenous schools are not allowed to change their script because the system is oppressing by the colonial government and students finishing school has to have a minimum standard of "knowledge." What is incredible to our understanding? There are many different forms of identification of Indigenous knowledge and Traditional knowledge but the recognition of the ways of knowing still a challenge to be changed inside the schools. Batiste (2000) argues that it is difficult to Eurocentric perspectives to understand that Indigenous knowledge is diverse, and this diversity throughout communities has a strong influence in schools system (p. 35). There is no school without walls, teacher-student relation, secretary, and principal, or books or writing systems because the way to recognize the knowledge is when this knowledge is written in a book and read by students behind desks set in a row. The way of knowing, the way children learn from family and members of an Indigenous community looks different from a western standardized school system.

So, how can we respect the Indigenous knowledge during the schooling process? First, we have to recognize a community-based curriculum where the Indigenous knowledge will be respected as the centre of all knowledge. Indigenous schools in Brazilian northeast have been suffering a very strong influence of the Western curriculum, pedagogy and framework which stratifies the knowledge based on a rationality resulted from a European development, rationality which does not accept the oral and holistic ways of thinking the World as a manner of rational thinking. Batiste (2000) points that, "[…] Eurocentric thought has created a mysticism around Indigenous knowledge that distances the outsider from Indigenous peoples and what they know" (p. 35). The Western colonial thought does not recognize the way of knowing is different from the Eurocentric way, which is established in a rationality based on the Enlightenment. For instance, Paulo Freire's idea of Pedagogy still being a critical thinking of teaching and learning process changed the perception of producing the knowledge.

Indigenous schools in northeast Brazil follows the mainstream society curriculum, pedagogy, and framework, even though according to Brazilian Education Law, Indigenous schools have autonomy to change, create, innovate and write your own curriculum. Does it change the reality? Many Indigenous schools still following the same curriculum and practices of non-Indigenous schools as a result not only of colonization but moreover, the consequence of colonization as a mindset change. It is difficult to create something different from Western schools. First, since the school has to follow the law dictated by the Government. Second, there is a hierarchy of power that should be respected. Third, to make a change implies to respect, to recognize, to work with a different way of knowing inside the school.

There is a hierarchy of rules, which all schools have to follow. The school board, school division, Education Ministry, all those compartmented offices analyze the student progress and the index of failure each year to decide the future of each school. The law is highly restrictive to open a way to change curriculum and frameworks inside Indigenous schools. The necessity to give the opportunity to Indigenous students the 'same' chances of enjoying the labor market as a non-Indigenous student is the alibi of white-colonial society to impose the fragmented curriculum and the Western way of knowing. Peter Cole (2016) shows a fascinating point of view, which represents the difference between ways of knowing. The curriculum technology and the idea of teaching being something untouchable, something that is impossible to see or feel give to us an opportunity to change. Students ask the teacher where is the teaching. They want something touchable, real, and alive. The reality and the imaginary seem in some Indigenous communities a very strong and close relationship to create knowledge and open the process of teaching-learning (p. 110). For example, the western-colonial school does not accept dream as an important instrument of knowledge. But in many different Indigenous communities' dreams have a specific and important place to understand the knowledge. Many different cultural aspects like respecting the animals before eating them, respect plants before using them, respecting the spiritual world and many different details show how different the western schools work for, and are prepared to annihilate the subjectivity of Indigenous people.

199

EDUARDO VERGOLINO

Is it possible to see the western knowledge in an Indigenous perspective? Schools and curriculums in Brazil and Canada are based on a Western perspective, which cannot be broken easily. "Epistemology is knowledge. Reclaiming cultural knowledge is fundamental to deconstructing ideas of the superiority of Western knowledge" (Lambert, 2014, p. 61). Decolonizing the Western curriculum is important to improve the contact with Indigenous knowledge inside the classroom, what in some communities is becoming rarer is the contact with Indigenous knowledge inside the classroom. According to Battiste (2013):

> Decolonization then is a process of unpacking the keeper current in education: its powerful Eurocentric assumptions of education, its narratives of race and difference in curriculum and pedagogy, its establishing culturalism or cultural racism as a justification for the status quo, and the advocacy for Indigenous knowledge as a legitimate education topic. It is the channel for generating a postcolonial education system in Canada and disrupting those normalized discourses and singularities and allowing diverse voices and perspectives and objectives into "mainstream" schooling. (p. 107)

It is not just a mere of increase the Indigenous knowledge inside the class but also the process of decolonizing the Western pedagogy inside Indigenous schools. It is more of recognize the Indigenous education as a genuine process of teaching and learning in another way. Frantz Fanon (1968) says, "Decolonization is truly the creation of new men. But such a creation cannot be attributed to a supernatural power: The 'thing' colonized becomes a man through the very process of liberation" (p. 2). According to Peter Cole (2006), "What kind of education might people in our community need?" (p. 120). It is important to note that school education is one part of all. Education is the whole process of teaching-learning, which all subjects are immersed in society every day and all moments of life. However, Education inside the Western school is a mere place where all the students are supposed to learn something useful and convenient to mainstream capitalist society. The primary goal of school education is the profitable possibility of students who are going to be pushed in labor market to learn useful abilities to work. Marx (2015) points out that, "[…] discovered that capital is not a thing, but a social relation between persons, established by the instrumentality of things" (p. 543).

The question now is if is it possible to merge the Western knowledge in an Indigenous perspective? The indigenization of schools in Canada and New Zealand show us that it is not an easy task but possible and necessary to work. It is not rare to see teachers and students working on the indigenization of curriculum through the process of setting Indigenous knowledge in a fragmented perspective to a Western curriculum. It is easy, in a certain way, to listen to elders talking stories and put that knowledge in a History class or Art class. But it is not easy to free the school, students, teachers, and community to decide and create their own way. Peter Cole (2006) points that, "We can choose or not to adopt innovation into our traditions, we are narrators narratives voices interlocutors of our own knowings, we can determine

200

for ourselves what our educational needs are" (p. 111). The problem that can be seen in Brazil and Canada is the opposite to accept the Indigenous knowledge as knowledge that has importance and meaning inside the rationalized society. In the Brazilian case, the way of knowing, the process of passing the knowledge to youth is compartmentalized and fragmented following the colonial rules. It is 'allowed' to Indigenous communities to include contents from their history, beliefs, nourishment, dances and others characteristics inside the curriculum but the Government's rules do not allow them to change the way, the process of teaching the knowledge, the way to teach and learn the contents. The school has to follow the pattern to build a community as close as possible to the standard that mainstream society demands. "When improvements in Indigenous education focus primarily on cultural programming, taught within the framework of current schooling practices, the initiatives do not expose or challenge power relationships within our society" (Goulet, 2014, p. 22). Indigenous schools are able to teach Indigenous history inside their classrooms following books, schedule, time, but are they allowed to teach western contents in an Indigenous perspective? Is the Indigenous school plenty of teachers able to teach Western contents inside the bush? In a canoe down the river? Looking the stars? Trapping a fox or a moose? This is the problem of the universalism of structure of schools, frameworks, and curriculum. Marie Battiste (2000) argues, "Universality creates cultural and cognitive imperialism, which establishes a dominant group's knowledge, experience, culture, and language as the universal norm" (p. 63). This does not need to be referring to the content of curriculum but the ways of curriculum and pedagogies are established inside the community. The attempt of the colonial framework is to fragment the Indigenous knowledge to be placed in a frame where universalization is the standard, in an effort to keep the main goal of colonization, which is the assimilation of Indigenous people.

Is it right to fragment the Indigenous knowledge to fit in the Western curriculum? It is important to note that Indigenous knowledge has been introduced in many Indigenous schools in a fragmented format around the World. Even in some non-Indigenous school, the content of Indigenous History has been teaching as a necessary content to society. However, our point here is to debate what is going to be in the future if we 'westernize' the Indigenous knowledge. Morra and Reder (2016) argue that "Tribal epistemologies are a way of knowing that does not debate the subjectivity factor in knowledge production – subjectivity is a given" (p. 97). In knowledge production based on an Indigenous community, spirituality has a strong and significant influence in the process of teaching and learning. Since Aristotle, the spirituality has been declined as a realm where rationality cannot accept as knowledge. Rationality has to be proven, statistically and data-based. Indigenous knowledge has a different process of knowing which respects the connection between humans and nature as one unique body, the living body, the natural and biologic being. Different epistemologies maybe not fit together in the same framework as schools are trying to do. "Indigenous methods do not flow from Western philosophy; they flow from tribal epistemologies" (Kovach, 2009, p. 36). Kovach also points that European way

EDUARDO VERGOLINO

of thought had for centuries a strong effect on Indigenous communities through the positivistic and reductionist rationality introduced by the schools. How can we fragment the spirituality from the Nature to fit in a classroom and with fifty minutes weekly to be explained? According to Kovach (2009), "further Indigenous knowledges could not be understood from a reductionist analysis because they could not be fragmented, externalized, and objectified. Without an appreciation for Indigenous ways of knowing, Indigenous people were excluded from knowledge construction as defined by Western thought" (p. 77). The point is the recognition of Indigenous knowledge respecting the methods of teaching and learning of each people. The standard of Western school education is still colonizing Indigenous people through the fragmentation of their knowledge.

The issue pointed here is the process of reclaiming Indigenous voice and autonomy to decide and create a school that represents what Indigenous people want. To respect Indigenous ways of knowing is to respect the subjectivity oppressed during centuries of colonization. It is not just a mere of introducing the 'content' (Indigenous syllabus) to the school curriculum structure but to change the main structure of Indigenous school to promote the voices and specific ways of knowing. To respect the specificity of each Indigenous people in Brazil and Canada go beyond the compartmentalized content, it needs to allow them to change the organizational structure of thinking, which the Western school is based. Memmi (1965) affirms that, "Colonial racism is built from three major ideological components: one, the gulf between the culture of colonialist and the colonized; two, the exploitation of these differences for the benefit of the colonialist; three, the use of these supposed differences as standards of absolute fact" (p. 71). Schools are an ideological space colonizing the subjectivity and the way of knowing the World being used by mainstream society to annihilate the individual of the Indigenous. According to Fanon (1968), the existence is the only possession of the colonized, which is dominated and oppressed by the colonialist. It is vital to (re)create Indigenous schools respecting the diversity of knowledge and ways of knowing from each specific people around the World. We should change the Indigenous schools to be a place where the respect to the knowledge is the purpose. Indigenous schools should be a place to Indigenous people with their own voices, and not a place where colonization still thrives. Schools currently are places of colonization and oppression reflecting the Western culture inside Indigenous communities.

REFERENCES

Battiste, M. (2000). *Reclaiming indigenous voice and vision.* Vancouver: UBC Press.
Battiste, M. (2013). *Decolonizing education: Nourishing the learning spirit.* Saskatoon: Purich Publishing Limited.
Battiste, M., & Henderson, J. Y. (2000). *Protecting indigenous knowledge and heritage: A global challenge* (Purich's Aboriginal Issues Series). Saskatoon: Zurich Publishing.
Cole, P. (2005). *Coyote raven go canoeing: Coming home to the village* (McGill-Queen's Native and Northern Series; 42). Montreal: McGill-Queen's University Press.

Fanon, F. (1968). *The wretched of the earth* (An Evergreen Black cat book; B-149). New York, NY: Grove Press.

Goulet, L., & Goulet, K. (2014). *Teaching each other: Nehinuw concepts and indigenous pedagogies.* Vancouver, University of British Columbia Press.

Hale, D. (2006). *The novel: An anthology of criticism and theory, 1900–2000.* Malden, MA: Blackwell Publishing.

Jameson, F. (1991). *Postmodernism, or the cultural logic of late capitalism.* Durham, NC: Duke University Press.

Kovach, M. (2009). *Indigenous methodologies: Characteristics, conversations, and contexts.* Toronto: University of Toronto Press.

Kulchyski, P. (2000). What is native studies? In R. Laliberte (Ed.), *Expressions in Canadian native studies* (pp. 13–26). Saskatoon: University Extension Press.

Lambert, L. (2014). *Research for indigenous survival: Indigenous research methodologies in the behavioural science.* Montana: Salish Kootenai College Press.

Marx, K. (2015). *Capital.* Moscow: Progress Publishers.

Memmi, A. (1991). *The colonizer and the colonized* (Expanded ed.). Boston, MA: Beacon Press.

Morra, L., & Reder, D. (2016). *Learn, teach, challenge: Approaching indigenous literatures* (Indigenous Studies Series). Waterloo: Wilfrid Laurier University Press.

Navin, K. S., & Jon, R. (2017, May 15). *Indigenous knowledge and pedagogy for indigenous children.* Retrieved from http://jan.ucc.nau.edu/~jar/HOC/HOC-4.pdf

Sahlins, M. (1972). *Stone age economics.* Chicago, IL: Aldine-Atherton.

Eduardo Vergolino
Federal University of Paraiba-Brazil &
University of Manitoba, Winnipeg, Manitoba

AMANDA APPASAMY, CASSANDRA SZABO, AND
JORDAN TABOBONDUNG

22. SURVEYING UNDERGRADUATE STUDENTS' PERCEPTIONS ON THE INDIGENOUS COURSE REQUIREMENT

INTRODUCTION

Background

"Professional Development and Training for Public Servants:

> 57. We call upon federal, provincial, territorial, and municipal governments to provide education to public servants on the history of Aboriginal peoples, including the history and legacy of residential schools, the United Nations Declaration on the Rights of Indigenous Peoples, Treaties and Aboriginal rights, Indigenous law, and Aboriginal–Crown relations. This will require skills based training in intercultural competency, conflict resolution, human rights and anti-racism." (p. 11, TRC Calls to Action)

The University of Winnipeg made national headlines when it stated that it would be "the first university in the country to mandate that all students will learn about Indigenous Peoples" (Lee, 2016). The Indigenous Course Requirement (ICR) passed by the Senate at the University of Winnipeg in November 2015, is the result of a student led initiative. The ICR has been structured as mandatory to graduate for incoming 2016 undergraduate students. These undergraduate students have the opportunity to choose from a broad range of Indigenous content courses across disciplines to fulfill this requirement towards their diploma. Kevin Settee, University of Winnipeg Student President, stated to CBC news in Sept 2016 that "[The] initiative was born out of the Aboriginal student council because of negative things that were happening on campus – racist texts on bathroom stalls, overall racism and negative experiences in classrooms" (Monkman, 2016).

The Truth and Reconciliation Committee has 94 calls to action (TRC, 2015), and within those 94 calls to action, was a recommendation that Post- Secondary Institutions teach younger generations about the history of First Nations people (Lee, 2016). The University of Winnipeg took this recommendation seriously, and a group of students rallied for this change (Lee, 2016). The students, the Faculty and The University of Winnipeg believe that education and awareness are the best ways to challenge racism and create stronger relationships (Lee, 2016). Literature has shown

© KONINKLIJKE BRILL NV, LEIDEN, 2018 | DOI 9789004367418_022

AMANDA APPASAMY ET AL.

that there are substantial misconceptions from non-indigenous Canadians towards Indigenous peoples, a lot of these misconceptions come from not being educated or informed about the realities that Indigenous peoples face (Assembly of First Nations, 2002). These misconceptions cause racism towards Indigenous peoples, and education is a tool to combat this.

Thus, this research project aimed to undertake the task of understanding students' perceptions and understandings of the ICR to see if it had a positive outcome and realizing the goal of lessening discrimination. It is crucial to do this research because education is key to reconciliation, and if it is found that the ICR is not having the desired outcome, it can be altered.

The research question was agreed upon before the researchers' involvement by the Indigenous Advisory circle. Research Question:

The University of Winnipeg is recognized nationally as a leader in Indigenizing the Institution. Starting in 2016, all undergraduate students must complete an Indigenous course requirement (ICR) in order to graduate. How do U of W students feel the ICR will impact their perspective on Indigenous Issues?

METHODS

Rationale

The methodology chosen for this research work was the quantitative method of collecting surveys. The collection of surveys enables the research to show measurements of typically unmeasurable data, such as perceptions, thoughts, and importance of a topic. In this research, we aimed to measure undergraduate students' feelings and perceptions towards the recently mandated ICR.

We saw many potential issues arising with the method of interviewing, and one of the issues we saw transpiring in conducting interviews, was the interviewer effect, where interviewer characteristics and presence would affect a respondent's answer (Bryman & Bell, 2012). In interviews, there is the tendency to exhibit social desirability bias and respond with the politically correct answer and not the answer the respondent believes (Bryman & Bell, 2012). We believed that due to the sensitive nature of the topic, this would be a likely phenomenon when conducting interviews, some respondents may feel embarrassed of the fact that they know little of Indigenous issues, or that they do not care to know. With a survey, we were confident that the respondents would feel comfortable telling the truth about these potentially embarrassing questions.

The type of survey that was used was a cross-sectional survey, in which collection of data occurred at a single point in time from a sample drawn from a specified population (Visser, Krosnick, & Lavrakas, 2003). It is suggested that this type of study is most often used to document the prevalence of particular characteristics in a population, for example, cross-sectional surveys are used to assess the frequency with which people perform certain behaviours, or the number of people who hold certain beliefs (Visser, Krosnick, & Lavrakas, 2003). This ability to assess relationships between variables amongst subgroups was of importance to the research. We wanted to see if certain demographic factors had a relationship with perceptions of the Indigenous Course Requirement. Thus, for the design of the survey we began with demographic questions, such as: "What program of study are you in?" "What is your age?" "What gender do you identify with?" "What ethnicity do you identify with?" These questions were included to cross-tabulate between the program of study and perception of the course requirement. For instance, if a particular program of study had the least interest or least positive reaction, further work could be done within that program to understand why.

The surveys were done using probability sampling in which the selection process is random. Each participant would theoretically have an equal chance of being selected; this is done to ensure that the selected sample is representative of the larger population from which it was drawn. It is also said that it permits researchers to estimate the amount of variance present in a given data set (Visser, Krosnick, & Lavrakas, 2003). However, the sample size used for this research was not of accurate scale. Therefore, the ability to estimate variance or accurate representation of the larger population is not truly accurate. The researchers collected 78 surveys out of a total undergraduate population of approximately 10,000. Hence, the true sample size would need to have been around 727 with a confidence level of 95% and a confidence interval of 3.5. Despite the limitation of not having an accurate sample size, probability sampling was still used, with simple random sampling and cluster sampling being implemented. Simple random sampling is when participants are drawn from at random. We also used cluster sampling where a population is dispersed over a large area, and the researchers collect data from certain areas of interest (Visser, Krosnick, & Lavrakas, 2003).

In this research, the population would have been dispersed widely throughout the campus' many buildings, and it would have been difficult to get an accurate representation. We collected data from the main campus at three locations.

Additionally, we used some aspects of convenience sampling, a non-probability sampling method. With random sampling a researcher would know that it would be random because they would know the exact population size and exact sample size, thus the probability of each participant being selected. Non-probability methods mean that the sampling method used was not random, and there is, in fact, a system for choosing participants. Thus, not all members of a population have an equal chance of being in the study (Sedgwick, 2013). Convenience sampling is when participants are selected because it is convenient and they are easily accessible (Sedgwick, 2013). In this research, the students that were approached to participate in the study were convenient due to their location on campus on that particular day. They were easily accessible because they were in the main buildings and not the smaller more obscure parts of the campus.

AMANDA APPASAMY ET AL.

Design

As mentioned previously, the survey was designed using a cross-sectional approach to examine attitudes, perceptions, and understandings of the ICR. The first step in creating the survey was reviewing other surveys of similar nature. We found a helpful resource that is the Statistics Canada guidebook. It had an extensive list of guidelines to use when conducting surveys (Statistics Canada, 2010). This resource gave us guidelines that we believe helped with getting a high response rate. Initially, we were only going to distribute 60 surveys. However, the students were easily filling out the surveys, which allowed us to get a total of 78. The planning of our survey is one reason why we acquired good response rates. Some of the crucial factors taken into consideration were: the length of the survey, appearance and organization of the survey, consideration of the characteristics of respondents, and reducing the burden to responding to survey. This resource also gave information on what types of questions should be included or not, such as: do not put jargon or technical terms, the answer should reflect an array of choices, limit open ended questions, allow respondents to skip questions that are not relevant. Once we reviewed other surveys, the aforementioned resource, and piloted the questions amongst ourselves, we created the first draft of the survey.

The survey was comprised of 13 closed-response and 1 open response question. The one open ended question invited the participants to reflect on their own beliefs about how the ICR would impact them. The closed-response questions included 4 demographic questions. There was then an attitudinal question to assess how perceptions were changed, and a question regarding whether they would take the course if it were not required. Finally, there was one open-ended question about how they feel an ICR would change perceptions. We felt that these questions would give us adequate information to assess the student's perceptions on the ICR.

Questions 5, 10 and 12 were measured using a Likert scale. Likert scales are a commonly used measurement when conducting research; the approach involves the presentation of a set of selected items that together measure one trait (Harpe, 2015), in this case: level of information, perspective, and interest. From a statistical standpoint, the different level a respondent chooses shows an interval level of measurement. It allows the ability to number certain phenomena using some rule. It is based on the idea that the phenomena can be measured by aggregating an individual's rating of his/her feelings, attitudes, and perceptions (Harpe, 2015). The Likert scale system was used in these questions because it allowed data to be collected on otherwise qualitative information, without having to use time-consuming methods to collect such data.

The survey was also designed being cognisant of ethics, seeing as the research needed to obtain approval from the ethics board at the University of Winnipeg. The wording and the way in which the questions were asked were mindful of this. The demographic questions were asked in a way that allowed a full spectrum of answers. Another key consideration in the design was trying not to show the researchers' bias

208

in the wording. The researchers all felt that the Indigenous Course Requirement was crucial. We knew that we could easily skew the survey wording and questions to represent our own beliefs. Therefore, the neutral wording was used, and certain questions were re-written due to the feeling that they showed bias.

Data Analysis

The data was analysed in excel using the simple survey data structure, in which the data from a single round survey is analysed. The data is considered "flat" in this type of analysis and is regarded as one of the easier methods of analysis. In a survey with numbered questions, the flat file has a column for each question and a row for each respondent. The data should then form a rectangular grid with a number in every cell (SSC, 2001). However, there are some challenges to this type of analysis, if respondents choose not to answer certain questions, or if there are skip questions, it means different sub-sets of people reply, or could mean the survey was not clear in instructions. These challenges were realized in the research, but a coding system was created to account for the non-respondents, and skip questions.

The coding system was formulated to enter all data into excel. For the demographic answers, the respondents were asked to provide one-word answers. These responses were then coded. For example, the question of "What ethnicity do you identify with?" gave responses of: Canadian, African, Indigenous, Asian, Latin American, European, Other. These answers were then given numbers from 1–7 providing a codebook, in which categories are listed, and codes are assigned to them (SSC, 2001). The process of assigning codes involved scanning the data to realize common themes that can be put into groups. This process was only done for the questions that could have variation in answers, such as the program of study, ethnicity, gender, age, and the open-ended question. For the questions that use the Likert scale, the scaling of 1–5 was coded with numbers as well.

Once all data was coded and entered into the excel sheet, each question and the possible responses were counted using a formula in excel. This allowed for the researchers to look at the data from individuals who appear in one column. These responses were then put into graphical representations to observe patterns easily. Following this, we were able to quickly profile the respondents, which is when data is drawn out from groups of respondents whose response profiles are similar to one another (SSC, 2001). This data was then used to interpret the results of the surveys and to make generalizations of the data collected.

Limits

When conducting research there are always limitations, and surveys, in particular, have specific limits compared to other research methods. One of the fundamental limitations being the respondents may not understand the questions and answer the questions incorrectly. Without the ability to clarify the questions, the data collected

AMANDA APPASAMY ET AL.

may not be accurate. There is also the risk of missing data due to not being able to probe, or due to the respondent skipping questions if they find it boring or irrelevant, which is a phenomenon, we saw with some of our respondents. (Bryman & Bell, 2012). Additionally, with using a survey as the primary method it is difficult to ask many questions due to respondent fatigue, or it may discourage the respondents from doing the survey altogether (Bryman & Bell, 2012). Our awareness of respondent fatigue limited our ability to include questions on the quality of the Indigenous course taken, quality of instructors, etc. It was also difficult to ask open ended questions because often respondents do not want to write great amounts, which limited many respondents resulting in one sentence answers.

Questions on a survey are also not independent of one another; one question may influence the response to another, or impact the respondent's overall opinion if they read the entire survey before answering the questions. Raising the possibility of question-order effect, in which a previous question primes a respondent to further questions. It is known that the order that questions appear on a survey can directly impact the responses. It is suggested that to test for this phenomenon, alternate surveys where questions are systematically rotated should be employed during the piloting (Bradburn & Mason, 1964). Surveys are also not appropriate for individuals who have disabilities, or those who do not speak the language the survey was written. Resulting in large portions of the population at the University of Winnipeg being missed.

In our particular research, we saw time constraints as the major limitation, due to the short period to collect and analyze data an accurate sample size was not achieved to make strong generalizations. Additionally, due to time constraints of respondents we were unable to ask as many questions as we would have liked to, in order to get a wider understanding of the views expressed. Furthermore, due to the time delay from the ethics board, we were unable to pilot the questions with students. Had we done this, we would have realized the design of our survey was not ideal and we could have made those changes to collect better data. We also could have asked those with whom we piloted questions with, if the questions resulted in the question-order effect.

A further limitation noticed in this research is the fact that the Indigenous Course Requirement was just recently mandated. Many of the students surveyed had not taken it, or had taken an Indigenous course that was required for their program only, or the students had taken the course out of interest. This skewed our data as we were only hoping to receive information on the recently mandated course requirement. This again would likely be another issue that could have been resolved with piloting the survey.

RESULTS

Demographics

The sample size surveyed is 78 undergraduate students. The majority of the students surveyed, i.e. 29% are enrolled in a Science program, followed by 23% of students in a social science program, where social science was seen as any program dealing with human society, such as Sociology, International Development, Conflict Resolution. 18% of the students are enrolled in an Arts program and 14% in the business faculty.

Age

The majority of the population surveyed was aged between 21 to 25 years old followed by 17–20 years old. In addition, 56.6 % of the population were female students, 40.8 % male and 2.6 % of the respondents identified as other gender.

Cultural Background

35% of the respondents are of European origins, 20% African, 16% Asian, followed by 13% Indigenous, 3 % Latin American and lastly, 7% other.

Knowledge of Indigenous Issues

11% of the population indicated that they have excellent knowledge of indigenous issues, 31% stated that they have an above average knowledge of indigenous issues followed by 37% indicating average knowledge and 21% of the population indicated moderate to little knowledge about the issue. Overall, 79% of the respondents surveyed indicate high to good knowledge of indigenous issues as compared to 21% with the low knowledge.

Source of Information about Indigenous Issues

30% of the population surveyed indicated that their source of information about Indigenous issues is from an educational institution, 28 % of the population obtained their information from social media, followed by 25% of the population from conversations with peer and 17 % of the population from mainstream media.

Percentage of Students Who Have Taken an ICR

Of the 78 students surveyed only 23% had taken an Indigenous Required course. Of the 23% of students who took and Indigenous Required course, 11% indicated that the course was a required course and 12% indicated that the course was an elective course. The target population of this study was first-year students, as only first year university students are required to take an indigenous Course Requirement as of 2016. However, it was difficult to obtain responses from first-year students only. Surveys from undergraduate students in their second and third year were also

AMANDA APPASAMY ET AL.

collected. Hence, the recorded number of respondents who took an ICR for this survey is low. In addition, since this course is a new requirement, there are not many students who have taken it as of yet. In the next year or two, there will be a higher percentage of students taking the ICR; this study may get more accurate responses then.

Perception Change of Students Who Took an ICR

Of the 23% of the respondents who took an ICR course, 43% indicated that their knowledge of Indigenous issues has increased and 43% of the students also indicated that taking an ICR course has had a transformative effect on their knowledge in the matter. It was also interesting to note that 7% of the population who took the course indicated that it was a negative experience. It would be significant to look further as to why taking the ICR has been negative for some, but overall the majority of students who took the course found that it has increased their knowledge. Therefore, based on this information, and from personal accounts of the students, it shows that education can be used a tool to increase the public's awareness and to change negative perception about Indigenous issues.

Would Students Have Taken the ICR If It Was Not Required?

For this question, we had 58 out of 78 responses. Out of the 58 responses, 45 % of the population indicated that they would *maybe* have taken the course if it was not required, 26% indicated that they would have definitely taken the course had it not been a required course and 29 % of the population indicated that they would not have taken the course if it was not required. Of the 78 students interviewed, 70 % indicated that they have a high or medium interest in learning about Indigenous issues, 30 % of the population indicated low to moderate interest in the issue as shown in figure 4. Based on this information, the majority of students have a high interest in learning about Indigenous issues.

Level of Interest vs. Program of Study

Cross-tabulating our results to compare the level of interest of students to their program of study found that students enrolled in a Social Science program have a higher interest in learning about Indigenous issues, followed by Criminal Justice, Business and Arts. We can conclude that the interests of students in learning about Indigenous issues may depend on their program of studies.

On the other hand, students who are in the Sciences and Computer Sciences have less interest in learning about Indigenous issues, because it is not crucial to their understanding of their field. Consequently, it can be assumed that to educate the entire population about Indigenous issues it would be important to make it mandatory; otherwise students enrolled in programs that do not focus on Social Issues or Indigenous issues would not make an effort in learning about the matter through an educational institution. As a result, they may have a high tendency of learning biased information about the issue through social media, mainstream media or conversation with peers jeopardizing the efforts of eliminating discrimination.

Importance of the ICR to Students?

35.5% of the population surveyed indicated that they believe it is important to them that the University of Winnipeg has included a mandatory Indigenous course in their program for all first-year students as of 2016. 22.4 % indicated that it is not important to them followed by 35.5% stated that they are indifferent as to whether the course is mandatory or not. The majority of students indicate that it is not important to them that there is a mandatory Indigenous course requirement. We have also cross-tabulated our results to compare students' knowledge of Indigenous Issues with whether the ICR is important to them.

We found that the ICR is insignificant to students with low to moderate knowledge about Indigenous issues. However, the ICR is important to those who claim to have good to excellent knowledge about indigenous issues. Based on this information, we could conclude that those students who have little knowledge of Indigenous issues would not make the effort to learn more about it or voluntarily take a course at the university level to educate them about the issue. Meaning many students will not be aware of Indigenous issues facing the people of Canada. Demonstrating that making the ICR a mandatory requirement is crucial to the elimination of discrimination against Indigenous peoples and to addressing the ignorance of the general public about the issue.

How Do You Think the ICR Will Change/Shape Your Behaviour When Approaching Indigenous Issues?

63% of the population surveyed indicated that implementing an ICR would increase their knowledge when approaching and reacting to Indigenous issues. 20% of the respondents indicated that they would approach Indigenous issues with less discrimination. 13 % of the population indicated that it is a hassle that the ICR has been implemented and 4% of the population indicated that they are unsure as to how the ICR will change their behaviour.

The majority of the respondents seems to agree that without the ICR, there will be continued discrimination towards Indigenous people in Canada and implementing this course will educate the public, which will then lead to reconciliation. Those students who indicated that implementing the ICR is a hassle may not be aware of how it applies to their program of study or could be misinformed about the ICR associating it with an additional course load and cost.

AMANDA APPASAMY ET AL.

DISCUSSION

This research has notable limitations; however, it can serve as a starting point for future research done on this topic. We believe the research would be beneficial if done on a larger scale with the correct sample size, and with a well-piloted survey. The data shows some areas of interest, such as the cross tabulation between the program of study and level of interest in Indigenous Issues. This question along with the question, which showed that 7% believe the course to be a hassle, would be important to understand further. There may be a lack of understanding about the Indigenous Course Requirement regarding how it affects a student's degree plan or could give clues to systemic issues of racism. Furthermore, it would be important to include more questions on the actual content of the course, the satisfaction of the instructor's ability, and other logistical aspects that were not included in this study, because these elements will affect how a student perceives the requirement.

The effect this course requirement has on instructors should also be noted, if an instructor is getting negative reviews of the course because students do not want to take it, then the instructor too will naturally show hesitations on teaching this course requirement. Perhaps the impact on instructors would be a different research project. However, it is worth noting.

We would also recommend that other methods be used to triangulate the results for stronger reliability. One method that would be helpful and that would lessen the interviewer effect would be focus groups. Interviews should also be conducted, but rigorous piloting of the questions should be done in order to avoid interview bias.

Lastly, we recommend that further research on this topic not be done until the Indigenous Course Requirement has been in effect for an established length of time. Much of the information we collected on student's perceptions of the course requirement was in relation to other Indigenous courses students have taken and not necessarily the required course. This while helpful, was not what the research was seeking to understand.

CONCLUSION

This research project showed that many students at the University of Winnipeg feel that the Indigenous Course Requirement will decrease discrimination towards Indigenous people in Canada, and increase awareness about Indigenous issues. It also showed us that students who have taken an Indigenous course felt that they had a significant change in perception as a result of the course. Thus, while the survey may have been done on a small scale, it gives valuable insights into future areas of research and interest. While showing although the course requirement is a key tool for reconciliation, there is still work that needs to be done in order manifest the benefits of the ICR to as many students as possible.

214

SURVEYING UNDERGRADUATE STUDENTS' PERCEPTIONS

REFERENCES

Assembly of First Nations. (2002). *Top misconceptions about aboriginal peoples*. Retrieved from http://tricitiesecd.ca/files/4013/3599/2965/FACTSandMisconceptions.pdf

Bradburn, N., & Mason, W. (1964). The effect of question order on responses. *Journal of Marketing Research, 1*(4), 57–61. Retrieved from http://www.jstor.org/stable/3150380?seq=1#page_scan_tab-_contents

Bryman, A., & Bell, E. (2012). *Social research methods* (pp. 66–140). Toronto: Oxford University Press.

Harpe, S. (2015). How to analyze likert and other rating scale data. *Currents in Pharmacy Teaching and Learning, 7*(6), 836–850. Retrieved from http://www.sciencedirect.com.libproxy.uwinnipeg.-ca/science/article/pii/S187712971520196

Lee, D. (2016). *University of Winnipeg makes indigenous course a requirement*. Retrieved from http://www.cbc.ca/news/canada/manitoba/university-of-winnipeg-makes-indigenouscourse-a-requirement-1.3328372

Monkman, L. (2016). *High hopes for mandatory indigenous courses set to start at U of W*. Retrieved from http://www.cbc.ca/news/indigenous/uof-w-mandatory-indigenouscourserequirement-1.3744485

Sedgwick, P. (2013). Convenience sampling. *Endgames*. Retrieved from https://fhs.mcmaster.ca/anesthesiaresearch/documents/Sedgwick2013Conveniencesampling.pdf

Statistical Services Center. (2001). *Approaches to the analysis of survey data*. Retrieved from https://www.reading.ac.uk/ssc/resources/ApproachesToTheAnalysisOfSurveyData.pdf

Statistics Canada. (2010). *Survey methods and practices*. Retrieved from http://www.statcan.gc.ca/pub/12-587-x/12-587-x2003001-eng.pdf

Truth and Reconciliation Commission of Canada. (2015). *Calls to actions*. Retrieved from http://www.trc.ca/websites/trcinstitution/File/2015/Findings/Calls_to_Action_English2.pdf

Visser, P., Krosnick, J., & Lavrakas, P. (2003). *Survey research* (pp. 223–246). Retrieved from http://web.stanford.edu/dept/communication/faculty/krosnick/Survey_Research.pdf

Amanda Appasamy
University of Winnipeg
Winnipeg, Manitoba

Cassandra Szabo
University of Winnipeg
Winnipeg, Manitoba

Jordan Tabobondung
University of Winnipeg
Winnipeg, Manitoba

PART 4

COMMUNITIES OF HEALING AND STRENGTH: REDIRECTION TO RESURGENCE

CHARLENE MOORE

23. MOCCASIN MAKING FOR COMMUNITY DEVELOPMENT

In York Factory First Nation

The people of York Landing have seen many changes over the years and yet they have maintained their proud cultural traditions adapting to major disruptions such as relocation, the loss of their traditional lands, and the impacts of major hydro- electric projects. Today, the people of York Factory First Nation are preparing for the future by re-establishing their connection with the land, and becoming more self-reliant again.[1]

INTRODUCTION

The activity of making moccasins in a communal setting contributes to community development among Indigenous Peoples. This is achieved through traditional methods of reciprocity, communal planning, and sharing. The purpose of this literature review is to find what information is available on moccasin making and community development. The findings will provide context for further research on a group of moccasin makers in York Factory First Nation called the 'Busy Beavers' who are looking to open a business to sell their art.

BACKGROUND

Despite the importance, there has been limited literature on moccasins and moccasin making as well as no research on how moccasin making can contribute to community development. However, there is a decent amount of discourse on community development from a Western and an Indigenous perspective. Imposed Western development has often had adverse effects and oppressed community initiatives. This literature review will try to answer the question of how moccasin making in York Landing will contribute to community development. Without the use of primary research this will be achieved through the available literature, and the gaps will be presented for future primary research.

The art of moccasin making has been a craft held closely to members of York Factory First Nation. The process and intricate designs require hard work that traditionally involves everyone in the community. The communal art is described as a way to hold people together as it creates "…one big happy family."[2] The skill was often passed on from generation to generation, creating intergenerational

© KONINKLIJKE BRILL NV, LEIDEN, 2018 | DOI 9789004367418_023

CHARLENE MOORE

benefits, and communal positivity.[3] Working together provided a means of healing, community development, and economic gain.[4]

With the arrival of European colonies to North America, Indigenous Peoples and their community institutions have been adversely affected by colonization.[5] The Western development paradigms are often highly hierarchical and based on economic development in an industrial sense.[6] Whereas Indigenous planning/ development follows different models based on communal benefit, reciprocity, and future generations.[7] The appearance of Western community development has proven to have unsatisfactory results for Indigenous Peoples' communities.[8] This is especially true when outsiders initiate projects that are thought up and constructed within a Western paradigm.[9] It is essential to understand the current development discourse and environment for Indigenous communities.

YORK FACTORY FIRST NATION

York Factory has a registered population of 1,332 members with 464 members living on reserve and 868 living off reserve. The community of York Factory was relocated in 1957 to York Landing, which, is located in northern Manitoba about 50–160 Km from the nearest service stations.[10] Average earnings equal $21,762 with the average income being $18,000. Significantly lower than Manitoba's average earnings ($37,579) and income ($36,696). In addition to this, the unemployment rate is also notably higher in York Factory (18.9) than in Manitoba (6.2). Currently, the community has little opportunity for economic growth due to its isolation and small population.[11]

Due to the imposition of government initiated development and policy it has been difficult for Indigenous communities to do their own community planning.[12] Specifically, York Factory has dealt with forced relocation, the imposition of residential schooling, and Manitoba Hydro Electric Dams.[13] These impositions have caused significant change and have drastically impeded on the community's traditional ways of subsistence living.[14]

However difficult it has been, York Factory, like other communities have still been able to remain resilient and successful in their pursuits.[15] Gordon Wastesicoot, a community member, stated, "I enjoyed my people and saw their willingness to accept things both good and bad and move on. It takes a lot of courage to do this."[16] When the community was relocated and found that the promise of housing had not been fulfilled, the community came together and built their own houses.[17] The community is now trying to combat this through moccasin making as a means to grow the local economy through new economic opportunities by creating and selling their art.

COMMUNITY DEVELOPMENT LITERATURE

There is literature on Indigenous planning/development, Western community development, and the combination of the two based on various topics like traditional

220

development and material culture.[18] There is also research on economic development and the different forms it can take in an Indigenous community.[19] In addition to this, there is research available about York Factory First Nation and their history.[20] All of these topics with their corresponding literature are important and guide this research on how moccasin making fits into community development for York Factory First Nation.

However, there appear to be several gaps in the literature in regards to moccasin making and community development. In a broad sense, there is highly limited information on moccasins in general[21] and minimal amounts on moccasin making as a form of community development.[22] There is also, absolutely no research on moccasin making in regards to the economic side of community development. Even more specifically, there is no information on moccasins and moccasin making in regards to the community of York Factory First Nation or how the community perceives community development.

Community-driven development within the current political context has been hard to achieve for many Indigenous Peoples. This struggle has resulted in the creation of research and literature to discuss the significance of the different strategies theorized and used to achieve community development. The existing literature will be used to discuss how material culture can be used by communities to self-determine their economic and social development to create context around moccasin making for community development in York Landing. These sources have been chosen based on academic merit (peer-reviewed) relevance in time (released no longer than ten years ago), and relevance to the research topic. In addition to this, importance has been put on variation in the field/research type/method/ of the source.

Three themes, each with sub-themes and their corresponding sources will be discussed in this literature review. Gaps found in the literature for each theme will be shown and explained. This will indicate what research is needed and how the current literature will supplement primary research with York Factory First Nation.

INDIGENOUS COMMUNITY DEVELOPMENT

As Matunga (2013) writes, since time immemorial Indigenous communities were planning according to their own traditions and practices, pre-dating settler colonies and illegal colonial government takeovers.[23]

> ...[M]anaging the environment and interactions between humans and the natural world were based on traditional knowledge, worldviews, and values. It used traditional approaches, processes, and institutional arrangements to implement decisions – including environmental decisions – and to determine appropriate resource use and allocation.[24]

Decisions were made through consensus/agreement with respect to traditional values and knowledge, Elders' wisdom, hospitality, and reciprocity.[25] There was considerable importance on equal improvement to the environment, social, economic, cultural, and political outcomes for all unlike Western imperial politics, economy, and social systems.[26] Assuming moccasin making assists in these qualities of Indigenous planning and therefore requires community control in the development process. This is the type of development York Factory First Nation is looking to create with their moccasin making efforts.

Community-Based

Works by Barraket (2005) and Mannell discuss the importance of the communal aspect of community planning. Also argued by Mannell (2013), is the importance of awareness in the community, higher standards and outspokenness, creativity, outside and local knowledge/support, as well as traditional knowledge.[27] The authors explore how community planning is done, and bring up ways to progress development strategies, indicating that communities have improvement to be made.

An example of community-based planning is collective work through moccasin making as exampled by Anderson (2011) and Theriault (2006), where moccasin making relied on the whole community and required strong relationships.[28] While Theriault looks more into the mechanics of moccasin making (providing insight into the multigenerational work, Anderson explains how this contributed to positive social development for the community. This activity may be similar to the moccasin making in York Factory First Nation.

Traditional Planning

In addition to this, Jojola (2013) and Matunga (2013) indicate that planning must also be placed-based with the use of traditional knowledge; this knowledge involves deep understanding of the present, while thinking of the future to liberate Indigenous Peoples.[29] Matunga argues that "[i]f Indigenous peoples were planned into oppression; equally they can be planned out of it."[30] York Factory First Nation is taking the opportunity to determine their development with traditional skills to create positive change.

Gap

There appear to be gaps in the information of how moccasin making can currently facilitate community planning. There are many communal benefits as exampled in the literature; however, there is no specific literature on utilizing moccasin making for the use of social development in Indigenous communities. In addition to this, there appears to be minimal information on the traditional knowledge that might correspond with the art of moccasin making.

Community planning can bring about positive change as exampled in the literature above. With an emphasis on communal needs and traditional knowledge, progressive innovations can be created, by the community, for the community. As we will learn later, it is important to understand this form of development as it has had a positive effect on communities who have used it. Community planning and its features largely contrast with Western community development features. These concepts are essential to understand how moccasin making can influence communities and their development strategy.

WESTERN COMMUNITY DEVELOPMENT

As indicated earlier, Western development equates mostly to economic development, relying on top-down decision-making and large-scale enterprises by the state or the private sector. Western development emphasizes labor productivity, creating a systematic underclass group twisted into poverty, unemployment, and lower rates of education.[31]

These things are representative of the Western assimilative behavior and the 'universal' understanding of progress and development.

> Industrial capitalism, the nation-state, and reason have shaped the modern world. They have made possible the production of great wealth, longer life, uncountable amenities, and freedoms from ancient tyrannies. Above everything else, they have given us the opportunity for choice, perhaps the defining characteristic of modernity. But they have exacted a price in human solidarity and agency.[32]

Although it is understood that there are negative aspects of the system, the system is still unquestioned. It is this belief that is dangerous to Indigenous communities. York Factory First Nation has often been adversely affected by Western development, and thus it is understandable why the community might withdraw from this paradigm.

Impacts

Despite even the best of interest from the government, there are still issues when outsiders try to control Indigenous community development. An example of this is the case of the Bamberton Sustainable Community Design Process.[33] Government plans to create social change often fails because of the government's controlling, objective behavior, and the tendency to misunderstand the people and their needs.[34] Boydell exemplifies this by discussing the failing current government structure and how new forms of government would do better.[35] He concludes that the government needs to change the stovepipe system (top to bottom) to a more flexible and cross-sectorial system with better communication. Boydell argues that all levels of government (federal, provincial, and municipal) should be working together to give communities more autonomy and social capital.[36]

Goodfellow-Baikie takes this further with a discussion on the problems with outsider community planning and in what ways it can fail.[37] Arguing a case study

CHARLENE MOORE

was done with seventy community members involved in the learning of traditional skills,[38] the study looks at how it failed and why.[39] He explains that northern communities require a combination of inside and outside resources, there are not enough people usually, and it is difficult to find an appropriate model of community economic development.[40]

Through the imposition of inappropriate Western community development methods aimed to assimilate and abrogate Indigenous social and economic systems, the Canadian State, like other States, has worked to demean and obliterate Indigenous Peoples self-determination.[41] There is also an issue with the spectrum of different levels and all of the actors involved in community development (cooperation's, local actors, and governments) specifically in dealing with land.[42] The authors' use a case study was done in Australia to argue that the colonizing practices that have taken place caused many tensions at the different levels of development.[43]

Balance

There is a common understanding that there is a need to reconcile tradition with innovation and the need to understand how Indigenous world-views and values impact upon enterprise.[44] To do this Hindle looks at casinos ran in partnership with non-Indigenous companies, and businesses owned solely by Indigenous members. Hindle looks at the positives and negatives of each as well as cultural impacts of this.[45] The author explains that these are equal but different and that heritage can be used in economic gains. Hindle argues that there does not need to be a paradox or the current false dichotomy.[46] Indigenous forms of community development and economic development are viable and do not need to be assimilatory and colonial by nature, exemplified by authors such as Benn and Onyx (2005) and Cardinal (2005).

Gap

There appears to be a gap in the literature about how Western economics can positively impact local moccasin making. Where do moccasins and other material culture stand in the Western market despite the negative aspects of its structure and theory? Does participating within the capitalist industry provide substantial benefit? Within all of these questions, there are even fewer answers when it comes to the specifics of York Landing.

Western development has caused damage to many Indigenous communities due to the foreign imposition. The high contrast between Indigenous worldviews of development and Western development has created an unbalanced relationship with tremendous tension. However, it is possible that these two ideologies can work together to create a cohesive and high functioning system to benefit Indigenous communities better.

Economic Development

Cahn argues that economics and business are often intertwined with social and cultural aspects of society. He indicates that Indigenous entrepreneurship is different regarding the context and goals the enterprise focuses on. Further, Indigenous enterprises are mostly community orientated rather than individualistic (like Western economics). In looking at micro-enterprises Cahn found that they relate to fa'aSamoa's concepts, and values.[47]

> [i]n Indigenous enterprises, fa'aSamoa is a motivating factor, an important asset, and a support mechanism that enhances entrepreneurial activity. In such enterprises, fa'aSamoa can reduce vulnerability. Ultimately, the success and sustainability of the micro-enterprises was strongly influenced by how successfully the entrepreneurial activity blended with fa'aSamoa and thus how 'indigenous' the enterprise was.[48]

It was found that money was an important outcome, as was the social and cultural capital that was developed through active engagement in values and expressions of fa'aSamoa, which were equally important to the micro-entrepreneurs.[49]

Exemplifying how Indigenous communities are evolving to incorporate Western concepts to survive and compete in today's society. It is clear that there are different options available through the examples in the literature discussed below. Traditional knowledge and systems of economic and social development are still valuable tools and concepts to be utilized. It appears that York Factory First Nation is looking to do similar development to fa'aSamoa.

Social Capital/Sustainability

Jojola discusses significant social capital, looking at the ethical, methodological, and epistemological approaches to community design and planning by Indigenous communities. He argues that these approaches are based on a seven-generation model.[50] A large part of communal wellness is relationships (collectivism and kinship), which are often achieved through collective work, including moccasin making as argued by Anderson.[51] This is supported by Theriault who indicates the importance of youth and passing on traditional knowledge.[52]

Traditional Skills

Kritsch's article is an indication of how traditional skills can be used to achieve positive development for Indigenous communities. The example of the Gwich'in people working on a caribou skin-clothing project explored culture and history, which raised the participants' pride.[53] Cardinal exemplifies the success of several Indigenous entrepreneurs in his article. [54]Arguing that their success came from how they "...utilized their traditional values to move their community into prosperity."[55]

CHARLENE MOORE

More specifically, Theriault also indicates that moccasin making was used as a form of survival, not only for clothing but also for trading or selling.[56] Thus demonstrating how traditional skills and material culture have been used for economic and social sustenance for a long time. This furthers my indication that traditional skills and knowledge are important to communities and individuals. Making the transference of the moccasin making knowledge an important and essential addition to any community. Especially when it comes to community led and community initiated development projects and plans.

New Paths

Hindle and Landsdowne explore the need to reconcile tradition with innovation and the need to understand how Indigenous world-views and values impact enterprise in the predominantly Western world.[57] They explain that these are equal but different and that heritage can be used in economic gains; there does not need to be a paradox or false dichotomy. In addition to this Tapsell and Woods explore self-organization theoretically from a social entrepreneurship perspective and under an Indigenous entrepreneurial understanding.[58] The authors argue that heritage is a positive option for moving forward with social enterprises for Indigenous peoples.[59] Furthermore, Jojola positions that Indigenous Peoples need to develop their own nationhood to maintain authority. Indicating that it is important to keep reclaiming cultural practices and sustainability. All of which must be done with the intergenerational participation of youth and elders (Jojola, pp. 468–470).[60] These are essential facets of moccasin making as indicated earlier. Thus, the moccasin making business could benefit a community's development in both social and economic ways.

Gap

The literature shows how traditional skills and material culture can contribute to community development. There are many opinions on how best to grow economically and socially in communities ranging from the Western paradigm to the Indigenous paradigm. The possibilities surrounding moccasin making as a form of economic and social support have not been discussed despite the range of paths moving forward. There also appears to be a gap in the traditional knowledge of moccasin making and how this can facilitate community growth economically and socially.

CONCLUSION

From the literature there appear to be three significant gaps: How can we apply moccasin making to social development in current society? What is the cultural and traditional knowledge of moccasin making (especially from the Cree of York Factory First Nation)? And finally, what are the ways in which Western development can positively affect the local moccasin making industry?

MOCCASIN MAKING FOR COMMUNITY DEVELOPMENT

A research project with York Factory First Nation will look at how moccasin making is positively affecting communities in a traditional and contemporary sense. This research should have interviews with the 'Busy Beavers' Chief and Council, as well as other interested community members, to find how the art has contributed economically and socially. There will be conversations on how this development can be taken further to create a more significant impact and benefit for community members. With this research, the gaps mentioned above will be fulfilled. Like York Factory First Nation, many communities are looking for ways to positively impact their communities and stimulate development through the use of traditional knowledge, intergenerational relationships, and economic gains. This research will not only be beneficial to York Factory First Nation, but it will also help other Indigenous communities find new ways to utilize traditional skills and knowledge for community development.

NOTES

[1] York Factory First Nation, *Kipekiskwaywinan (Our Voices)* (York Landing, 2012), 67. The York Factory First Nation Community is currently living in York Landing. The Band was relocated from York Factory.

[2] Madeline Katt Theriault, *Moose to Moccasins: The Story of Ka Kita Wa Pa No Kwe* (Ontario: Dundurn Group, 2006), 59.

[3] Theriault, "Moose to Moccasins," 13–25, 54–61.

[4] Kim Anderson, *Life Stages and Native Women: Memory, Teachings, and Story Medicine 2011*, (Winnipeg: University of Manitoba Press, 2011), pp. 104–110, 112–117.

[5] Bill Lee, "Colonization and Community: Implications for First Nations Development," *Community Development Journal* 27, no. 3 (1992): 211–214, 216–218.

[6] Jnanabrata Bhattacharyya, "Theorizing Community Development," *Journal of the Community Development Society* (2004): 13, 26.

[7] Ted Jojola, "Indigenous Planning: Towards A Seven Generations Model," in *Reclaiming Indigenous Planning 2013*, by Theodore S. Jojola, David C. Natcher and Ryan Christopher Walker (Montreal; Kingston: McGill-Queen's University Press, 2013), pp. 465–470; Hirini Matunga, "Theorizing Indigenous Planning," in *Reclaiming Indigenous Planning 2013*, by Theodore S. Jojola, David C. Natcher and Ryan Christopher Walker (Montreal; Kingston: McGill-Queen's University Press, 2013), pp. 4–10, 14–22.

[8] Suzanne Benn and Jenny Onyx, "Negotiating Interorganizational Domains: The Politics of Social, Natural, and Symbolic Capital," in *A Dynamic Balance: Social Capital and Sustainable 2005*, by Ann Dale and Jenny Onyx (Vancouver: UBC Press, 2005), pp. 99–102; Tony Boydell, "The Challenges of Traditional Models of Governance in the Creation of Social Capital," in *A Dynamic Balance: Social Capital and Sustainable Community Development 2005,* by Ann Dale and Jenny Onyx (Vancouver: UBC Press, 2005), pp. 227–228, 238–241.

[9] Robin L. Goodfellow-Baikie and Leona M. English, "First Nations and Community Economic Development:A Case Study," *Community Development Journal* (2006): 223–228).

[10] Aboriginal Affairs and Northern Development Canada, "First Nation Profiles," last modified March 28, 2017, http://fnp-ppn.aandcaadnc.gc.ca/fnp/Main/Search/FNMain.aspx?BAND_NUMBER= 304 lang=eng

[11] Ibid.

[12] Bhattacharyya, "Theorizing Community Development"; Boydell, "Challenges of Traditional Models of Governance."

[13] York Factory First Nation, "Kipekiskwaywinan," pp. 51–65.

[14] Ibid., pp. 86–91.

CHARLENE MOORE

[15] Cheryl Cardinal, "Cando Economic Developer of the Year Awards: Utilizing Traditional Knowledge to Strive Toward Unity," *The Journal of Aboriginal Economic Development*, (2005): 14–20.

[16] Gordon Wastesicoot in York Factory First Nation, "Kipekiskwaywinan," 59.

[17] York Factory First Nation, "Kipekiskwaywinan," 55, 57.

[18] Jo Barraket, "Enabling Structures for Coordinated Action: Community Organizations, Social Capital, and Rural Community Sustainability," in *A Dynamic Balance: Social Capital and Sustainable Community Development 2005*, by Ann Dale and Jenny Onyx, 2005; Benn and Onyx, "Negotiating Interorganizational Domains"; Boydell, "Challenges of Traditional Models of Governance"; Kevin Hindle and Michele Lansdowne, "Brave Spirits on New Paths: Toward a Globally Relevant Paradigm of Indigenous Entrepreneurship Research," *Journal of Small Business & Entrepreneurship* 18, no. 2 (2005); Jojola, "Indigenous Planning"; Laura Mannell, Frank Palermo, and Crispin Smith, "Community-Based and Comprehensive: Reflections on Planning and Action in First Nations," in *Reclaiming Indigenous Planning* (Montreal; Kingston: McGill-Queen's University Press, 2013); Matunga, Theorizing Indigenous Planning.

[19] Steven Dinero, "Analysis of a "Mixed Economy" in an Alaskan Native Settlement: The Case of Arctic Village" *The Canadian Journal of Native Studies* XXIII, 1 (2003); Martha. Dowsley, "The Value of a Polar Bear: Evaluating the Role of a Multiple-Use Resource in the Nunavut Mixed Economy" *Arctic Anthropology* 45, no. 1 (2010); Gérard Duhaime, Edmund Searles and Peter J. Usher, "The Household as an Economic Unit in Arctic Aboriginal Communities, and its Measurement by Means of a Comprehensive Survey," *Social Indicators Research: An International and Interdisciplinary Journal for Quality-of-Life Measurement* 61, no. 2 (2003); Sylvia Van Kirk, "The Role of Native Women in the Fur Trade Society of Western Canada, 1670–1830," *Frontiers: A Journal of Women Studies* 7, no. 3 (1984); George W.Wenzel, "Canadian Inuit in a Mixed Economy: Thoughts on Seals, Snowmobiles, and Animal Rights," *Native Studies Review* 2, no. 1 (1986).

[20] Aboriginal Affairs and Northern Development Canada, "First Nation Profiles"; Ann M. Carlos and Frank D. Lewis, "Trade, Consumption, and the Native Economy: Lessons From York Factory, Hudson Bay," *The Journal of Economic History* 61 no. 4 (2001); York Factory First Nation, "Kipekiskwaywinan."

[21] David Sager, "The Rose Collection of Moccasins in the Canadian Museum of Civilization: Transitional Woodland/Grassland Footwear," *The Canadian Journal of Native Studies* 14, no. 2 (1994); Van Kirk, "The Role of Native Women in the Fur Trade."

[22] Anderson, "The Women's Circle"; Theriault, "Moose to Moccasins."

[23] Matunga, "Theorizing Indigenous Planning," 3, 5, 18–19.

[24] Ibid., p. 11.

[25] Ibid., pp. 19–21.

[26] Ibid., pp. 22–27.

[27] Mannell, Palermo, and Smith, "Community-Based and Comprehensive," 117–123, 133.

[28] Anderson, "The Women's Circle," 104–110, 112–117; Theriault, "Moose to Moccasins," 59.

[29] Jojola, "Indigenous Planning," 465–468; Matunga, "Theorizing Indigenous Planning," 27–29.

[30] Jojola, "Indigenous Planning," 31.

[31] Bhattacharyya, "Theorizing Community Development," 26.

[32] Boydell, "The Challenges of Traditional Models of Governance," 20–21.

[33] Ibid., pp. 227, 230–238.

[34] Ibid., pp. 227–228, 237–238.

[35] Ibid., pp. 227–228, 238–241.

[36] Ibid., pp. 235, 238–240, 241.

[37] Goodfellow-Baikie and English, "First Nations and Community Economic Development," 223.

[38] Ibid., pp. 225–228.

[39] Ibid., pp. 226–227, 228–229.

[40] Ibid., pp. 229–230.

[41] Jojola, "Indigenous Planning," 457–464; Bill, "Colonization and Community," 211–214, 216–218.

[42] Benn and Onyx, "Negotiating Interorganizational Domains," 87–89, 92–98.

[43] Ibid., pp. 99–102.

MOCCASIN MAKING FOR COMMUNITY DEVELOPMENT

[44] Hindle and Lansdowne. "Brave Spirits on New Paths," 131, 132–134, 136–137.
[45] Ibid., pp. 134–136, 138.
[46] Ibid., pp. 138.
[47] Miranda Cahn, "Indigenous Entrepreneurship, Culture and Micro-Enterprise in the Pacific Islands: Case Studies From Samoa," *Entrepreneurship & Development* 20, no. 1 (2008): 1–3.
[48] Cahn, "Indigenous Entrepreneurship, Culture and Micro-Enterprise," 16–17.
[49] Ibid., pp. 17.
[50] Jojola, "Indigenous Planning," 457.
[51] Anderson, "The Women's Circle," 104–110, 112–117.
[52] Theriault, "Moose to Moccasins," 13–25, 59–61.
[53] Ingrid Kritsch and Karen Wright-Fraser, "The The Gwuch'in Traditional Caribou Skin Clothing Project: Repatriating Traditional Knowledge and Skills," *Artic Institute of North America*, (2002): 205, 208–209.
[54] Cardinal, "Cando Economic Developer of the Year," 14–19.
[55] Ibid., 20.
[56] Theriault, "Moose to Moccasins," 58, 62–74, 93, 96–97.
[57] Hindle and Lansdowne, "Brave Spirits on New Paths," 131, 132–134, 136–138.
[58] Paul Tapsell and Christine Woods, "Social Entrepreneurship and Innovation: Self-Organization in an Indigenous Context." *Entrepreneurship & Regional Development* 22, no. 6 (2010): 536, 539–544.
[59] Tapsell and Woods, "Social Entrepreneurship and Innovation," 547–550.
[60] Jojola, "Indigenous Planning," 468–470.

REFERENCES

Aboriginal Affairs and Northern Development Canada. (2017, March 28). *First nation profiles*. Retrieved from http://fnp-ppn.aandc-aadnc.gc.ca/fnp/Main/Search/FNMain.aspx?BAND_NUMBER=304&lang=eng

Anderson, K. (2011). Adult years: The women's circle. In K. Anderson (Ed.), *Life stages and native women: Memory, teachings, and story medicine* (pp. 97–125). Winnipeg: University of Manitoba Press.

Barraket, J. (2005). Enabling structures for coordinated action: Community organizations, social capital, and rural community sustainability. In A. Dale & J. Onyx (Eds.), *A dynamic balance: Social capital and sustainable community development* (pp. 71–86). Vancouver: University of British Columbia Press.

Benn, S., & Onyx, J. (2005). Negotiating interorganizational domains: The politics of social, natural, and symbolic capital. In A. Dale & J. Onyx (Eds.), *A dynamic balance: Social capital and sustainable* (pp. 87–104). Vancouver: University of British Columbia Press.

Bhattacharyya, J. (2004). Theorizing community development. *Journal of the Community Development Society, 34*(2), 5–34.

Boydell, T. (2005). The challenges of traditional models of governance in the creation of social capital. In A. Dale & Onyx, J. (Eds.), *A dynamic balance: Social capital and sustainable community development* (pp. 227–242). Vancouver: University of British Columbia Press.

Cahn, M. (2008). Indigenous entrepreneurship, culture and micro-enterprise in the Pacific Islands: Case studies from Samoa. *Entrepreneurship & Regional Development, 20*(1), 1–18.

Cardinal, C. (2005). Cando economic developer of the year awards: Utilizing traditional knowledge to strive toward unity. *The Journal of Aboriginal Economic Development*, 13–20.

Carlos, A. M., & Lewis, F. D. (2001). Trade, consumption, and the native economy: Lessons from York factory, Hudson Bay. *The Journal of Economic History, 61*(4), 1037–1064.

Dinero, S. (2003). Analysis of a "mixed economy" in an Alaskan native settlement: The case of Arctic Village. *The Canadian Journal of Native Studies, 23*(1), 135–164.

Dowsley, M. (2010, July 17). The value of a polar bear: Evaluating the role of a multiple-use resource in the nunavut mixed economy. *Arctic Anthropology, 45*(1), 39–56.

Goodfellow-Baikie, R. L., & English, L. M. (2006). First nations and community economic development: A case study. *Community Development Journal, 41*(2), 223–233.

229

CHARLENE MOORE

Hindle, K., & Lansdowne, M. (2005). Brave spirits on new paths: Toward a globally relevant paradigm of indigenous entrepreneurship research. *Journal of Small Business & Entrepreneurship, 18*(2), 131–141.

Jojola, T. (2013). Indigenous planning: Towards A seven generations model. In T. S. Jojola, D. C. Natcher, & R. C. Walker (Eds.), *Reclaiming indigenous planning* (pp. 457–472). Montreal: McGill-Queen's University Press.

Ingrid, K., & Wright-Fraser, K. (2002). The Gwuch'in traditional caribou skin clothing project: Repatriating traditional knowledge and skills. *Artic Institute of North America, 55*(2).

Lee, B. (1992, July). Colonization and community: Implications for first nations development. *Community Development Journal, 27*(3), 211–219.

Mannell, L., Palermo, F., & Smith, C. (2013). Community-based and comprehensive: Reflections on planning and action in first nations. In R. Walker, T. Jojola, & D. Natcher (Eds.), *Reclaiming indigenous planning* (pp. 113–140). Montreal: McGill-Queen's University Press.

Matunga, H. (2013). Theorizing indigenous planning. In T. S. Jojola, D. C. Natcher, & R. C. Walker (Eds.), *Reclaiming indigenous planning* (pp. 3–32). Montreal: McGill-Queen's University Press.

Tapsell, P., & Woods, C. (2010). Social entrepreneurship and innovation: Self-organization in an indigenous context. *Entrepreneurship & Regional Development, 22*(6), 535–556.

Theriault, M. K. (2006). *Moose to moccasins: The story of ka kita wa pa no kwe.* Toronto: Dundurn Group.

Usher, P. J., Duhaime, G., & Searles, E. (2003). The household as an economic unit in arctic aboriginal communities, and its measurement by means of a comprehensive survey. *Social Indicators Research: An International and Interdisciplinary Journal for Quality-of-Life Measurement, 61*(2), 175–202.

Van Kirk, S. (1984). The role of native women in the fur trade society of Western Canada, 1670–1830. *Frontiers: A Journal of Women Studies, 7*(3), 9–13.

Wenzel, G. W. (1986). Canadian inuit in a mixed economy: Thoughts on seals, snowmobiles, and animal rights. *Native Studies Review, 2*(1), 69–82.

York Factory First Nation. (2012, June 13). *Kipekiskwaywinan (our voices).* Manitoba: York Landing.

Charlene Moore
Department of Indigenous Studies
University of Winnipeg
Winnipeg, Manitoba

ROBIN QUANTICK

24. ELDERS AND INDIGENOUS HEALING IN THE CORRECTIONAL SERVICE OF CANADA

A Story of Relational Dissonance, Sacred Doughnuts, and Drive-Thru Expectations

For over thirty years, the Government of Canada has made it a priority to hire Elders to lead intervention and healing programs for the expanding community of offenders of Aboriginal descent held in Canada's federal prisons (Sapers, 2012). The Elders' placement is embedded in a general policy aimed at successful community reintegration, the intended impact of which is to reduce the disproportionate representation of Aboriginal offenders held under federal warrant. Put another way, Elders are hired by the Correctional Service of Canada (CSC) in the restorative justice belief that, with their participation, fewer offenders of Aboriginal descent will return to prison.

The pursuit of successful community integration is central to the ebb and flow of daily institutional life. To transfer through the system and eventually secure a parole offenders are compelled to navigate a series of colonial structures, assumptions, and concepts. Power, knowledge, and compliance are the principle concepts that define the prison (Foucault, 1977) and, by extension, from the CSC's perspective, the process that leads to successful community reintegration. For theorists there is a well-documented relationship between power, knowledge, and compliance in the retributive prison. This work isolates a binary question that preoccupies theorists and places role, place, and function of Elders in an academic context: Is compliance with generally understood, retributive, dominant-culture values and attitudes sufficient to meet the requirement for successful community reintegration? Or are Indigenous understandings of individual, internalized self-awareness, recognition, and responsibility essential requirements? If the latter is true, then the retributive colonial prison cannot produce successful community reintegration as a substantive or measurable visible outcome. It is within this dichotomy that Elders do their work and that decolonizing theoretical concepts are enacted.

The research question that connects the purpose and rationale was as follows: What is the role, place, and function of Elders in the delivery of Indigenous healing programs within Canadian federal prisons?

© KONINKLIJKE BRILL NV, LEIDEN, 2018 | DOI 9789004367418_024

ROBIN QUANTICK

THEORETICAL CONTEXT/LITERATURE REVIEW

The outcome of the theoretical context for this study is best understood as an internalized sequence of understandings. These understandings guide, isolate and confirm the dichotomy presented in two different world-views – a dichotomy that serves as firewall to the efforts of an entire community of staff, incarcerated adults, and researchers who occupy the space that this study inhabits.

The study confirms an imperative in which each person in the community has a responsibility to recognize, remedy, and address injustice. In the words of Cora Weber-Pillwax (2001), "I cannot be involved in research and scholarly discourse unless I know that such work will lead to some change (out there) in that community, in my community" (p. 169). With this understanding, I selected a series of theoretical lenses: from dominant-culture understandings, to decolonizing understandings, to restorative-justice understandings, and culminating in Indigenous understandings.

The exploration of theory in this study confirms the outcome effects of two distinctly different world-views: the dominant culture and the Indigenous. The theoretical understanding of the dominant culture applies assumptions about the nature of the world that are vested in a colonial, paternal, and punitive process. Conversely, the roots of understanding in Indigenous theory are concentrated on consensual assumptions that require a decolonizing process of collaboration and cooperation to produce recognition, responsibility, restitution, and reconciliation.

The theoretical context of this study is best understood as a ritual protocol that requires internalization. For me, the product of internalization is self-awareness; it is a decolonizing process that empowers and transforms. It is a call to arms that is best expressed by Thomas King (2003):

> So here are our choices: a world in which creation is a solitary, individual act or a world in which creation is a shared activity; a world that begins in harmony and slides towards chaos or a world that begins in chaos and moves towards harmony; a world marked by competition or a world determined by co-operation. (pp. 21–25)

OVERVIEW

Success for the Correctional Service of Canada is measured by its capacity to produce successful community reintegration for the adults entrusted to their care. The colonizing architecture of secure custody facilities operated by the Correctional Service of Canada (with their panopticon assumptions and heritage) and the ritual systems required to sustain carceral surveillance in pursuit of unqualified compliance serve as a barrier to meeting the Government of Canada mandate to achieve successful community reintegration. In fact, successful community reintegration cannot be achieved with the current colonizing architecture maintained and sustained by the Correctional Service of Canada.

ELDERS AND INDIGENOUS HEALING IN THE CORRECTIONAL SERVICE OF CANADA

Conversely, Elder-led healing programs employ decolonizing principles of consensual design and delivery – focused on the role of relationship, balance, and self-awareness – to arrive at internalized recognition and responsibility. The aim in this consensual decolonizing approach is for each person to find an internalized path to restitution and, to the extent possible, community reconciliation. In this approach ritual and ceremony are essential methodologies.

The CSC cannot produce successful community reintegration because the structural and cultural anatomy of the organization does not align with the mandate. The image that comes to mind is the flying fish. The flying fish can, with astounding effort, launch itself out of the water; from a distance, it appears to fly at altitudes of over one meter and to cruise at this altitude for distances of up to 200 meters. In point of fact, the flying fish does not fly; it glides. But not really ... to glide as a bird does, the flying fish would require both the capacity to make use of thermal air currents to rise and fall and a whole new respiratory system so that it could exist out of water. Ultimately, the flying fish does not fly; it does not really even glide. To paraphrase the Disney character Buzz Lightyear ... it falls with style. With respect to the Government of Canada mandate on successful community reintegration, the CSC is a flying fish reacting to external demands beyond their control.

With this image in mind, the disproportionate representation of men and women of Aboriginal descent who are held under federal warrant must be understood to be the result of more than just systemic discrimination. The volume of people of Aboriginal descent in the Canadian federal criminal-justice system illustrates two things: that there is a disconnection in the processes that govern transfer and parole for incarcerated men and women of Aboriginal descent; and that, when successful reintegration does occur, it is an anomaly. My career in correctional programs began in 1986. In the 29 years that I worked in and around the CSC, I have never met anyone who went to work intending to visit harm on another person and yet that is undeniably what the current system does. The operational rituals, assumptions, beliefs, and practices are not designed to achieve successful community reintegration for any of the people assigned to the CSC's care.

The central, operational, institutional ritual that frames the role, place, and function of all of the people who inhabit the institutional space is the morning meeting. It is the ground in which the essential disconnections between aspirations and operations are unwittingly planted, nurtured, and harvested.

The collective assumptions brought to bear at the morning meeting have consequence. Among the binary and adversarial assumptions that drive the endeavour is what I have come to think of as the 3% assumption: While less than 3% of the offenders held under warrant are categorized as dangerous offenders (people like Paul Bernardo or Russell Williams) the morning meeting compels its participants to assume that every offender is understood to be a dangerous offender.

The consequence of the 3% assumption permeates every layer of the system. To achieve positions of authority, personnel are compelled to become experts in navigating the ebb and flow of the morning meeting. Consciously or unconsciously, the experience of the morning meeting impacts the negotiation between aspirations and operations. In this context, the experience of the morning meeting serves as a touchstone in the selection of the emerging generations of CSC leadership, thus perpetuating adversarial relationships between staff and offenders.

A Day in the Life

To put the self-fulfilling impact of the process into more concrete terms, let us imagine the process from the perspective of a young man of Aboriginal descent held under federal warrant. Based on statistics collated and published in 2013 by Public Safety Canada in its annual *Corrections and Conditional Release Statistical Overview* (CCRSO) the young man is probably below the average age of offenders in the general population. Statistically, it is likely he did not finish high school. It is also very likely that he was under the influence of drugs or alcohol when the offence occurred.

In this scenario, the young man meets the statistical averages of the system. He is likely to have entered the CSC's daily institutional orbit as part of a plea bargain. On this basis, he will serve his sentence; as he accepted a plea bargain, there are no available avenues of appeal for him.

His first CSC stop is the Reception Assessment Centre where, for three to four months, he will be evaluated and exercised and locked down in a process that culminates in a correctional plan. If he follows the plan as presented, it is presumed

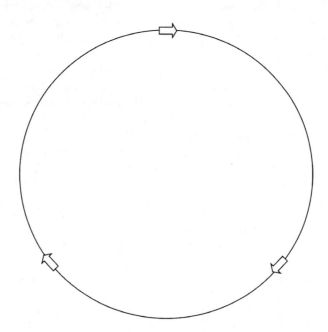

Figure 1. Daily operations orbit

he will cascade through the system to achieve successful community reintegration. At this point in the process, the system divides itself between the logistic challenges of feeding, housing, and clothing people and producing an individualized correctional plan from which to manage their care.

The daily operations orbit (see Figure 1) cannot focus on the needs of the individual because the reactive logistics of feeding and housing people effectively serve as a barrier to applying proactive, individualized responses. The system must rely on a binary process of checklists that are defined and administered around the warrant; the terms of reference, processes and acronyms applied in the administration of the sentence are very likely akin to new learning a new language. In this scenario, the young man remains invisible until the day he is assaulted while on the exercise yard. At that moment, he leaves the daily operations orbit; he is now on the agenda at the morning meeting.

The video record reflects that he did not initiate the altercation and the security staff assigned to his range (cell block) report that he has been keeping to himself. He is sent to hospital, where he is examined and then assigned to a different area of the institution. All of this is noted on the offender management system, documenting that his constitutionally mandated due process/*Charter of Rights and Freedoms* requirements have been observed and respected (see Figure 2).

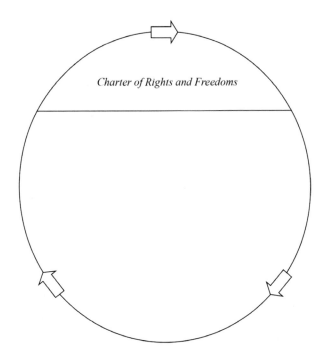

Figure 2. Charter of rights and freedoms

The systemic dialogue of the morning meeting moves on to the offenders' personal safety in relation to the *Commissioners Directives and Institutional Exigencies* (see Figure 3). Ultimately, this raises paternal questions for the meeting: How do we keep him off the agenda for the next morning meeting? Will he become an ongoing concern? Where do we put him?

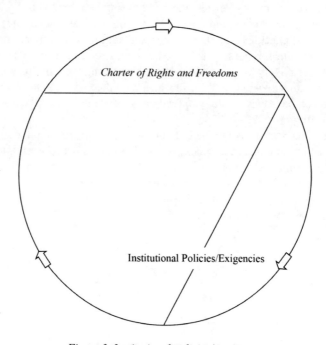

Figure 3. Institutional policies/exigencies

In this scenario, the correctional-plan process is accelerated in the name of dynamic security. In accordance with the findings published in the CCRSO, the exigencies of time and penitentiary placement mean that no *Corrections and Conditional Release Act* (CCRA) section 84 Gladue report will be completed. Statistically, it is unlikely that one will ever be completed. This is a fact that the offender is unlikely to appreciate, although he will undoubtedly live with the consequences, including decreased opportunity for community reintegration. The absence of a Gladue report thus directly contributes the disproportionate representation of persons of Aboriginal descent held under federal warrant.

With the Charter and exigency challenges of housing and safety sorted, the process is now primarily defined by the warrant in relation to the *Corrections and Conditional Release Act* (see Figure 4). If the offender can demonstrate, manufacture, or simulate the appropriate volume of remorse in the various meetings and hearings, he can proceed according to schedule and in relative anonymity.

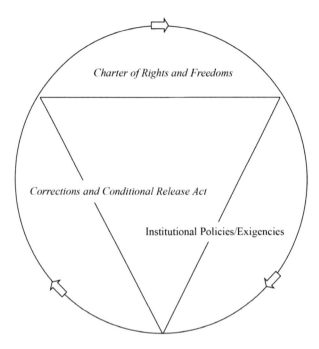

Figure 4. Corrections and conditional release act

As an outcome effect, the institutional process is compelled to focus on logistics, groups and trends. Our young man can anticipate that he will spend more time in segregation than his non-Aboriginal peers. As time passes, he is unlikely to be transferred to minimum security at the same rate as his non-Aboriginal peers. More significantly, he is unlikely to be granted day or full parole: He will have to wait until his statutory release date to secure a place at a halfway house.

Once at the halfway house, he is more likely to have his parole revoked than non-Aboriginal parolees. For offenders of Aboriginal descent, the daily operations orbit is not a circle; it is an oval engineered to impede successful community reintegration. It is the personification of relational dissonance. This conflicts with the aims, objectives, methods, and philosophy of Elder-led healing programs.

The logistical processes of all CSC facilities grew from a panopticon model that places unqualified compliance as the goal. As such, it should come as no surprise when the established institutional-operations model proves itself expert at producing myopic and retributive results that are substantially disconnected from the spirit of the principle of least restriction. Where then do Elder-led healing programs fit into this image?

Elders and healing programs exist in the space inside the large triangle. In fact, given their consensual approach to communication, they function in the centre of a smaller daily operations orbit (see Figure 5). Their first task is to bring the individual

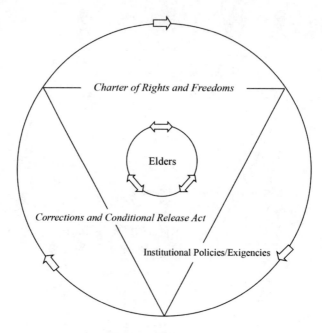

Figure 5. Elders' circle

to a level of self-awareness in which detention and deterrence are irrelevant to decisions regarding personal behaviour. This requires that, on a case-by-case basis, they break through the binary noise of institutional life to fundamentally change individual attitudes and values. As they establish the participant circle, they introduce a new triangle grounded in Indigenous knowledge, ritual and ceremony.

The circle they function within does not touch the planes of the interior triangle they rely on for program space and time. They begin a bottom-up process of effort concentrated on the whole person in which Indigenous knowledge and ritual and ceremony circles back and forth.

Ultimately, the work of Elders begins in a consensual bottom-up process that introduces Indigenous knowledge to the individual through the grey noise that is the daily operational cycle (see Figure 6). In this process, the Elder treats the offender as he/she might treat any other person they might encounter in their home community. As the program participant allows the Elder to push through the exigencies of the daily operational cycle, the Elder can begin to introduce ritual to the relationship. This is a stark contrast to the carceral approach that puts dehumanization above self-actualization.

In this model and over time, the relationship between the offender and the Elder begins to take root. As the offender becomes more comfortable, ritual is practiced more overtly in relation to Indigenous knowledge and in reference to the detention/deterrence objectives of the daily operational cycle. This is practiced as one might learn to play a musical instrument, with teacher and student engaged in a

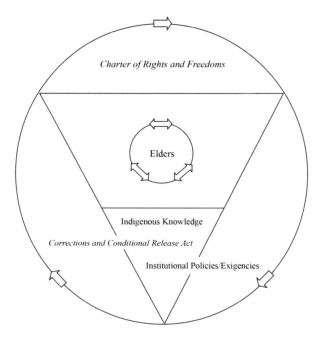

Figure 6. Indigenous knowledge

call-and-response process until it becomes engrained and second nature. Over time it will become an interchangeable process between ritual and Indigenous knowledge (see Figure 7). When these moments begin to emerge, the Elder introduces ceremony as a means to internalize the teaching.

As ceremony begins to take root, the Elder and offender move back and forth, in no particular order between the daily orbit, Indigenous knowledge, ritual, and ceremony. In this movement, the objective is that each person will integrate the process into recognition and responsibility, restitution and reconciliation in ways that internalize and confirm the teachings that emerge in ceremony (see Figure 8).

The aim of the process is not to manufacture a sense of guilt from which the system can measure some kind of deterrence. Rather, the object is for the individual to find an internalized and self-initiating desire to seek restitution for his or her own sake. In the case of federally incarcerated men and women, it is entirely likely that the restitution they make will only ever be symbolic, as the individual has probably violated the peace of their community in ways that cannot be reconciled. The object of the Elder-led healing program is better aligned with successful community reintegration because its objective is to work with each person, one person at a time, to help that person reach a state of self-awareness in which grace and objectivity are possible and the parole that may be extended by the National Parole Board ceases to be the primary objective.

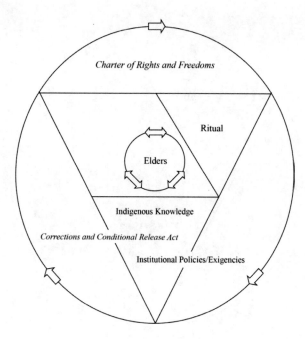

Figure 7. Ritual

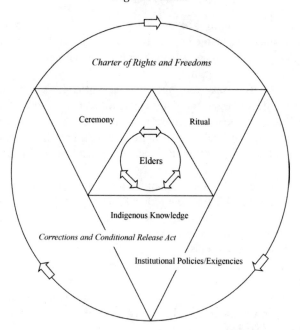

Figure 8. Ceremony

ELDERS AND INDIGENOUS HEALING IN THE CORRECTIONAL SERVICE OF CANADA

CRITICAL POLICY REVIEW

The Correctional Service of Canada is a complex, retributive organization with pockets of restorative justice and Indigenous justice innovation that defy the carceral reality of the prison. As a matter of policy oversight, the CSC was given a mandate to operationalize either a restorative or Indigenous justice paradigm. Contained in the principle of least restriction was the expectation that the CSC would be unreservedly fixed on achieving successful community reintegration for each of the citizens held under federal warrant.

In the current dominant culture model only when something has happened in a program area that requires the attention of the management and security staff are the typifications of the prison challenged (Berger & Luckmann, 1967). Ultimately, the foundational carceral assumptions of the CSC compel its participants to assume that every offender is a dangerous offender. These assumptions drive a wedge between restorative aspirations and retributive operations.

The CSC's statistical results are a reflection of its retributive roots. Currently, 70% of offenders assigned to the CSC are held in federal institutions, while 30% are serving their sentences in community-supervision settings. Between 1992 and 2012, if the CSC had met the standard of "least restrictive measure" as defined in the CCRA, these proportions would have been reversed, with 30% held in federal institutions and 70% serving sentences in community-supervision settings. This would have meant closing two-thirds of existing prisons and replacing them with community-based treatment/supervision facilities modeled on the concept of healing lodges.

ELDERS' PERSPECTIVES

The Elders' words bring into relief their world-view and understanding of their role, place, and function in the provision of healing programs. Their words express an understanding that they are engaged in a process of reciprocal learning. It begins with a rejection of a dominant-culture colonial understanding of status and place. Elder is a Government of Canada term that is rejected by the people who design and deliver healing programs. If they refer to themselves in connection with their responsibilities, they call themselves helpers. This reflects both a difference in world view and an acknowledgement that to refer to themselves as Elders would be entirely inconsistent with community practice. In this vein, the incarcerated adults who participate in healing programs routinely refer to them as Elders; this is entirely consistent with community practice. Participants understand healing programs as extensions of the traditional community they aspire to rejoin.

Over time, the process by which the Government of Canada appoints individuals to the role of Elder has changed. In the early years, it was entirely by word of mouth. Current practice is far more formal. The common ground in all appointments is that the individual who applies does so at the suggestion of others. The outcome of

ROBIN QUANTICK

this process is the raised accountability and increased authority that comes from a community nomination.

Elders are engaged in a process of reciprocal healing. It begins with the understanding that anyone can find themselves is a state of crisis. For healing to happen, Elders must first make space to acknowledge their place in the universe. Elder Elizabeth notes, "I realized I was out of balance." They must then make space for emotions that grow things; Elizabeth describes the process: "It is hard work but at the same time … there's laughter and there's teasing." Alexander describes how healing happens when Elders fulfill a duty of care to challenge participants:

> Sometimes I'm a conscience, bringing things to light maybe that sometimes we as human beings just want to keep in dark places and not admit that these are dark things that we've done or think or do. … I'm also encouraging them, trying to encourage them to have the bravery to look. And then, asking them to tell me what they see.

The implication of this journey is the impact on the offenders when they are provided a model from which to sculpt their own healing. Elders understand that their primary function in the healing paradigm is to teach; sometimes the responsibility requires them to teach the same lesson over and over again. Elders' knowledge is concentrated in the Indigenous knowledge that flows from the teachings. The language of the teachings does not concern itself with the language of the theorist or, for that matter, the language of policy makers.

CONCLUSIONS

If successful community reintegration is to be more than a lofty goal, the CSC and the Government of Canada needs to engage in a process that reviews and renews the Continuum of Care with communities to ensure it has not inadvertently become a colonizing pan-Indian approach to program delivery. Inuit men and women should not be compelled to participate in Cree teachings or Mohawk sweat lodges as part of their healing program because it's the only option available to them. Each offender must be recognized as the person they are. In accordance with the Supreme Court of Canada decision in *Gladue*, each offender is entitled to a healing program that incorporates his or her culture and community.

The small size of this study's interview group limits the ability to reach generalized conclusions. A national study of Elders is needed to explore the role, place, and function of Elders in different settings – from region to region and community to community.

The CSC needs to build community supervision facilities that will support and promote both healing and successful community reintegration. Within their own best practices, the CSC operates two facilities that are templates for healing and successful community reintegration. They are the Oki Ma Ochi Healing Lodge located in Maple Creek Saskatchewan and the Henry Trail Community Corrections Centre on the grounds of Collins Bay Institution in Kingston Ontario. For men and women

242

ELDERS AND INDIGENOUS HEALING IN THE CORRECTIONAL SERVICE OF CANADA

whose needs are a challenge to anticipate and supervise, the Henry Trail Centre facility model partnered with a healing lodge represents a transformative model better designed and engineered to produce successful community reintegration.

Elder-led healing programs represent an opportunity to build on something that works – something that is aligned with who we are in our best moments. The work is not easy; it requires grit. It is best illustrated in the words of Elder Elizabeth as she explores the challenges of acknowledgement and forgiveness:

You're coming from two worlds ... two different world-views. That's how it was at the beginning and it's still going on now ... It's not about blaming and shaming, it's about enlightening ourselves to what things were done ... We need to look at the past as a teaching. We need to look back to what has brought us here and (ask ourselves) how we can change that ...

REFERENCES

Battiste, M. (2000). *Reclaiming indigenous voice and vision.* Vancouver: University of British Columbia Press.

Baxter, J., & Eyles, J. (1997). Evaluating qualitative research in social geography: Establishing rigor in interview analysis. *Transactions of the Institute of British Geographers, 222,* 505–525.

Berger, P., & Luckmann, T. (1967). *The social construction of reality: A treatise in the sociology of knowledge.* New York, NY: Knopf Doubleday.

Braithwaite, J. (2003a). Principles of restorative justice. In A. von Hirsch, J. V. Roberts, A. E. Bottoms, K. Roasch, & M. Schiff (Eds.), *Restorative justice and criminal justice: Competing or reconcilable paradigms?* (pp. 1–20). Oxford: Hart.

Braithwaite, J. (2003b). What's wrong with the sociology of punishment? *Theoretical Criminology, 7*(1), 5–29.

Cajete, G. (1994). *Look to the mountain: An ecology of indigenous education.* Rio Rancho, NM: Kivaki Press.

Chilisa, B. (2012). *Indigenous research methodologies.* Thousand Oaks, CA: Sage Publications.

Christie, N. (2004). *A suitable amount of crime.* London: Routledge.

Corrections and Conditional Release Act. (1992). *Government of Canada.* Ottawa: Queen's Printer of Canada.

Corrections and Conditional Release Statistical Overview. (2013). *Ministry of public of safety.* Ottawa: Queen's Printer of Canada.

Cousins, M. (2005). Aboriginal justice: A Haudenosaunee approach. In W. D. McCaslin (Ed.), *Justice as healing* (pp. 141–159). St. Paul, MN: Living Justice Press.

Couture, J. (1983). *Traditional aboriginal spirituality and religious practice in federal prisons.* Saskatoon: Queen's Printer of Canada.

Couture, J. (1994). *Aboriginal behavioral trauma: Towards a taxonomy.* Saskatoon: Queen's Printer of Canada.

Dumont, J. (1996). Justice and aboriginal people. In *Bridging the cultural divide: A report on aboriginal peoples and the criminal justice system in Canada* (p. 69). Ottawa: Royal Commission on Aboriginal People.

Farmer, T., Robinson, K., Elliott, S. J., & Eyles, J. (2006). Developing and implementing a triangulation protocol for qualitative health research. *Qualitative Health Research, 16,* 377–394.

Foucault, M. (1977). *Discipline and punish: The birth of the prison.* New York, NY: Random House.

Garland, D. (1990). *Punishment and modern society: A study in social theory.* Chicago, IL: University of Chicago Press.

Garland, D. (2001). *The culture of control.* Chicago, IL: University of Chicago Press.

Huculak, B. (2005). Restorative justice and the youth criminal justice act. In W. D. McCaslin (Ed.), *Justice as healing* (pp. 161–166). St. Paul, MN: Living Justice Press.

ROBIN QUANTICK

Jackson, M. (2002). *Justice behind the walls: Human rights in Canadian prisons*. Vancouver: Douglas & McIntyre. Retrieved from http://www.justicebehindthewalls.net/resources/arbour_report/arbour_rpt.htm

King, T. (2003). *The truth about stories: A native narrative*. Toronto: House of Anansi Press.

Kirchheimer, O. (1968). *Punishment and social structure*. London: Transaction.

Lee, G. (2005). Defining traditional healing. In W. D. McCaslin (Ed.), *Justice as healing* (pp. 308–312). St. Paul, MN: Living Justice Press.

McCaslin, W. D. (2005). *Justice as healing: Indigenous ways, writings on community peacemaking and restorative justice from the native law centre*. St. Paul, MN: Living Justice Press.

Melton, A. (2005). Indigenous justice systems and tribal society. In W. D. McCaslin (Ed.), *Justice as healing* (pp. 108–120). St. Paul, MN: Living Justice Press.

Mertens, D. M. (2009). *Transformative research and evaluation*. New York, NY: Guilford.

Mission of the Correctional Service of Canada. (1997). *Correctional service Canada*. Ottawa: Queen's Printer of Canada.

Monchalin, L. (2016). *The colonial problem: An indigenous perspective on crime and injustice in Canada*. Toronto: University of Toronto Press.

Response to the Office of the Correctional Investigator's Report. (2012). *Spirit matters: Aboriginal people and the corrections and conditional release act*. Ottawa: Correctional service Canada.

Roadmap to Strengthening Public Safety. (2007). *Government of Canada*. Ottawa: Queen's Printer of Canada.

Ross, R. (2006). *Returning to the teachings, exploring aboriginal justice*. Toronto: Penguin.

Royal Commission on Aboriginal Peoples. (1996). *Bridging the cultural divide: A report on aboriginal people and criminal justice in Canada*. Ottawa: Minister of Supply and Services Canada.

Rudin, J. (2005). *Aboriginal justice and restorative justice, new directions in restorative justice: Issues, practice, evaluation*. Portland, OR: Wilan.

Said, E. W. (1978). *Orientalism*. New York, NY: Pantheon.

Sapers, H. (2012). *Spirit matters: Aboriginal people and the corrections and conditional release act*. Ottawa: Office of the Correctional Investigator, Government of Canada.

Smith, L. T. (1999). *Decolonizing methodologies*. Dunedin: Otago University Press.

Supreme Court of Canada. (1999). *Gladue v. Canada* (Attorney General). S.C.R. 688.

Supreme Court of Canada. (2002). *Sauvé v. Canada* (Attorney General). 3 S.C.R. 519.

Umbreit, M. (1999). *Restorative justice in Canada: Research framework for a review of communiity justice in Yukon*. Paper produced for the Yukon Territory Community Justice Review, Government of the Yukon, Yellowknife. Retrieved from www.gov.yk.ca/fr/pdf/02-1_History.pdf

Waldram, J. (1997). *The way of the pipe, aboriginal spirituality and symbolic healing in Canadian prisons*. Toronto: Broadview Press.

Weber-Pillwax, C. (2001). What is indigenous research? *Canadian Journal of Native Education, 25*, 166–174.

Williams, P. (2004, March). *Believing in the covenant chain: Haudenosaunee justice*. Paper presented at The Baldy Centre for Law and Social Policy, State University of New York, Buffalo, NY.

Wilson, S. (2008). *Research is ceremony, indigenous research methods*. Halifax: Fernwood.

Yazzie, R. (2005). Healing as justice: The Navajo response to crime. In W. D. McCaslin (Ed.), *Justice as healing* (pp. 121–133). St. Paul, MN: Living Justice Press.

Youngblood Henderson, J. S. (2005). Warriors of justice and healing. In W. D. McCaslin (Ed.), *Justice as healing*, (pp. 20–23). St. Paul, MN: Living Justice Press.

Zehr, H. (1990). *Changing lenses: A new focus on crime and justice*. Intercourse, PA: Good Books.

Zehr, H. (2002). *The little book of restorative justice*. Intercourse, PA: Good Books.

Robin Quantick
Department of Indigenous Studies
Trent University
Peterborough, Ontario

MIRIAM PERRY

25. INDIGENOUS VOICES FOR WELL-BEING IN NORTHERN MANITOBA

An Exploratory Study

INTRODUCTION

It is well known that Indigenous Peoples of Canada have endured and continue to endure a damaging colonial legacy, which has resulted in many ongoing structural, social, political and cultural challenges for the people today. It is further known that the Indigenous People's 'situation', in all aspects of life, history, governance, health and education have largely been viewed through the lens of the dominant society. For example, Western (used to refer to the dominant, European-ancestry-based culture) academics, civil servants and politicians, have produced studies, analysis and many subsequent economic, political and wellness strategies in their effort to facilitate progress and development for Indigenous Peoples. It is further part of the common narrative that the vast majority of the world's Indigenous populations have not experienced nearly enough positive benefits from these efforts largely led by the dominant society. It is unjust in a country such as Canada's, which repeatedly makes it to the top 10 on the Human Development Index (Human Development Index, 2015) and World Happiness Report (World Happiness Report, 2016) that the First Peoples are not benefitting equally in this country's prosperity.

It has been increasingly acknowledged that the lack of effective Indigenous recognized development and progress is largely due to the lack of involvement of Indigenous Peoples in both the decision-making process as well as the research policy is based on. Research is more fundamental to facilitating progress because how something is researched leads to a certain way of framing the issues and translates into not only factual and academic understanding, but also evolves into the common narrative of which we all prescribe to. This study's purpose is to address this gap by exploring local perceptions of the issues of importance for wellbeing in the communities of Pukatawagon and Sherridon through direct conversation-style engagement. Other goals are accountability and reciprocity with the communities, promoting positive social change; providing insight for future studies on local issues; to influence policy as it pertains to the worlds Indigenous Peoples; and lastly, to allow for views that have in the past, been largely dominated by those from the outside.

© KONINKLIJKE BRILL NV, LEIDEN, 2018 | DOI 9789004367418_025

MIRIAM PERRY

METHODOLOGY

I conducted this study using an Indigenous Research Paradigm (IRP). A paradigmatic approach can be defined as a set of beliefs that shape the research process. A Western-based research framework has been criticized by Indigenous researchers such as Kovach (2009) as one that drives colonialist and imperialist notions of identifying the Other, such as those from a different culture, from a particular ideological framework and consequently has resulted in "an investigative and classifying apparatus that can only respond to the unknown in terms that further compound both difference and difficulty," (Willis & Saunders, 2007, p. 99). IRP offers an approach that places Indigenous Peoples, epistemology and beliefs at the forefront.

I used the common IRP principles of the acceptance of a non-structured, fluid methodology; willingness to be reflexive; relationship-building and relational accountability; and respect and reciprocity. My data gathering method included primarily utilizing a Conversational Method (Kovach, 2010), in which emphasizes informal as opposed to structured interviews, the sharing of stories and the building on relations. I also used participation observation, grounded theory, and thematic content analysis.

In order to briefly locate myself in relation to this research I will make it known that I have Northern Manitoba Cree roots, as well as am part of Southern Manitoba Saulteaux and a mix of Eastern and Western European ancestry. I grew up practicing many land-based cultural activities such as berry gathering, spending time at trap lines and hunting and fishing. My immediate and extended family from my mother's side have lived in Sherridon and surrounding areas for many generations.

FINDINGS

Within my strategy of inquiry, I focused on both areas for improvement as well as strengths. By focusing on the challenges, I aimed to be both relevant and responsible to the communities such that local perspectives of the issues were brought forward to be understood both locally and to a wider audience with the hopes of being adequately addressed. In focusing on the strengths, relevancy and responsibility were also the aim of a strength-based approach as they may be beneficial for future community use, such as in areas to focus or build on. Furthermore, in highlighting strengths, it may offer a differing illustration to the greater narrative of Indigenous Peoples and their communities to the one that has often been consumed with negativity.

Areas for Improvement Concern for Youth

The broad theme of 'Concern for Youth' for both children and young adults was brought up as an issue in differing contexts by the vast majority of the participants. Within 'Youth', there are two sub-themes that emerged including lessening (mainstream) educational quality, and broad distress concerns.

246

Perspective of lower education quality. Many people expressed concern that the education system was not as good as those found out of the reserve, in neighboring towns for example. For instance, one mother relayed, "If I had the chance to move, I'd move, because I want to take my kids to have an education, when we first moved in 2002 to The Pas, my kids were tested, they were higher in Puk, but two grades lower over there."

Two other families described how much they like living in the community and the only reason they would move would be for their children's education. One mother stating, "I was just thinking about it [moving]" and another mother saying she would "move somewhere for my kid's education, but would want to stay if education was better."

There was also a sense of the importance of education. For example one man spoke passionately regarding the next generation: "we have nothing today, we have to give freedom to the next generation, we got to pass it on to them, if we don't have education, we're going down, because no one will be a leader... me, not enough education, all these jobs I had... not enough." He further spoke of his life growing up on the trapline and all the things he learned such as hunting and trapping and living off the land, and stated: "Now we need education to do something – but not a lot of us have that because we were raised on the trapline, there's lots of us... don't have much education, but lots of trapping!"

Youth distress issues. Many people spoke of the youth in concerning terms. For example, some people in Pukatawagan spoke of the gangs that emerged in the neighborhoods and how sometimes it's scary to walk out at night because of fear of being jumped. Many gave instances of someone they knew that had got attacked and had been badly hurt recently. In Sherridon people voiced concerns that many kids don't care to attend school consistently and seem "disrespectful". From both communities there was a sense that youth were misguided or heading in a wrong direction such as not knowing where to invest their energy.

An elder who has cared for many foster kids as well as has many children and grandchildren said she noticed a difference in the youth in terms of the respect they had toward their elders and their attitudes to help out around the house. In speaking with her and other family members, they described the youth that they cared for: "They'll get mad even if you tell them to wash the dishes, it's not hard to wash the dishes I'll tell her... she'll get mad." Then insights from another family member went as follows: "we had it rough ... they [younger generation] think it's pretty easy for them, like growing up ... they don't think how we were brought up... they don't respect the adults and how they were brought up and what they are trying to teach them ..."

Another woman in her fifties offered her input concerning youth describing the apparent differences between her generation and the current: "This generation say 'I don't have anything'... they are not sharing... we used to share, kill a moose, even fish – I don't sell them, I always give to elders... this generation, they don't go to

MIRIAM PERRY

camps, they'll go for a ride and want to go back home, they don't even know how to fish."

A man in his forties spoke of the issues of the youth and young adults in the community as being one of the biggest concerns from his perspective. He relayed his perspective of young parents: "Some of them have very little to no parental skills, and I find these are the ones getting drunk on family allowance... and you know children are struggling to eat and realize what their parents are doing, and they're a burden and you know they lash out."

I inquired for his perspective on what he thought the cause of these young parents doing that, he stated: "That's where the whole residential school problem is with these kids, because I'd say it's been about 2–3 generations now ... loss of family values."

A few people spoke directly of mental stress and mentioned many youth suicide attempts in the community of Pukatawagan. One woman in her thirties stated: "There are lots of mental health issues, attempted suicides, I've seen it."

The topic came up again with a couple in their fifties, I asked, "I wonder why suicide attempts?" A man in his fifties replied: "Because they do drugs, feel different, like a choke... get hurt, can't go anywhere, get frustrated... because of that train... forget it, I'll just die," emphasizing the isolation of the community especially in the summer when the limited running train is the only main accessible mode out of the community by most people.

A man in his forties brought up the gangs as well and his reasoning for where they came from: "Some of them boredom... feels better to belong to a group... I would also say a lot didn't get to go out [to camps or traplines], some lucky enough to go out, I think there's a lot less doing stuff, some have no opportunity to go out on the boat."

Another man in his forties offered his view: "some of our youth go into the system [juvenile detention or jail] and end up back here and bring things they learn out there."

Governance & Development Issues

The broad theme of governance and development were issues of concern expressed by most of the people in both communities.

In one conversation with a couple in Sherridon, the issue of the conflict that was known at the time to be going on with members of council arose. The wife said the fighting is a problem and that "people are not working together."

A woman in her forties in another conversation offered her reasons for the conflict:

We have no elders... all the elders are teachers, the teachers are all gone, like when I was growing up, we had [she listed ten elder's names]... when they got together, like when something needed to be discussed you find a lot of the elders at one person's home, discussing things talking about you know like what we should do about this, this is getting bad, this is getting worse, and then they would have one person that they would choose someone to be the speaker for them, to say you know we need this, or if they needed the whole group, the whole group was there to talk to the people...

Many people also spoke of governance in a more pointed way as in toward the federal government. For instance in a conversation with a man in his forties regarding my inquiry on what is looked at as important for his community stated:

There needs to be a change, there needs to be a meaningful desire to work together in this country... the government has to accept the fact that we are a partner and that we will have to be a partner on how we develop as a nation ... and they have to accept the fact that we have our own authority, they have to enshrine that and accept it and move forward with us in that way because that is what we are wanting to do...

Another man explained his take on the 'system': "The current government system has been streamlined from the time of colonization, so it has in effect, become effective in what they have been trying to do and that is to keep us down."

He further stated: "It's easy for someone who is living in Canadian suburbia, 'oh why can't they go out and get a job' or you know, go out and get their education, they don't know the social aspect, they don't know this persons' life..."

Another man in his forties stated his view of the economic development happening in their territories, which he pointed out is under the Treaty Land Entitlement negotiation, and that has made "some CEO somewhere down south millions... from resources on our territories, meanwhile we don't have enough houses for everyone and can't put all the kids who want to go to school through," emphasizing the struggles that the community has due to lack of funding.

In another conversation with a couple in their fifties, the husband was describing his family's history of how they moved from their trapline to the community and came to be placed in government housing. He explained that his dad misunderstood and they thought they would own their own house and not the current government-housing situation they are not in. He further described his family's understanding of the treaty agreements and the changes made to the trapline set-up and states: "We are trying to fight for our land, but a lot of issues to deal with from the back... it is set that way and hard to change..."

The next section highlights the minor themes that arose in the conversations.

Drugs & Alcohol Issues

Drugs and alcohol issues were brought up a number of times. In one conversation with a group of four family members they discussed the issues brought on by drugs and alcohol: "People start fights with each other... it's mostly with family." Another family member agreed: "I'm brave enough to express my anger when I'm drinking... I would fight my own family only, I wouldn't fight anyone else."

MIRIAM PERRY

Another woman stated how she witnessed people being sent out for alcohol treatment and that once "they get out they'll start drinking again, I've seen that many times."

In another conversation I had with a woman in her fifties, she described the negative experience she had in residential school, calling it "like a nightmare." She then explained how she drank for 30 years directly because of her experience: "I would be angry with the people I was drinking with... I'm glad I let go." She further explained that she tries to help her friends, those who attended the school with her and said many have already died from drinking and many have aged, "they look ten years older than they are," and "they can't forget." She expressed that she wishes she could help them.

Residential School Issues

The next minor theme that arose in many conversations with participants from both communities was related to residential school experiences.

One woman in her sixties described at length her experience and how she felt about being at residential school. She described being strapped and said, "I didn't want them to see me crying... that's why there's no emotions now, didn't want to give them that satisfaction." She further recalls both girls and boys being taken away at night and offered her assessment of the effects: "That's why men in that generation are angry and drink and pass it on... it's a cycle."

This woman is a Cree language teacher, and I inquired how she was able to keep her strong cultural ties and language, she replied, "I was stubborn I didn't want to lose my language... I got strong traditions from my grandparents."

In another conversation I had with woman in her fifties, she also described at length her negative experience at residential school: "The memories stayed with me... I had nightmares for 30 years, that's why I was drinking heavy... When I finally told the lawyer I let it all out, I felt better, and we had to tell our story... I didn't tell everything, they knew I didn't tell everything. Today I don't have nightmares, they went away."

She further described her friends' current situations that attended the school with her and stated: "I keep in touch with my friends from school, quite a few passed away from alcohol [under fifty years old]... The ones I see back home, it's like they aged twice... they can't forget... they do talk to me... today I see them, they're still the same."

Two women described their experiences with those that raised them. The first woman recalled painful memories of her grandpa and the angry verbal and physical outbursts toward family members that would occur frequently. The other women also spoke of her dad's extreme anger, she stated: "I didn't even know he went to residential school, he didn't talk about it, but when I found out, I felt better, I didn't think it was right [how she and her siblings were treated], but at least I understood."

250

INDIGENOUS VOICES FOR WELL-BEING IN NORTHERN MANITOBA

Reviving & Re-learning Culture & Traditions

The last minor theme involves people speaking of what they know of their culture and traditions. Many expressed not being taught by their parents or as part of their education and that cultural knowledge and identity come to them later in life either through seeking it out for themselves or from the influence of family and friends.

In a conversation I had with a woman in her thirties who was raised by her grandparents, she explained her observation of the erosion of speaking Cree: "Even in my grandparent's generation it was already lost." She described how her grandparents would only speak to the friends of their generation and speaks only English to their kids and grandkids. She said she understood Cree, but she did not pass it on to her kids and stated, "Now it stops with me."

This woman further explained that growing up cultural concepts such as Cree or Métis were not known to her in the way that they are now: "I didn't even know I was half-white, or whatever, wasn't taught to me, I thought I was just a human being... I didn't know all the culture was important... it didn't matter before, but now it matters."

Another woman in her forties spoke of how growing up she was not aware of many of the cultural traditions that she is learning now such as the Sundance. She also described traditional medicines such as sweet grass, and said of them: "It is scary to learn all about that stuff, got to respect everything, or else Karma."

In my inquiry into how it was for her growing up she stated: "I didn't know I was an Indian... I was ashamed because what we learned in school, the Indians were the ones who always died." I asked when she learned, she replied: "About grade five... but now I'm proud to be an Indian."

Community Strengths

Youth cultural continuation. Many people spoke of instances pertaining to youth cultural continuation such as pride in their ability to speak and understand Cree and the traditions they carry on associated with respect and hunting and sharing wild food.

In one visit with a family I noticed the grandma asking her grandson questions in Cree every now and then. I commented, "he understands well hey?" The grandma replied yes and her daughter said that all the grandkids do, which were close to fifty.

I spent the day with another family where we went to a place by the lake to pluck ducks and have a cookout. All the kids participated in plucking the ducks and watched on as they were gutted and cleaned by their mom and extended family. One boy spoke excitedly that he wanted to get his picture on their family's 'wall of fame', which is a display of pictures of each family member who had shot a moose. After returning to their house for supper (duck soup), the mother relayed a story of her experience of commercial fishing and how everyone often speaks Cree. In one instance, one young boy was told in Cree to clean his nose, and he misunderstood

MIRIAM PERRY

and thought he was told to throw the fish back in the water, so he started throwing the suckers back in the water. She then stated: "So that is why it is good for parents to speak Cree to their kids on every little thing, cause that's where they get lost when they're growing up without hearing it."

In another conversation with a mother in her forties, she spoke of her young son going duck hunting and that he had just come back from giving away a few to a neighbor, she described how she teaches him not to ask for anything in return such as money. Another younger family member agreed, "My mom raised us to help others and don't expect anything in return – 'you don't ask for anything!' She would say…"

Perspective of Life & Community

Arising out of many of my conversations, the theme of family connectedness, peace in their communities and love of the bush life arose as dominant themes for what people love about living in their communities. It was clear speaking with many people that what they enjoyed doing were mainly traditional land-based activities that their parents and grandparents used to do.

In a conversation with a couple from Sherridon, they relayed that they would only move if they had to, such as for health reasons, and expressed because: "Here there is no trouble, quiet, no really bad stuff… and people like doing stuff, going out in the bush, out in the lake."

Another woman in her thirties who had lived in larger urban areas for more than five years and then returned relayed: "Here it is different every day, in the city, it is the robotic life – work, work, and work – and people need to money to do things [entertainment]…" She went on to further point out that the nature of entertainment is different in the bush and the need to rely on money is not the main factor.

Other people spoke of their experiences when they would leave for a short time to visit relatives in larger urban areas and thus allowed them to express what they missed when leaving home. One woman said, "I can only last so long in the city," and she went on to explain her appreciation for returning home, describing how she can go down to the lake to watch the sunset or go for nature walks right outside her door.

A man in his thirties described going to The Pas for two weeks, a community of approximately fifty five hundred people: "I'm one of those bushed out Indians, I swear, I went to The Pas, haven't been there in years, I went into culture shock because everything was so different… I had to go run to the bridge to look at the open water and the trees and breathe." I inquired on what it was that got to him. He replied: "It was the concrete, everything comes in on you, the hustle and bustle, I'm used to this… [points to the gravel road where we were walking, the lake within eyesight, trees, rocks in the background, and houses scattered around]… people were swearing, kids crying, mom yelling… all that…"

Upon my further inquiry about what are the best things he likes about living in the community he replied: "The best thing about living out in Puk is you're able to do anything you want no matter what the season is ... cause it's not just any one thing ... cause I was going to say, my one time that I get to jump into the lake ... like what we're doing now, having a conversation in the bush at the beginning of fall ..." I inquired further what exactly he meant 'doing anything', he said "well you can't go have a fish fry in the middle of Main Street! [Referring to Flin Flon]" emphasizing his land-based point of view.

A woman in her thirties who had lived in both communities stated: "I feel like there's a lot of good that can be done in each of these communities and there's a lot of good people that still have the values..."

CONCLUDING REMARKS

I have used my relations as well as utilized an Indigenous Research Paradigm in this exploratory study with the aim of gaining a richer understanding of the issues that matter to the people in Sherridon and Pukatawagan.

My observations and the tone and conversational topics lead me to conclude that there is direct evidence of a need for individual and community level healing. This is based on the many accounts of youth distress, stories of residential school experiences and effects, the issues with drugs and alcohol, development and governance issues and the fact that there is need and desire for cultural renewal with many people. There are clear ongoing historical, structural and social challenges, such as the legacy of cultural loss due to direct government policy of residential schools and the link between generations, the ongoing political and structural struggles related to land rights and the intergenerational trauma associated with these matters. It is clear that many of the issues are cumulative and on-going, or as one man put it "[we] a lot of issues to deal with from the back."

The concept of Environmental Repossession which is described by Big-Canoe and Richmond (2014) as "social, cultural and political process by which Indigenous peoples and communities are reclaiming their traditional lands and ways of life... [which is a] concept [that] is rooted centrally in the idea that Indigenous peoples' health, way of living, and Indigenous knowledge systems are dependent on access to their traditional land and territories" (p. 133), can be a productive way of framing the future direction based on what many people have expressed.

It is also important that Indigenous-led research and utilizing an Indigenous Research Paradigm be front and center when it comes to understanding and responding to developments and well-being. In the Western context, well-being indicators commonly incorporate such things as job statistics and income, which may lead to policy that contributes to people leaving the community to work and get a 'Western' education. In a study with Aboriginal people in Australia on subjective well-being, it was found that those living in remote compared to non-remote areas appeared to have higher levels of emotional well-being, with likely reasons being related to language retention and the greater likelihood of engaging in cultural activities (Biddle, 2014). These studies highlight the importance of understanding

MIRIAM PERRY

the differences in worldviews and the trade-off to leave communities and family connections to fulfill Western notions of development and wellness for Indigenous Peoples.

Numerous studies point to the benefits of traditional healing approaches such as sweat lodges and the Sun Dance ceremony and Indigenous spirituality for those directly and indirectly affected by residential schooling and deliberate government policies of assimilation. Given the connection Aboriginal people have with the land and the ongoing resurgence of cultural revitalization amongst Indigenous Peoples of Canada, which were both revealed here, it is essential for people to be connected to cultural empowerment initiatives.

What is needed is a rounded approach that addresses underlying issues through understanding the bigger picture as opposed to the symptoms associated with a damaging colonial legacy, along with working to build on the strengths expressed in this study. I end with a quote from one of the woman in the community which expresses the potential of both communities: "I feel like there's a lot of good that can be done in each of these communities and there's a lot of good people that still have the values..."

REFERENCES

Biddle, N. (2014). Measuring and analyzing the wellbeing of Australia's indigenous population. *Social Indicators Research, 116*(3), 713–729.

Big-Canoe, K., & Richmond, C. A. M. (2014). Anishinabe youth perceptions about community health: Toward environmental repossession. *Health & Place, 26,* 127–135.

Human Development Index. (2015). *United nations development programme.* Retrieved from http://hdr.undp.org/en/content/human-development-index-hdi

Kovach, M. (2009). *Indigenous methodologies: Characteristics, conversations, and contexts.* Toronto: University of Toronto Press.

Kovach, M. (2010). Conversational method in indigenous research. *First Peoples Child and Family Review, 5*(1), 40–48.

Willis, J., & Saunders, M. (2007). Research in a post-colonial world: The example of Australian aborigines. In M. Pitts & A. Smith (Ed.), *Researching the margins: Strategies for ethical and rigorous research with marginalised communities* (pp. 96–113). Hampshire: Palgrave Macmillan.

Wilson, S. (2008). *Research is ceremony: Indigenous research methods.* Black Point: Fernwood Publications.

World Happiness Report. (2016). Retrieved from http://worldhappiness.report/wp-content/uploads/sites/2/2016/03/HR-V1_web.pdf

Miriam Perry
Centre for Integrated Studies
Athabasca University
Athabasca, Alberta

KARA PASSEY

26. SCALING DEEP

Arts Based Research Practices

INTRODUCTION

Art has been used to document and illustrate our cultural climate, empower vulnerable communities, and challenge systems long before the era of community development began. Art is at the root of all communities who thrive, whether it is through the songs shared between generations to communicate knowledge and values, or woven into the textiles that swaddle babies, art is innovation. It can tell a story without words so that it's impact can be felt across borders – those that are physical and those that are created by unjust systems or the division between social classes.

Participatory action research is a method that promotes the direct participation of the community being investigated, including support for community members to then either take action in the research process or the development of projects as a result of the research findings (Bergold & Thomas, 2012). Artistic methods are a valuable approach in participatory research and development because artistic tools are accessible to those who may not have institutional knowledge or training in development practices. Art can be integrated within any step of a research and development framework, including community consultations, documentation, design, evaluation, and scaling processes. The Winnipeg Boldness Project[1] an example of a research and development initiative, which has heavily embedded art within their process.

The Winnipeg Boldness Project has a bold goal: to dramatically transform the wellbeing of children living in the Point Douglas area. Winnipeg is the home to the largest urban population of Indigenous peoples in Canada (Statistics Canada, 2006), the highest concentration of which live within Point Douglas, known in more affectionate terms to locals as the North End of Winnipeg (City of Winnipeg, 2006). The North End, whose boundaries run along the Red River, CPR Winnipeg Train Yards, McPhillips Street and Carruthers Avenue has historically been host to the highest concentration of poverty within Winnipeg (Silver, 2010). As determined by the Early Development Instrument (EDI) (Santos et al., 2012), many families living in Point Douglas are finding that their children aren't ready for kindergarten, despite their love and hard work to support their development.

The neighbourhood is also host to the majority of Winnipeg's Community Based Organizations (CBOs), outreach programs, resource centres, and grassroots

© KONINKLIJKE BRILL NV, LEIDEN, 2018 | DOI 9789004367418_026

KARA PASSEY

initiatives. Residents have long been engaged in programming, as well as participatory processes related to poverty reduction within the North End. By acknowledging the practices and approaches that are already implemented by families, community leaders, and CBOs located within the North End, the Winnipeg Boldness Project has developed a wholistic Early Childhood Development model that is grounded in the rich Indigenous cosmology that is present within the neighbourhood, known as the Ways of Knowing, Being, Feeling, and Doing. This model also informs the project's Knowledge Mobilization Framework (The Winnipeg Boldness Project, 2016), which ensures that the community guides the process of the project along every step of the way including research, summary, design, evaluation, and testing. One of the ways that the project ensures community involvement throughout these processes is by removing barriers to participation, as well as designing accessible methods such as arts based research methods.

Community leaders have described this way of working as the acknowledgment of the interconnectedness of all living things, and the employment of a wholistic approach when supporting families. Community leaders have stressed the importance of working within a model that places the child at the centre, and maintains the balance of the interconnectedness between their immediate families and caregivers, relatives, elders, community, environment, and infrastructure that surrounds them (The Winnipeg Boldness Project, 2016). By engaging in a participatory and iterative manner, the project is able to ensure a meaningful community knowledge mobilization process, which will deliver supports directly to families, in a way that is determined and designed by them. This approach places the wisdom of families and community as the centre of personal, familial, community and systemic change.

RESEARCH

Point Douglas has been painted with a broad brush – media portrayal and normalized prejudice from outsiders to the community has created a narrative that concentrates on the negative attributes of the community. Intergenerational poverty, addictions, poor infrastructure, and family or gang related violence are common themes when outsiders iterate their stigma against the community. Social programs are usually designed as a response to crisis, offering – extremely necessary – resources as short-term solutions, instead of long-term investment to sustainable change, as dictated by the community. As part of a communications and community engagement strategy, the Winnipeg Boldness Project sought to bring forward the other side of the story. Who are the heroes of the North End? The grandmothers? The leaders? The future? By identifying the strengths of the community and providing them a platform to grow, the project can identify points of impact and thus influence change up, out, and deep.

The photovoice project, a visual storytelling art installation based on photography and written narratives created by community residents, was the first tool used by the project to highlight a strengths-based narrative. The use of this tool was inspired by the work of Heather Castleden and Theresa Garvin (2008) in collaboration with Huu-ay-aht First Nation, who adapted the participatory research method of the photovoice as a tool to ensure that communities remained empowered throughout the research or consultation process. Castleden and Garvin (2008) emphasize the importance of acknowledging the long history of anthropological research *on* Indigenous peoples, as opposed to *with* them, and how this dynamic has created power imbalances and even inaccurate findings. Further, communities are wary of researchers who arrive for a brief visit, gather data which they might not be entitled to, and disappear to never be heard from again. Using art in research methods, such as the photovoice method, allows control by the community being represented, and enforces accountability of the researcher to do something with their findings – if there is no final product created in the art process, the participant can clearly see that the researcher has not been accountable to their process.

The project provided digital cameras to community members, advised them how to use them, and gave two weeks for each participant to take photographs of people, places, and things they found meaningful within Point Douglas. Each participant took a minimum of one hundred photos, and narrowing them down to their favorites was a difficult but engaging process. Final photos used in the art piece included pictures of their children, community parks, pets, smiling friends and families, resources, and images representing aspects of Indigenous culture. The final product was situated around a large map of Point Douglas, where each photo was mounted near it, with a thread connecting the photo to it's corresponding point on the map. Participants also all provided biographies and statements for each individual photo. All the photos shared resounding themes of love, and family togetherness. There were no representations of the poverty and violence, themes that might have been expected by outsiders to the community.

The final piece, titled *"Through My Own Eyes: A visual narrative of life in the North End"* was presented back to the community in a gallery setting, and community members were interviewed by local media on their participation. Paired with the small tour that the piece took to surrounding universities, government buildings and city services, the project as well as its knowledge and strength was shared with the rest of the city. Community members express pride in the final product, and continual point back to it as a way that they contributed to the Winnipeg Boldness Project.

ACCESSIBILITY

Despite the plethora of researchers and academics conducting various projects on poverty reduction, the social exclusion to those without access to academic spaces is often over looked. More and more often, communities are requesting more control over the research done within their spaces. Why can't they be included on a board of ethics? A funding proposal? An evaluation process? Why not hire their own experts, or utilize their own methods? The Winnipeg Boldness Project utilizes a board of

KARA PASSEY

community caregivers – known as the Parent Guide Group – who are the most robust and engaged group of all the guiding groups involved in the project (The Winnipeg Boldness Project, 2016). These community caregivers help to bridge the gap of communication from the academics, funders, and leaders associated in the project, to the other community members whose livelihood are directly affected by the impact of the project. This group is regularly consulted and helps to test prototypes, and design research and evaluation processes. The relationship between this group and the project is reciprocal – the local team learns how to more effectively communicate and improve their engagement processes, and the community caregivers increase their capacity to advocate on behalf of themselves and their community. The equal exchange of ideas and labour between project staff and community members ensures that the project follows in time with the beat of the communities' heart, and ensures community ownership.

Another way that The Winnipeg Boldness Project seeks to increase accessibility is through the documentation of their process. While it's necessary, as it is with any research project, to develop lengthy reports catered to funders or members or a board of directors, the project strives to share the content of these reports in a variety of ways as to: A. remain transparent to the community they are serving, and B. ensure inclusive accountability to those from all sectors. By using graphic design the project has been able to create visual representations of the ways of working that have been embedded in the community for decades and communicate these models in a way that translates across sectors including business, non-profit, government, and community. By developing short documentary style videos to showcase our models, guiding groups, and research processes and hosting them on a platform such as YouTube, the project is able to be transparent and communicate our processes in a way that is accessible to everyone, not just those who have access to our reports. Sharing video interviews done with community members and leaders who have participated in our processes shows accountability to the experiences and feedback that we have been given by those directly impacted by our work.

DESIGN

As a social innovation project, The Winnipeg Boldness Project uses an innovation design process that begins with a gathering of diverse knowledges. This process, used at the beginning of each activity stream, is known as a co-creation session. These sessions take place after the community consultation and the community validation of research findings, where issues are brought to a cross-sector group (i.e. community members, service providers, healthcare providers, policy makers, business, political sector, etc.) in order to discuss and design potential solutions. Since these sessions have such a diverse array of people, it is important to utilize a variety of facilitation tools to ensure active participation from all parties. These tools can include work sheets, facilitated discussions with the aid of flip charts and post it notes, and – of course – arts based approaches.

258

The very first co-creation session undertaken by the project included representatives from funders, the United Way, Winnipeg Regional Health Authority, representatives from the business sector, various CBOs, as well as representatives from the project's Parent Guide Group. It was apparent through the course of the 2-day session that some voices more easily dominated the conversation over others. In particular, one of the fathers from the Parent Guide Group, who is always soft spoken, didn't engage with the majority of the activities. Despite efforts to check in and include him in conversation, he sat dis-engaged from the process, watching everyone else participate. One of the final activities for the session included art supplies: plasticine, pipe-cleaners, glitter, markers, craft foam, etc. When these supplies were put on the table, many of the service sector representatives were put off, confused as to how to begin. The previously disengaged father jumped to action, designing a prototype of the community he wanted for his family. This activity silenced the voices of the policy makers and those who normally dominate these conversations, and allowed a platform for the community members – who are normally excluded from these spaces – to participate. Everyone thinks and communicates in different ways, by allowing participants in our designing processes to draw or sculpt their input we provide a platform for participation that may be overlooked for those not comfortable speaking out in these spaces.

EVALUATION

Evaluation is a crucial step of the Winnipeg Boldness Project's knowledge mobilization framework; once a prototype is developed and tested, it must be evaluation and then further reassessed, and even retested, until the prototype is successful. Surveys and interviews can lack a layer of conceptualization that really tells a story. Quantitative numbers are necessary in some forms of reporting, but can lack the intersectional impact experienced by families. Evaluation methods like the photovoice activity provide insight into the emotional and cultural impact that these prototypes can have – this is where we are able to highlight themes of wellbeing, a sense of belonging or identity, cultural safety, relationship building and trust which are often overlooked when only collecting data in the sense of numbers.

The project continues to engage in arts based activities throughout it's lifespan in order to: A. continue to build the strengths based narrative which drives the project forward, B. continue to build relationships and remain engaged with the community, and C. to evaluate the processes under taken by the project. Are we remaining engaged? Are we accessible to the community? Are we listening to their voices? Are we learning from our earlier mistakes?

A year and a half after unveiling the initial photo voice project, the project presented the third addition to the strengths based narrative being built in partnership with the community: "*Community Star Blanket*" a while hanging made in a star blanket style, decorated with illustrations created community members. The Parent Guide Group were the creative leaders responsible for this project, and decided on

KARA PASSEY

the research question, "What do we need in order to maintain healthy relationships with our families, partners, and community?" Local team and guide group members attended programming at various CBOs as well as community events in order to ask this question, and have community members draw their response. The blanket was presented back to the community along with a star blanket teaching, where Elder Cheryl Alexander shared that the star blanket teaching validates the child-centered model used by the Winnipeg Boldness Project.

The process of embarking on this project required local team to evaluate past processes: what worked and what didn't? How can we ensure to be more successful in our engagement, execution, and sharing of this project? The original photovoice was complicated in its construction and the format it was delivered in wasn't always appropriate for every setting, and needed to be re-created several times. Participants involved in the photovoice didn't all understand the process of the project, and the blanket needed to be more transparent and accessible. The original photovoice had difficulty engaging participants and needed to be adapted in order to ensure greater engagement, resulting in just fewer than 20 participants – the blanket's approach was much more engaging, and receiving just over 100 participants. Even further, having an elder present the blanket back to the community with a teaching contributed to the evaluation process. Receiving the star blanket teaching in conjunction with completing the blanket helped to validate the process, and the models adopted by the project.

CONCLUSION

As mentioned previously, the Winnipeg Boldness Project believes that by identifying the strengths of the community and providing them a platform to grow, the project can identify points of impact and thus influence change up, out, and deep. Darcy Riddell and Michele-Lee Moore (2015) introduced this three-part concept of scaling in a report prepared for the J.W. McConnell Foundation and Tamarack Institute. "Scaling out" describes the action of sharing results across sectors to be adapted into other communities, thus sharing the impact at a further radius. "Scaling up" describes policy change at a higher level, most likely within the political sector. "Scaling deep," describes the impact and change that can happen within peoples' hearts and minds, by challenging social constructs that are deeply embedded into us (Riddell & Moore, 2015). Consider how art has made commentary on political unrest, world war, violence, poverty, or gender and race inequality. Consider the volume it speaks at without having to actually articulate a single word in one solitary language. Art has historically challenged mindsets of those who oppress others, and art is an invaluable tool in the act of scaling deep.

Art allows us to embrace vulnerable processes, experiment, and try new things. The most successful artists are those who allow themselves to fail in order to re-evaluate their process and try something new. We all look to art to see representations of ourselves, something we can connect with, something that

260

SCALING DEEP

makes us feel. The Winnipeg Boldness Project has only scratched the surface on the range of possibilities available when using arts based methods in community research and development. In addition to visual art forms such as photography or drawing, mediums such as performance, writing, and music are still areas waiting to be explored. Future projects might ask how can smells, touch, or sound contribute to approaches in participatory action research. It is important to explore these other mediums in order to explore the strengths and limitations of all who participants – one art form might be more accessible to some and less to others.

NOTE

[1] http://www.winnipegboldness.ca/

REFERENCES

Bergold, J., & Thomas, S. (2012, January). *Participatory research methods: A methodological approach in motion.* Retrieved from http://www.qualitativeresearch.net/index.php/fqs/article/view/1801/3334
Castleden, H., Garvin, T., & Huu-ay-aht First Nation. (2008, March). *Modifying photovoice for community-based participatory indigenous research.* Retrieved from http://www.sciencedirect.com.libproxy.uwinnipeg.ca/science/article/pii/S0277953607005813
City of Winnipeg. (2006). *City of Winnipeg neighbourhood cluster profiles.* Retrieved from http://winnipeg.ca/census/2006/clusters/
Riddell, D., & Moore, M. L. (2015, October). *Scaling out, scaling up, scaling deep: Advancing systemic social innovation and the learning processes to support it.* Retrieved from https://www.dunstan.org.au/docs/Scaling_Up,_Out,_Deep.pdf
Santos, R., Brownell, M., Ekuma, O., Mayer, T., & Soodeen, R. (2012, May). *The Early Development Instrument (EDI) in Manitoba: Linking socioeconomic adversity and biological vulnerability at birth to children's outcomes at age 5.* Retrieved from http://mchp-appserv.cpe.umanitoba.ca/deliverablesList.html
Silver, J. (2010, January). *Winnipeg's North end: Yesterday and today.* Retrieved from https://canadiandimension.com/articles/view/winnipegs-north-end
Statistics Canada. (2006). *The urban aboriginal population.* Retrieved from http://www.statcan.gc.ca/pub/11-402-x/2008/10000/ceb10000_002-eng.htm
The Winnipeg Boldness Project. (2016). *Strengthening a foundation for success and wellbeing: Reflecting back in order to journey forward.* Retrieved from http://www.winnipegboldness.ca/wcm-docs/docs/wpgboldnessproject_2yrreview_finalweb.pdf

Kara Passey
Indigenous Development Program
University of Winnipeg
Winnipeg, Manitoba

MONIKA M. KOWATSCH, COURTNEY BELL,
MARGARET ORMOND, AND KEITH R. FOWKE

27. DRAWING BACK THE CURTAIN[1]

*Community Engagement Prior to Basic Science Research Improves
Research Questions and Assists in Framing Study Outcomes*

INTRODUCTION

Community engagement is critical to creating well-designed, human participant research studies and an essential part of the research process. This holds especially true when research is conducted in partnership with underserved communities in Canada, notably Indigenous communities. Community engagement and knowledge translation (KT) with Indigenous partners offers the opportunity to collaborate with community partners in order to improve Indigenous health and well-being (Canadian Institutes of Health Research (CIHR), 2009). According to the CIHR's guidelines on Aboriginal KT, KT can be defined as, "a dynamic and iterative process that includes the synthesis, dissemination, exchange and ethically sound application of knowledge to improve health, provide more effective health services and products and strengthen the healthcare system (Straus, Tetroe, & Graham, 2013, p. 3).

Based on this definition, there are two main methods of KT: (1) end-of-grant KT and (2) integrated KT. In end-of-grant-KT, knowledge or findings gained from a study are most often shared through publication in an academic journal or in the grey literature (Canadian Institutes of Health Research, 2009; Straus et al., 2013). While it is the most common form of KT, end-of-grant KT does not leave room for Indigenous and/or community partners to influence or guide the direction of the study or the research questions being asked during the planning or implementation stages of the study. In contrast to end-of-grant-KT, integrated KT, also called community-based participatory action (Woolf, 2008), occurs throughout the duration of the entire research study. Integrated KT engages the community in meaningful ways throughout the research process, and acknowledges strengths and experiences of the different partners (Horowitz, Robinson, & Seifer, 2009). In this way, integrated KT is a community-based bi-directional exchange of knowledge that requires participatory action from the partners from the development of the research question till the end of the study (Straus et al., 2013). Based on a knowledge-to-action model proposed by Graham et al., proper integrated KT brings the community and the researchers into a full collaborative partnership(Canadian Institutes of Health Research, 2009) which aims to ensure that the community partner's voice is heard and valued during

© KONINKLIJKE BRILL NV, LEIDEN, 2018 | DOI 9789004367418_027

MONIKA M. KOWATSCH ET AL.

the design and planning stages of the study. This approach allows the research study to be tailored to the questions, concerns and interests of community partners, and ensures that priorities of the community are meaningfully incorporated into the research study design (Graham et al., 2006; Straus et al., 2013, pp. 2–3).

The importance of engaging in research in partnership with Aboriginal communities is addressed in the Truth and Reconciliation Commission of Canada: Calls to Action (2012). Within this document, the call states:

> We call upon the federal government, in consultation with Aboriginal peoples, to establish measurable goals to identify and close the gaps in health outcomes between Aboriginal and non-Aboriginal communities and to publish annual progress reports and assess long-term trends. Such efforts would focus on indicators such as infant mortality, maternal health, suicide, mental health, addictions, life expectancy, birth rates, infant and child health issues, chronic diseases, illness and injury incidence, and the availability of appropriate health services. (Truth and Reconciliation Commission of Canada, 2012)

It is the responsibility of researchers to respond to the calls put forward by Indigenous partners in order to help close existing gaps in health outcomes. Some examples of this health gap include rates of diabetes (Reading, Ph, & Director, n.d.), HIV/AIDs (human immunodeficiency virus/acquired immunodeficiency syndrome) (Public Health Agency of Canada, 2014) and tuberculosis (Reading et al., n.d.). Research can help to close the gap in health outcomes by asking research questions that Indigenous partners are invested in, and by ensuring that the knowledge gained from research studies serves to improve the health and well-being of Indigenous partners. To ensure that research questions are designed with the intention of closing gaps in both knowledge and health outcomes, the research questions must address community priorities as articulated by community members themselves. This process requires engaging in bi-directional integrated KT in addition to end-of-grant KT.

Trust is a key component of integrated KT. Without trust, the authentic questions and concerns of the community may not be brought forward (Lakes et al., 2014). As trust is a key component of a respectful integrated KT research study, the logical question to follow is how one would create and maintain a trusting relationship between a community and a research lab. In community member interviews exploring perceptions on research, Lakes et al. (2014) found that a mutual learning environment, including participants' knowledge and understanding of how their samples, in this case, interview transcripts, would be handled and processed, was an important component of building a trusting relationship (Lakes et al., 2014). To further support this conclusion, Holzer, Ellis, and Merritt found mistrust to be a barrier to KT which ultimately decreased the dissemination of results within the community (Holzer, Ellis, & Merritt, 2014), such as in end-of-grant KT. They suggested that integration of community members into the research planning process during the initial stages of the study would increase trust and ensure the research

264

findings would be relevant to the community (Holzer et al., 2014). In addition, they found that integrated KT demonstrated respect for the community partners and ensured their values, interests, and experiences were integral to the study design (Holzer et al., 2014).

While it is easy to acknowledge the importance of integrated KT in research studies involving Indigenous partners, the methodology around how to conduct such community engagement remains less clear. In the following sections, we will outline one such attempt at integrated KT as a form of community engagement between a community partner and a research lab.

THE INITIAL ENGAGEMENT

When beginning a research project in collaboration with a community partner, in this case a community-based organization, it is important to ensure that the project is congruent with the mission statement of the community. The research study described in the following sections was carried out in partnership between the University of Manitoba and Sunshine House, located in Winnipeg, Manitoba. Sunshine House is a community-based health promotion organization that provides services to groups in Winnipeg that have been historically underserved, such as individuals affected by HIV/AIDS, individuals who use substances, individuals exploring gender and sexual identity, and individuals experiencing homelessness (Sunshine House Inc, n.d.). The vast majority of participants in Sunshine House programs identify as Indigenous. The mission statement of Sunshine House is to be a place where people can grow. To achieve this, Sunshine House aims to: "act as a community resource, addressing determinants of health for the benefit of the neighbourhood and poly drug users who are entirely or mainly homeless" (Sunshine House Inc, n.d.). It is also important to note that while Sunshine House itself is not an Indigenous organization, within their guiding principles, it states that, "Sunshine House respects the complex histories and traditions of Indigenous participants and their communities. We are committed to the philosophy and practice of decolonization in the programs we develop" (Sunshine House Inc, n.d.).

One aspect of decolonization for Sunshine House is the use of participatory action through ongoing community consultation and a commitment to being responsive to participant-identified needs and interests; this ensures that all programs developed at Sunshine House are developed *for* the community *by* the community. Reflecting this model of program development and delivery, in pursuing a research project with Sunshine House, an Integrated KT approach allowed for the incorporation of a participatory action approach to ensure that the study objectives matched with the mission statement and needs of the group by incorporating the community's voice into the study design and asking questions of importance to the community (Straus et al., 2013). When entering into a relationship built through integrated KT, it is important to tailor the approach to the specific partner community (Graham et al., 2006). To do this, there must be understanding of the context of both the community's and research lab's experiences. In this case, the engagement occurred between a research lab and a community of individuals who chronically use solvents and access programs at Sunshine House. These individuals' experiences have included homelessness, long histories of episodic solvent use, along with high levels of stigma and social exclusion as a result of their substance use (including experiences at health clinics, with other street-involved groups, and in wider society). In this case, the research lab is an academic lab at the University of Manitoba focused on how the body, particularly the immune system, responds to viral infection, such as HIV (human immune deficiency virus). The research lab was interested in determining what, if any, effects solvent use had on the immune system. However, the first priority was establishing a relationship with the community to determine their interests, needs and attitudes towards research.

At the suggestion of the special projects manager of Sunshine House, in 2010, she, research lab members, and community members at Sunshine House came together to begin to establish a relationship. The primary goal of these meetings was to get to know each other and secondarily to determine the community's interest in research. During these meetings, Sunshine House participants and research lab members came together over a meal and discussed various issues including their perspectives surrounding experiences regarding health concerns, research studies, and KT (Bell, 2013). Through these dinners, the community and research team got to know one another, thereby initiating a relationship. At these dinners, it was also determined that members of the community were interested in their own health and that they would be willing to participate in research that addressed questions relevant to their interests. To more specifically determine their interests, a mixed method approach was agreed upon, involving individual interviews, key informant discussions, and a focus groups. Interviews with several focus groups of people who use solvents were held to discuss the research project design, as well as potential applications of the research and methods of end-of-grant-KT (Bell, 2013). Following the focus group discussions, interviews with participants of Sunshine House programs were conducted, in addition to interviews with key informants, such as service providers and physicians associated with the community of interest, to discuss interest in health research and social constructs of health (Bell, 2013). From these meetings and interviews, the lab and community were able to establish a long lasting partnership as well as define "solvent use" and gatehr information about who, in the context of Sunshine House and to a larger extent Winnipeg, are the people using solvents. Finally, during these meetings it came to light that not only was the community open to research, they were satisfied with methods proposed for the laboratory-based, or basic science, portion of the study.

A good research study is one that is mutually beneficial, where the questions being asked, and answers that are derived, are relevant to the community and meet their priorities and interests (Government of Canada, 2015). Through the meetings and dinners between the community at Sunshine House and the research team, several questions of interest were brought forward. One such question that was of interest to the research team was the investigation into the effects of chronic solvent use on the immune system. This question was of particular interest to the Sunshine House participants and the research laboratory as they specialise in immune studies and had the skills and tools required to address the question. During the meetings with the Sunshine House participants, it became clear that not only was the community interested in participating in laboratory-based research, the effects of chronic solvent use were of particular interest to them. In this way, the interests of both the community and the research lab came together to form the final study question. Following the initial engagement period and meetings with Sunshine House participants, several data verification meetings took place both before and after analysis of the data generated. This ensured the community's perspectives on the research was included in the final analysis prior to dissemination of the results and conclusions (Bell, 2013). With a targeted research question agreed upon, the community members and research team were ready to begin the second phase of the research study, which involved drawing blood from Sunshine House participants who use solvents in order to conduct immune studies. Through this initial engagement and meetings, we found that community engagement prior to study onset improved research questions and created important relationships between the community and research team resulting in higher quality research.

DRAWING BACK THE CURTAIN

Prior to the onset of the biological portion of the research study, in early 2015, the second round of engagement with the Sunshine House community occurred. This second round of engagement was deemed a necessity by both the research team and staff at Sunshine House because several members of the original research team had changed and it was crucial that Sunshine House participants had a relationship with all current members of the research team.

This second round of engagement meetings served to strengthen the relationship between members of the community and the research team, both new and old, as well as bring the concerns and questions of the community to the forefront of the study. For example, Sunshine House participants were interested to know how solvent use affected their health. By ensuring the questions of the Sunshine House participants were at the heart of the study, the relevance of the research questions were improved. In addition, engagement based on integrated KT allowed a higher quality of research to be obtained by seeking to answer a community-driven question thus directly serving the community. In order to facilitate transparency throughout the project, and to further develop community participants' understanding of the research process and exactly what would happen with their blood samples once transported to the lab, in this second round of engagement the Sunshine House participants were invited to visit the research lab. At the lab facility, the Sunshine House participants and the research team sat together and discussed health research, their respective understandings of the immune system, and how a research study proceeds. Basic science, or the science of understanding how things work, does not inherently include dissemination and KT beyond the scientific field. Due to this normative practice, basic science can be perceived as being surrounded by a black curtain of complicated language and specialized facilities that block the general public or community members from fully knowing how or why research is conducted. However, in order to truly partake in integrated KT, this curtain must be drawn back. In other words, researchers must translate the basic science knowledge that is generated into knowledge that can be used by the community partner. The discussion that was held in the research space between community members and the research team strove to remove this curtain by answering questions such as: *What do researchers do with the samples? Are the samples respected? How are samples handled and disposed of? Can samples be returned when finished with? And, how do researchers generate their answers?* While a general discussion and description of how a research study proceeds helped alleviate some of these concerns, we found that community members participating in a tour of the lab with hands-on demonstrations was also an effective form of knowledge exchange. During the tour, Sunshine House participants received a demonstration of how samples collected during a research study are processed and analysed, along with information about where the samples would be stored and how they would be disposed of at the end of the study period. This demonstration helped answer the questions participants had posed during the discussion period. Demonstrating how the samples would be handled, where they would be stored along with how they would be disposed, showed respect for the samples. This tour tailored to Sunshine House participants' questions helped to demonstrate the key role that transparency in the research process and sample processing can play in building trusting relationships during basic science research.

The final question remaining, *how do researchers generate their answers*, can be more challenging to effectively explain. To address this question, Sunshine House participants were able to come into the lab and perform science experiments of their own where they learned how infectious agents, such as HIV, are detected in the lab. This engagement process allowed the Sunshine House participants to step into the researchers' shoes and experience how answers are generated and collected during a basic science research study. Through the second engagement experience, most notably via increasing the transparency around basic science research processes and truly demonstrating how research is conducted in the laboratory, a trusting relationship continued to build with the community participants. As an additional benefit to our engagement process, the participants became informal advocates of the research and returned to Sunshine House enthusiastic for the study. This enthusiasm resulted in increased awareness about the study and aided in study enrollment. In summary, this period preceding study-onset fostered trust between the Sunshine House community and the researchers and, provided ongoing opportunities to gauge the levels of the community's interest in health research and the research questions posed.

DISSEMINATION OF RESULTS

Proper integrated KT requires the community to be a partner in the interpretation and review of the research findings prior to publication of the study results (Graham et al., 2006). For this reason, following the laboratory-based portion of the study, the findings were orally presented to the Sunshine House participants and a community discussion was held where the study results and implications were discussed. One goal of the dissemination of the results was to present the findings in a way that would provide community members with a greater understanding of their immune system in order to facilitate discussions with their healthcare providers. To achieve this aim, the results of the basic science study were presented using an analogy of the immune system that was used in laboratory visit discussions. For example, if a community house, such as the Sunshine House, represents our body then the fence surrounding this space represents our skin. Immune cells, whose job is to patrol the body for invading bacteria, were depicted as a guard dog protecting a common space. The analogy was supplemented with the use of pictures to illustrate the various components of the immune system. The use of the analogy was adapted to change unfamiliar terms, such as immune cell names and functions, into recognisable characters. This allowed the discussion to flow more easily as little to no memorization of cell roles or functions were required. The use of a familiar analogy provided a common format for discussion, a platform to share study results, and, most importantly, provided an environment where everyone could contribute to the conversation and understand the results being presented. Uptake of the information being presented was evaluated based on comments and questions that occurred throughout the process. Following the presentation of the study results, a discussion between the researchers and Sunshine House participants took place during which the potential implications for the results were considered as well as future directions and new avenues the study could pursue. Questions that were sparked during this follow-up discussion period included; "do solvents kill bacteria?" and "does solvent use affect our lungs?" these questions were recorded as potential future research avenues to pursue due to the community's expression of interested in these topics.

CONCLUSION

Community engagement through integrated KT is a crucial step in all population-based research studies. KT should be carried out prior to the onset of study enrollment and sample collection and sustained until study completion. There are many forms of community engagement that can be tailored to the many different communities and research questions being addressed. While tailoring community engagement to a specific community is important, it can also be difficult. It is crucial to remember that the community is the best guide, responding to their questions/requests/interests can be an effective way to begin community engagement. Basic science research has the unique challenge of drawing back the curtain of complex

MONIKA M. KOWATSCH ET AL.

language and specialised facilities, and turning the unknown, or perhaps the never explained, processes of generating answers from a biological sample, into a process that can be more easily understood. Critical aspects of the integrated KT process include: cultivating a trusting relationship with community partners and opening the laboratory doors to members of the community to see firsthand exactly how samples in the research study are processed and respected; engaging the community within their area of comfort, Sunshine House, through dinners and meetings both prior to and upon study conclusion. In this way, the research team has been able to increase the transparency of basic science research and, together with the community partner, continue the journey of mutually meaningful knowledge creation and translation. Engaging in research with a community partner means supporting, as much as possible, their priorities regardless of whether they relate directly to the research project. Longitudinal supportive relationships between the community partner and the research team provide a context in which new questions/needs that arise from either side can be discussed, supported and investigated. For example, the research team supported Sunshine House's production of a music CD featuring the Sunshine House Band and arranged a gig for the band. The band was established during a separate activity at Sunshine House: The Solvent User's Recreation Project (SURP) (Sunshine House, 2014). Community engagement through KT is instrumental to the study design and must be incorporated early on in the research process. Community engagement helps to refine the research questions, assist in study enrollment, and increases the study relevance. This improves the study quality by ensuring the research study is directly addressing issues that are important to the community.

NOTE

[1] The chapter has been edited by Chelsea Jalloh.

REFERENCES

Bell, C. P. (2013). *Investigating biological and social factors influencing the HIV epidemic in Manitoba.* Winnipeg: University of Manitoba.

Canadian Institutes of Health Research. (2009). *Aboriginal knowledge translation: Understanding and respecting the distinct needs of aboriginal communities in research.* Retrieved from http://www.cihr-irsc.gc.ca/e/8668

Government of Canada. (2015). *Research involving the first nations, Inuit and Métis peoples of Canada.* Retrieved from http://www.pre.ethics.gc.ca/eng/policy-politique/initiatives/tcps2-eptc2/chapter9-chapitre9/

Graham, I. D., Logan, J., Harrison, M. B., Straus, S. E., Tetroe, J., Caswell, W., & Robinson, N. (2006). Lost in knowledge translation: Time for a map? *Journal of Continuing Education in the Health Professions, 26*(1), 13–24. Retrieved from https://doi.org/10.1002/chp.47

Holzer, J. K., Ellis, L., & Merritt, M. W. (2014). Why we need community engagement in medical research. *Journal of Investigative Medicine: The Official Publication of the American Federation for Clinical Research, 62*(6), 851–555. Retrieved from https://doi.org/10.1097/JIM.0000000000000097

Horowitz, C. R., Robinson, M., & Seifer, S. (2009). Community-based participatory research from the margin to the mainstream: Are researchers prepared? *Circulation, 119*(19), 2633–2642. Retrieved from https://doi.org/10.1161/CIRCULATIONAHA.107.729863

Lakes, K. D., Vaughan, E., Pham, J., Tran, T., Jones, M., Baker, D., Swanson, J. M., & Olshansky, E. (2014). Community member and faith leader perspectives on the process of building trusting relationships between communities and researchers. *Clinical and Translational Science, 7*(1), 20–28. Retrieved from https://doi.org/10.1111/cts.12136

Public Health Agency of Canada. (2014). *HIV/AIDs among aboriginal people in Canada: HIV/AIDs epi updates*. Retrieved from http://www.caan.ca/wp-content/uploads/2015/02/Chapter-8-Epi-Update_ENG_Web-2.pdf

Reading, J. (n.d.). *The crisis of chronic disease among aboriginal peoples: A challenge for public health, population health and social policy*. Retrieved from https://dspace.library.uvic.ca:8443/bitstream/handle/1828/5380/Chronic-Disease-2009.pdf?sequence=1&isAllowed=y

Straus, S. E., Tetroe, J., & Graham, I. D. (2013). *Knowledge translation in health care* (2nd ed.). Chichester: John Wiley. Retrieved from http://ebookcentral.proquest.com/lib/umanitoba/reader.action?docID=1207850

Sunshine House. (2014). *Solvent users' recreation project*. Retrieved from https://sunshinehousewpg.files.wordpress.com/2014/03/supr-book-interior-v5-low.pdf

Sunshine House Inc. (n.d.). *Sunshine house*. Retrieved from https://sunshinehousewpg.org/

Truth and Reconciliation Commission of Canada. (2012). *Truth and reconciliation commission of canada: Calls to action*. Winnipeg. Truth and Reconciliation Commission of Canada. Retrieved from http://www.trc.ca/websites/trcinstitution/File/2015/Findings/Calls_to_Action_English2.pdf

Woolf, S. H. (2008). The meaning of translational research and why it matters. *JAMA, 299*(2), 523–526. Retrieved from https://doi.org/10.1001/jama.2007.26

Monika M. Kowatsch
Medical Microbiology
University of Manitoba
Winnipeg, Manitoba

Courtney Bell
College of Medicine
University of Manitoba
Winnipeg, Manitoba

Margaret Ormond
Sunshine House,
Winnipeg, Manitoba

Keith R. Fowke
Medical Microbiology
University of Manitoba
Winnipeg, Manitoba

MARION J. KIPROP

28. RESEARCH ETHICS REVIEW, RESEARCH PARTICIPANTS, AND THE RESEARCHER IN-BETWEEN

When REB Directives Clash with Participant Socio-Relational Cosmologies

INTRODUCTION

The process of regulating research to ensure that researchers adhere to the principles of autonomy, beneficence, and justice is essential in ensuring that research participants and communities are "treated with respect, protected from harm, and saved from embarrassing exposure" (Bosk & de Vries, 2004, p. 256). The way that ethics oversight is structured, however, has proven to be problematic for non-experimental research. The bureaucratic nature of the regulatory ethics system has, thus, invited critical discussions amongst researchers who, for the most part, challenge its efficacy for qualitative research (e.g., Dingwall, 2012; Israel, 2016). The challenges that have been identified specifically with the bureaucratic review of ethnographic research result from the application of biomedical and other experimental research protocols – that approach research with a linear frame – onto qualitative research (see Bosk & de Vries, 2004; Fassin, 2006; Katz, 2006; Lederman, 2006; Tolich & Fitzgerald, 2006). The general consensus amongst these authors is that the linear hypothetico-deductive assumptions underlying the structuring of research ethics review often affects the quality and the direction of research because it is difficult to predict how qualitative research fieldwork will unfold and, subsequently, the kinds of ethical dilemmas a researcher might encounter. In this chapter, I reflect on the challenges I encountered while translating "procedural ethics" – which refers to the process of applying for ethics approval (Guillemin & Gillam, 2004, p. 263) – to "situational ethics" – which refers to the "daily ethical and moral challenges and decisions encountered when interacting with participants" (Ellis, 2007, p. 7) – during my PhD ethnographic research in a non-western context. The on-field dilemmas I encountered pertained to my positionality and subsequent contextual power dynamics, the extent to which my chosen research problem was reasonable to research participants, and the cultural relevance – or irrelevance – of the informed consent process to research participants.

© KONINKLIJKE BRILL NV, LEIDEN, 2018 | DOI 9789004367418_028

MARION J. KIPROP

CHOICE OF RESEARCH QUESTION AND RESEARCH CONTEXT

For my Ph.D. ethnographic research, I proposed to explore generational differences in the approach to conflict and conflict resolution. The choice of my research problem derived from an academe-tradition driven need to contribute to the progress science cumulatively. While the daily practice of conflict resolution exists in all societies, the discipline of Peace and Conflict Studies developed in the west. As a result, its prototypical theories and models of analysis and practice remain, to a large extent, western-oriented. Conflict researchers who have taken an interest in the question of culture have sought to account for cultural variance in conflict and conflict resolution by either developing comparative models of classification (e.g., Abu-Nimer, 1996; Augsburger, 1992) or by exploring holistic single-case studies (e.g., Cook, 1997; Robarchek, 1997). Despite these efforts, research studies that focus on the question of culture in conflict remain few and far between. My proposed research was, therefore, decidedly crucial in introducing a nuanced approach to the question of culture in conflict, that is, exploring sub-cultural – generational – variations in conflict formation, behaviour, and resolution processes within a culture-sharing group.

While my chosen research problem was scientifically driven, the selection of my research location – Kisima[1] – was mostly strategic. Considering the question of non-western culture in conflict and conflict resolution called for an ethnographic study of a non-western culture. Born into a non-western cultural group, the Tugen of Kenya, I reckoned that it would be easier to gain physical and social access into Kisima – my ancestral home – given my pre-established networks and points of contact. While I never domiciled in Kisima, I made frequent – one to two month – visits to the location to see my extended family during school holidays. Over the years, specifically, after I joined university, my visits to Kisima became shorter – hours to less than a week – and far between. In my early visits to Kisima, I developed linguistic competence in Kalenjin – the Tugen native tongue. I, also, developed cultural competence in the socio-cultural and relational fabric of the community which, I thought, would allow me develop focused interview questions that would be effective in soliciting participant responsiveness. These considerations influenced my selection of Kisima as a convenient research site.

POWER, THE REB PROCESS, RESEARCH PARTICIPANTS, AND I

As I draft my dissertation report, I am compelled to engage in what Jackson (2004) calls "rigorous reflexivity" (p. 33) on my nuanced positionality while considering the power dynamics that were manifest as I negotiated the ethics of data collection and after arriving at the field site. With my ethics review application process, the task of establishing credibility with the REB to secure approval to conduct research was overwhelming; on the field site, I engaged with participants commanding a different yet meaningful type of power. Becker (1967) conceptualizes the "hierarchy of credibility" to illuminate on the experience of being caught in between an established system of hierarchy (p. 242). van den Scott (2016) uses Becker's (1967) notion of the "hierarchy of credibility" to illustrate how the ethics process is stratified. van den Scott (2016) critiques the placing of ethics boards, students, and participants in the research ethics review system of hierarchy. She writes: "…ethics boards are placed higher in the hierarchy of credibility than students. Researchers, too, occupy a lower stratum of credibility than ethics boards…. research participants…occupy a yet lower place in the hierarchy of credibility than researchers" (p. 233). In this system of hierarchy ethics boards, without direct contact with researchers and/or participants, make decisions about the researcher's capability, based on written applications, to successfully mitigate ethical liabilities during research (van den Scott, 2016). Researchers are, thus, often compelled to feign expertise on matters that pertain to participants, which in turn "silences the participants' own expertise in their own lives, stripping away their autonomy – the pinnacle of disrespect – by privileging the researcher's understanding of the participants' world" (van den Scott, 2016, p. 235).

Despite the lower positioning of research participants in the hierarchy of credibility before fieldwork, my research participants reversed that hierarchy placing my university at the bottom and placing themselves at the top during fieldwork. During early consent conversations, I was introduced to a retired teacher, Mzee Gideon whose primary vocation now entails gathering and documenting data about Tugen material, social, and ideological culture for heritage preservation purposes. Mzee Gideon would become my primary research guarantor. As we got to know each other through the duration of my fieldwork, we had lots of conversations about each of our endeavours. We spoke about my life in Canada, my Ph.D. research, and my future research goals and his current research work, his heritage preservation undertaking, and his hopes for the younger members of the community to embrace Tugen socio-cultural values. One time, Mzee Gideon told me a story that, he said, would make me aware of my positionality in relation to the community.

Approximately 15–20 years ago, there was word of a visiting European researcher, Mr. Spade, seeking to conduct cultural research with residents of a neighbouring village. Given the distrust of strangers, specifically of foreign heritage, the community in question shunned Mr. Spade telling him that he was not entitled to cultural knowledge since he was a stranger and that strangers are generally considered enemies. Mr. Spade, curious to know how one might be accepted as a friend, not seen as an enemy, was informed that communal membership rested on kinship ties established by birth or through marriage. Mr. Spade, after his first rejection, left the village but would return several months later asking for one of the village girls' hand in marriage. The circumstances of their courtship remain unclear. Following family deliberations and traditional marriage proceedings, Mr. Spade became a village son. Mr. Spade built a small house in the village for his new bride. Gradually, Mr. Spade was permitted to attend to communal activities, participate in communal traditions and rituals, and partake in family and communal decision-making. After a couple of

MARION J. KIPROP

years, Mr. Spade informed his new family that he needed to make a trip to Europe to attend to some business and family matters. He asked the family to take care of his wife while away. Mr. Spade left and was never heard from again.

The story illustrates the dilemmas associated with researcher positionality and the subsequent ethics of representation in writing. During early consent conversations and throughout data collection, communal gatekeepers and some of my participants communicated the privilege and responsibility that came with my belongingness. "You are not Mr. Spade, you are not a stranger, you are a child of this community, and you are allowed access to our culture," Mzee Gideon summed up the story. He explained that having access to "our culture" is a privilege that comes with responsibility. "Us Tugens, have classified information," he continued. In essence, one is afforded 'insider' access to Tugen community by virtue of belongingness. Insiders are thus entrusted with communal knowledge, and it is every member's responsibility to safeguard it and in the words of one of my participants, "not expose our secrets." The sentiment concerning the sheltering of classified information was echoed several times. One instance stands out. In preparing for a focus group discussion, and in the spirit of checking for continuous consent, I re-explained the nature of my research. Generally, the group was pleased that I was returning "to my roots" after travelling to a foreign country and being away for so long. They also expressed, while echoing Mzee Gideons's stance on classified information, that as their "communal ambassador" to the world, I am responsible for packaging written information in a way that brings honour and respect to the community.

In addition to dictating how they wished to be presented in publications, research participant wishes informed my fieldwork questions. The purpose of my proposed research, when I applied for ethics, was to explore generational differences in the approach to conflict and conflict resolution. Specifically, I proposed to explore the differences in the way cross-sectional age-set groups approach conflict and conflict resolution. In line with academe-driven priorities, I developed an inductive-model research proposal but framed it deductively. Tolich and Fitzgerald (2006) contend that since researchers, during the ethics review process, are expected to "describe their project as if they had [advance knowledge of the literature]" and to draft "the ethics application as if the outcome were more predictable," qualitative researchers often develop strategies to get through a review process that does not take into account the emergent and unpredictable nature of qualitative research (p. 73). One such strategy is the use of a "deductive frame" – that "has clearly stated hypotheses leading to a linear data collection and analysis that is both transparent and straightforward" (Fitzgerald, 2006, p. 73). While my proposed research was not based on a hypothesis, when I got to the field site, I realized that I had an implied hypothesis in my research question. In seeking to explore generational differences in conflict, I was working under the presumption that there are in fact generational subcultures and generational differences in the ways individuals respond to conflict.

As I interacted with participants, I learned that a lot of them were interested, just like Mzee Gideon, in seeing the documentation of Tugen culture for heritage preservation.

276

Some of my participants worried that the cultural holders of knowledge were dying of old age and that the young members of the community might, as a result, not have a chance to receive cultural knowledge. They also expressed disappointment in existing scant literature about the Tugen. Existing Tugen literature, to a large extent, focuses on colonial and post-colonial economic development (e.g., Anderson, 2002; Coy, 1988). There is some literature about the Kalenjin and other Kalenjin sub-groups specifically the Nandi (e.g., Chesaina, 1991; Hollis, 1969). Since the Tugen belong to the larger Kalenjin speaking group, there has been a tendency to assume cultural similarities with other Kalenjin sub-groups. The lumping of Tugen with other – more researched – Kalenjin speaking groups displeased a majority of my participants. Most times, I would ask questions, based on the literature I had read about other Kalenjin speaking groups (mostly the Nandi and Kipsigis) and some of the responses I got included: "No, I have never heard of that in Tugenland" or "That is not a Tugen tradition" or "They do that among the Kipsigis or Nandi; we do not do that." As a result of guarantor's, gatekeepers' and some of my research participants' wishes for cultural preservation through documented research, I was challenged to start reflecting on the implications of my chosen research question and considering ways in which I could let data emerge inductively.

CLASHING VALUES ON THE PROCESS OF OBTAINING WRITTEN INFORMED CONSENT

Obtaining informed consent is one of the most critical components of research ethics practice. Most researchers work to obtain written informed consent from participants. While TCPS 2 recognizes that some instances do not call for written consent, applicants are asked to provide "valid reasons" for deviating from the norm of written consent (CIHR, NSERCC, & SSHRCC, 2010, p. 140). Bell (2016) argues that the phrase "valid reasons" is vague and its ambiguity serves the purpose of shifting more power to the review board, which has to determine what "valid reasons" constitute and if an applicant has successfully demonstrated that they are justifiable (p. 196). In light of Bell's (2016) point and in trying to avoid a lengthy review process, I stated my intent to obtain written consent.[2] On my consent forms, I was required to include a detailed description of my research question and specific data collection techniques, a statement on potential risks and benefits, a statement on confidentiality and anonymity, a statement on mandatory reporting, and a statement on voluntariness.

During fieldwork, I found that continued consent conversations undermined local expectations on relational concepts of respect, trust, and good faith. A central feature of Tugen life is the relationship system with a select group of people called the *tilie*, which means 'relations.' The *tilie* is used to describe all those that are bonded by kinship ties established at birth or through marriage. The *tilie* is a framework that establishes a code of behaviour determining how community members will relate to each other, that is, it provides a foundation for socio-political organization and

MARION J. KIPROP

modes of interaction. The first set of questions individuals often ask when they meet each other for the first time have to do with lineage, for example, "Whose home do you belong to"? "Who are your parents?" Once one's lineage is determined, individuals often seek to determine if and how they share *tilia*. One might say for example, "my sister is married to someone from your clan, which means that you and are *tilia.*" Once *tiliandi* is established, individuals proceed on to other matters knowing that from that point on they are obligated to respect and to look out for each other by virtue of being *tilia* – related.

The history of deceitful contractual agreements within the Kenyan context may be one of the reasons that participants were skeptical about consent forms. One research participant reminded me of the Lenana Treaty – signed by a Maasai chief with the British during colonial expansion (Anderson, 2002) – when I mentioned the signing of consent forms. Maasai pastoralists controlled the vast lowland plains of the Rift Valley province, including Kisima. Other groups including the Tugen seasonally grazed their livestock from the top of the hills in Rift Valley to the edges of the Maasai controlled lowlands (Anderson, 2002). In 1904, Chief Olanana signed a colonial land treaty allowing British settlers to seize control of the land in Rift Valley (Anderson, 2002).

The informed consent was also frowned upon because the formalized and bureaucratic nature of interaction often associated with colonialism and attributed to the prevailing cultures in western societies not only makes relationships impersonal but also breaches the *tilie* principle of respect. During a consent conversation, one participant was perplexed by the multi-paged document I was referring to when communicating the components of the informed consent form. He shook his head in disapproval saying: "these things of *wazungu* (white people)." He proceeded to ask if I had any friends in Canada and if I ever visit their homes. On affirming, "You must first report to them that you are coming, right?" he asked. "I know for sure that in the world of white people, you have to write a letter or call them to inform them that you are coming to see them… back in the day, they wrote letters, maybe now they make phone calls to inform," he continued and then proceeded to tell me a story:

> Long ago, I wanted to go visit a friend of mine. He was hosting European missionaries. I informed him that I would stop by for a visit and he told me that I had to write a letter to express my interest to visit. "To visit your home?" I asked. He informed me that that is what the missionaries had requested; for people to inform him when they would be visiting his home. I asked my son to write the letter for me. I was given a specific date to go to my friend's house. When we got there – there was a group of us who had been told to go on that day – it was already getting dark. A man pulled out a piece of paper and started calling out our names one by one like they call out school children. He checked our names, and only then were we allowed into the house where we met the missionaries who started praying for us. At this point, most of us were

RESEARCH ETHICS REVIEW, RESEARCH PARTICIPANTS, AND THE RESEARCHER

annoyed because we are adults and they treated us like school children lining up for food. I have never forgotten how disrespected I felt that day and I was very disappointed in my friend.

On asking why he felt disrespected, he told me that the formality of relationships is not only foreign to Tugen culture but is also associated with the condescending and paternalistic nature of interaction established by colonial administrators over locals.

In addition to undermining the *tilie* principle of respect, asking people to sign a document of consent, also undermined the principle of mutual trust. Mutual trust amongst members is fundamental to the preservation of *tiliandi*. One of the ways the principle of mutual trust manifests is by taking someone's word; it is a show of good faith to believe that an individual/group will do as they say they will. On my ethics application, I indicated that I would hold continued consent conversations. Some of my participants expressed annoyance as a result of the repetitive nature of conversations about consent and voluntariness. "What is [wrong with] this child? I already said I want to teach you about our culture. Why do you keep asking? I am an adult, when I say I will do something, it means that I intend to do it," one participant told me in frustration.

There were other challenges I encountered with the contents of the consent form. Some participants picked out the statement on benefits for clarification and renegotiation at the early stages of fieldwork. During consent conversations with potential focus group participants, I was probed about my allegiance and responsibility to my Canadian university *vis* a *vis* to my ethnic community. "So, they have sent you here to write about our people and about our culture" one participant said. "Who will write about them and their culture?" he asked. "Other than for the reason that you belong to this community, why else should we give you this information?" he continued. During such consent conversations, I found that the top-down approach of ethics regulations and the misconceived linearity of the research process prevents researchers from working with communities, especially those overseas, to determine how research projects should be approached and how those research projects might benefit participating communities; this disregards the fact that research participants are better positioned to determine how and if a research project will be of benefit to their community.

CONCLUSION: LOOKING FORWARD

The linear approach to research ethics disallows researchers from contacting participants before ethics approval making it difficult to anticipate how participants will respond to a research project. One major problem with the linear approach is the disregard of participant cultural and relational cosmologies. Often ethical principles clash with participant ethical and cultural mores. As a result, researchers might find themselves caught in between two conflicting cultural and ethical expectations: that of their institution and the group they interact with for their research. The mismatch

279

MARION J. KIPROP

between "procedural ethics" (Guillemin & Gillam, 2004, p. 263) and "situational ethics" (Ellis, 2007, p. 7) may be particularly problematic for researchers in western institutions doing research amongst members of communities in non-western societies. Research participants in non-western communities are more prone to exploitation and researcher ethical impropriety given the varying approaches to ethics – from country to country – and the lack of continued ethical conversations after ethics approval.

There are no easy solutions to the dilemmas I have alluded to in this chapter. However, I do hope that my reflections will prompt other graduate students to not only reflect on "ethically important moments" (Guillemin & Gillam, 2004, p. 261) as they interact with research participants but to, also, publish reports on on-field ethical dilemmas and the strategies they might employ in mitigating unforeseen contingencies. From these publications, other graduate students, navigating through research ethics may be able to anticipate, as far as it is possible, the spontaneous ethical contingencies of fieldwork. Additionally, research ethics boards should re-think the linear approach to ethnographic research. To solve the mismatch that exists between procedural and situational ethics, researchers should be allowed to consult with participants about participant cultural ethics and if possible work with communal gatekeepers and/or leaders in drafting ethics applications.

NOTES

[1] Location and individual names are pseudonymised.
[2] In retrospect, given how fieldwork unfolded, I should have applied to use verbal consent. I am, however, not sure if the review board would have approved a verbal consent in a language other than English as I have not been able to identify precedent practice to this effect in literature.

REFERENCES

Abu-Nimer, M. (1996). Conflict resolution approaches: Western and Middle Eastern possibilities. *The American Journal of Economics and Sociology, 55*(1), 35–52.

Anderson, D. (2002). *Eroding the commons: The politics of ecology in Baringo, Kenya 1890–1963.* Nairobi: East African Educational Publishers.

Augsburger, D. (1992). *Conflict mediation across cultures.* Louisville, KY: Westmister John Knox Press.

Becker, H. S. (1967). Whose side are we on? *Social Problems, 14*(3), 239–247.

Bell, K. (2016). The more things change, the more they stay the same: The TCPS 2 and the institutional ethical oversight of social science research in Canada. In W. C. Hoonard & A. Hamilton (Eds.), *The ethics rupture: Exploring alternatives to formal research ethics review* (pp. 189–205). Toronto: University of Toronto Press.

Bosk, C., & de Vries, R. (2004). Bureaucracies of mass deception: Institutional review boards and the ethics of ethnographic research. *Annals of the American Academy of Political and Social Science, 595*, 249–263.

Chesaina, C. (1991). *Oral literature of the Kalenjin.* Nairobi: East African Educational Publishers.

CIHR, NSERCC, & SSHRCC. (2010). *Tri-council policy statement: Ethical conduct for research involving humans* (2nd ed.). Ottawa: Interagency Panel on Research Ethics.

Cook, H. K. (1997). Conflict resolution in native margariteno society. In D. Fry & K. Bjorkqvist (Eds.), *Cultural variance in conflict resolution: Alternatives to violence* (pp. 69–77). Mahwah, NJ: Lawrence Elrbaum Associates, Inc.

280

RESEARCH ETHICS REVIEW, RESEARCH PARTICIPANTS, AND THE RESEARCHER

Coy, M. (1988). Tugen monopoly: Capitalism and conflict in the mountains of Kenya. *Anthropology and Humanism Quartely, 13*(2), 40–47.

Dingwall, R. (2012). How did we get into this mess? The rise of ethical regulation in the social sciences. *Studies in Qualitative Methodology, 12*, 3–26.

Ellis, C. (2007). Telling secrets, revealing lives: Relational ethics in research with intimate others. *Qualitative Inquiry, 13*(1), 3–29.

Fassin, D. (2006). The end of ethnography as collateral damage of ethical regulation? *American Ethnologist, 33*(4), 522–524.

Guillemin, M., & Gillam, L. (2004). Ethics, reflexivity, and "ethically important moments" in research. *Qualitative Inquiry, 10*(2), 261–280.

Hollis, A. (1969). *The Nandi: Their language and folk-lore.* Oxford: Clarendon Press.

Israel, M. (2016). *Research ethics and integrity for social scientists: Beyond regulatory compliance.* Los Angeles, CA: Sage Publishing.

Jackson, J. L. (2004). An ethnographic flimflam: Giving gifts, doing research, and videotaping the native subject/object. *American Anthropologist, 106*(1), 32–42.

Katz, J. (2006). Ethical escape routes for ethnographic researchers. *American Ethnologist, 33*(4), 499–506.

Lederman, R. (2006). The perils of working at home: IRB "mission creep" as context and content for an ethnography of disciplinary knowledges. *American Ethnologist, 33*(4), 482–491.

Robarchek, C. (1997). A community of interests: Semai conflict resolution. In D. Fry & K. Bjorkqvist (Eds.), *Cultural variation in conflict resolution* (pp. 51–77). Mahwah, NJ: Lawrence Erlbaum Associates, Inc.

Tolich, M., & Fitzgerald, M. H. (2006). If ethics committees were designed for ethnography. *Journal of Empirical Research on Human Research Ethics, 1*(2), 71–78.

van den Scott, L. K. (2016). The socialization of contemporary students by ethics boards: Malaise and ethics for graduate students. In W. C. Hoonard & A. Hamilton (Eds.), *The ethics rupture: Exploring alternatives to foral research ethics review* (pp. 230–247). Toronto: University of Toronto Press.

Marion J. Kiprop
Peace and Conflict Studies
University of Manitoba
Winnipeg, Manitoba

PATRICIA SINIIKWE PAJUNEN

29. AN ACT OF ANISHINAABE RESISTANCE

Boozhoo. Siniikwe ndigo. Patricia ndishinakaaz. Opwaaganasiniing nitoonci. Hello. Siniikwe is what they call me. My name is Patricia. I'm from Opwaaganasiniing near Thunder Bay, Ontario. Miigwetch. Thank you for taking time to read my story.

It has been the case – and still is – that philosophy largely disregards pan-Indigenous[1] thought as not philosophy or something lesser than philosophy. Learning involves storytelling, a method of learning that is largely frowned upon in philosophy. Storytelling would be akin to anecdotes, and most philosophical advice recommends one stay away from anecdotes. Pan-Indigenous philosophy as storytelling is still philosophy. It is a method of learning and questioning that Western cannon philosophy[2] does not understand. The problem for Indigenous philosophers is colonial academic institutions deciding to leave out pan-Indigenous thought or deciding to 'translate' pan-Indigenous thought into the Continental or Analytic traditions, removing the necessary things that make pan-Indigenous thought Indigenous philosophy.

Hence, what you will find in this work is a mixture of storytelling as concept analysis and an academic translation of the storytelling. What you will find in this work is my voice presented in two distinct ways: my storytelling voice and my philosopher voice. Hence, you will find my stories to be more colloquial; I will use, for instance, 'don't' rather than 'do not'. My philosopher voice, however, will be formal and technical. This style choice is important in the reclamation of my Anishinaabe voice in my philosophical work. My stories are for everyone and the colloquial style represents how I would tell my stories in person. In the act of storytelling as philosophy, I resist the oppressive nature of academia which forces a grammatical and formal style that is not necessary for argument construction and my discipline which seeks to eradicate all sorts of anecdotes from philosophical work. I was told by a professor that I couldn't use anecdotes in my work unless I was Martha Nussbaum, meaning that I couldn't get away with using anecdotes unless I was a well situated and known philosopher. Being a Masters student at the time I was told this strange advice, I took it that there was some sort of privilege that I didn't have in virtue of being a student. Now at the Ph.D. level, I still have professors reminding me that anecdotes are detrimental to academic work. From my perspective, an Anishinaabe philosopher, anecdotes lend credence to the application of abstract concepts to the real world. I was told to use hypothetical people instead. To me, this does not make any sense when there are actual people, situations, and

© KONINKLIJKE BRILL NV, LEIDEN, 2018 | DOI 9789004367418_029

stories that can exemplify (or understand differently) these abstract concepts. So, by doing the translation from storytelling to academic, philosophical jargon, I aim to teach my discipline that storytelling is a strong way of teaching the tough, abstract concepts found within this work.

In this work, I will tell stories to illustrate oppression, oppressors, oppressed, and two categories of bystanders. The stories/concept analysis could stand alone without the philosophical jargon. However, to show the merit of storytelling as philosophy, this work will be a weaving of Western cannon concept analysis and storytelling as concept analysis. As much as this is an act of resistance against oppressive systems and people, this is also an opportunity to practice the seven grandfather teachings: nibwaakaawin, zaagi'idiwin, minaadendamowin, aakode'ewin, gwayakwaadiziwin, dabaadendiziwin, and debwewin.[3] Translating from Anishinaabemowin to English, these teachings are wisdom, love, respect, bravery, honesty, humility, and truth. Attempting to build a bridge which will allow pan-Indigenous thought to enter the academe as it is and become a part of the knowledge base that philosophy draws from, I welcome you on this journey. Please respect the seven grandfathers while we explore these highly charged topics.

Taiaiake Alfred and Jeff Corntassel start their article, *Being Indigenous: Resurgences against Contemporary Colonialism*, with the line, "Indigenousness is an identity constructed, shaped and lived in the politicized context of contemporary colonialism" (2005, p. 597). It is no different in academia. Western cannon philosophy presents itself as the par excellence of what can be considered philosophy. Everything that western cannon philosophy is necessarily closes itself off from voices like mine because my Anishinaabe voice doesn't sound like western cannon philosophy. To be accepted, I need to suppress my Anishinaabe voice. To participate in philosophy, I need to speak in a voice that is not mine or that is abstracted from how I would speak to an audience. Hence, this is an act of resistance; resistance against the oppressor that is my own discipline: a discipline that wants to assimilate Indigenous Philosophy, a discipline that wants to do Indigenous Philosophy as if it were western cannon, a discipline filled with philosophers who uphold Western cannon as the only way to do philosophy.

Two preliminary notes:

- Trigger warnings: I will be talking about and referring to residential schools, assimilation, oppression, suppression, death, genocide, and bullying.
- Spoiler alert: as I tell my story, I would like everyone to keep in mind Bernard Boxill's (2010) categorization of those involved in oppression and what resistance looks like for each group. Boxill defines resistance from the perspectives of three groups: the oppressors, the bystanders, and the oppressed (1). The oppressors are meant to resist committing acts of oppression (Boxill, 2010, p. 1). The bystanders are meant to resist being bystanders – being complicit in oppression (Boxill 1). The oppressed, however, are meant to do whatever they can to frustrate their oppressors (Boxill, 2010, p. 8).

And this is where my story starts. Survival. I think it's fair to say the Indigenous people have moved beyond survival and into resistance. But survival is a form of resistance. Everything the colonizers and the religious people did to my ancestors is deplorable. My ancestors resisted enough, they held on enough, to get to this point. It's 2017 and Indigenous people are still here; it may not matter whether it is by our own definition or by the colonial one because, by reclaiming identity, we are resisting. We, I think, have moved beyond mere survival. We are here, and we are strong. This work will speak to some of that.

I determined it would be best to begin the story before my birth to speculate on what might be plausible causes of my present situation. No, I will not recount 500 years of colonial history. I want to start with my Nana. When I was born in 1977, my mum's mum was the only grandparent I had left. My Nana was born in 1932. For at least 19 years she had to shun her Anishinaabe practices or face going to prison. Her father was an RCMP officer. I don't know much about him or their lifestyle, but his career choice must have had influence on cultural practices and language use. My mum told me that Nana probably understood Anishinaabemowin when she was younger, but she rarely spoke Anishinaabemowin. I remember her saying 'aaniina' a lot. When I am home with my family, I say it, too. Loosely, it translates into English as 'that's silly'. Nana also used to say 'miigomanjigo after dark'. My mum thinks it translates to 'I don't know after dark' which can be understood as 'I'm not sure what happens after dark/when the lights go out'. I suppose my Nana was superstitious.

By the time I was born, the family environment was immersed in the Roman Catholic church rather than the Anishinaabe culture. Because my great grandfather was an RCMP officer and because it was illegal for Anishinaabe people to practice cultural ceremonies and speak the language, it makes sense that I didn't know I was Anishinaabe until some point after my Nana died. I was 11. Even though my Nana was too old by the time the 60s Scoop happened and did not end up in the local residential school with some of her siblings, she was already firmly under the oppressive finger of colonization. So, it's not too much of a mystery of why she suppressed her identity and refused to participate in Anishinaabe ways.

I was born and raised in Nipigon, Ontario. It's a small town about an hour away from Thunder Bay. My mum's reserve was just a quick jaunt down the highway. Because my Nana didn't live on the reserve, my mum didn't either. We rarely visited our family on the reserve. I really don't remember going to the reserve often until after Nana died. So, I didn't truly recognize myself as Anishinaabe when I was growing up. To make matters worse, I didn't realize how horrible it was for Indigenous people until high school. In grade school, I remember doing projects on Christopher Columbus and retelling his story of 'discovering' North America. I also remember bullying the 'rez kids'. What I grew up to believe was that living on the rez was bad and living off the rez was good. No one ever said this explicitly; it was in the attitudes of everyone around me. The educational structure never explicitly said that the Indigenous people were bad and ought to be avoided at all costs; those in charge of the structure never had to. There was so much around me that silently

PATRICIA SINIIKWE PAJUNEN

screamed to stay away from Indigenous people and the rez that I avoided it like the plague and made fun of it when the opportunities came. The historical account of Canada was such that we needed to pity, coddle, and hate the Indigenous people. When the historical account refuses to publish the voices of the people who were almost eradicated by 'discovery', we tend to grow up wondering why this group of people complains so much.

Because I'm a mixed breed, I ended up being too white for the Indigenous kids and too Indigenous for the white kids. Trying to carve a niche out for myself in either group was a difficult chore, so I adapted to whichever group I was a part of in the moment and worked toward alienating the other group from me so I could appear to fit in. It all backfired: both sides hated me. I found friendship with a couple of other mixed kids. They were able to maintain a sort of kinship with both sides and I wasn't. As those two friendships drifted away, I decided that I didn't need any friends. This explanation is not justification for what I've done. I know I was not a good kid. I know I have a lot of healing to do within myself and within my community. It would be easy to pass responsibility onto my Nana, the kids who bullied me, the education system, colonialism, or many other things. Regardless of how young I was, it was all my doing and I need to acknowledge, accept, and account for that. It's time to accept the truth of it, call upon wisdom, love, and bravery, and humbly apologize for what I did. I must be honest and respect all involved including myself. Just one more step toward decolonizing myself is to apologize for what I did in accepting the colonial lies and perpetuating them for as long as I did.

So, what happened in high school? I ended up befriending two ostracized young Anishinaabe women who helped me gain something I wanted since I was a kid: an identity; a group to be a part of; and acceptance. At the same time, my sister, who had quit school two years before, was with an Indigenous man who owned a copy of *500 Nations*[4] – a documentary about Indigenous peoples. It's been 23 years since I watched it – even then I spent more time passing notes to my two friends than watching it in the only Native Studies class my high school had, taught by a white woman who admitted to having to no clue how to teach it. So, I asked my sister's partner to borrow the series.

The reason watching this mini-series was so significant was because the parts I did watch were tremendously horrid. The murder, the oppression, and the subjugation (even though I didn't have these words while in high school) all punched me in the heart. The effects were not immediate; the effects took years to develop. The horrible atrocities explained in the video were of those things that I never learned about when I was younger. The celebrations we had for Columbus seemed like a cruel joke. The formation of this country was based on attempted genocide (and continued genocide through erasure rather than murder, mostly). My Nana was a survivor of this. This is a long history of colonizers and settlers making decisions and putting structures and systems in place to make sure First Nations, Inuit, and Metis people were stricken from the historical record and lost to history like the library of Alexandria. The colonizers didn't want us here because they wanted everything to themselves.

And they probably believed it was theirs due to their religious affiliations. They used that Doctrine of Discovery[5] to justify every single atrocity that was done to the First Nations, Inuit, and Metis people. After switching from murder to erasure, the education system was set up to make sure that the colonizers were seen as heroes to the Indigenous people. That was my education. White heroes to look up to; savage relatives I needed to stay away from.

Out of curiosity, I looked at new Ontario curricula for adding in Indigenous content in grade school. Largely, the guideline is from the voice of colonization.[6] The guide reads as if all Indigenous peoples are the same and hold the same cultural symbols. They focus on only a handful, at most, of groups and refer to only two as language-based (endnote 6). On page 9 of that guide, however, the colonial language rears its ugly head:

> Cultural similarities were not the only factors that came into play when different *First Nation groups were deciding with whom they would align.* Some of the variables included, but were not limited to, geographic proximity, language, lifestyle, the degree to which *First Nation groups chose to convert to Christianity*, and the degree to which *groups saw themselves as useful to one another's goals.* (my italics; endnote 6)

This language is problematic since it erases the coercion used in gaining alliances and it erases the forced conversion to Christianity or Catholicism. It also implicitly says that the Indigenous groups saw themselves as tools to help colonizers achieve their goal of colonization. The language makes it seem as if these things happened because the Indigenous people wanted them to happen. Perhaps some alliances were chosen. Perhaps all alliances were made in order to stay alive in some fashion. Yes, this is speculation. With the historical account controlled by the colonizers, I remain sceptical of what is passed off as knowledge of what occurred over the last 500+ years.

It is a tricky situation to figure out the oppressors and bystanders during my grade school and high school years. Because written history was controlled by the colonizers – who then set up the educational structures which made it as if Indigenous people didn't exist, were happy about helping the 'settlers', or 'chose' to convert to Christianity – it could be argued that the original colonizers and the structures that still exist are the oppressors and all other people involved are bystanders. Because Indigenous peoples were not eradicated completely, the descendants of the colonizers could have done more in narrowing in on an account of history that is not one-sided rather than maintain the one-sided narrative that we continue to receive in schools. Most of the teachers I had could be seen as oppressors since they were following in their forefathers' footsteps with the maintenance of the historical account. It is not unreasonable to call out those who oppress as oppressors even if the current social structure tells them they are not oppressing. The marginalized are not ignorant of the oppression they face. Oppressors, on the other hand, can sometimes be ignorant of the oppression they are the cause of. This ignorance, however, is no excuse against

PATRICIA SINIIKWE PAJUNEN

culpability. Make no mistake here, the consequences of culpability are on a sliding scale just like the consequences of breaking the law: the consequences for a first offence are not the same for repeated offences. Someone who utters a racial slur the first time will be educated on the problems with uttering such words. Someone who continues to utter a racial slur may be accused of hate speech. There is a sliding scale here.

Concerning bystanders, Boxill claims that "there can be oppression without bystanders [but] there cannot be oppression without oppressed people" (2010, p. 6). Bystanders are not necessary to have instances of oppression; however, bystanders can assist the oppressed in resisting oppression. When bystanders are identified, their role in resistance is to intervene and stop oppression when possible (Boxill, 2010, p. 1). When bystanders do nothing, they are complicit in oppression. Hence, Rachel McKinnon suggests we abandon the term 'ally' in favour of another category of bystander: the active bystander (2017, p. 172). McKinnon's distinction adds depth to Boxill's account of the bystander since it puts the bystander on a spectrum from complicity to resistance. Concerning the Active Bystander, McKinnon says,

> The idea is that if one develops strategies for how to respond to discrimination and harassment when one sees it happen, one will be more likely to (hopefully) appropriately intercede and assist the disadvantaged person. Importantly, active bystanders can be in-group or fellow out-group members of the disadvantaged person. A trans woman can thus act as an active bystander to another trans woman. (2017, p. 172)

McKinnon's push for cultivating active bystanders rather than 'allies' is an important move. Where many 'allies' believe they are doing good for disadvantaged, marginalized, and oppressed people, they often are committing microaggressions and macroaggressions against the people they claim to support. Also, these 'allies' tend to go on the attack when called out for committing these aggressions, reminding the person affected that they are an 'ally'. Also known as a gross form of gaslighting.

Bystanders, then, can come in two flavours: active and passive. When Boxill points out that the bystanders are meant to resist oppression by attempting to stop acts of oppression (2010, p. 1), he would be referring to McKinnon's Active Bystander. A passive bystander would not be attempting to stop acts of oppression. The culpability a bystander faces is a bit more complicated than it seems. One day in high school, a white boy pushed me against the lockers and threatened to punch me repeatedly. All the kids watching this happen might have suffered the punches instead of me if they had interfered. Thankfully, no one suffered punches that day. Just like a little bird that fluffs up its feathers to look bigger and tougher, I gathered myself and walked toward the boy. He quickly dropped his 'tough-guy' act and left me alone. The question raised by this situation is whether it is appropriate to expect bystanders to be active bystanders in every situation of oppression? It is not farfetched to expect bystanders to do everything they can to resist oppression. The other kids could have run for a teacher. No one moved. I can appreciate the precarious position the bystanders are in. However, the bystanders have access to

288

the greatest of excuses to refuse to resist oppression: the bystanders did not want to put themselves in danger. Can we fault them for self-preservation? I will not be able to answer these questions here. It is enough right now to realize how complicated these categories are and we need to remember that all three of Boxill's categories are responsible for resisting oppression.

After being out of academia for many years, going back was a struggle. I am now immersed in the same colonial education system that has been maintained and perpetuated since the opening of western, colonial schools on Turtle Island. I have started a Ph.D. in Philosophy in the midst of Philosophy Departments everywhere jumping on the Indigenous Philosophy bandwagon. So here I am presenting a story as a test run for what assignments in Indigenous Philosophy might look like. We take these complex concepts like 'oppression' and we tell our stories about them. This is not Western cannon. This is neither continental nor analytic. This certainly is not an ancient philosophy that is no longer practiced; Indigenous philosophy is alive. Pan-Indigenous thought is a wealth of knowledge intimately tied to many different ways to live life. Indigenous philosophy is taking the practice of storytelling as concept analysis. This is not Western cannon. These two ways of doing philosophy are not opposed to each other; however, they diverge in significant ways. These ways need to be honoured and respected. We don't want or need any more assimilation of Indigenous thought into Western cannon. There is no reason why we cannot do both.

And here I am, carving out my place within the Western cannon, doing what I can to frustrate oppression at every turn. I exist. I am Anishinaabe. I am two-spirit. I am vocal about Indigenous issues and how they intersect with other groups. And I do what I can to add my unique perspective into my work. I end up with something that is not Western cannon philosophy and that is the whole point. Philosophy is built around the colonial structures and necessarily subjugates Indigenous voices and knowledges. As an act of resistance, this project is meant to frustrate. This is my resistance against a structure that intends to silence people and disallow personal knowledges. I could have written the standard philosophy paper and left my experiences out of it, but I am done subjugating myself to satisfy oppression. I fully realize, however, that this act of resistance has little chance of stopping the subjugation of Indigenous voices. This is one small step in the direction of knowledge and practice liberation. As a member of the subjugated group, this is what I can do right now to resist the continuation of systematic subjugation. I appreciate your persistence in joining me on this journey; I realize that you may feel troubled or feel uncomfortable right now. I understand; telling my story isn't comfortable for me either. Being uncomfortable is the first step to being aware of oppression. Resisting oppression cannot happen if we are not aware of it. Miigwetch. Thank you for your time.

NOTES

[1] I am using 'pan-Indigenous' here to recognize the variety in Indigenous thought. Indigenous Philosophy, as a banner or branch of philosophy would be more like Hellenistic Philosophy: a branch

PATRICIA SINIIKWE PAJUNEN

of philosophy with the schools being branched from the main heading. So, Indigenous Philosophy would be the main heading with Anishinaabe Philosophy, for example, as a particular school. However, it is wrong to think of Indigenous Philosophy as an ancient period of time that is now gone, as would be done with the Hellenistic Philosophies. There is no neo-Indigenous Philosophy. Indigenous philosophy is ancient as well as current. Indigenous peoples, cultures, and practices are typically lumped together into one giant melting pot. This is not what I am doing here.

[2] What I mean by Western Cannon philosophy are the three dominant ways of categorizing, studying, and doing philosophy in Canada: ancient philosophy, continental philosophy, and analytic philosophy. While ancient philosophy typically refers to Ancient Greece, this categorization could include Ancient Chinese philosophies and Indian philosophies. In my seven years of learning philosophy, not once has any of these three categorizations recognized pan-Indigenous philosophies. With the push to adopt UNDRIP and the TRC recommendations, philosophy departments all over the 'Canada' portion of Turtle Island are moving to bring in Indigenous Philosophy under one of these banners. I am resisting this move since it would be easy for settler philosophers to stuff Indigenous Philosophy under the ancient philosophy heading, rendering Indigenous philosophy as juvenile and having no 'real world' application. The move, then, would be to make Indigenous philosophies recognized as current and worthy of their own category rather than being subsumed by the existing colonial ones.

[3] http://rrib.ca/~wwwrrib/our-culture/

[4] https://www.youtube.com/watch?v=m6K4ar1nm5A

[5] http://www.oktlaw.com/ditching-doctrine-discovery-means-canadian-law/

[6] http://www.edu.gov.on.ca/eng/aboriginal/Guide_Toolkit2009.pdf

REFERENCES

Alfred, T., & Corntassel, J. (2005). Being indigenous: Resurgences against contemporary colonialism. In R. Bellamy (Ed.), *The politics of identity* (pp. 597–614). Oxford: Blackwell Publishing.

Boxill, B. (2010). The responsibility of the oppressed to resist their own oppression. *Journal of Social Philosophy, 41*(1), 1–12.

McKinnon, R. (2017). Allies behaving badly: Gaslighting as epistemic injustice. In I. J. Kidd, G. Pohlhaus, & J. Medina (Eds.), *The Routledge handbook of epistemic injustice* (p. 167). New York, NY: Routledge.

Patricia Siniikwe Pajunen
Department of Philosophy
University of Guelph
Guelph, Ontario

JENNIFER MARKIDES

30. RECONCILING AN ETHICAL FRAMEWORK FOR LIVING WELL IN THE WORLD OF RESEARCH

How can I live well in an academic setting steeped in colonial traditions – built upon a Western worldview that values individualism over collectivity; promotes competition over collaboration; and perpetuates conformity over diversity?
Herein lies my struggle.

INTRODUCING MYSELF

I am a member of the Métis Nation and resident of High River, Alberta. My father's parents and grandparents are Métis (Swampy Cree and English), Welsh, Irish, and Coast Salish. My mother's parents and grandparents are Swedish, Belgian, and Scottish. I was raised in northern British Columbia in the town of Smithers, between the territories of the Wet'suwet'en and Gitxsan peoples. My Indigenous and non-Indigenous heritages factor heavily into how I negotiate the world and my understanding of it; at times, my conflicted identity and worldview(s) mirror the cultural unrest I see in Canadian society writ large.

I am an educator and have taught in a variety of school settings: from elementary Montessori classes to undergraduate programs in education. In my research, I am interested in the stories of struggle and hope in response to trauma, specifically looking at the experiences of youth in the aftermath of the 2013 High River flood.

While this type of introduction still feels unnatural to me, after thirty plus years of education and inculcation in Western systems of education and academic writing traditions, I know it is necessary.

Absolon and Willett (2005) share the importance of *putting ourselves forward* in our work. This is common practice in many Indigenous communities, identifying who we are and where we are from. It holds us accountable to a history and future, people and place. Introductions are the starting point for communication and dialogue, and form the basis of relationships. The act of sharing personal details in an introduction is also risky. By doing so, I make myself vulnerable.

I am exposed.

The practice of introducing one's familial relations – specific to ancestries, histories, and places – is less common in colonial institutions. Following Western

© KONINKLIJKE BRILL NV, LEIDEN, 2018 | DOI 9789004367418_030

JENNIFER MARKIDES

academic conventions, the third person voice is more prevalent and denotes a formal, authoritative distancing/presence.

> *Over time, I have grown more cautious about trusting unnamed sources of*
> *information. Now I ask questions, such as: Who owns this news station? Did*
> *the drug company sponsor the doctor's research? What were the researcher's*
> *interests and intentions for working in that community, on that project?*
> *It helps to know.*

Disrupting Eurocentric consciousness, Graveline (1998) outlines the importance of first person voice, speaking the truth, and telling our own stories.

> *I can only speak for myself – from my own experience and knowledge.*
> *For these reasons, I am in my work.*

ALLYING MYSELF

In preparation for this research, I struggle to find myself – *or to fit myself* – in the traditional Western academic frames. I read books and journal articles based in scientific method and positivist paradigms that talked about "hope" as though it were a reducible *thing*. Some scholars identified and named specific *types* of hope (Webb, 2007; Snyder, 2000); while others described ways to measure hope through standardized assessment tools (Snyder, Harris, Anderson, Holleran, Irving, Sigmon, Yoshinobu, Gibb, Langelle, & Harney, 1991; Magaletta & Oliver, 1999).

> *I found these readings to be distant/removed, and, in many ways, hope-less.*
> *They talked about hope in isolation, rather than in connection.*

These examples illustrate how a Western worldview is the hegemonic norm of research practices in Western institutions. The existing academic structures and frameworks act as gatekeepers that limit the diversity of ideas that are allowed/ accepted within the academy.

> *I fear that this narrowing of allowable/acceptable scholarship – and in turn,*
> *permissible/recognized scholars – has contributed to the unhealthy and*
> *unsustainable competitive underpinnings of present-day academic life.*
> *It has fostered the 'publish or perish' mentality that necessitates and favours*
> *streamlined research methods, presented as: controllable and objective, rather*
> *than complex inquiry approaches, seen as: unpredictable and subjective.*

Ermine (1995) observes, "In viewing the world objectively, Western science has habitually fragmented and measured the external space in an attempt to understand it in all its complexity" (p. 103). In addition, Little Bear (2000) underscores that, "Even though observation and measurement are both necessary to science, measurement is stressed and emphasized. If something is not measureable, then it is not scientific…. Objectivity concerns itself with quantity and not quality" (pp. 82–83).

RECONCILING AN ETHICAL FRAMEWORK FOR LIVING WELL IN THE WORLD

As much as I hope otherwise, I get the sense that qualitative research continues
to be undervalued; the belief that quantitative research is more valid persists.
Many of these research traditions – concerned with power – aim to control
risks and unknowns? But what if our questions cannot be answered in these
authoritative and normative ways?

Cruikshank (1998) cautions:

Academics too often frame the experience of others with reference to scholarly
norms. Yet unless we put ourselves in interactive situations where we are
exposed and vulnerable, where these norms are interrupted and challenged,
we can never recognize the limitations of our own descriptions. It is these
dialogues that are most productive, because they prevent us from becoming
overconfident about our own interpretations. (p. 165)

A standardized hope assessment test might generate a number on a scale, but
what will that tell of the person and their situation? In what ways can we mis/
interpret this disconnected information?
How can it tell the person's story with context, history, voice, and agency?
How can it paint a bigger picture? With detail and nuance?

In a Western worldview, "hope" becomes fragmented and measureable –
acceptable research. While in an Indigenous worldview, hope research becomes,
necessarily, wholistic, relational, and hermeneutic – *context specific and*
contested. One example of this is Lear's (2006) examination of *radical hope* –
His research is *grounded* in a historical context, *legitimized* through richly
detailed storytelling, and *strengthened* by the many connections to past and present
issues.

Because Indigenous research does not readily fit the Western paradigm,
the value of the scholarship is widely debated – held to a higher, or
different, standard.

Fortunately, many Indigenous scholars have *proven* themselves – their work
passing rigorous scrutiny and rising to meet long-established standards. Cole (2006)
broke from the accepted/expected conventions of scholarly writing and produced a
poetic masterpiece that challenged Eurocentric academic tradition in ways that are
easier to show, than to describe:

in order to enter those realms of anointed power
those racially predestined orbs those p/reserves of academ(ent)ia
those places where I can be of immediate help for my nation
it is deemed I am to follow western epistemologies
cast like the commandments of moses [or the manifesto of andré breton]
into petrified substantiation   transited like retrograde orbiting planets

293

JENNIFER MARKIDES

with us as indigenous people caught in the thrall
like occulted satellites eclipsed step sibs   ellipses to the indian acts and
treaties. (p. 450)

Cole's work was both controversial and highly effective. Four Arrows (2008) ambitiously created and richly described an entire fictitious conference to showcase competing Western and Indigenous epistemologies, in *The Authentic Dissertation: Alternative Ways of Knowing, Research and Representation*. Cruikshank (1990) led the way by fighting to include the names of the three Yukon Native elders as collaborators on the publication of her dissertation, which appeared in print as *Life Lived like a Story: Life Stories of Three Yukon Native Elders*, by Julie Cruikshank in collaboration with Angela Sidney, Kitty Smith, and Annie Ned. King (2003, 2014) bravely shared personal stories of not fitting into Indigenous stereotypes; and boldly wrote a fictional narrative, drawing attention environmental, societal, and cultural issues brought about by the financially motivated and progress driven impulses of Western civilization.

Indigenous scholars are successful in breaking Western academic traditions, so long as their work is exceptional. [I recognize that the word "exceptional" implies an "exception" to the rule; thus, strong Indigenous scholars are often considered rare and exoticized or showcased within their institutions. This is problematic.]
As a beginning scholar, I see their examples as both daunting and emboldening. Maybe now, in a time of truth and reconciliation, we can reach a critical mass of exceptional Indigenous scholars – to become less rare – towards mutual sustainability.

These scholars have shown innovation, courage, and resolve – staying true to their selves and remaining accountable to their communities. They have successfully navigated alternative forms of data representation (Eisner, 1997) where, "Not all forms of data representation have been considered legitimate in the context of research" (p. 5). Cole, Four Arrows, Cruikshank, King, and so many others have taken risks, allowed themselves to be vulnerable, and pushed boundaries to prove the merit of their work, expanding the realm of the possible for generations of scholars to come.

Instead of simply standing alone to stand out – by looking for *new and better* answers – Indigenous researchers are strong in their moves to stand together – by connecting to those who came before them, in shared *ways of knowing, being, and doing* (Martin & Mirraboopa, 2009; Aluli-Meyer, 2008). These *ways* respect relationships, protocols, and responsibilities beyond the research.

Relatedness holds us in check.
Relatedness holds us up.
Relatedness holds us together.

RECONCILING AN ETHICAL FRAMEWORK FOR LIVING WELL IN THE WORLD

ACKNOWLEDGING RISK

I want to explore and share the stories of others. These stories are not my own.

I will need permissions – approval and authority – from my participants to tell of their experiences.
I will need to earn, maintain, and care for these permissions/relationships.

RELATING AND CARING ETHICALLY

In academia, ethics review boards govern research. They review, question, and approve or disallow projects based on the ethical merits of the research proposal. In theory and practice, the ethics review process is in place to protect the participants, the researchers, the institutions, and the community.

The permissions I need, to tell someone else's story, go beyond the scope of an ethics review board.

I see the responsibility I have to my research participants as more than collecting a signature on a consent form, beyond an approved list of question, and beyond member checking. As an Indigenous doctoral student I have *relational accountability* (Wilson, 2008) for how I conduct my research, specifically in regard to how I build and maintain relationships through every stage of the process (p. 107), from inception of the topic to presentation of the findings and beyond. As Weber-Pillwax (2004) put it:

> The most serious consideration for me as a researcher is the assurance that I will be able to uphold the personal responsibility that goes along with carrying out a research project in the community I have decided to work within. Once the decision has been made to enter a community with the intention of 'doing formal research,' I am accepting responsibility and accountability for the impact of the project on the lives of the community members with whom I will be working. (p. 79)

I want my research to respect and honour the participants.
I want my work to make a difference in their/our communities.

The participants and I are interconnected in the work. Our work together is the product of the relationships we establish – relationships built on care, trust, and obligation.

As in teaching, I have a duty of care to the participants involved in my research.

Gilligan (1982) describes *ethics of care* as recognizing relationships – complex *webs* of connectivity – that influence women's decision-making and moral judgements. *Care ethics* also involve attentiveness, recognition, receptivity, response, and reciprocity (Noddings, 1984, 2012). In these ways, care becomes an ethical *way of being* in relationships. Little Bear (2000) shares an Indigenous worldview, one that

295

JENNIFER MARKIDES

regards all things as animate – spiritual and knowledgeable – beings belonging to kinship circles in a *spider web* of relations. This wholistic worldview acknowledges that all relationships are co-implicated in care.

I would argue that care is fundamental for living well in the world of research – to consider the wellbeing of self, others, and the world.

Care complicates and muddies the researcher's objectives by sharing power in the relationship with participants. It puts the researcher in a weak and vulnerable position; but this *weak* position opens up possibilities that might not otherwise have been afforded (Biesta, 2013), creating a strong research potential.

Beyond research, I believe that sharing power in any relationship has the potential to expand possibilities for learning and growth.

GATHERING MY THOUGHTS

Embarking on this journey, I am aware of the challenges and potential consequences – scrutiny and critique – that may come from using *alternative/* [Indigenous] research methods in an academic culture that continues to be steeped with "concern for verification, truth, and precision" (Eisner, 1997, p. 7).

Ironically, these standards can be far less rigorous than the relational accountability I am held to within my communities – the spider web of connections holds me to All My Relations, and I am responsible to them.

BRACING FOR REJECTION

Presently, there is a push to "Indigenize" the academy. In theory, for this to happen, the dominant Western worldview – that has conceptualized, implemented, and maintained the norms and traditions within academic institutions – needs to reconcile with Indigenous worldviews, through dialogue – marked by an openness and generosity of spirit – to create an *ethical space of engagement* (Ermine, 2007) and possibility.

I fear that indigenization will only happen on the academy's terms, and therefore, will not at all.
But I am hopeful.

The ethical space needs to be the starting place. Ermine (2007) explains:

It is argued that the ethical space, at the field of convergence for disparate systems, can become a refuge of possibility in cross-cultural relations and the legal order of society, for the effect of shifting the status quo of an asymmetrical social order to a partnership model between world communities. The new partnership model of the ethical space, in a cooperative spirit between Indigenous peoples and Western institutions, will create new currents of thought that flow in different directions and overrun the old ways of thinking. (p. 203)

296

RECONCILING AN ETHICAL FRAMEWORK FOR LIVING WELL IN THE WORLD

Further to an ethical space, decolonizing the academy will also require an *ethical relationality* that acknowledges "the particular historical, cultural, and social contexts" (Donald, 2012, p. 45) from which the differing perspectives arose. Donald (2012) also stresses that Indigenous wisdom traditions and philosophies need to be brought to the fore – to shift the power, privilege, and voice – in decolonizing and reframing Indigenous-Canadian relationships that were forged in *unethical relationality* (p. 45).

What if academic institutions approached Indigenous partnerships and decolonization projects with the same reverence that Weber-Pillwax has for research relationships?
Could greater possibilities for learning and growth be afforded?

COMING TO A FRAMEWORK FOR LIVING WELL IN THE WORLD OF RESEARCH

Initially I struggled to 'see' myself in the academic institution.

I am grateful to have found Indigenous scholars and scholarship that re-imagines research in relationally grounded and sustainable ways. These lessons are ongoing, and I have many teachers. In particular, Elder Bob Cardinal of the Enoch Cree Nation (personal communications, September 2016 to present) has taught me the importance of slowing down – becoming better attuned to my place in the world; attending to people, places, and other sentient beings; and being disciplined, to know what matters – to listen, and to learn with my mind, body, and spirit.

In these ways, I can live well with/in my surroundings.

For me, this journey has led to an ethical framework for living well in the world of research. It starts with *knowing myself*: who I am, where I come from, where I am going, and what my responsibilities are (J. Ottmann, personal communication, September-December, 2016). Knowing myself is not fixed, but fluid. It involves reflexivity, as Martin & Mirraboopa (2009) describe:

Reflexivity in research design affords the 'space' to decolonize western research methodologies, then harmonise and articulate Indigenist research. Reflexivity is a process that allows us to work from Aboriginal centres and ensure we work with relatedness of self and Entities. Reflexivity challenges us to claim our shortcomings, misunderstandings, oversights and mistakes, to re-claim our lives and make strong changes to our current realities. Being reflexive ensures we do not compromise our identity whilst undertaking research. (p. 212)

Being reflexive requires humility and introspection.

This reflexive practice is also intertwined with my responsibilities to the people with whom I am *allying myself*. The scholars I draw upon have not chosen me to share their work; I have chosen them. In allying myself with their work, I do so with

297

JENNIFER MARKIDES

reverence, respect, and responsibility. These are my role models and teachers. I have a lot to learn. When I *re*-present their work, I am responsible for staying true to their message and intent to the best of my ability. I am drawing connective lines between their ideas and my own, in a web of relationality.

With both the scholars and research participants, I am *holding myself accountable* to them. I have a responsibility that goes beyond formal ethics approval, to an implicit protocol of ethical relationality. This, for me, is based in care. Holding myself accountable also comes with the knowledge that my familial communities, my research communities, and the academic community are holding me responsible for my work. In these ways, I feel both the weight and support that comes with being held in relational care.

To meet these relational tensions and pressures, I am *holding myself to a high standard*. I must stay true to my self and my community – to think through a decolonizing lens, consistently and mindfully. As I learn from the Indigenous scholars that I admire and aspire to honour in my work, I feel heartened that I am "finding [my] face, finding [my] heart, and finding [my] foundation" (Kelly, 2010, p. 82; Cajete, 1994) in the Indigenous research community. I have big work ahead, and I am committed to rising to the challenges entrusted to me.

Will my scholarship meet the academic standards and strictures?

Only time will tell.

Will my work be given approval and authority from the participants?
Will it honour them?
Will it matter in our communities?

I can only hope.

REMAINING CONCERNS

In a climate of Indigenization and reconciliation, I am hopeful that Indigenous worldviews and epistemologies will be more broadly accepted by academic institutions – moving beyond commodification and tokenism of indigeneity, to understanding new ways of being and living well in the world. Many Indigenous scholars lead by example in the charge to decolonize the academy. Some work from within the institution, chipping away at deeply entrenched, Western: beliefs, norms, and ideals. While others leave the academy – when the *fit* is too disparate – and return to their communities, continuing to publish and present their work with great determination and renewed resilience from outside of the academy's walls.

In the diverse community of Indigenous scholars, I see an interminable resistance and a desire for change in post secondary institutions. The existing structures cannot simply subsume, ignore, or assimilate our "alternative" ways of knowing. Institutions are *being called* to evolve – looking back and living forward – and our communities are holding them accountable, with guidance, expectation, and leadership.

298

RECONCILING AN ETHICAL FRAMEWORK FOR LIVING WELL IN THE WORLD

How might our struggles now transform these dissonant places for the generations to come?
Where differences of worldview and pedagogy are recognized as essential for mutual sustainability?

Looking for hope anew, I turn to the wisdom Grande's (2004) *Red pedagogy*:

Finally, what distinguishes Red pedagogy is its basis in hope. Not the future-centred hope of the Western imagination, but rather, a hope that lives in contingency with the past – one that trusts the beliefs and understandings of our ancestors as well as the power of traditional knowledge. A Red pedagogy is, thus, as much about belief and acquiescence as it is about questioning and empowerment, about respecting the space of tradition as it intersects with the time frames of the (post)modern world. Most of all, it is a hope that believes in the strength and resiliency of indigenous peoples and communities, recognizing that their struggles are not about inclusion and enfranchisement to the "new world order" but, rather, are part of the indigenous project of sovereignty and indigenization. It reminds us that indigenous peoples have always been peoples of resistance, standing in defiance of the vapid emptiness of the bourgeois life. (pp. 28–29)

I see academic life is a privilege and a gift.
As a researcher, I hold a position of power that necessitates great ethical care, responsibility, and reverence for All My Relations.
In Indigenous scholarship, I have found hope renewed.

REFERENCES

Absolon, K., & Willett, C. (2005). Putting ourselves forward: Location in aboriginal research. In L. Brown & S. Strega (Eds.), *Research as resistance: Critical, indigenous, and anti-oppressive approaches* (pp. 97–126). Toronto: Canadian Scholar's Press.

Aluli-Meyer, M. (2008). Indigenous and authentic: Native Hawaiian epistemology and the triangulation of meaning. In N. Denzin, Y. Lincoln, & L. Smith (Eds.), *Handbook of critical and indigenous methodologies* (pp. 217–232). Thousand Oaks, CA: Sage Publications.

Biesta, G. J. (2013). *The beautiful risk of education*. Boulder, CO: Paradigm.

Cajete, G. (1994). *Look to the mountain: An ecology of indigenous education*. Durango, CO: Kivaki Press.

Cole, P. (2002). Aboriginalizing methodology: Considering the canoe. *International Journal of Qualitative Studies in Education, 15*(4), 447–459. doi:10.1080/09518390210145516

Cruikshank, J. (1990). *Life lived like a story: Life stories of three Yukon Native elders*. Lincoln, NE: University of Nebraska Press.

Cruikshank, J. (1998). *The social life of stories: Narrative and knowledge in the Yukon Territory*. Vancouver: UBC Press.

Donald, D. (2012). Forts, curriculum, and ethical relationality. In N. Ng-A-Fook, & J. Rottmann (Eds.) *Reconsidering Canadian Curriculum Studies: Provoking Historical, Present, and Future Perspectives* (pp. 39–46). New York, NY: Palgrave Macmillan.

Ermine, W. (1995). Aboriginal epistemology. In M. A. Battiste & J. Barman (Eds.), *First nations education in Canada: The circle unfolds* (pp. 101–112). Vancouver: UBC Press.

JENNIFER MARKIDES

Ermine, W. (2007). The ethical space of engagement. *Indigenous Law Journal, 6*(1), 193–203.
Four Arrows (aka Jacobs, D.T.). (2008). *The authentic dissertation: Alternative ways of knowing, research and representation.* London: Routledge.
Gilligan, C. (1982). *In a different voice.* Cambridge, MA: Harvard University Press.
Grande, S. (2004). *Red pedagogy: Native American social and political thought.* Lanham, MD: Rowman & Littlefield.
Graveline, J. (1998). *Circle works: Transforming eurocentric consciousness.* Winnipeg: Fernwood Publishers.
Kelly, V. (2010). Finding face, finding heart, and finding foundation: Life writing and the transformation of educational practice. *Transnational Curriculum Inquiry, 7*(2), 82–100.
King, T. (2003). *The truth about stories: A native narrative.* Toronto: House of Anansi Press.
King, T. (2014). *The back of the turtle.* Toronto: HarperCollins Publishers.
Lear, J. (2006). *Radical hope: Ethics in the face of cultural devastation.* Cambridge, MA: Harvard University Press.
Little Bear, L. (2000). Jagged worldviews colliding. In M. Battiste (Ed.), *Reclaiming indigenous voice and vision* (pp. 77–85). Vancouver: UBC Press.
Magaletta, P. R., & Oliver, J. M. (1999). The hope construct, will, and ways: Their relations with self-efficacy, optimism, and general well-being. *Journal of Clinical Psychology, 55*(5), 539–551.
Martin, K., & Mirraboopa, B. (2009). Ways of knowing, being and doing: A theoretical framework and methods for indigenous and indigenist research. *Journal of Australian Studies, 27*(76), 203–214.
Noddings, N. (1984). *Caring: A feminine approach to ethics and moral education.* Berkeley, CA: University of California Press.
Noddings, N. (2012). The language of care ethics. *Knowledge Quest, 40*(4), 52–56.
Snyder, C. R. (Ed.). (2000). *Handbook of hope: Theory, measures, and applications.* San Diego, CA: Academic Press.
Snyder, C. R., Harris, C., Anderson, J. R., Holleran, S. A., Irving, L. M., Sigmon, S. T., Yoshinobu, L., Gibb, J., Langelle, C., & Harney, P. (1991). The will and the ways: Development and validation of an individual-differences measure of hope. *Journal of Personality and Social Psychology, 60*(4), 570–585.
Webb, P. (2007). Modes of hoping. *History of the Human Sciences, 20*(3), 65–83.
Weber-Pillwax, C. (2004). Indigenous researchers and indigenous research methods: Cultural influences or cultural determinants of research methods. *Pimatisiwin: A Journal of Aboriginal and Indigenous Community Health, 2*(1), 77–90.
Wilson, S. (2008). *Research is ceremony: Indigenous research methods.* Halifax, NS: Fernwood Publishing.

Jennifer Markides
Werklund School of Education
University of Calgary
Calgary, Alberta